TOKYO GHOUL

SUI ISHIDA

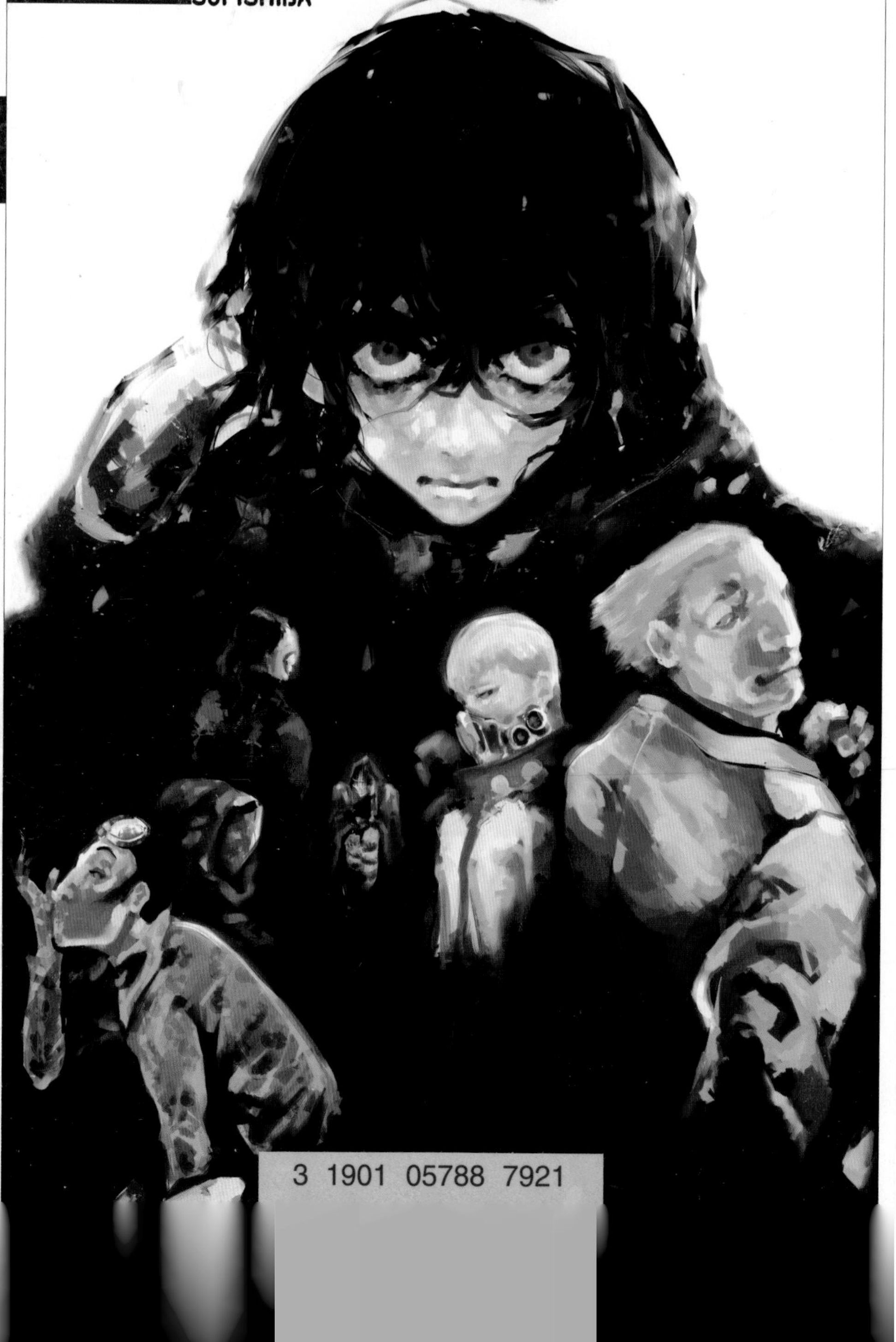

AYATO KIRISHIMA

霧 嶋 絢 都 （ キ リ シ マ　ア ヤ ト ）

BORN July 4th   Cancer

High-ranking Aogiri Tree member

BLOOD-TYPE: O

Size : 159cm   49 kg   FEET 25.0 CM

Likes : Fighting, tropical fish, **RABBITS**

Dislikes : Ghoul Investigators, weak people

Rc Type : Ukaku

ARATA KIRISHIMA

霧 嶋 新 （ キ リ シ マ　ア ラ タ ）

BORN January 1st   Capricorn

BLOOD-TYPE: A

Size : 174 cm   60kg   FEET 27.0 cm

Likes : Cooking, socializing, studying

Loves : Wife, Touka, Ayato

Rc Type : Kokaku

Unique States : Kakuja

SUI ISHIDA was born in Fukuoka, Japan. He is the author of *Tokyo Ghoul* and several *Tokyo Ghoul* one-shots, including one that won him second place in the *Weekly Young Jump* 113th Grand Prix award in 2010. *Tokyo Ghoul* began serialization in *Weekly Young Jump* in 2011 and was adapted into an anime series in 2014.

東京喰種

TOKYO GHOUL

TOKYO GHOUL

SUI ISHIDA

T O K Y O G H O U L

sui ishida

8

TOKYO GHOUL
TOKYO GHOUL

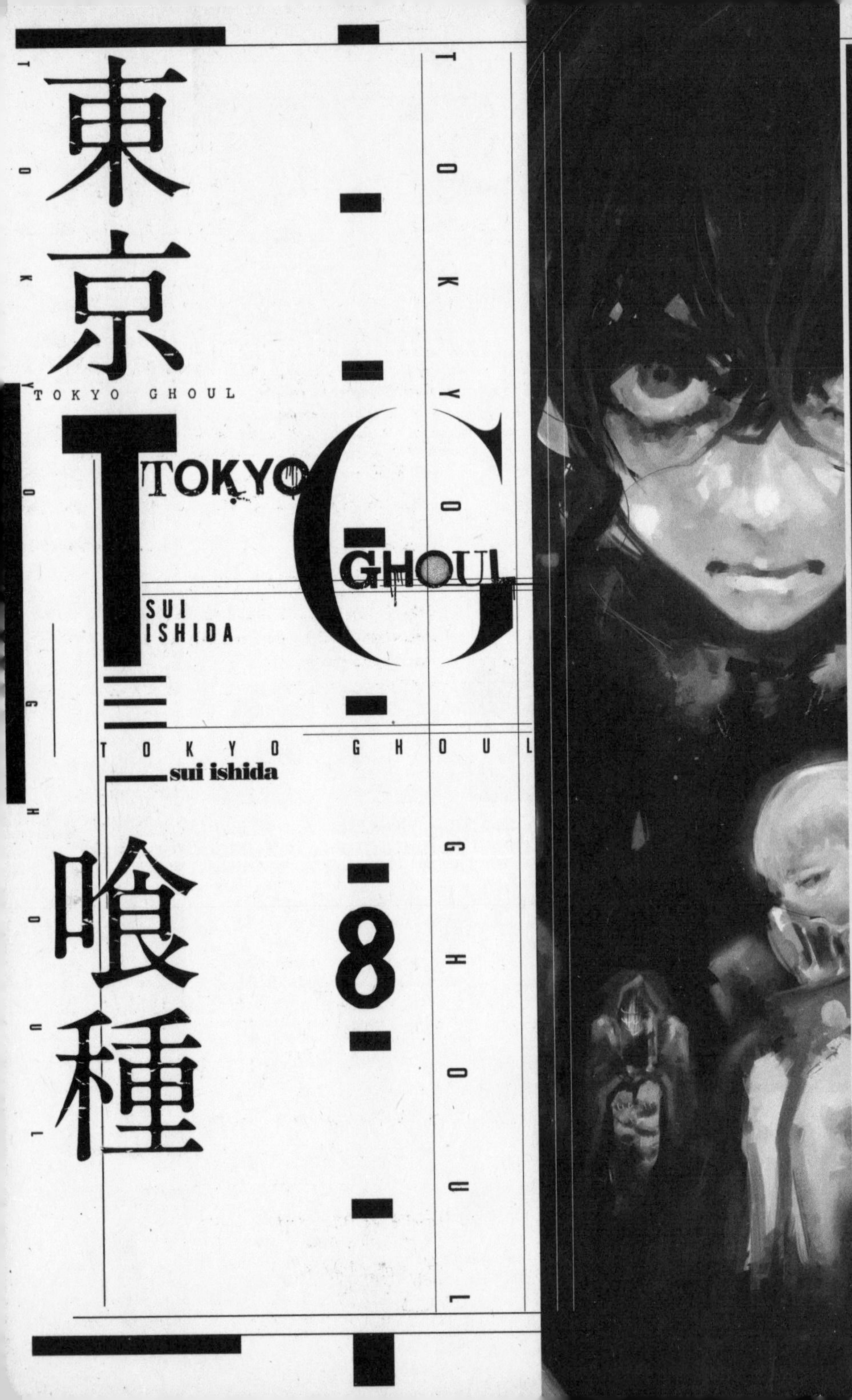

TOKYO GHOUL SO FAR

喰 GHOULS 種

ANTEIKU

The café where Ghouls gather. Known for their slow-brewed coffee. Has many human fans as well. Helping each other is the Ghouls' motto.

20TH WARD

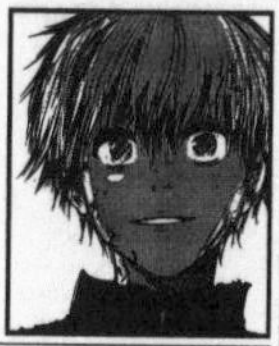

KEN KANEKI
(KANEKI)

An ordinary young man with a fondness for literature who meets with an accident and has Rize's organs transplanted into him. Becomes a half-Ghoul. Struggling to find his place in the world. After being abducted by the Aogiri Tree, the Ghoul inside him awakens.

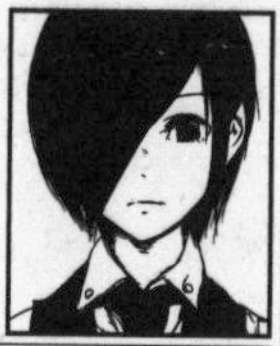

TOUKA KIRISHIMA
(TOUKA)

A conflicted heroine with two sides, rage and kindness. Ayato's older sister. Longs to become human. Hates investigators...?

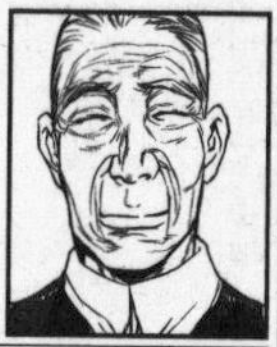

YOSHIMURA
(MANAGER)

The owner of Anteiku. Guides Kaneki so he can live as a Ghoul. Often works with Yomo. Shrouded by mystery.

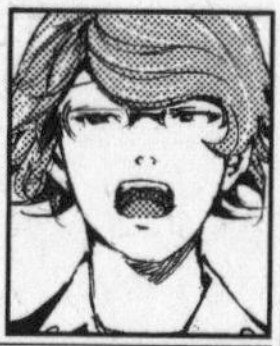

NISHIKI NISHIO
(NISHIKI)

Studious. Adept at blending into human society. Eats *taiyaki* with no difficulty. Has a human girlfriend, and a compassionate side.

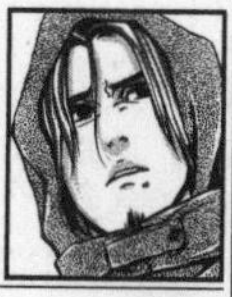

RENJI YOMO
(YOMO)

Does not appear out in the open that often. Taciturn and unfriendly, but is trusted by many. Frequently works with Yoshimura. Concerned about Kaneki's condition.

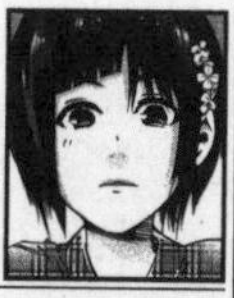

HINAMI FUEGUCHI
(HINAMI)

An orphan whose parents were killed by the CCG. Displays tremendous power when she is awakened. Living with Touka.

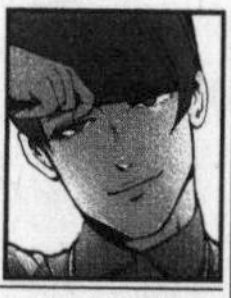

SHU TSUKIYAMA

A Gourmet who seeks the taste of the unknown. Obsessed with Kaneki, who is a half-Ghoul.

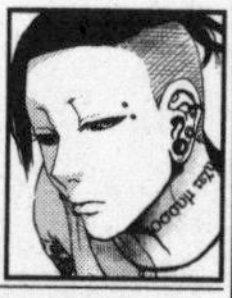

UTA

Owner of HySy Artmask Studio, a mask shop in the 4th Ward. Has a troubled history with Yomo.

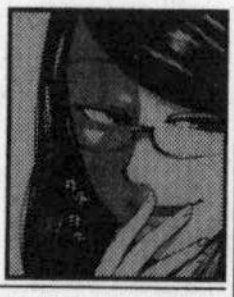

RIZE KAMISHIRO
DECEASED **(RIZE)**

Freewheeling Binge Eater who despised boredom. Previously lived in the 11th Ward. Met Kaneki in the 20th Ward and then had an accident. There are rumors she used an alias to hide her true identity.

[GHOUL]

A creature that appears human yet consumes humans. The top of the food chain. Finds anything other than humans and coffee unpleasant. Releases a highly lethal natural weapon unique to Ghouls, known as Kagune, from their body to prey on humans. Can be cannibalistic. Only sustains damage from Kagune or Quinques that are made from Kagune.

AOGIRI TREE 11TH WARD

A group of Ghouls with the ambition of ruling Ghouls and humans with force. Appoints a Ghoul called the One-Eyed King as their leader, but much is still unknown.

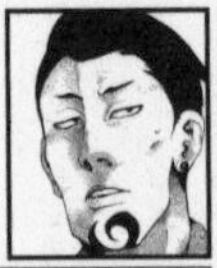

KAZUICHI BANJO

Former leader of the 11th Ward who admires Rize. Plans an escape with Kaneki that ends in failure after having doubts about the Aogiri Tree.

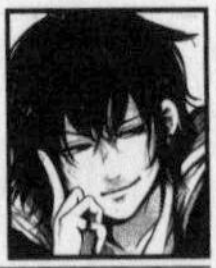

AYATO KIRISHIMA

Touka's younger brother. Even more hot-blooded than his sister. Recruited by Aogiri because of it. Has disdain for his sister and the 20th Ward.

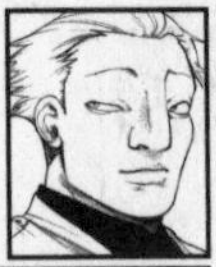

YAMORI

Possesses unrivaled combat skills. Feared as the 13th Ward's "Jason" for his brutal nature. Confines and tortures Kaneki, but is eventually defeated.

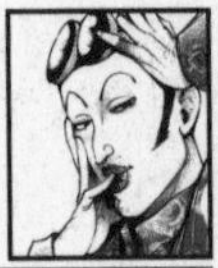

NICO

Yamori's partner. Has a keen sense of smell.

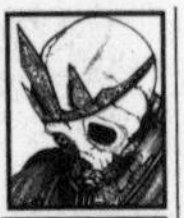

ONE-EYED KING

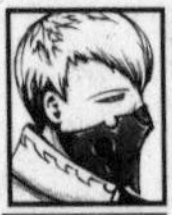

TATARA

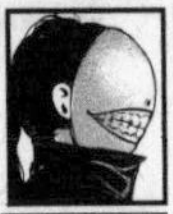

NORO

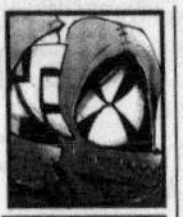

BIN BROTHERS

人 HUMANS 間

CCG GHOUL INVESTIGATORS

11TH WARD SPECIAL TASK FORCE

A government agency founded by the Washu family. Develops Ghoul extermination specialists at the Academy to maintain peace in the wards. Its principal functions include the development and improvement of Quinques, which can kill Ghouls.

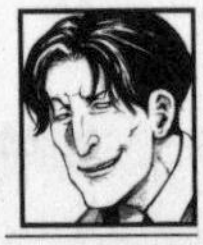

ITSUKI MARUDE (SPECIAL INVESTIGATOR)

Commands the 11th Ward Special Task Force. Biding his time for a promotion. Has an aversion to Quinques.

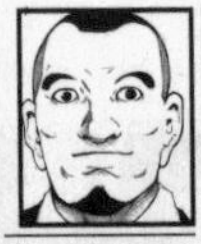

YUKINORI SHINOHARA (SPECIAL INVESTIGATOR)

Ex-Academy instructor. A onetime colleague of Mado and Amon's drill instructor. Appears easygoing, but…

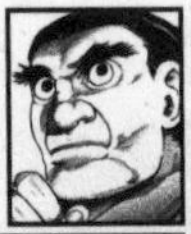

IWAO KUROIWA (SPECIAL INVESTIGATOR)

Lieutenant Commander of the 11th Ward Special Task Force. His rough-hewn looks match his rock-solid-sounding name. Called Iwaccho by Shinohara.

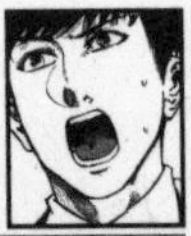

KOTARO AMON (RANK 1 INVESTIGATOR)

An Investigator with a very strong sense of justice. Determined to eradicate Ghouls. Dedicated to avenging Mado's loss through his ongoing battle with Kaneki.

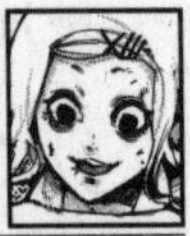

JUZO SUZUYA (RANK 3 INVESTIGATOR)

An eccentric who joined the CCG under special dispensation. Enjoys killing and longs for exceptionally lethal Quinques.

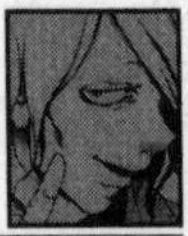

KUREO MADO DECEASED

An investigator with an unusual obsession with Quinques. Loathed the Ghouls who killed his family. Eventually lost his life.

Summary

Kaneki, an average student, is fated to live as a Ghoul when Rize's organs are transplanted into him. While questioning and struggling with the existence of creatures that take human lives to survive, he searches for an answer to how the world should be. One day while at Anteiku, he is abducted by members of the 11th Ward's Aogiri Tree organization. While being help captive and viciously tortured by Yamori, he accepts that he is a Ghoul. Meanwhile, Touka, who had infiltrated the Aogiri Tree's hideout to rescue Kaneki, encounters her younger brother.

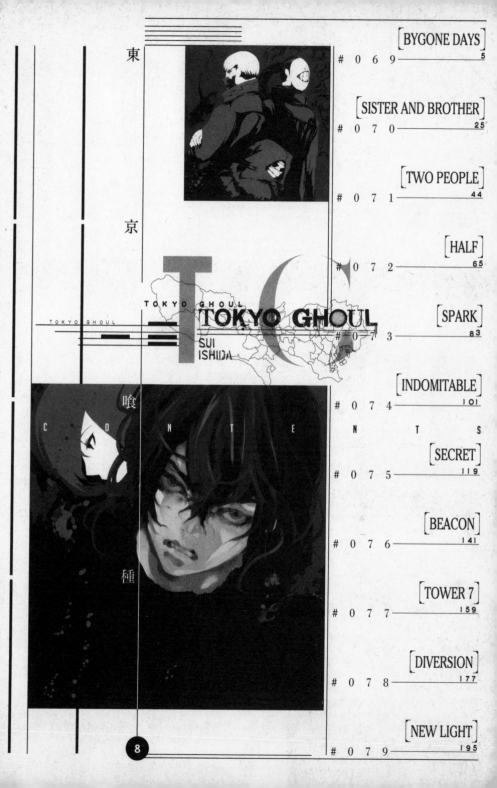

東

京

喰

種

TOKYO GHOUL

TOKYO GHOUL

SUI
ISHIDA

CONTENTS

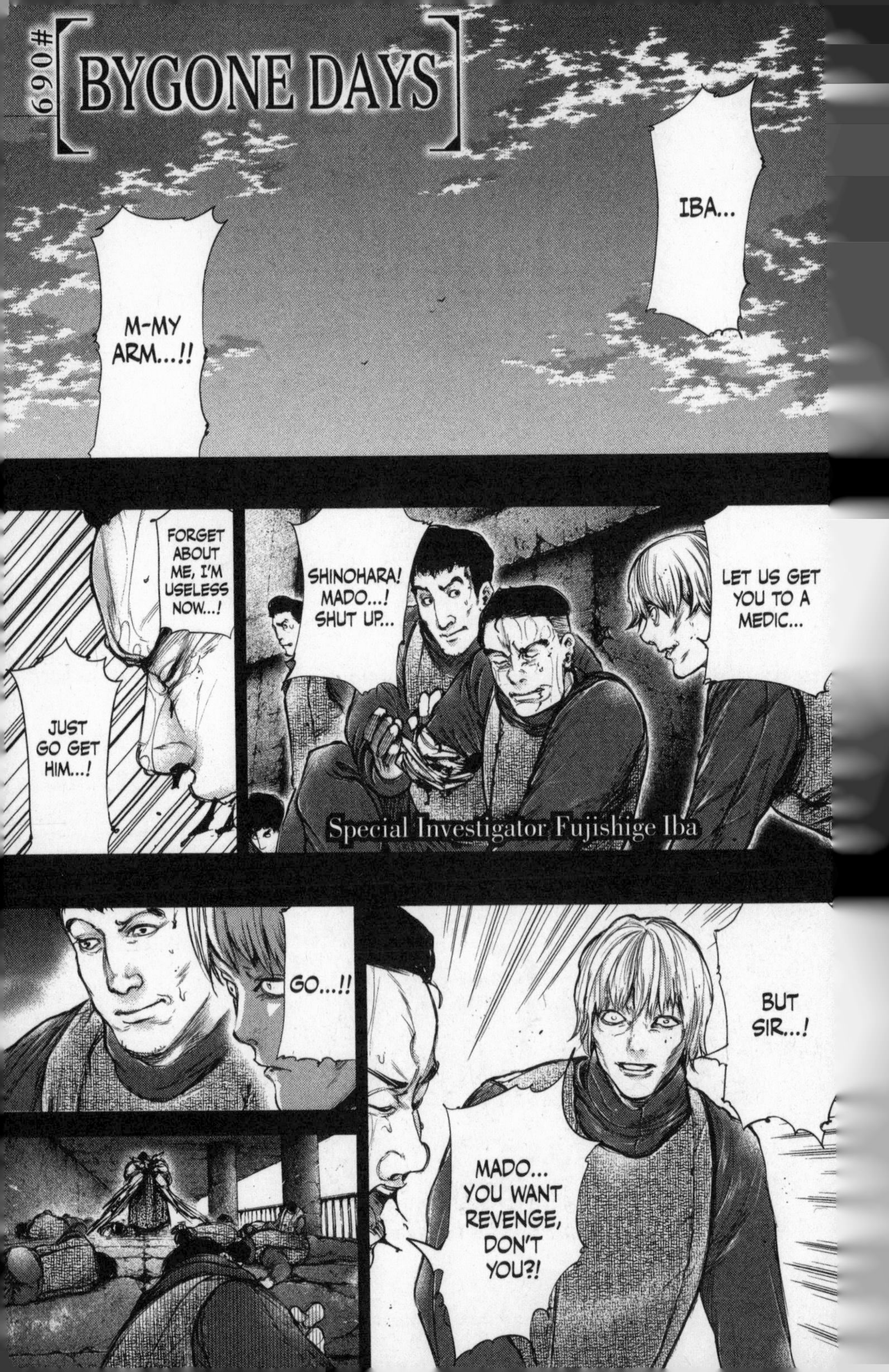
#069 [BYGONE DAYS]
IBA...
M-MY ARM...!!
LET US GET YOU TO A MEDIC...
SHINOHARA! MADO...! SHUT UP...
Special Investigator Fujishige Iba
FORGET ABOUT ME, I'M USELESS NOW...!
JUST GO GET HIM...!
BUT SIR...!
MADO... YOU WANT REVENGE, DON'T YOU?!
GO...!!

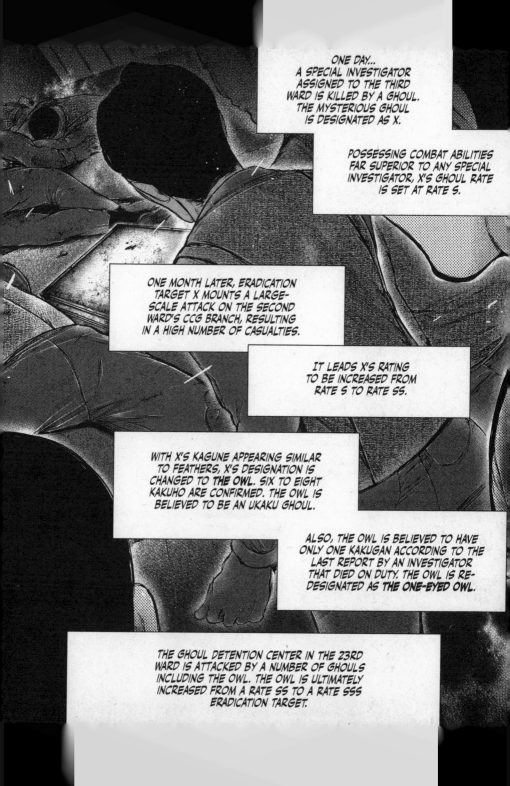

ONE DAY...
A SPECIAL INVESTIGATOR
ASSIGNED TO THE THIRD
WARD IS KILLED BY A GHOUL.
THE MYSTERIOUS GHOUL
IS DESIGNATED AS X.

POSSESSING COMBAT ABILITIES
FAR SUPERIOR TO ANY SPECIAL
INVESTIGATOR, X'S GHOUL RATE
IS SET AT RATE S.

ONE MONTH LATER, ERADICATION
TARGET X MOUNTS A LARGE-
SCALE ATTACK ON THE SECOND
WARD'S CCG BRANCH, RESULTING
IN A HIGH NUMBER OF CASUALTIES.

IT LEADS X'S RATING
TO BE INCREASED FROM
RATE S TO RATE SS.

WITH X'S KAGUNE APPEARING SIMILAR
TO FEATHERS, X'S DESIGNATION IS
CHANGED TO **THE OWL**. SIX TO EIGHT
KAKUHO ARE CONFIRMED. THE OWL IS
BELIEVED TO BE AN UKAKU GHOUL.

ALSO, THE OWL IS BELIEVED TO HAVE
ONLY ONE KAKUGAN ACCORDING TO THE
LAST REPORT BY AN INVESTIGATOR
THAT DIED ON DUTY. THE OWL IS RE-
DESIGNATED AS **THE ONE-EYED OWL.**

THE GHOUL DETENTION CENTER IN THE 23RD
WARD IS ATTACKED BY A NUMBER OF GHOULS
INCLUDING THE OWL. THE OWL IS ULTIMATELY
INCREASED FROM A RATE SS TO A RATE SSS
ERADICATION TARGET.

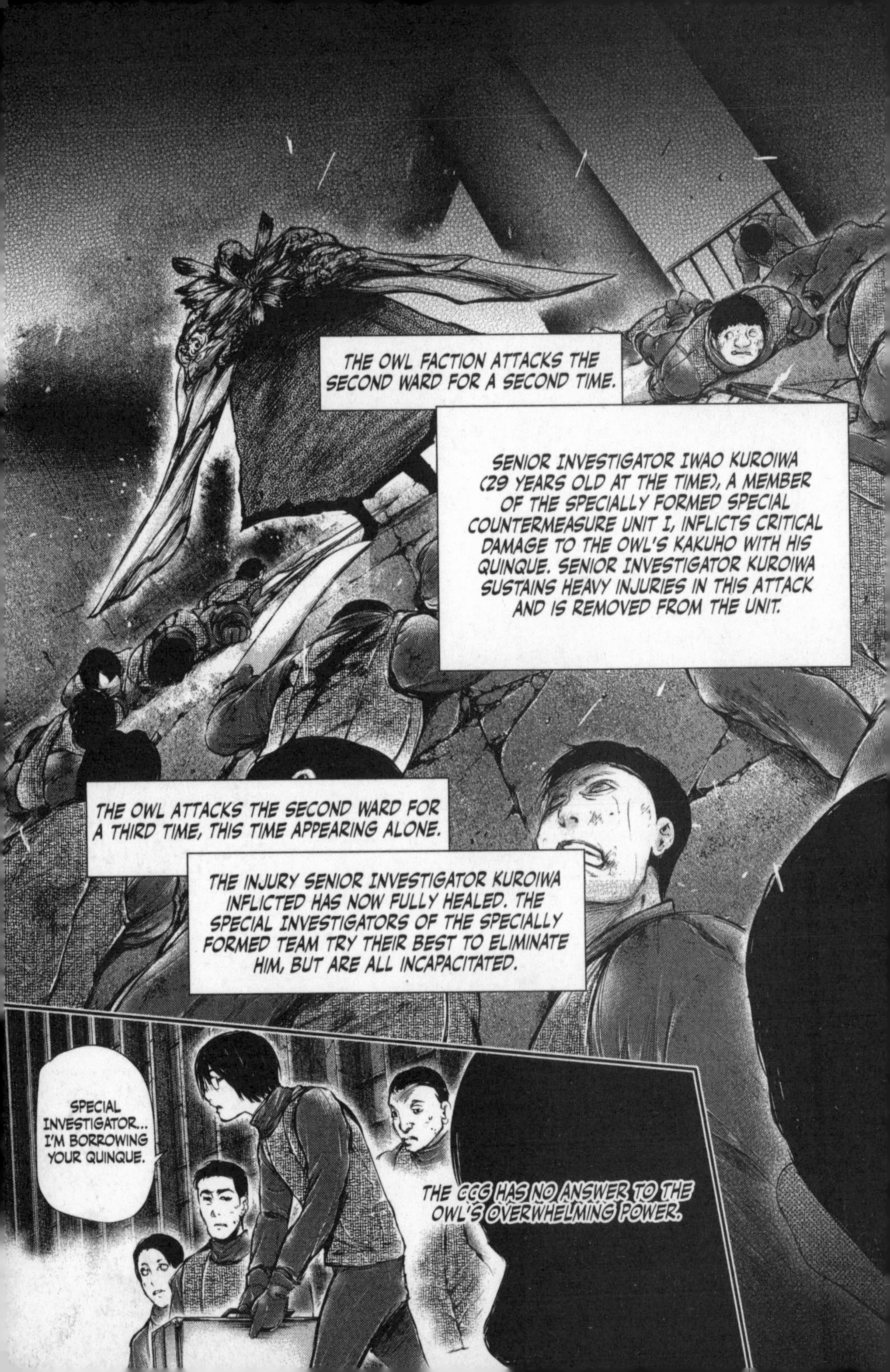
THE OWL FACTION ATTACKS THE SECOND WARD FOR A SECOND TIME.
SENIOR INVESTIGATOR IWAO KUROIWA (29 YEARS OLD AT THE TIME), A MEMBER OF THE SPECIALLY FORMED SPECIAL COUNTERMEASURE UNIT I, INFLICTS CRITICAL DAMAGE TO THE OWL'S KAKUHO WITH HIS QUINQUE. SENIOR INVESTIGATOR KUROIWA SUSTAINS HEAVY INJURIES IN THIS ATTACK AND IS REMOVED FROM THE UNIT.
THE OWL ATTACKS THE SECOND WARD FOR A THIRD TIME, THIS TIME APPEARING ALONE.
THE INJURY SENIOR INVESTIGATOR KUROIWA INFLICTED HAS NOW FULLY HEALED. THE SPECIAL INVESTIGATORS OF THE SPECIALLY FORMED TEAM TRY THEIR BEST TO ELIMINATE HIM, BUT ARE ALL INCAPACITATED.
THE CCG HAS NO ANSWER TO THE OWL'S OVERWHELMING POWER.
SPECIAL INVESTIGATOR... I'M BORROWING YOUR QUINQUE.

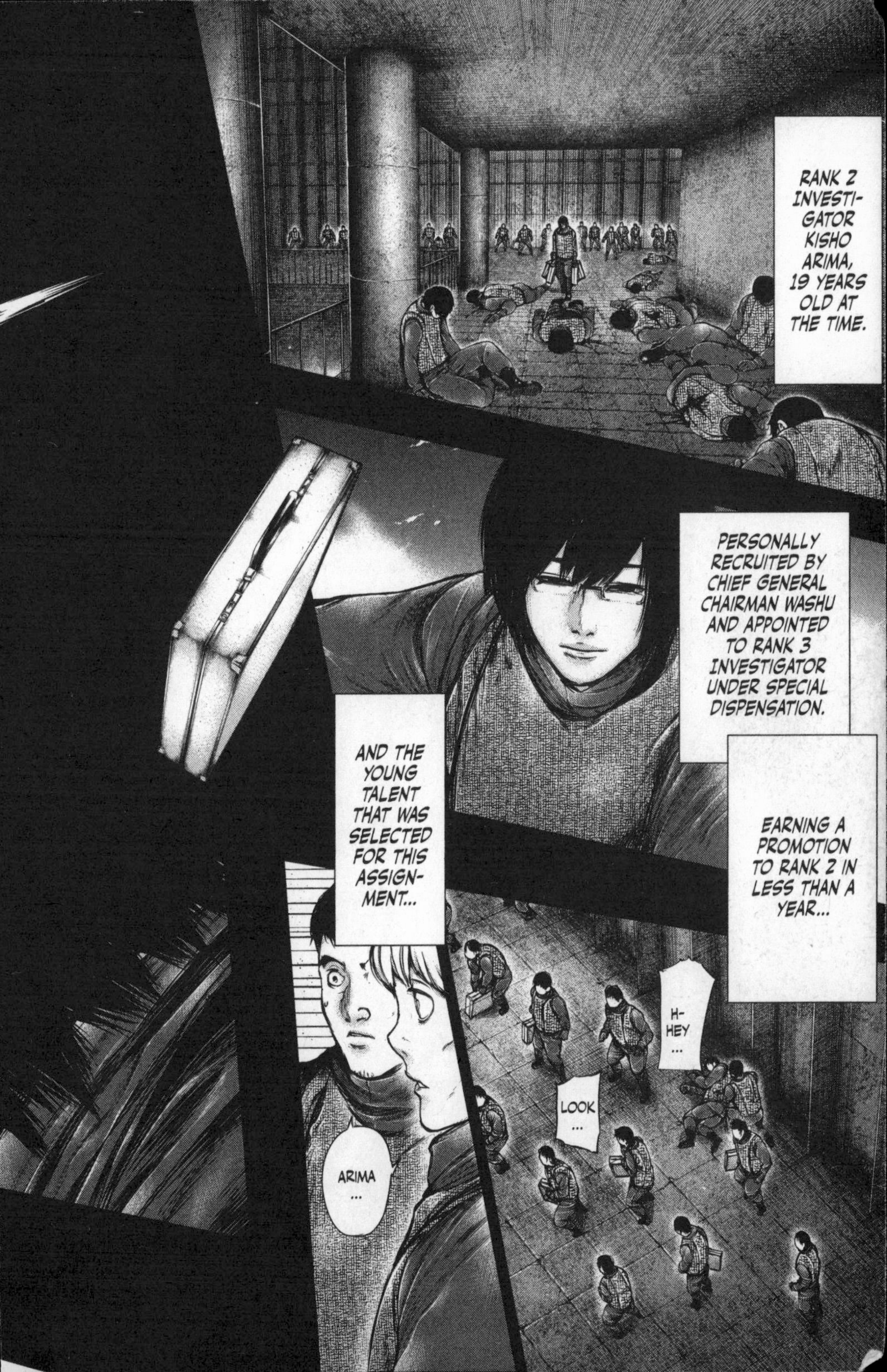
RANK 2 INVESTIGATOR KISHO ARIMA, 19 YEARS OLD AT THE TIME.
PERSONALLY RECRUITED BY CHIEF GENERAL CHAIRMAN WASHU AND APPOINTED TO RANK 3 INVESTIGATOR UNDER SPECIAL DISPENSATION.
EARNING A PROMOTION TO RANK 2 IN LESS THAN A YEAR...
AND THE YOUNG TALENT THAT WAS SELECTED FOR THIS ASSIGNMENT...
H-HEY...
LOOK...
ARIMA...

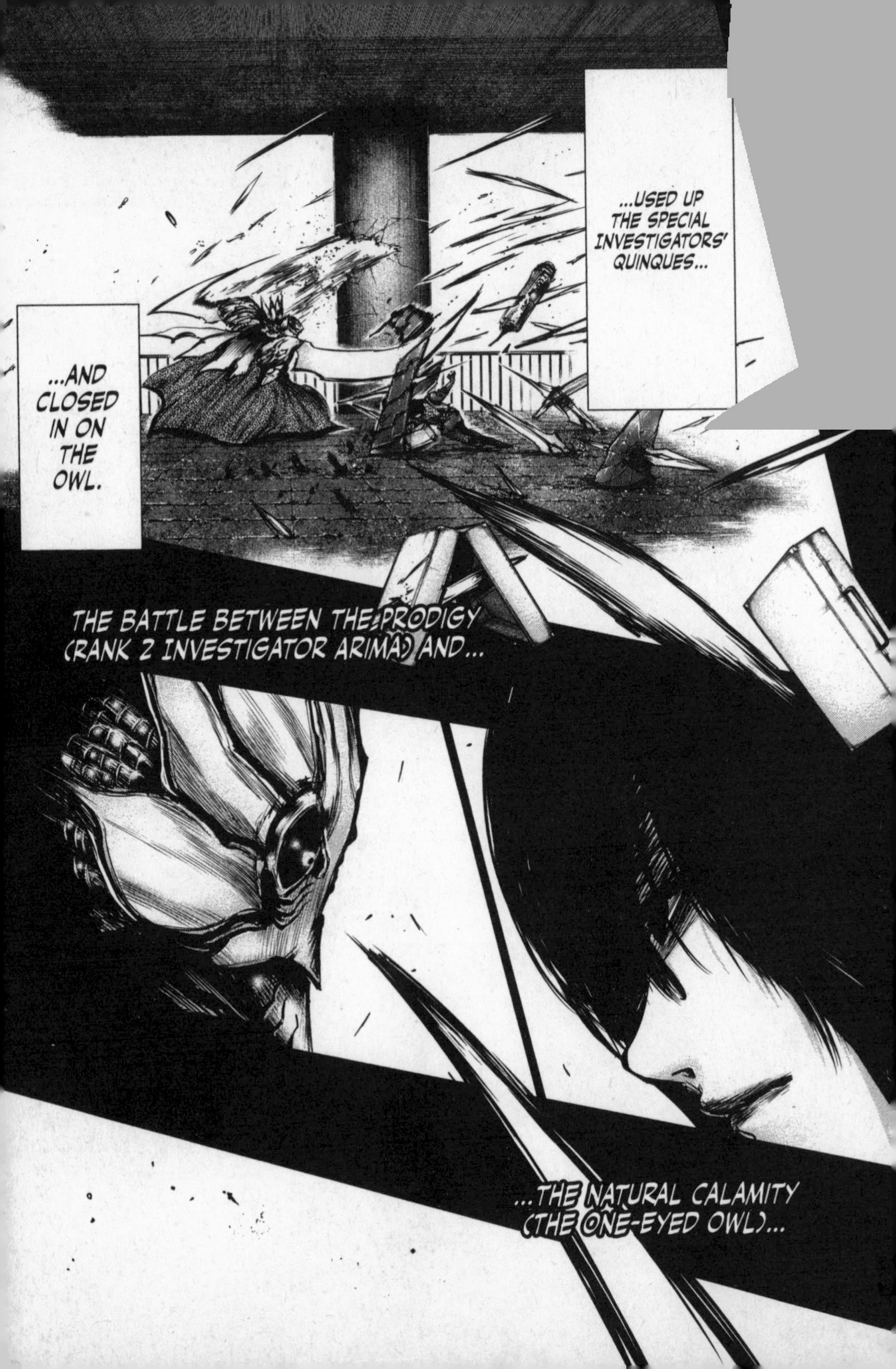
...USED UP THE SPECIAL INVESTIGATORS' QUINQUES...
...AND CLOSED IN ON THE OWL.
THE BATTLE BETWEEN THE PRODIGY (RANK 2 INVESTIGATOR ARIMA) AND...
...THE NATURAL CALAMITY (THE ONE-EYED OWL)...

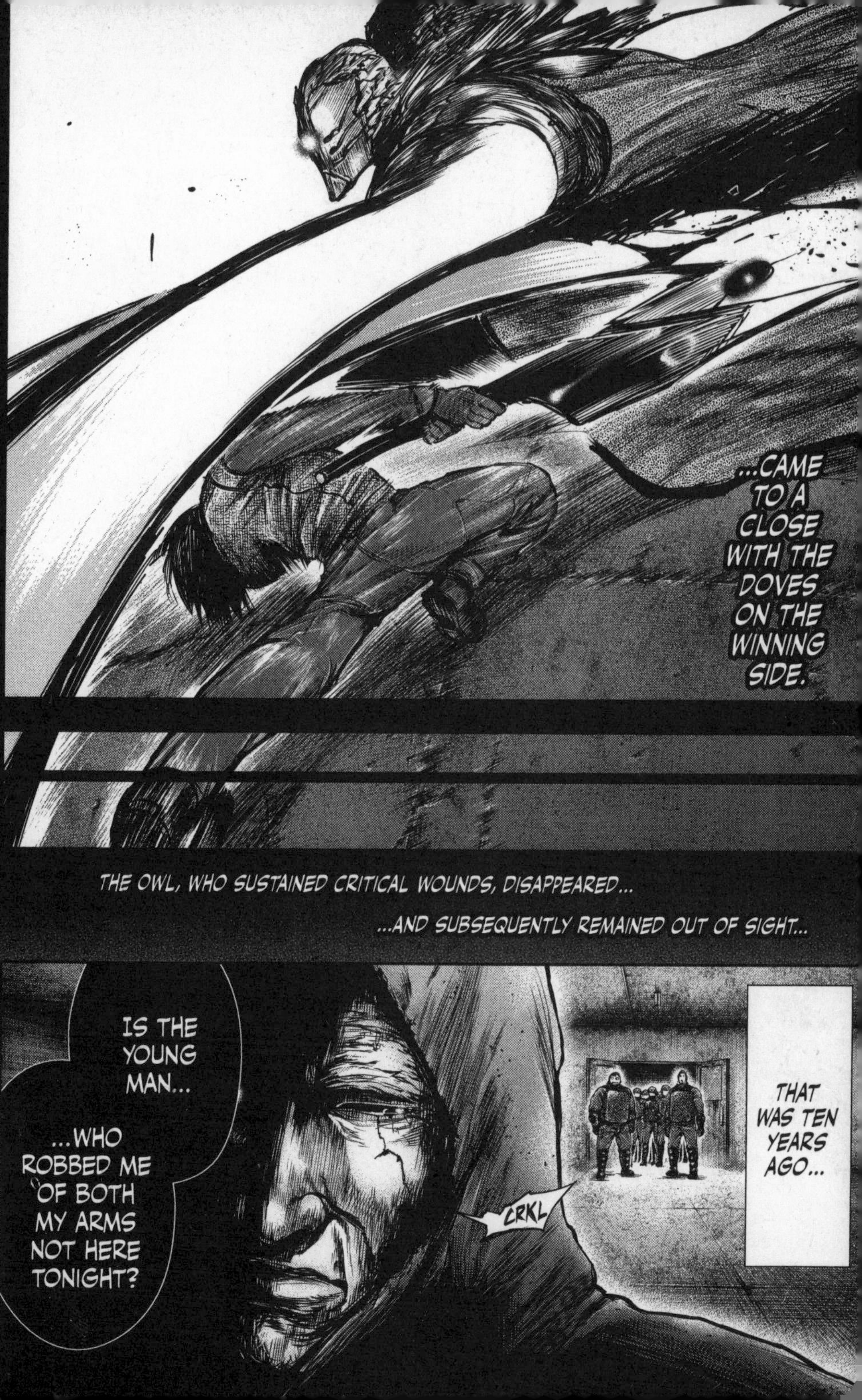
...CAME TO A CLOSE WITH THE DOVES ON THE WINNING SIDE.
THE OWL, WHO SUSTAINED CRITICAL WOUNDS, DISAPPEARED...
...AND SUBSEQUENTLY REMAINED OUT OF SIGHT...
THAT WAS TEN YEARS AGO...
IS THE YOUNG MAN...
...WHO ROBBED ME OF BOTH MY ARMS NOT HERE TONIGHT?
CRKL

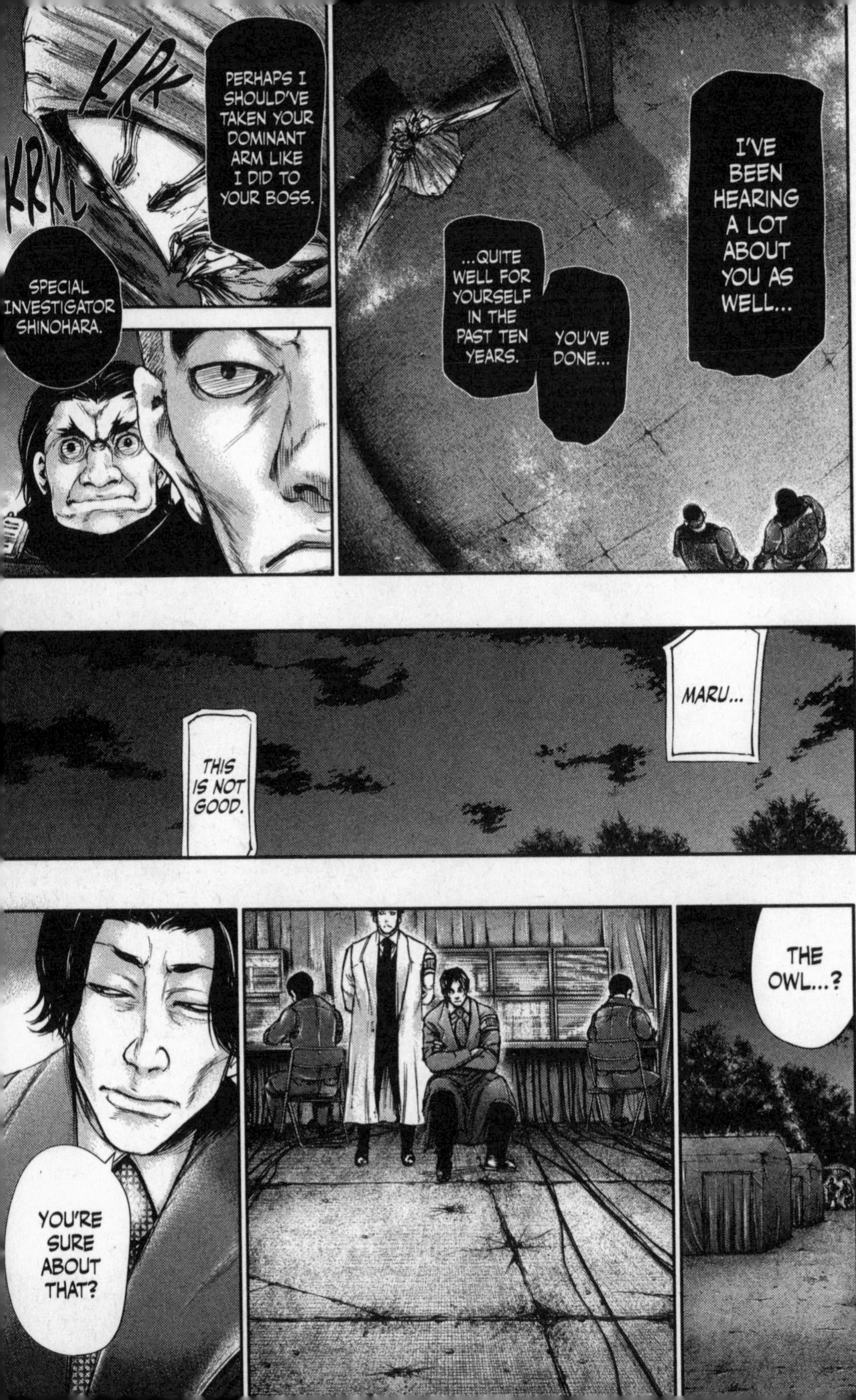
I'VE BEEN HEARING A LOT ABOUT YOU AS WELL...
YOU'VE DONE...
...QUITE WELL FOR YOURSELF IN THE PAST TEN YEARS.
PERHAPS I SHOULD'VE TAKEN YOUR DOMINANT ARM LIKE I DID TO YOUR BOSS.
KRK
KRKL
SPECIAL INVESTIGATOR SHINOHARA.
MARU...
THIS IS NOT GOOD.
THE OWL...?
YOU'RE SURE ABOUT THAT?

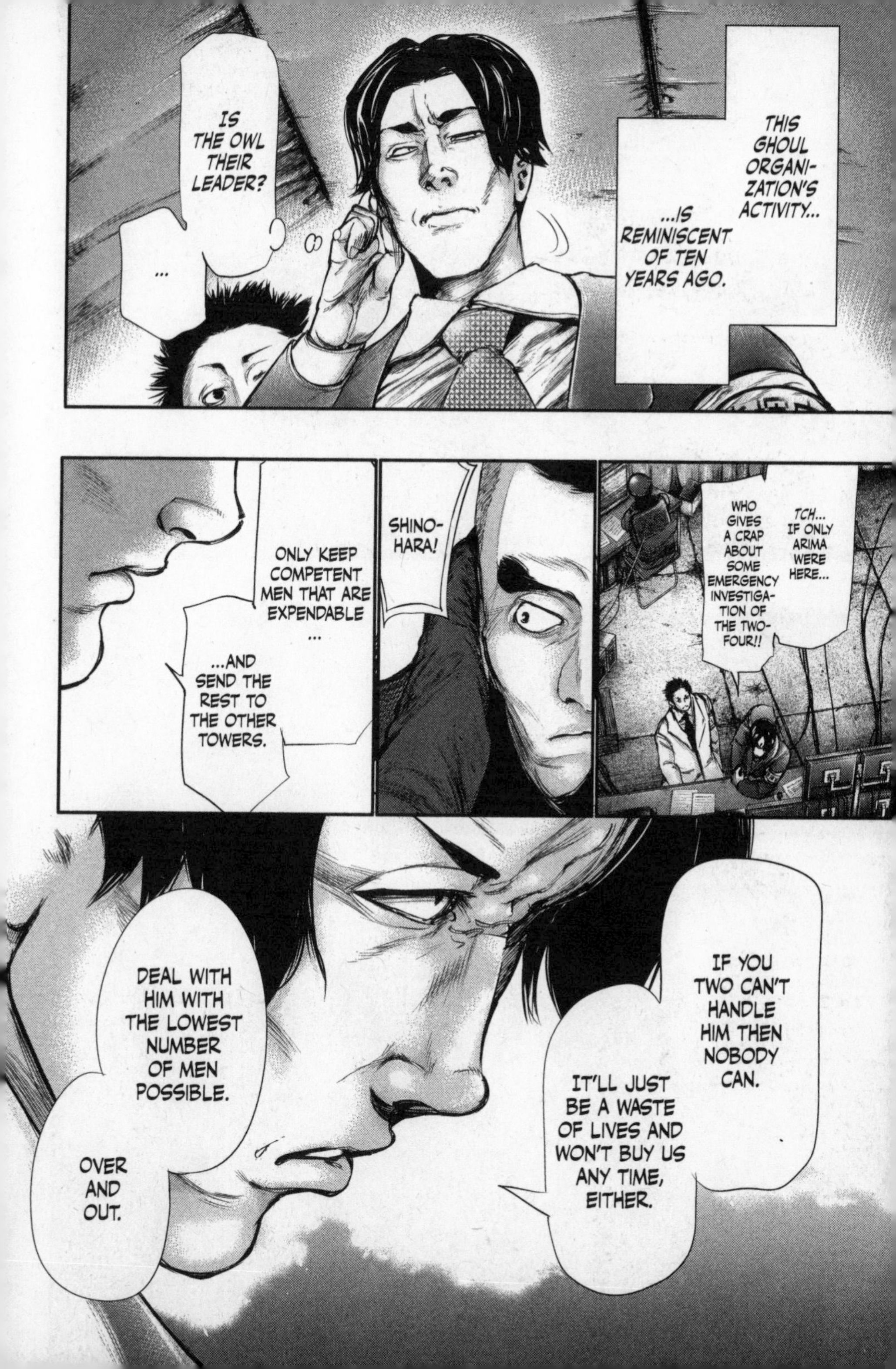
THIS GHOUL ORGANIZATION'S ACTIVITY...
...IS REMINISCENT OF TEN YEARS AGO.
IS THE OWL THEIR LEADER?
...
TCH... IF ONLY ARIMA WERE HERE...
WHO GIVES A CRAP ABOUT SOME EMERGENCY INVESTIGATION OF THE TWO-FOUR!!
SHINOHARA!
ONLY KEEP COMPETENT MEN THAT ARE EXPENDABLE...
...AND SEND THE REST TO THE OTHER TOWERS.
IF YOU TWO CAN'T HANDLE HIM THEN NOBODY CAN.
IT'LL JUST BE A WASTE OF LIVES AND WON'T BUY US ANY TIME, EITHER.
DEAL WITH HIM WITH THE LOWEST NUMBER OF MEN POSSIBLE.
OVER AND OUT.

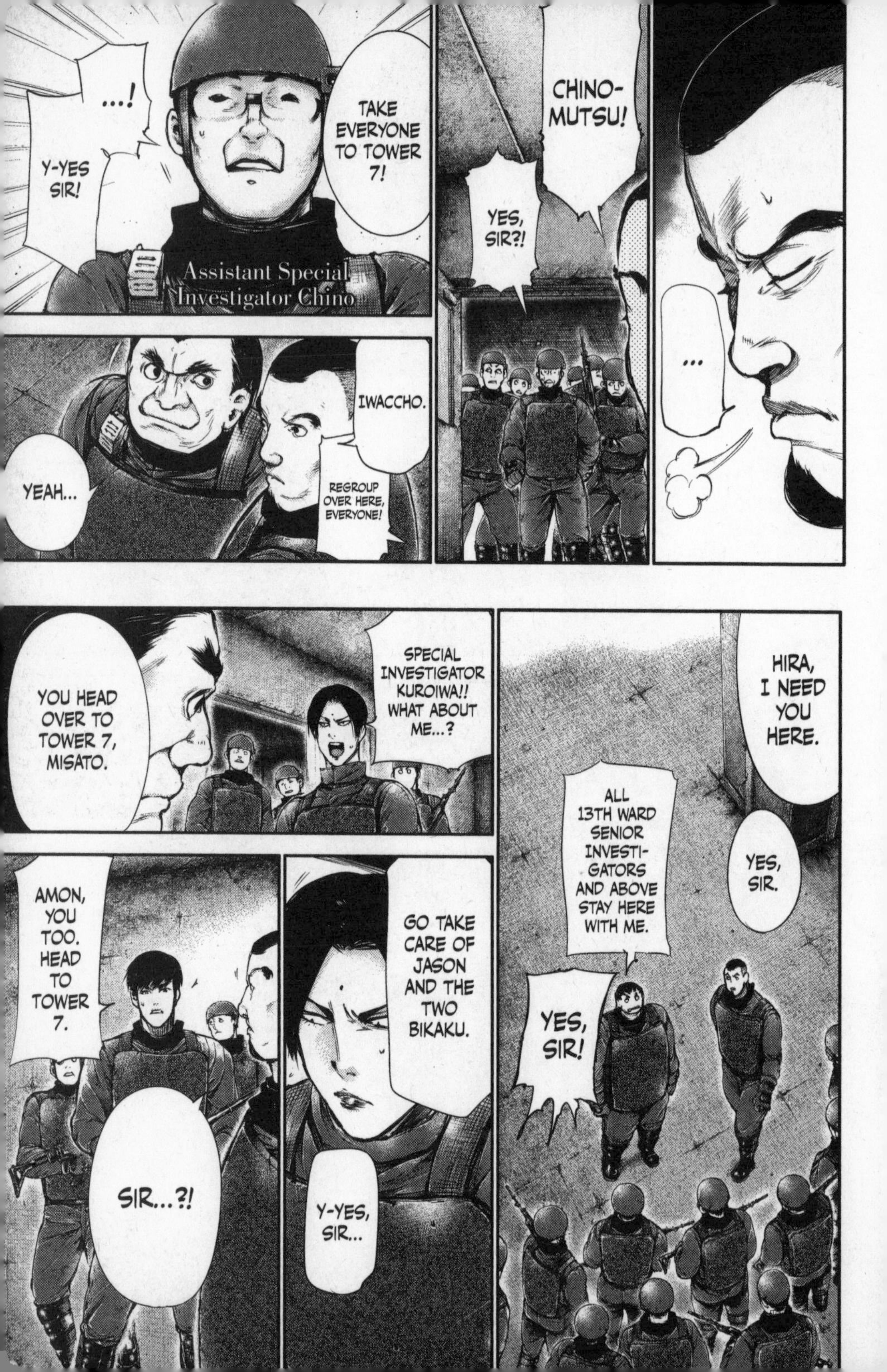
...
CHINO-MUTSU!
YES, SIR?!
TAKE EVERYONE TO TOWER 7!
...!
Y-YES SIR!
Assistant Special Investigator Chino
IWACCHO.
REGROUP OVER HERE, EVERYONE!
YEAH...
HIRA, I NEED YOU HERE.
YES, SIR.
ALL 13TH WARD SENIOR INVESTI-GATORS AND ABOVE STAY HERE WITH ME.
YES, SIR!
SPECIAL INVESTIGATOR KUROIWA!! WHAT ABOUT ME...?
YOU HEAD OVER TO TOWER 7, MISATO.
GO TAKE CARE OF JASON AND THE TWO BIKAKU.
Y-YES, SIR...
AMON, YOU TOO. HEAD TO TOWER 7.
SIR...?!

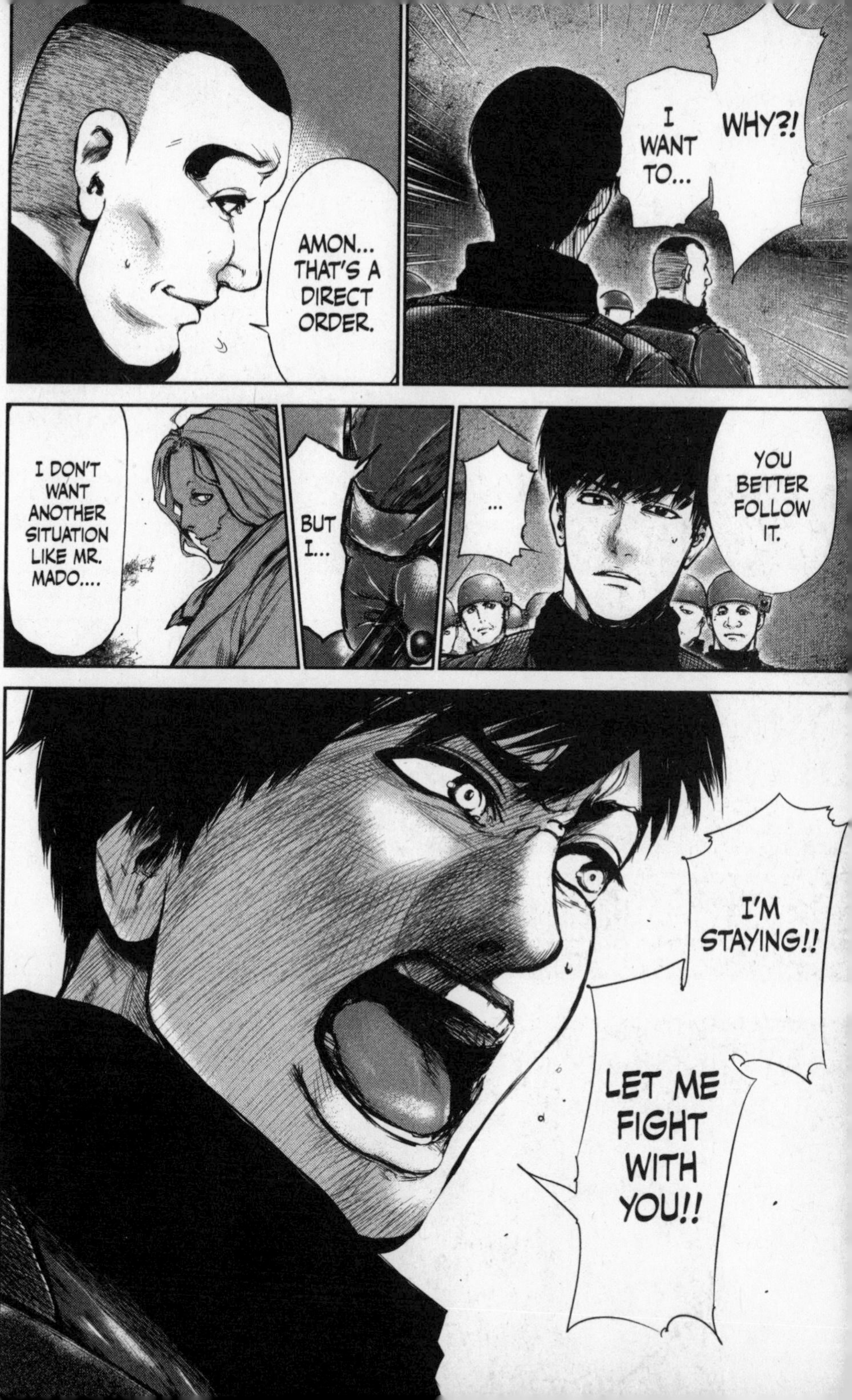
WHY?!
I WANT TO...
AMON... THAT'S A DIRECT ORDER.
YOU BETTER FOLLOW IT.
...
BUT I...
I DON'T WANT ANOTHER SITUATION LIKE MR. MADO....
I'M STAYING!!
LET ME FIGHT WITH YOU!!

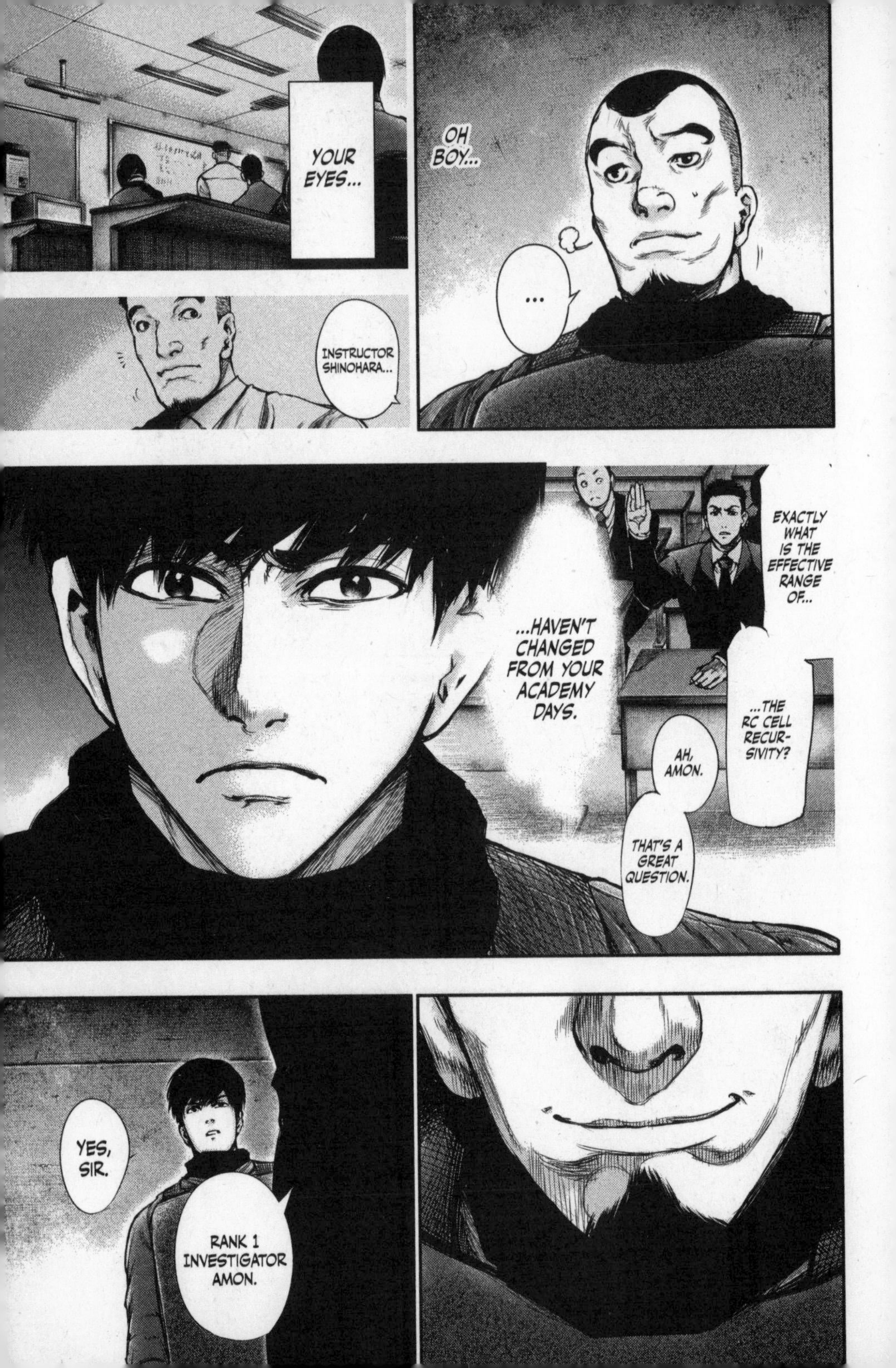
OH BOY...
...
YOUR EYES...
INSTRUCTOR SHINOHARA...
EXACTLY WHAT IS THE EFFECTIVE RANGE OF...
...THE RC CELL RECURSIVITY?
AH, AMON.
THAT'S A GREAT QUESTION.
...HAVEN'T CHANGED FROM YOUR ACADEMY DAYS.
RANK 1 INVESTIGATOR AMON.
YES, SIR.

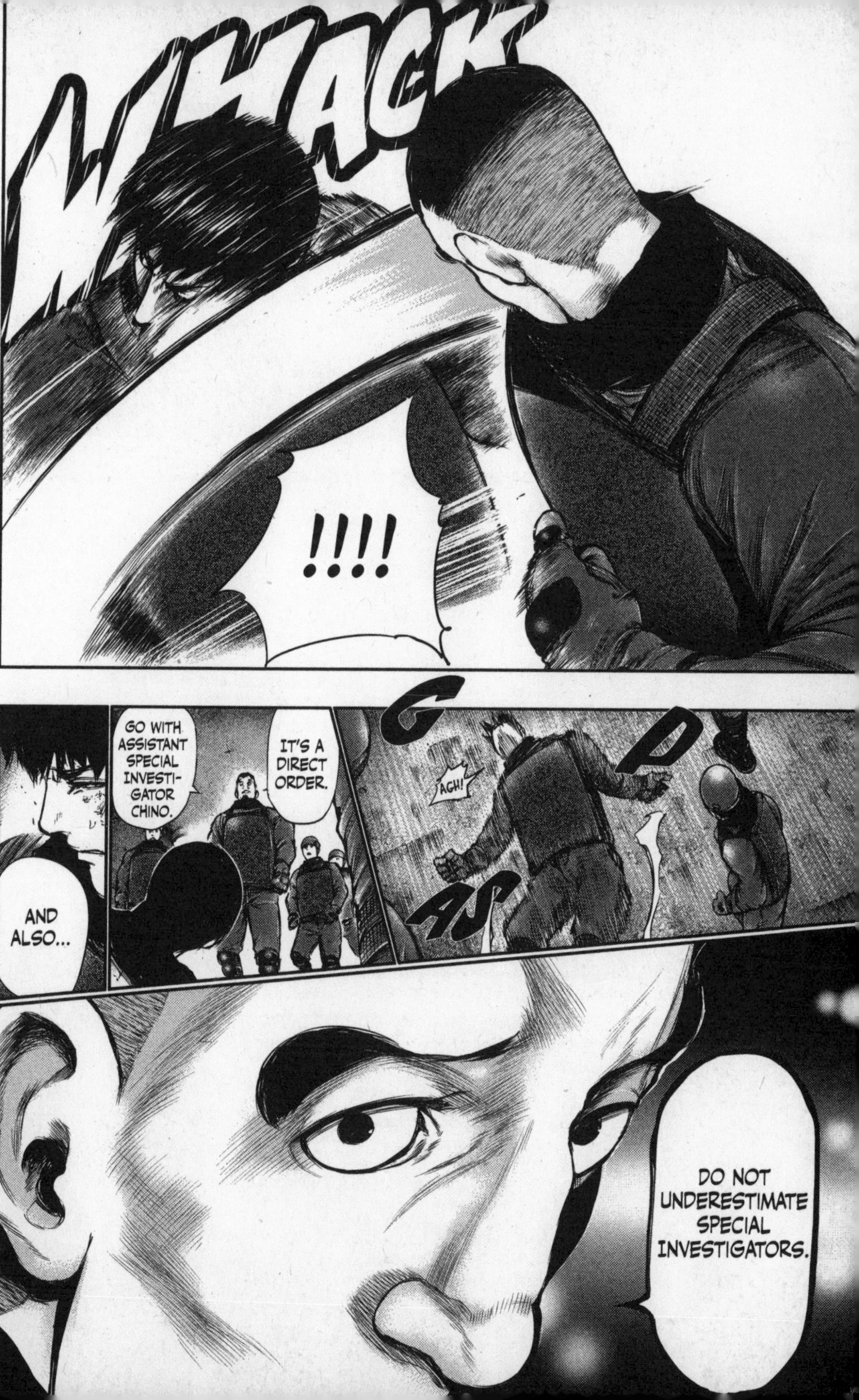
WHACK
!!!!
AGH!
G
D
AS
IT'S A DIRECT ORDER.
GO WITH ASSISTANT SPECIAL INVESTIGATOR CHINO.
AND ALSO...
DO NOT UNDERESTIMATE SPECIAL INVESTIGATORS.

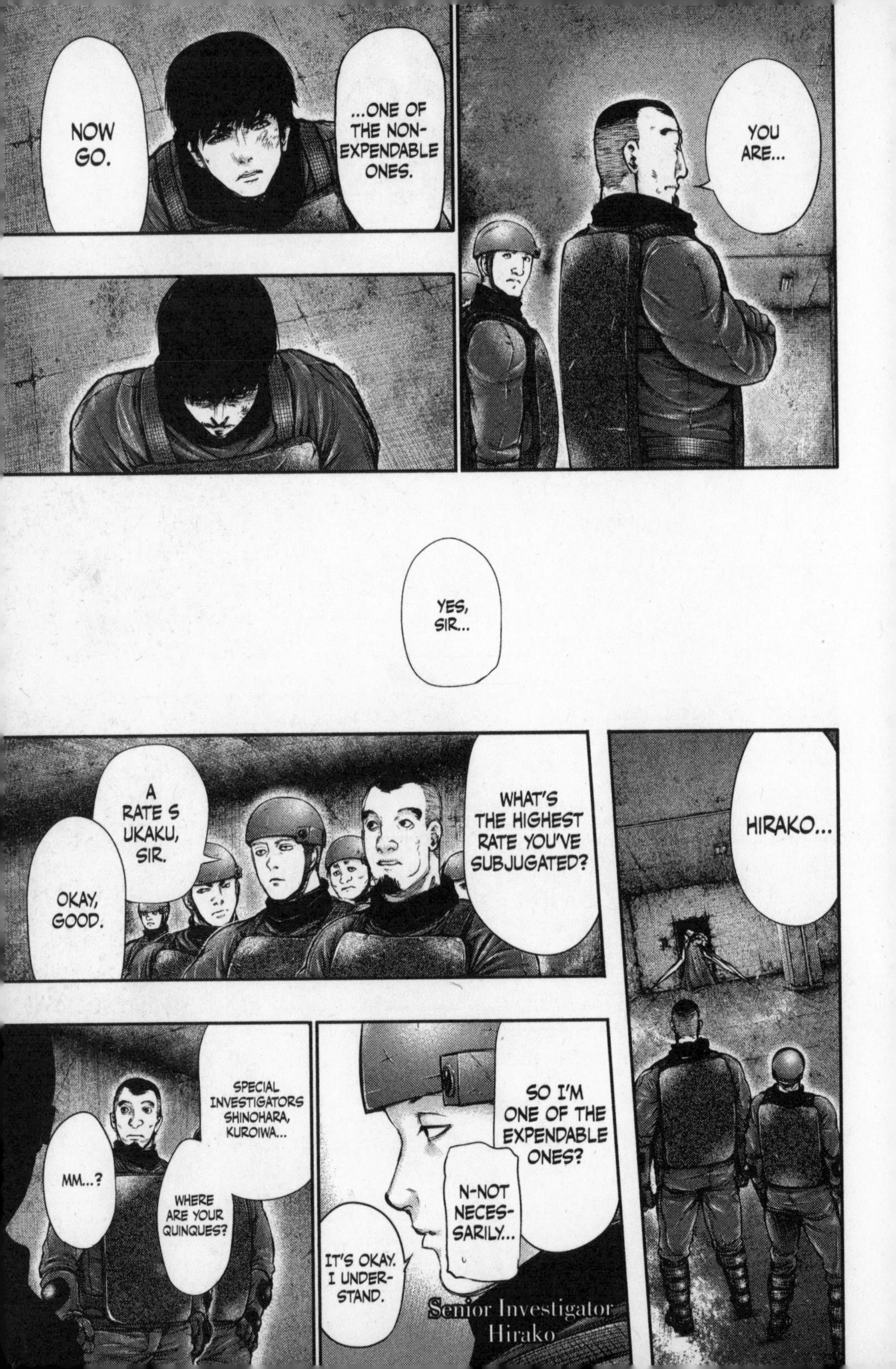

YOU ARE...
...ONE OF THE NON-EXPENDABLE ONES.
NOW GO.
YES, SIR...
HIRAKO...
WHAT'S THE HIGHEST RATE YOU'VE SUBJUGATED?
A RATE S UKAKU, SIR.
OKAY, GOOD.
SO I'M ONE OF THE EXPENDABLE ONES?
N-NOT NECES-SARILY...
IT'S OKAY. I UNDER-STAND.
Senior Investigator Hirako
SPECIAL INVESTIGATORS SHINOHARA, KUROIWA...
MM...?
WHERE ARE YOUR QUINQUES?

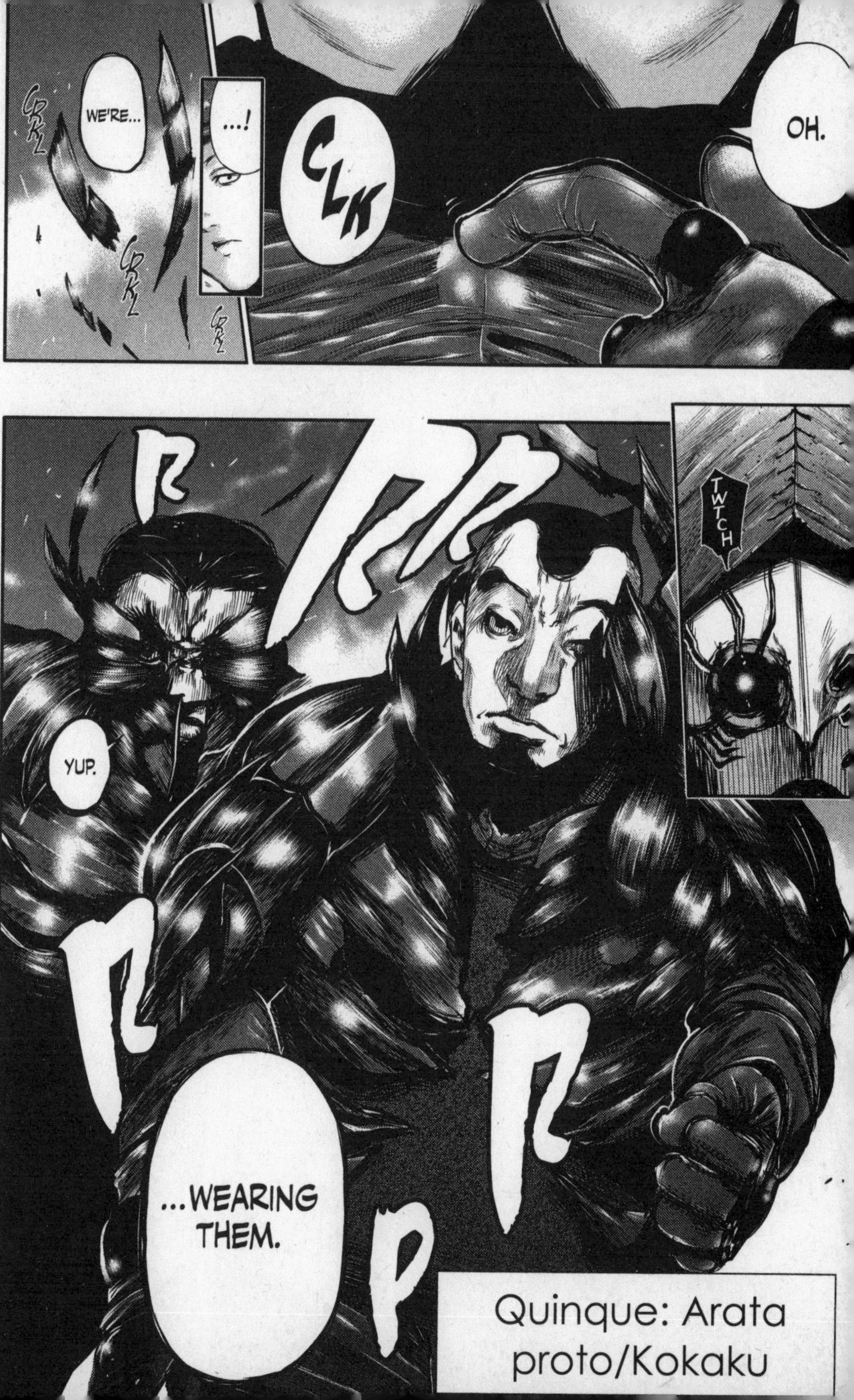

OH.
CLK
...!
WE'RE...
CRKL
CRKL
CRKL
TWTCH
YUP.
...WEARING THEM.
Quinque: Arata proto/Kokaku

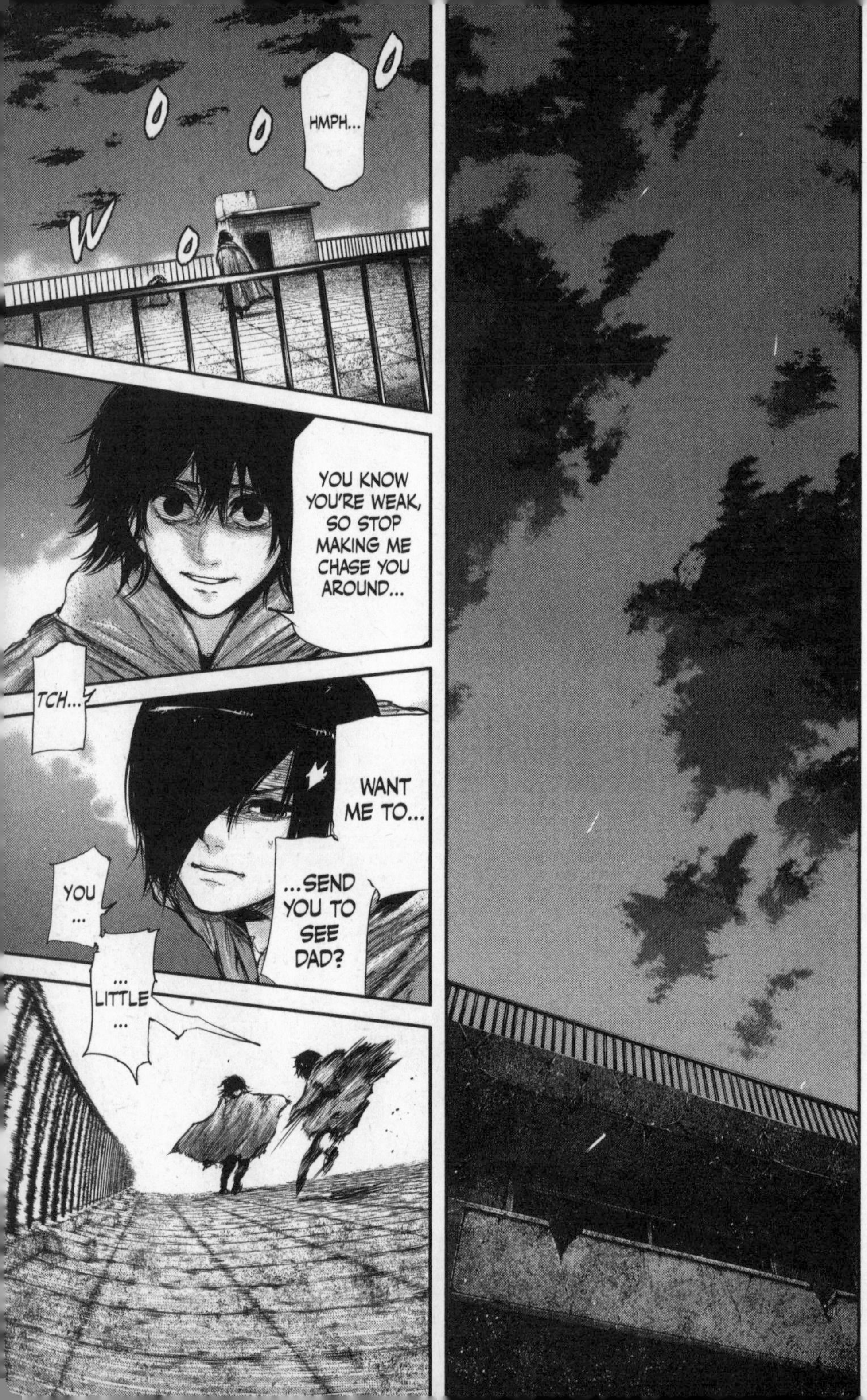
WOOOO
HMPH...
YOU KNOW YOU'RE WEAK, SO STOP MAKING ME CHASE YOU AROUND...
TCH...
WANT ME TO...
...SEND YOU TO SEE DAD?
YOU ...
... LITTLE ...

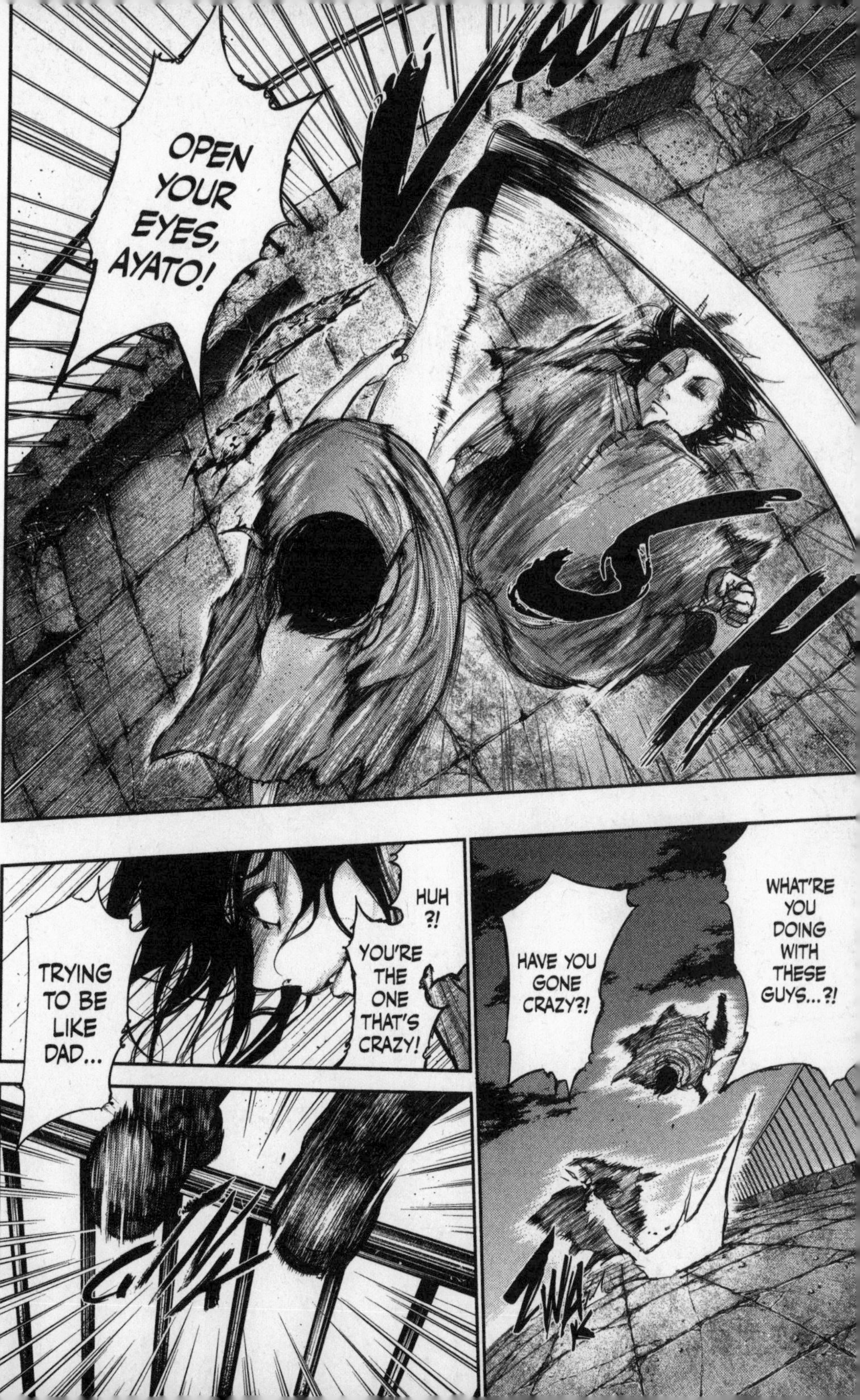
OPEN YOUR EYES, AYATO!
WHAT'RE YOU DOING WITH THESE GUYS...?!
HAVE YOU GONE CRAZY?!
ZWAK
HUH ?!
YOU'RE THE ONE THAT'S CRAZY!
TRYING TO BE LIKE DAD...

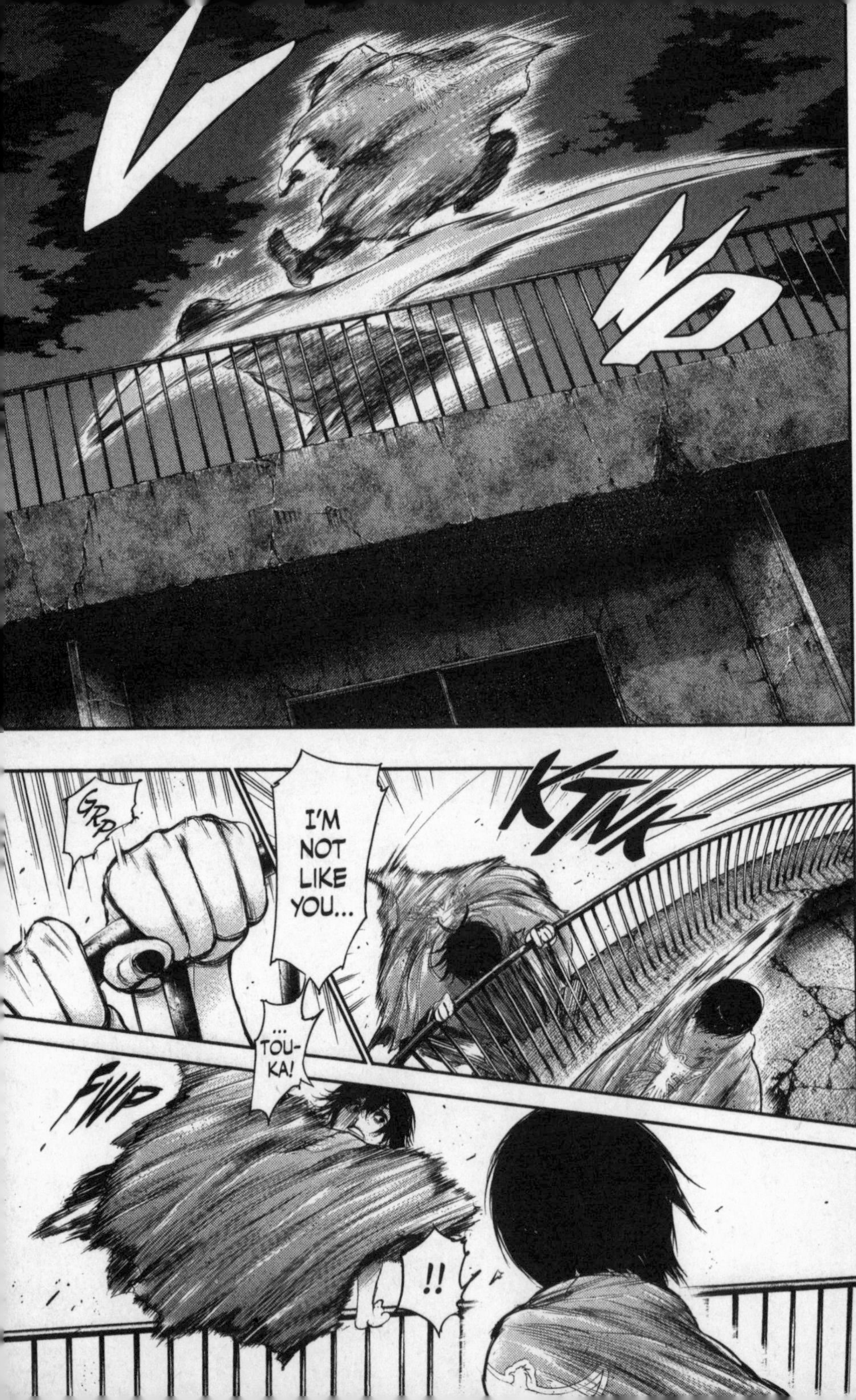
KTNK
I'M NOT LIKE YOU...
GRP
...TOU-KA!
FWP
!!

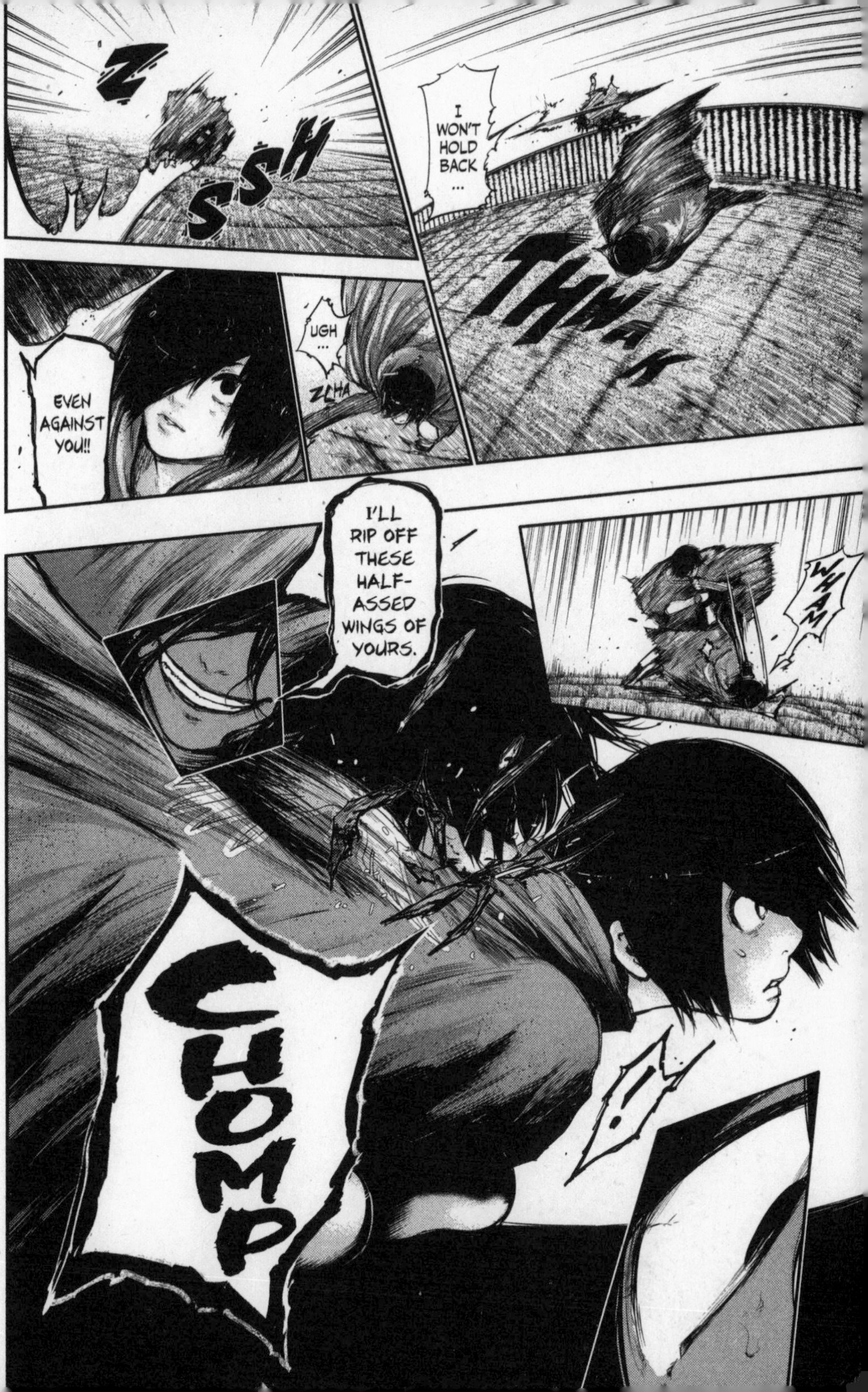
I WON'T HOLD BACK ...
THWACK
ZSSSH
UGH ...
ZCHA
EVEN AGAINST YOU!!
WHAM
I'LL RIP OFF THESE HALF-ASSED WINGS OF YOURS.
CHOMP
!

東京
トーキョーグール
喰種
Tokyo
Ghoul

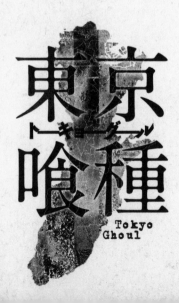

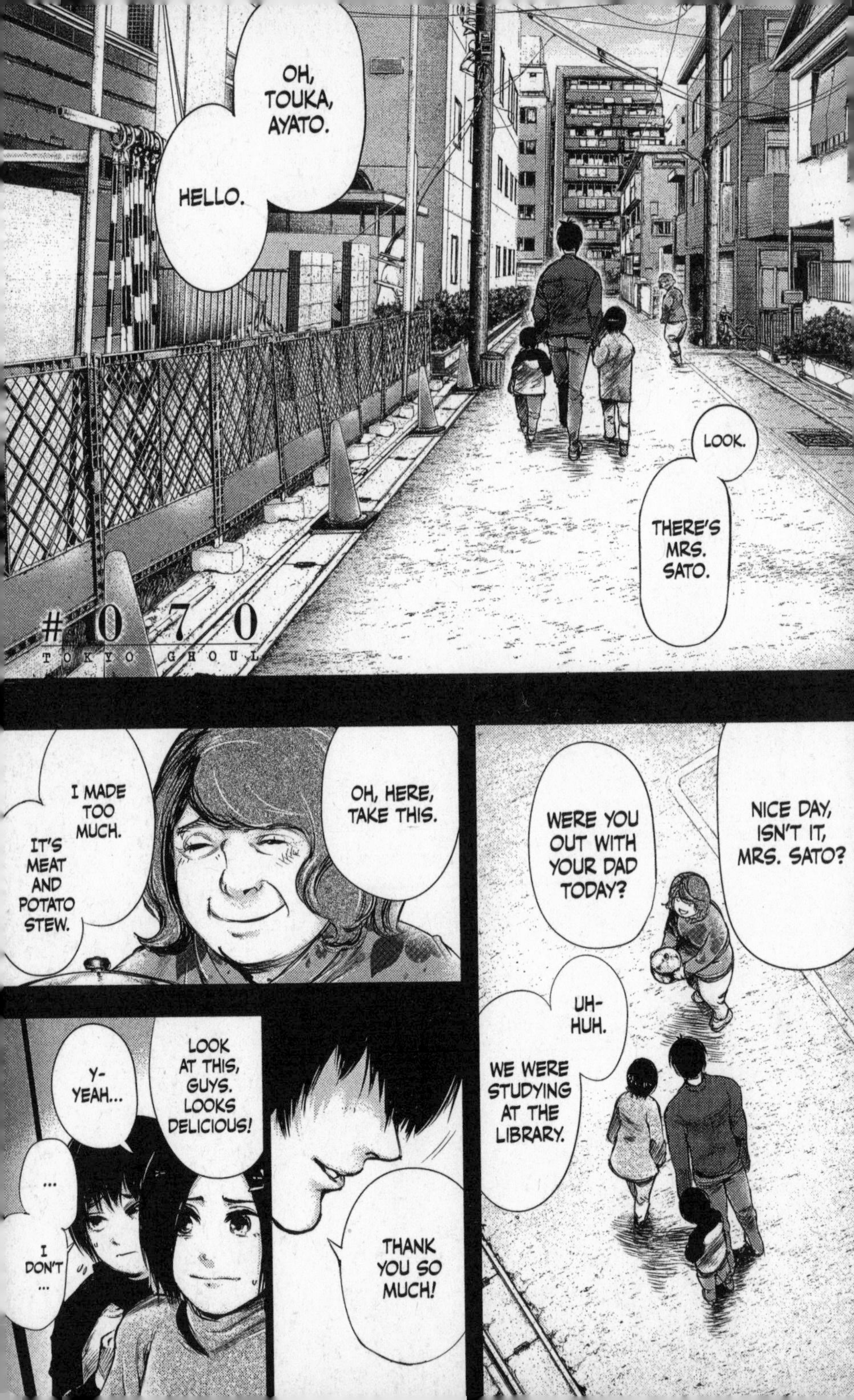
LOOK.
THERE'S MRS. SATO.
OH, TOUKA, AYATO.
HELLO.
#070
TOKYO GHOUL
NICE DAY, ISN'T IT, MRS. SATO?
WERE YOU OUT WITH YOUR DAD TODAY?
UH-HUH.
WE WERE STUDYING AT THE LIBRARY.
OH, HERE, TAKE THIS.
I MADE TOO MUCH.
IT'S MEAT AND POTATO STEW.
THANK YOU SO MUCH!
LOOK AT THIS, GUYS. LOOKS DELICIOUS!
Y-YEAH...
...
I DON'T ...

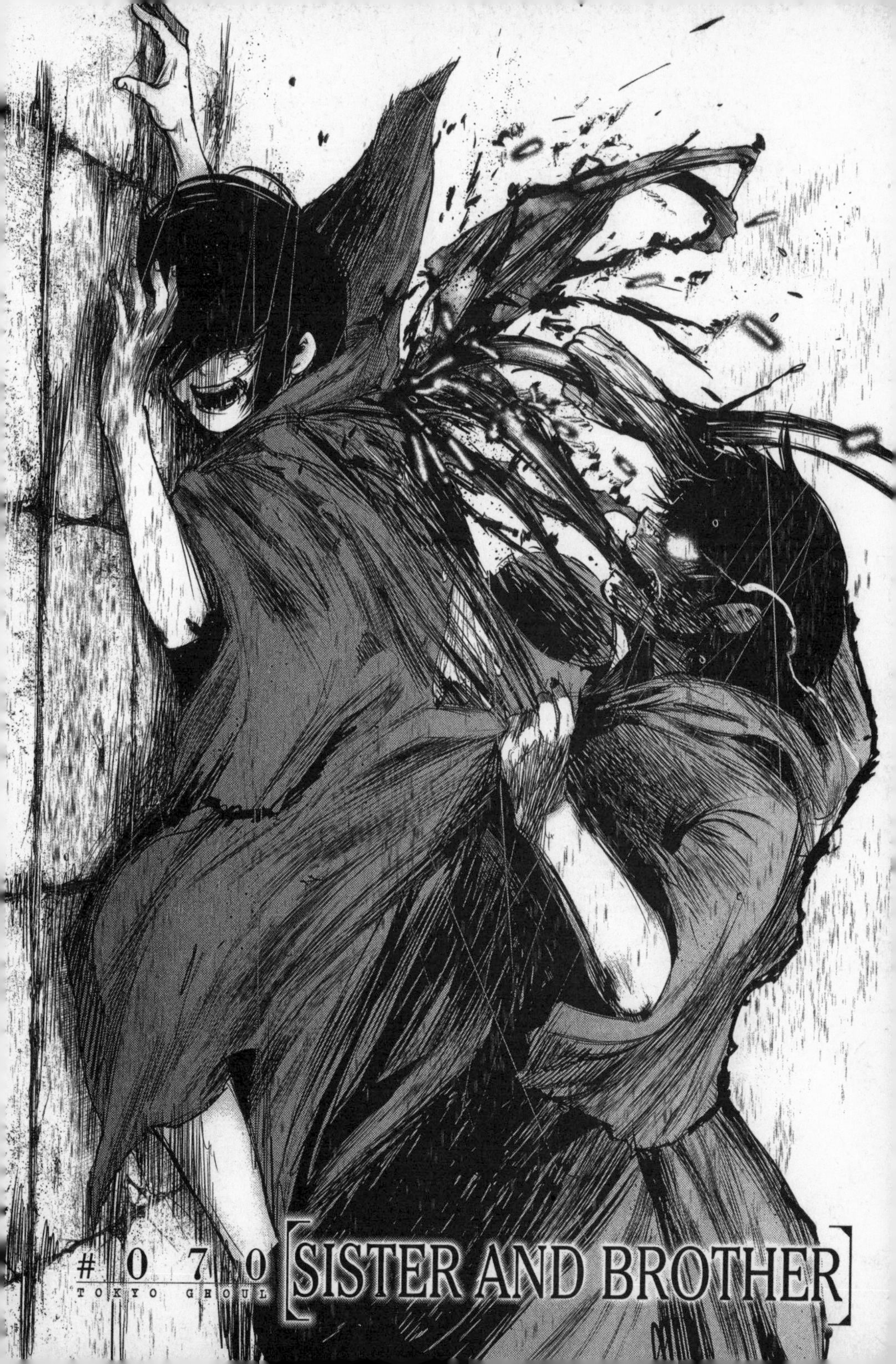

0 7 0 [SISTER AND BROTHER]
TOKYO GHOUL

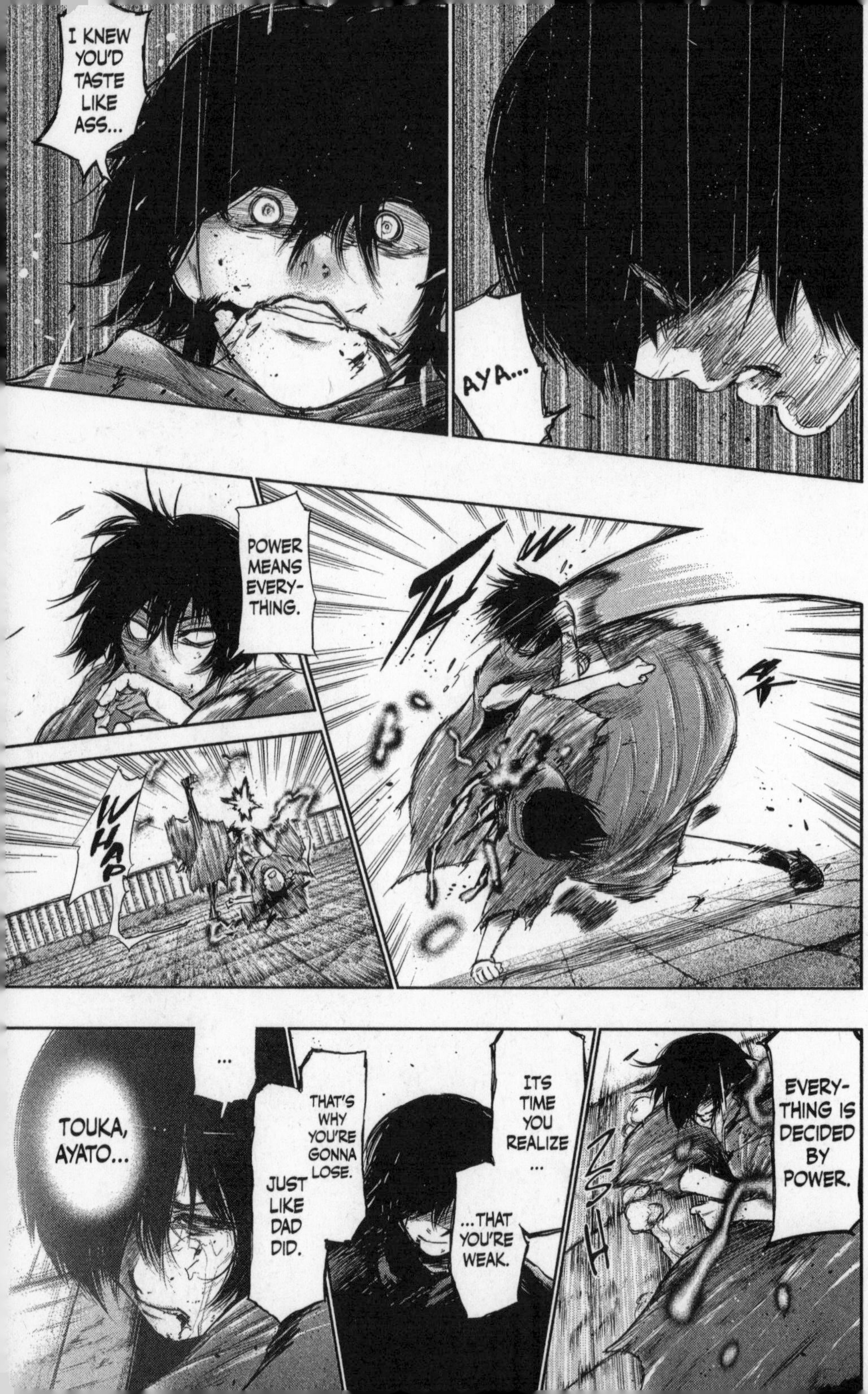
AYA...
I KNEW YOU'D TASTE LIKE ASS...
POWER MEANS EVERY-THING.
WHAP
EVERY-THING IS DECIDED BY POWER.
ITS TIME YOU REALIZE...
...THAT YOU'RE WEAK.
THAT'S WHY YOU'RE GONNA LOSE.
JUST LIKE DAD DID.
...
TOUKA, AYATO...

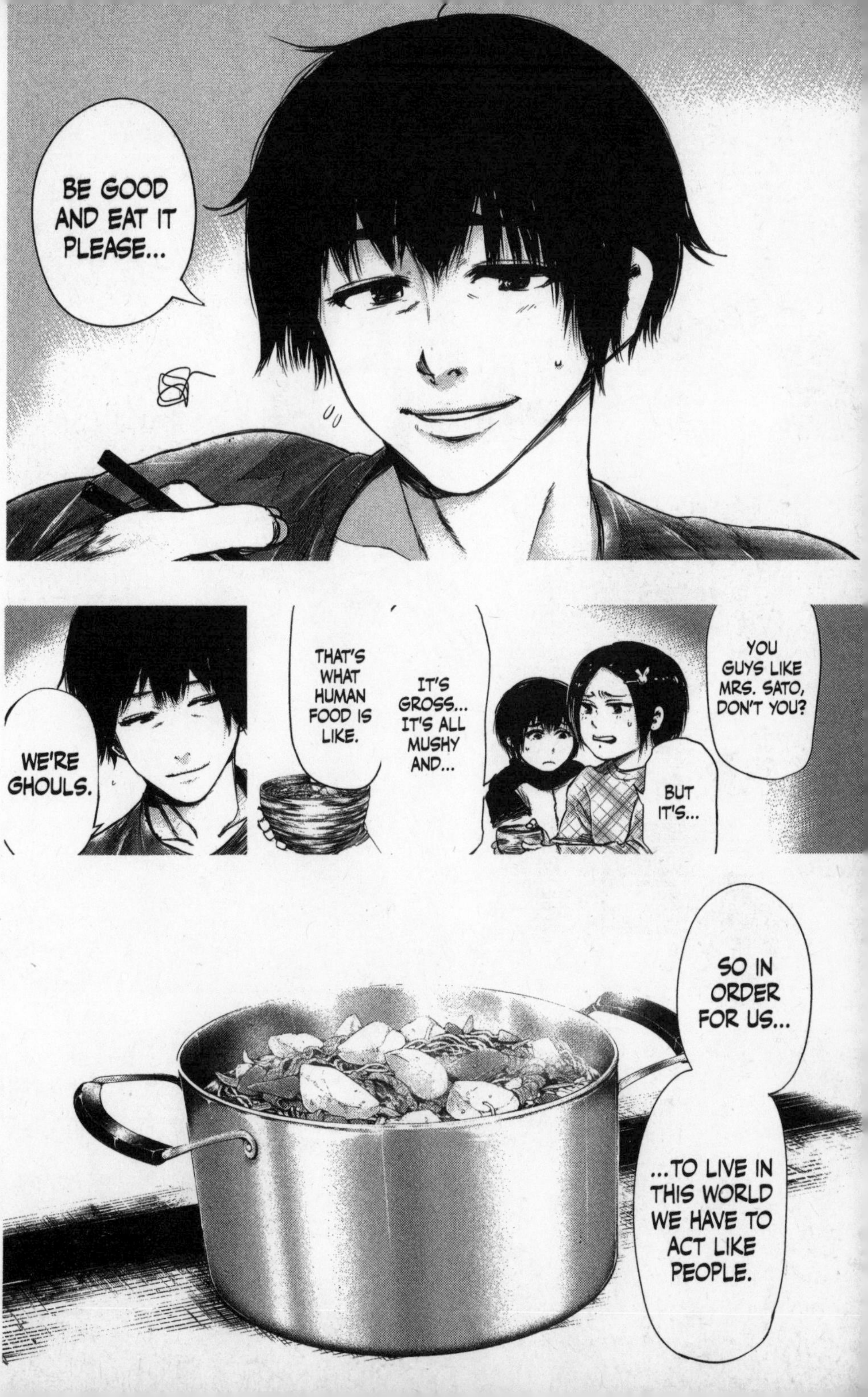
BE GOOD AND EAT IT PLEASE...
YOU GUYS LIKE MRS. SATO, DON'T YOU?
BUT IT'S...
IT'S GROSS... IT'S ALL MUSHY AND...
THAT'S WHAT HUMAN FOOD IS LIKE.
WE'RE GHOULS.
SO IN ORDER FOR US...
...TO LIVE IN THIS WORLD WE HAVE TO ACT LIKE PEOPLE.

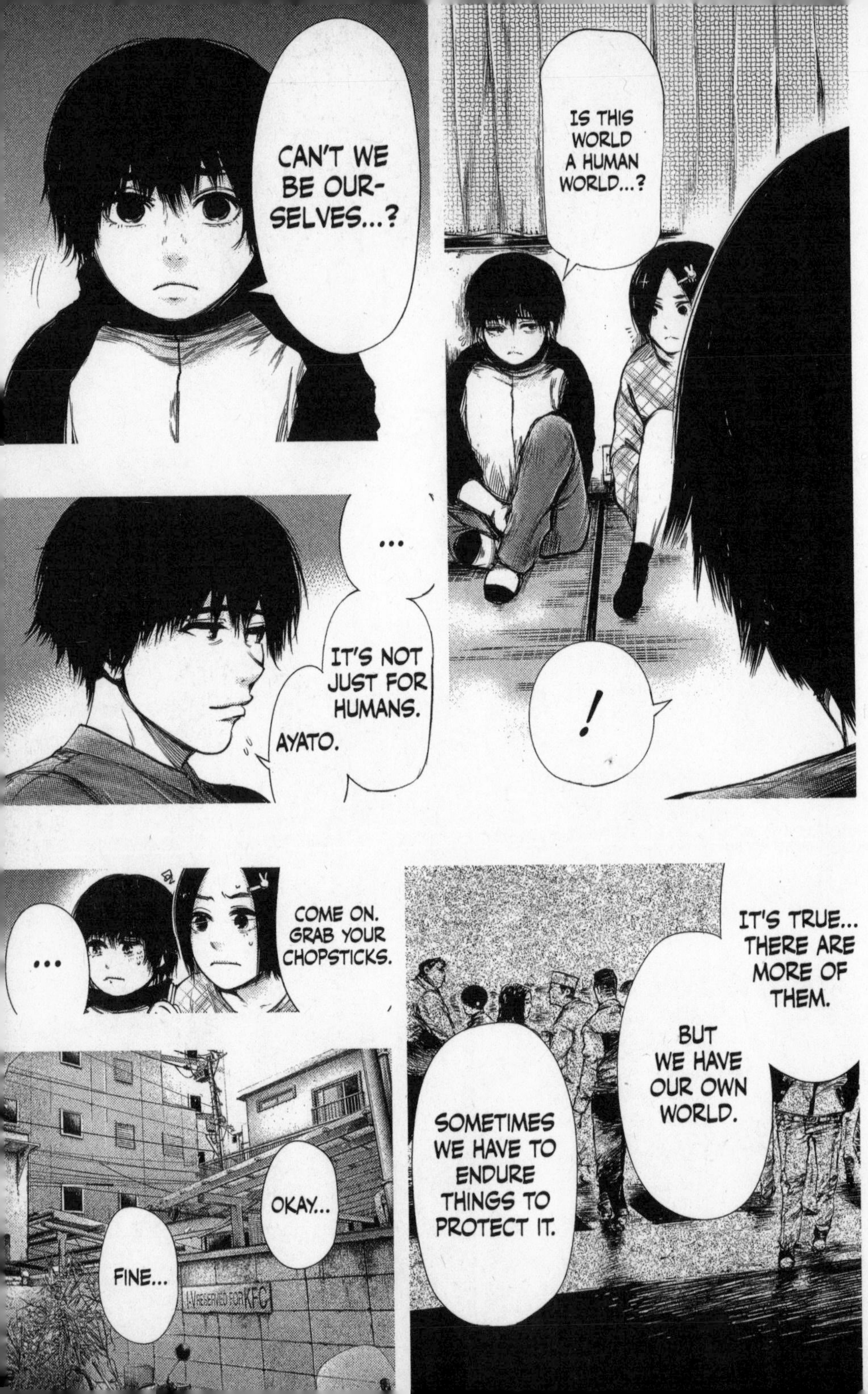
IS THIS WORLD A HUMAN WORLD...?
!
CAN'T WE BE OUR-SELVES...?
...
IT'S NOT JUST FOR HUMANS.
AYATO.
IT'S TRUE... THERE ARE MORE OF THEM.
BUT WE HAVE OUR OWN WORLD.
SOMETIMES WE HAVE TO ENDURE THINGS TO PROTECT IT.
COME ON. GRAB YOUR CHOPSTICKS.
...
OKAY...
FINE...

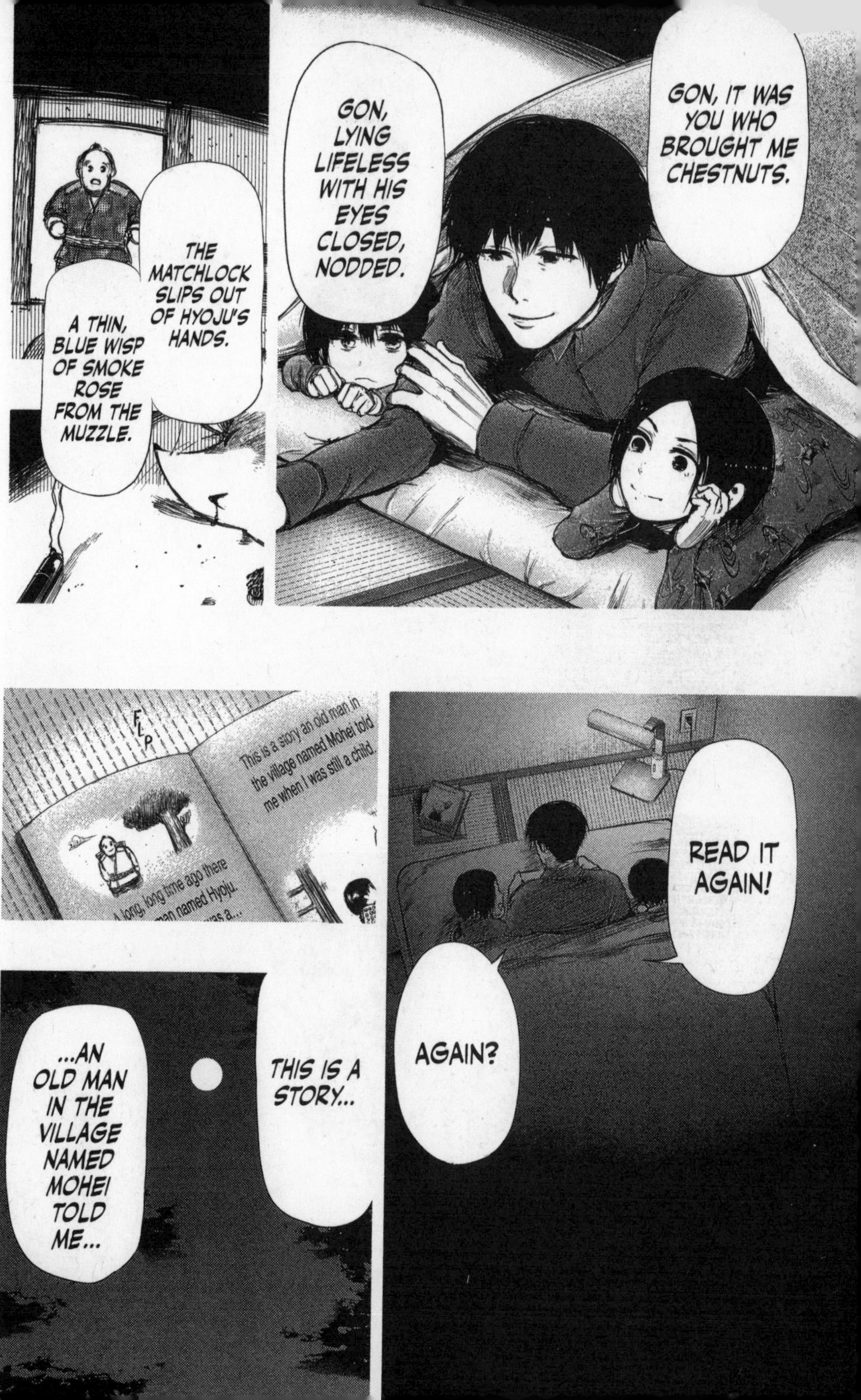
GON, IT WAS YOU WHO BROUGHT ME CHESTNUTS.
GON, LYING LIFELESS WITH HIS EYES CLOSED, NODDED.
THE MATCHLOCK SLIPS OUT OF HYOJU'S HANDS.
A THIN, BLUE WISP OF SMOKE ROSE FROM THE MUZZLE.
READ IT AGAIN!
AGAIN?
FLP
This is a story an old man in the village named Mohei told me when I was still a child.
THIS IS A STORY...
...AN OLD MAN IN THE VILLAGE NAMED MOHEI TOLD ME...

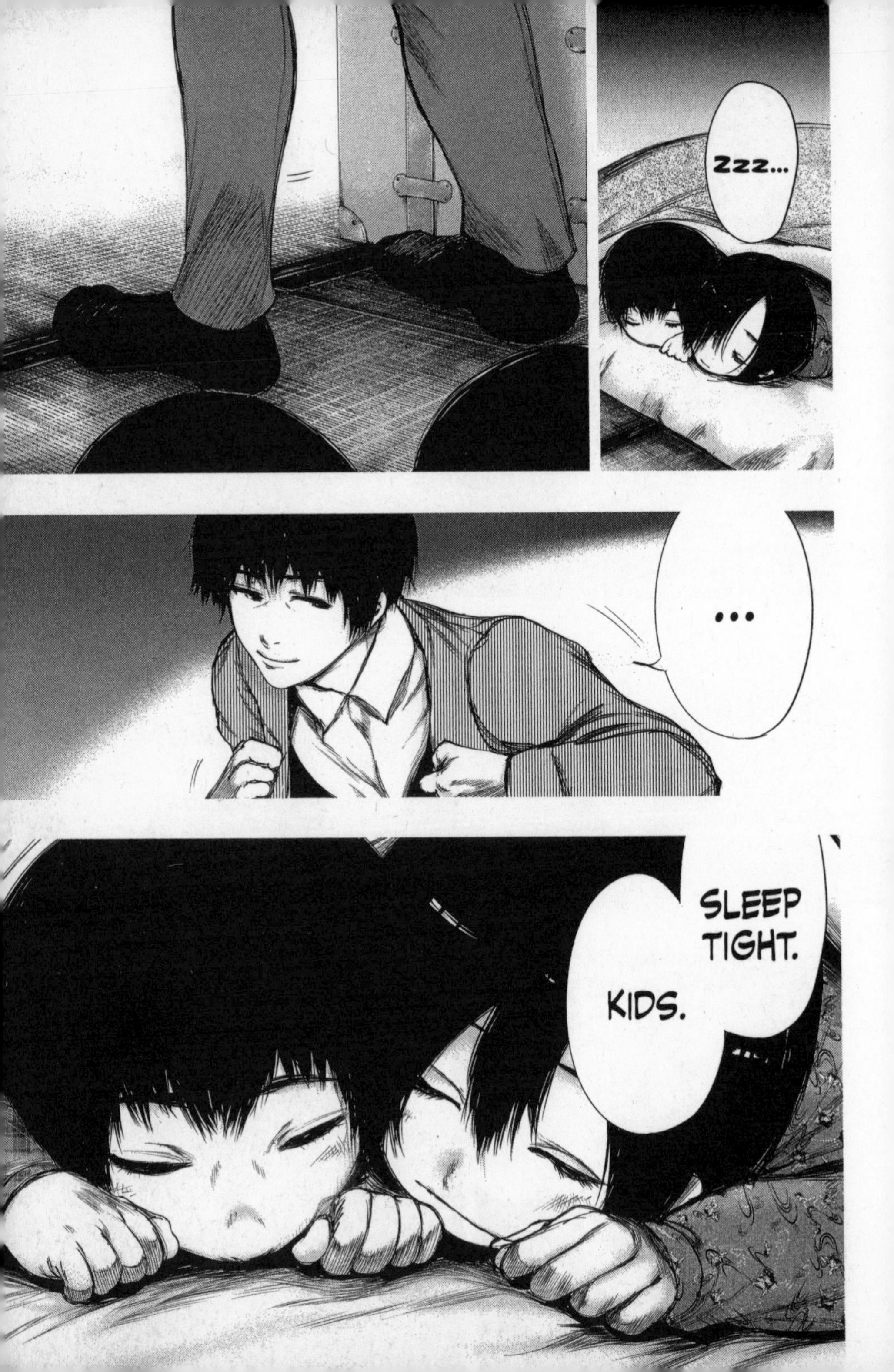
Zzz...
...
SLEEP TIGHT. KIDS.

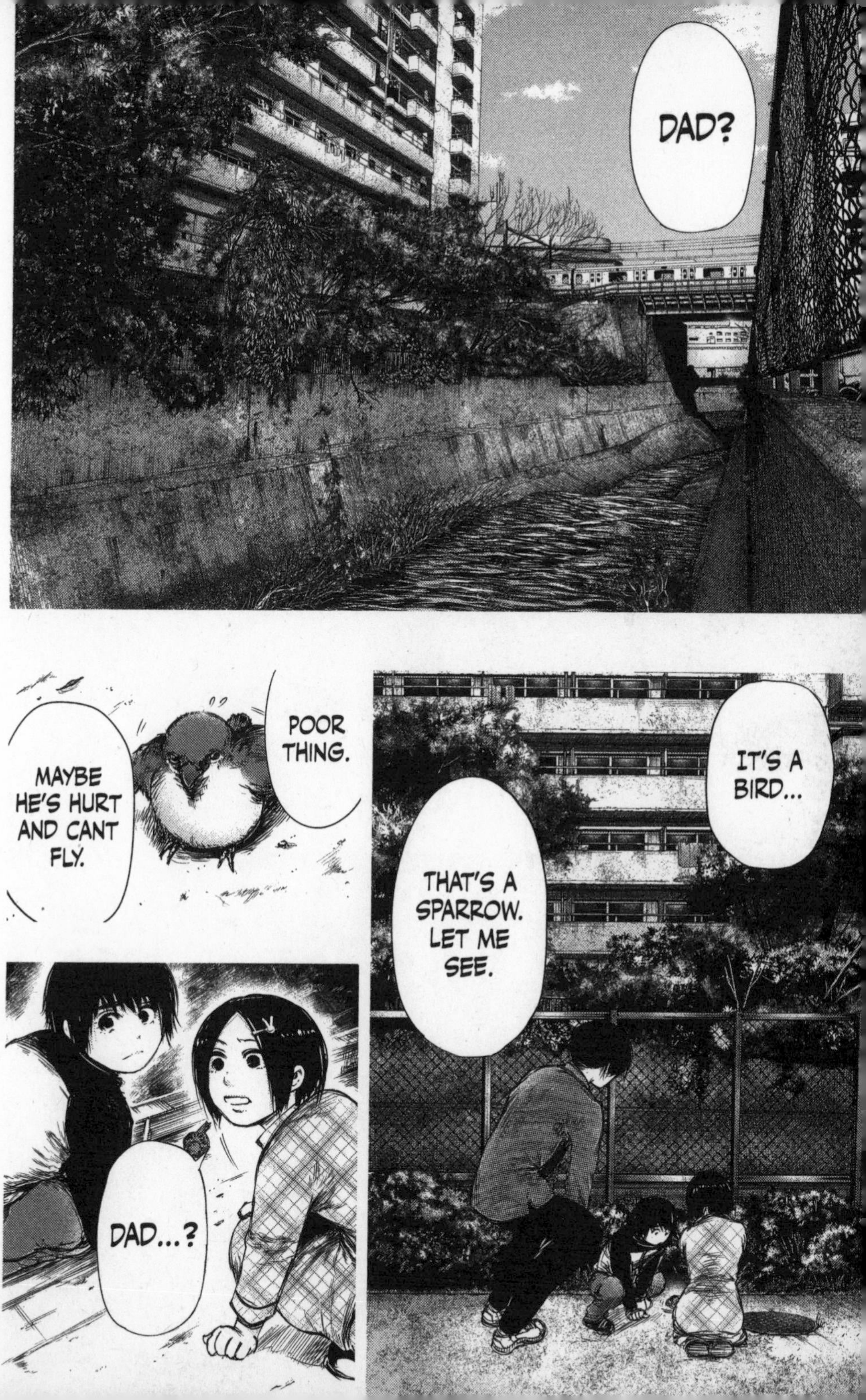
DAD?
IT'S A BIRD...
THAT'S A SPARROW. LET ME SEE.
POOR THING.
MAYBE HE'S HURT AND CANT FLY.
DAD...?

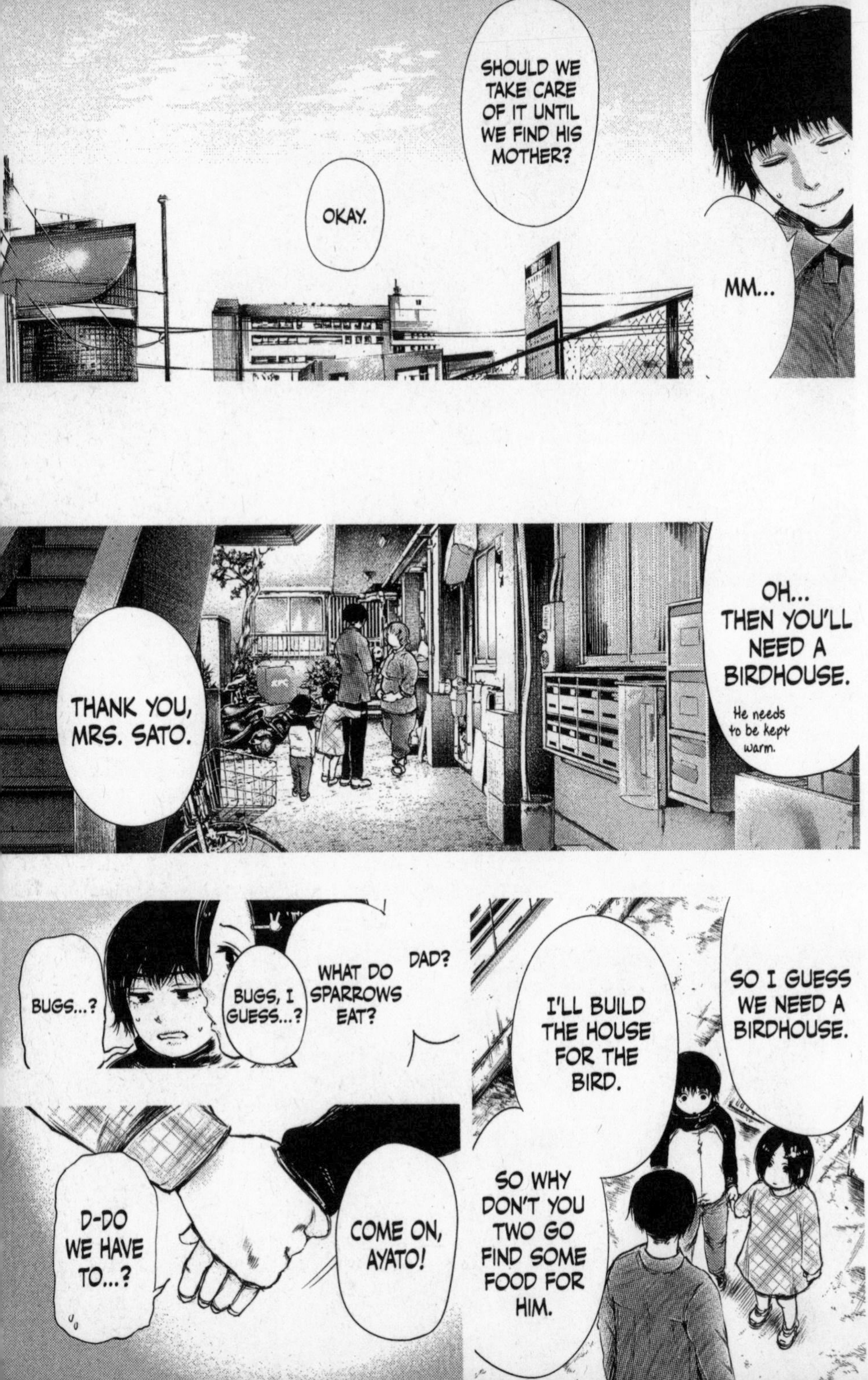
MM...
SHOULD WE TAKE CARE OF IT UNTIL WE FIND HIS MOTHER?
OKAY.
OH... THEN YOU'LL NEED A BIRDHOUSE.
He needs to be kept warm.
THANK YOU, MRS. SATO.
SO I GUESS WE NEED A BIRDHOUSE.
I'LL BUILD THE HOUSE FOR THE BIRD.
SO WHY DON'T YOU TWO GO FIND SOME FOOD FOR HIM.
DAD?
WHAT DO SPARROWS EAT?
BUGS, I GUESS...?
BUGS...?
COME ON, AYATO!
D-DO WE HAVE TO...?

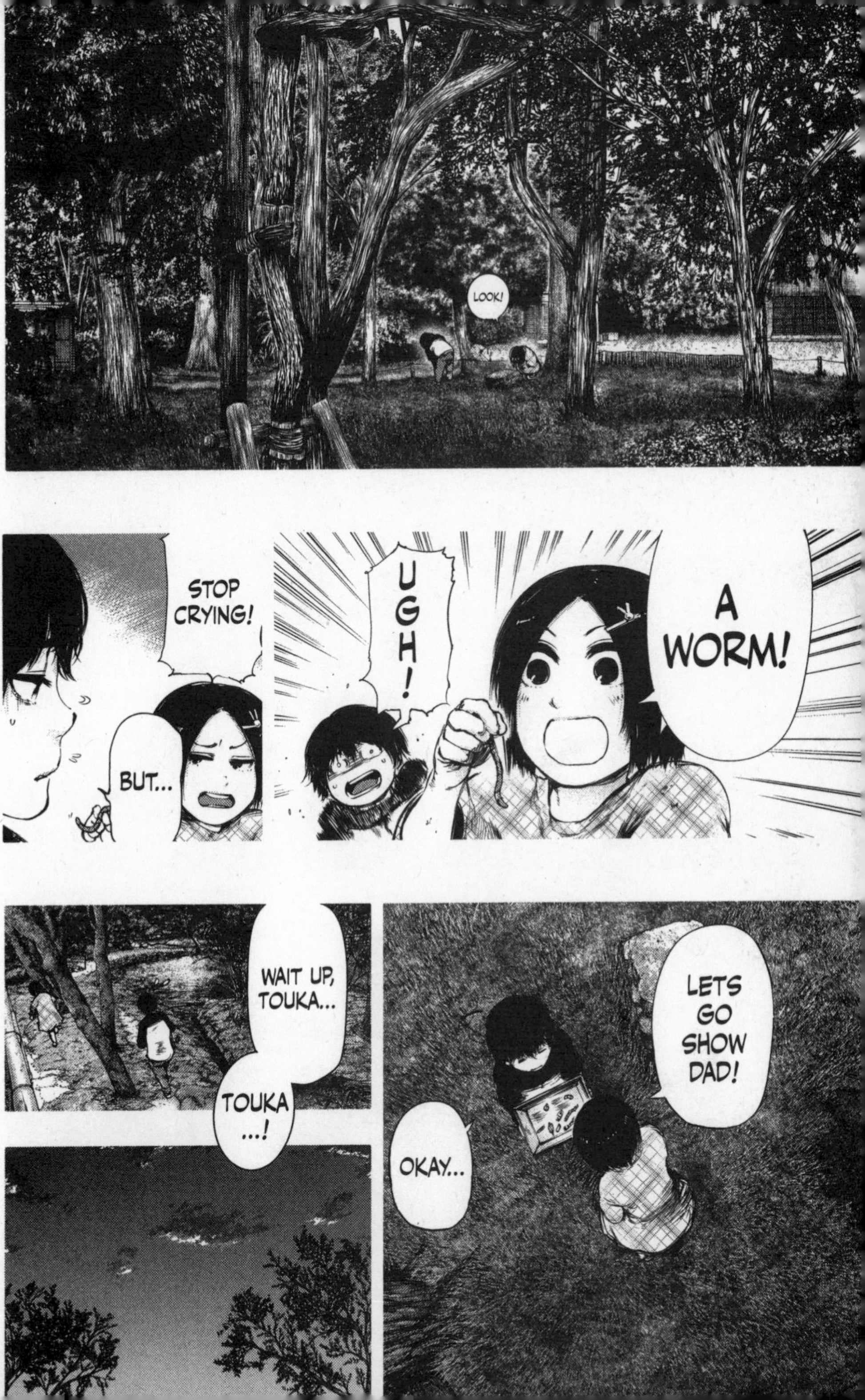
LOOK!
A WORM!
UGH!
STOP CRYING!
BUT...
LETS GO SHOW DAD!
OKAY...
WAIT UP, TOUKA...
TOUKA ...!

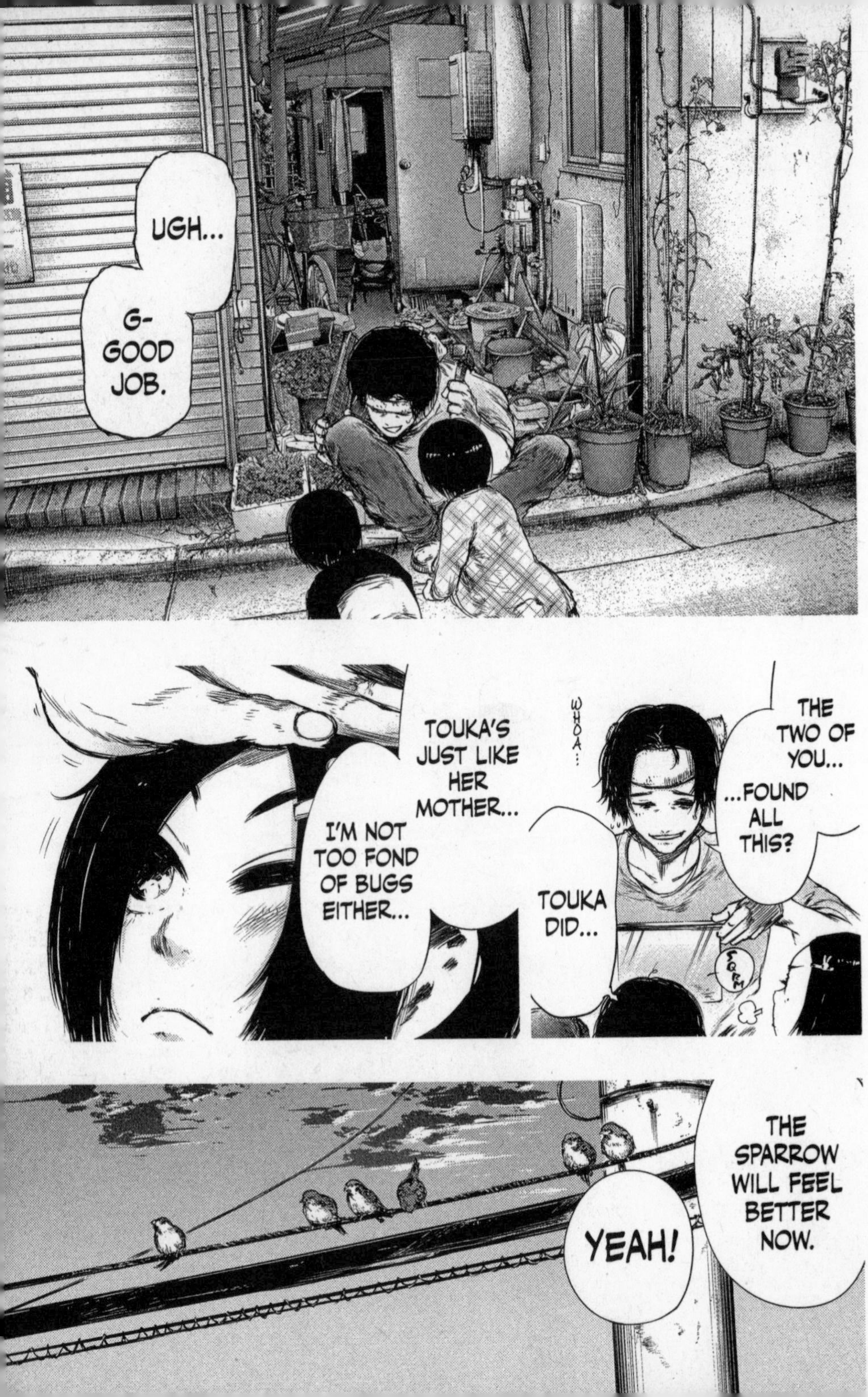
UGH...
G- GOOD JOB.
THE TWO OF YOU...
...FOUND ALL THIS?
WHOA...
TOUKA DID...
SQRM
TOUKA'S JUST LIKE HER MOTHER...
I'M NOT TOO FOND OF BUGS EITHER...
THE SPARROW WILL FEEL BETTER NOW.
YEAH!

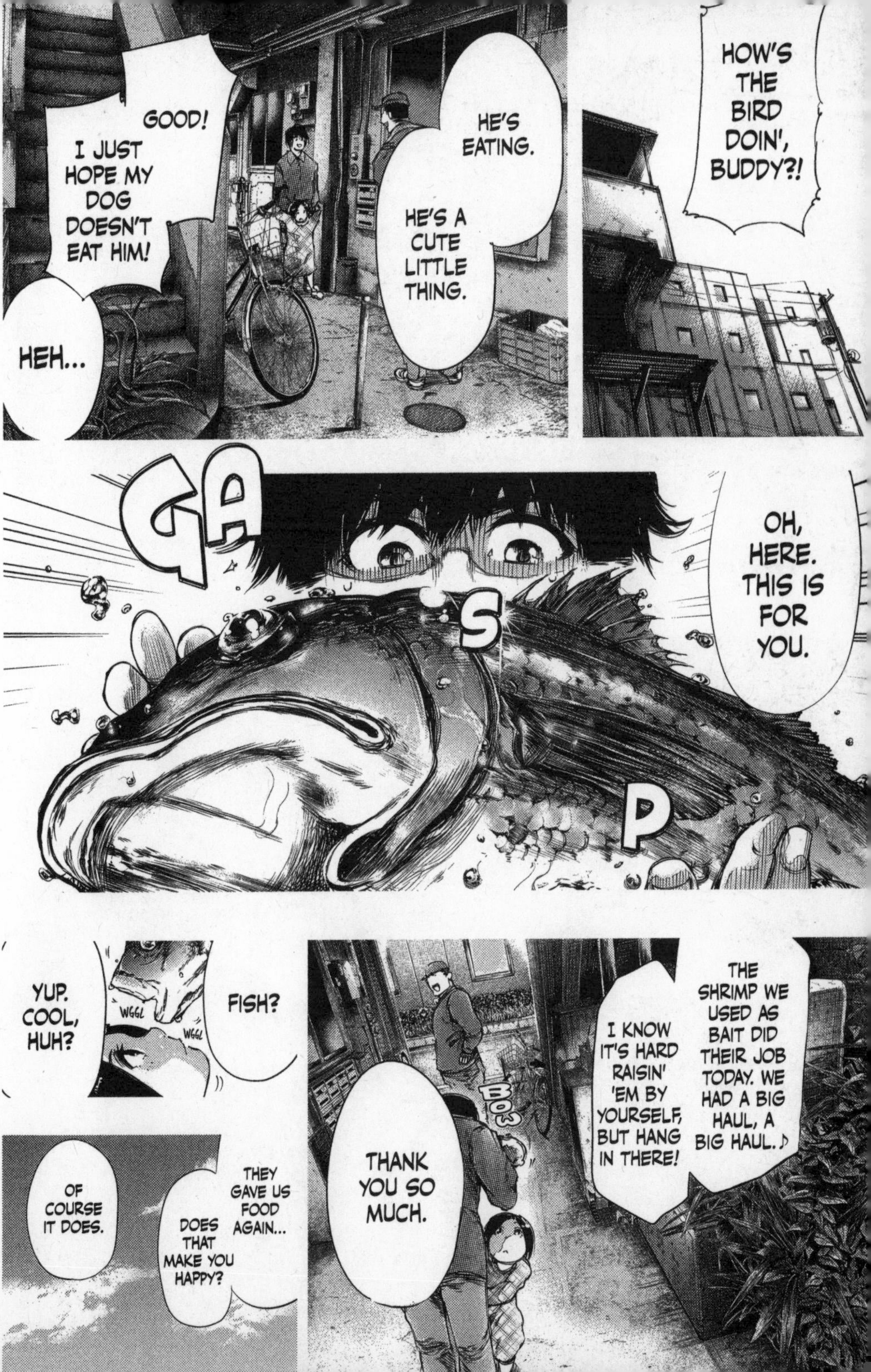
HOW'S THE BIRD DOIN', BUDDY?!
HE'S EATING.
HE'S A CUTE LITTLE THING.
GOOD! I JUST HOPE MY DOG DOESN'T EAT HIM!
HEH...
OH, HERE. THIS IS FOR YOU.
GASP
THE SHRIMP WE USED AS BAIT DID THEIR JOB TODAY. WE HAD A BIG HAUL, A BIG HAUL.♪
I KNOW IT'S HARD RAISIN' 'EM BY YOURSELF, BUT HANG IN THERE!
BOW
THANK YOU SO MUCH.
FISH?
WGGL
WGGL
YUP. COOL, HUH?
THEY GAVE US FOOD AGAIN...
DOES THAT MAKE YOU HAPPY?
OF COURSE IT DOES.

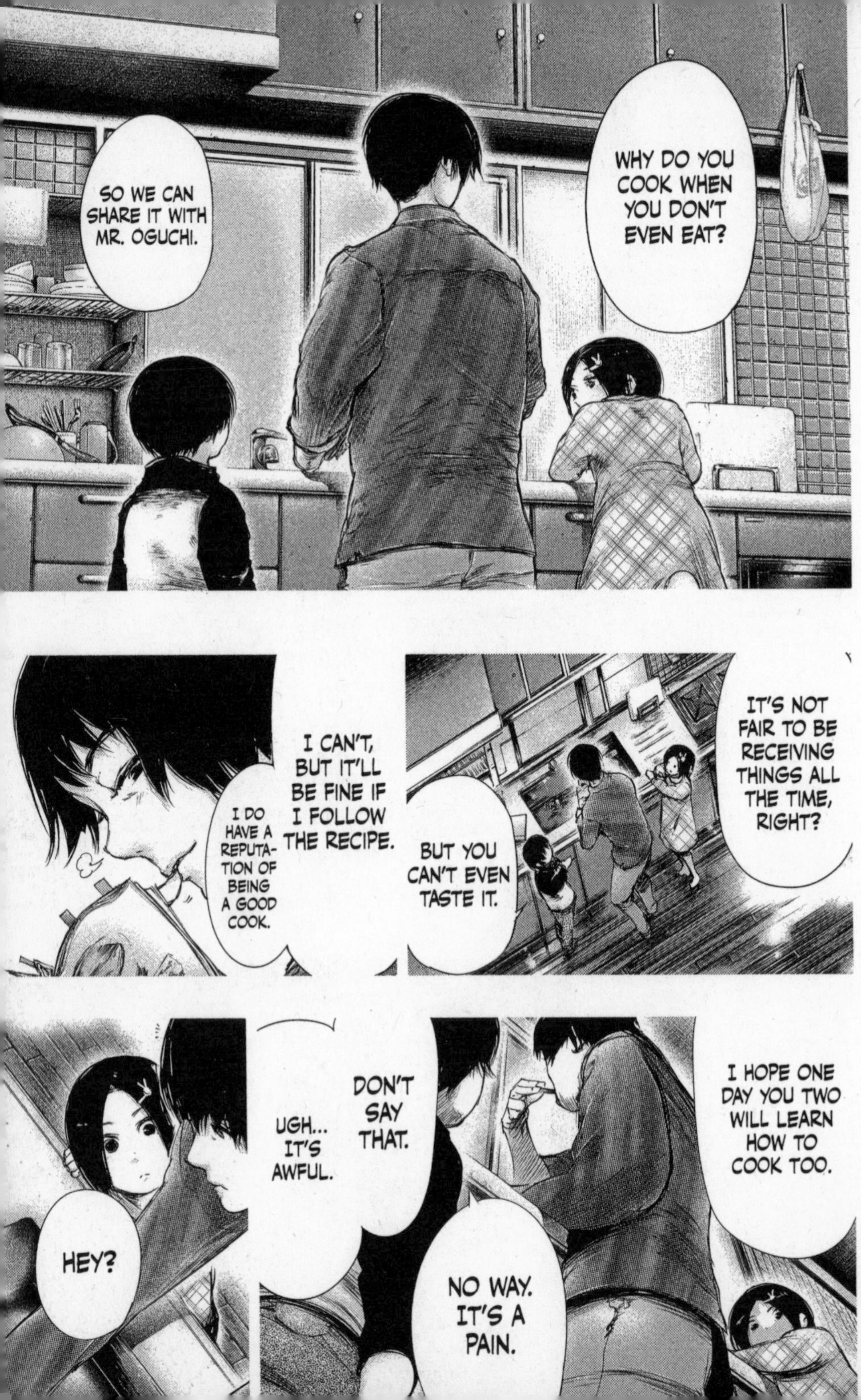
WHY DO YOU COOK WHEN YOU DON'T EVEN EAT?
SO WE CAN SHARE IT WITH MR. OGUCHI.
IT'S NOT FAIR TO BE RECEIVING THINGS ALL THE TIME, RIGHT?
BUT YOU CAN'T EVEN TASTE IT.
I CAN'T, BUT IT'LL BE FINE IF I FOLLOW THE RECIPE.
I DO HAVE A REPUTATION OF BEING A GOOD COOK.
I HOPE ONE DAY YOU TWO WILL LEARN HOW TO COOK TOO.
NO WAY. IT'S A PAIN.
DON'T SAY THAT.
UGH... IT'S AWFUL.
HEY?

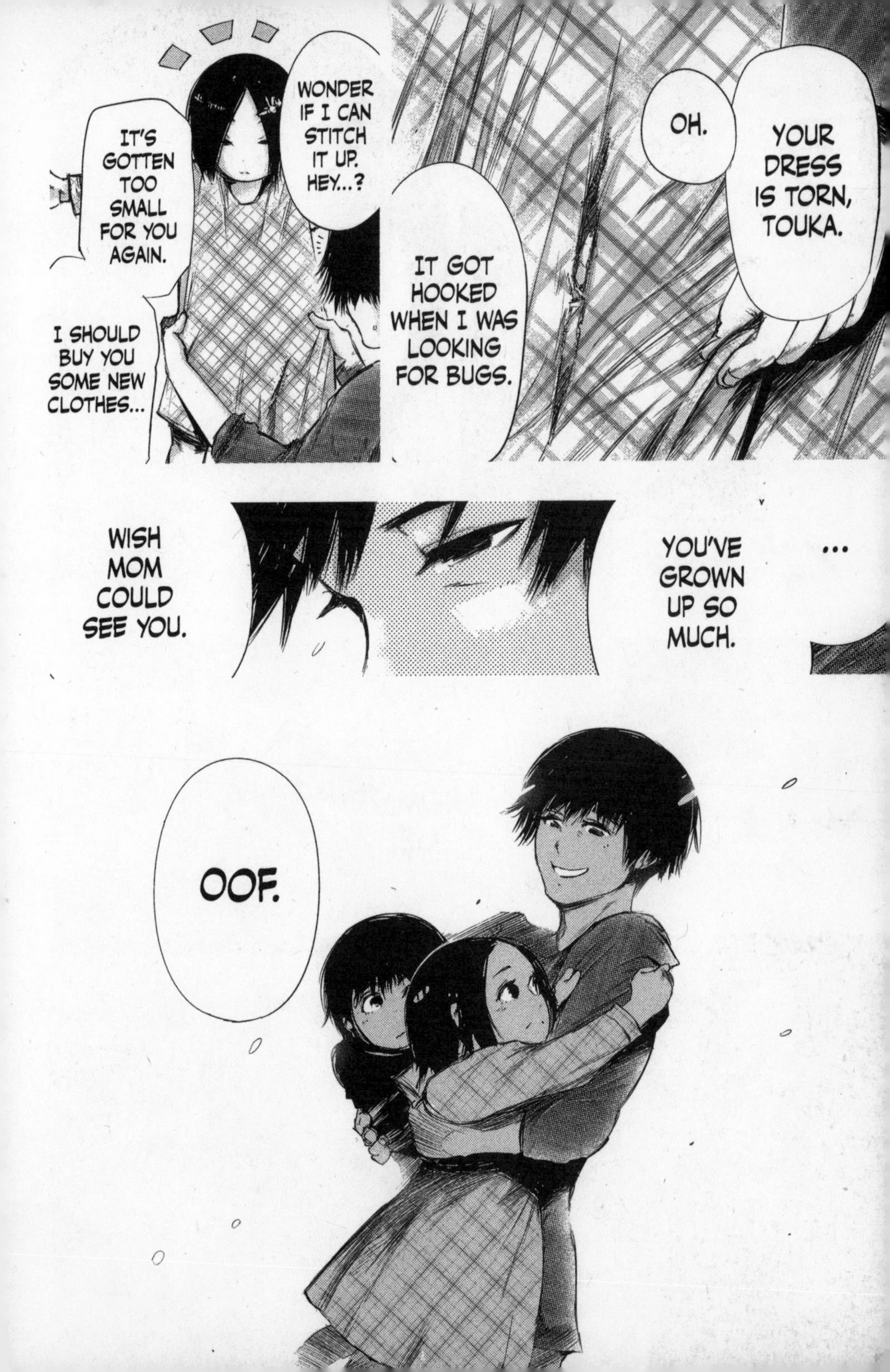
YOUR DRESS IS TORN, TOUKA.
OH.
IT GOT HOOKED WHEN I WAS LOOKING FOR BUGS.
WONDER IF I CAN STITCH IT UP. HEY...?
IT'S GOTTEN TOO SMALL FOR YOU AGAIN.
I SHOULD BUY YOU SOME NEW CLOTHES...
...
YOU'VE GROWN UP SO MUCH.
WISH MOM COULD SEE YOU.
OOF.

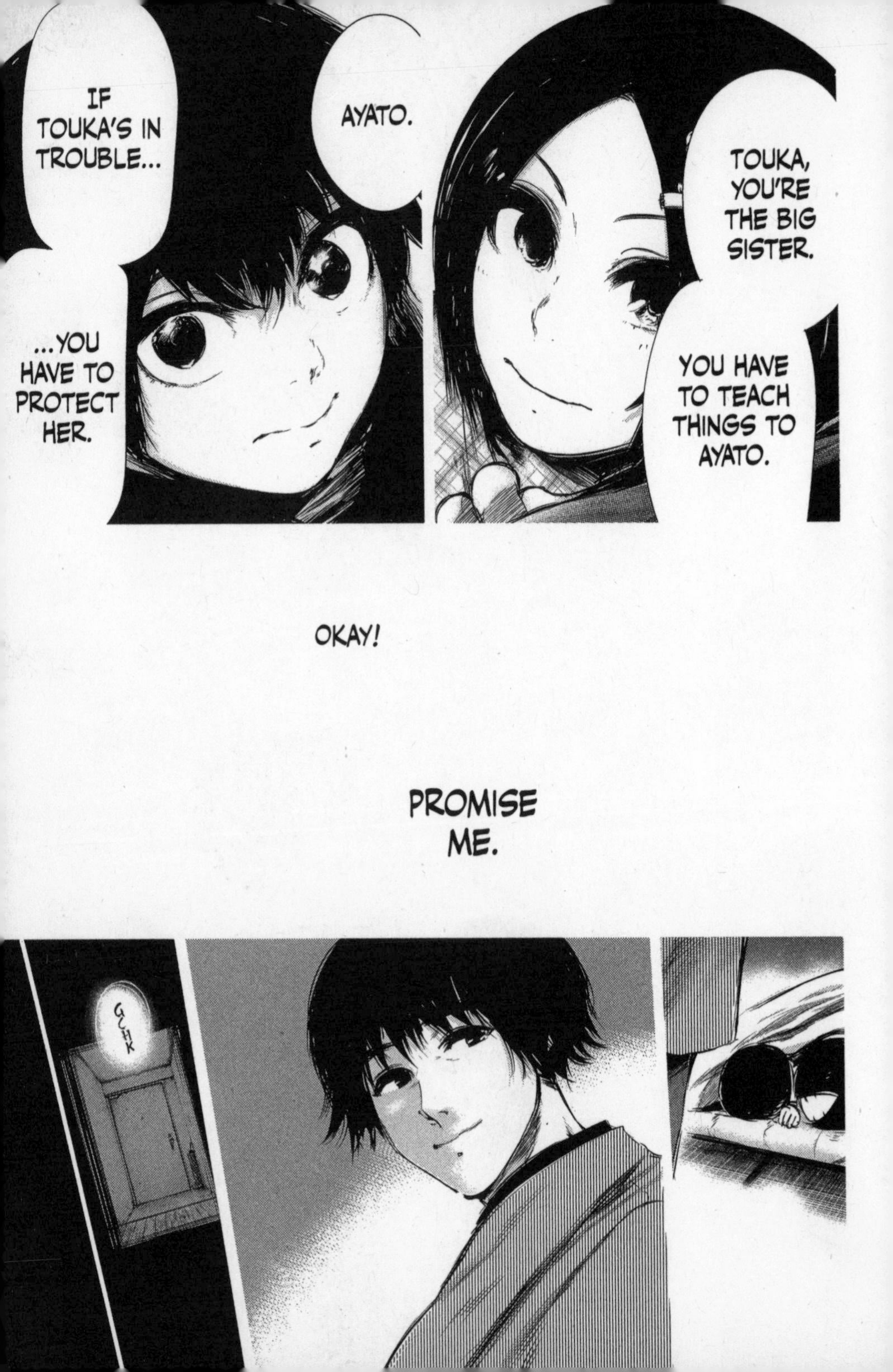
TOUKA, YOU'RE THE BIG SISTER.
YOU HAVE TO TEACH THINGS TO AYATO.
AYATO.
IF TOUKA'S IN TROUBLE...
...YOU HAVE TO PROTECT HER.
OKAY!
PROMISE ME.
GCHK

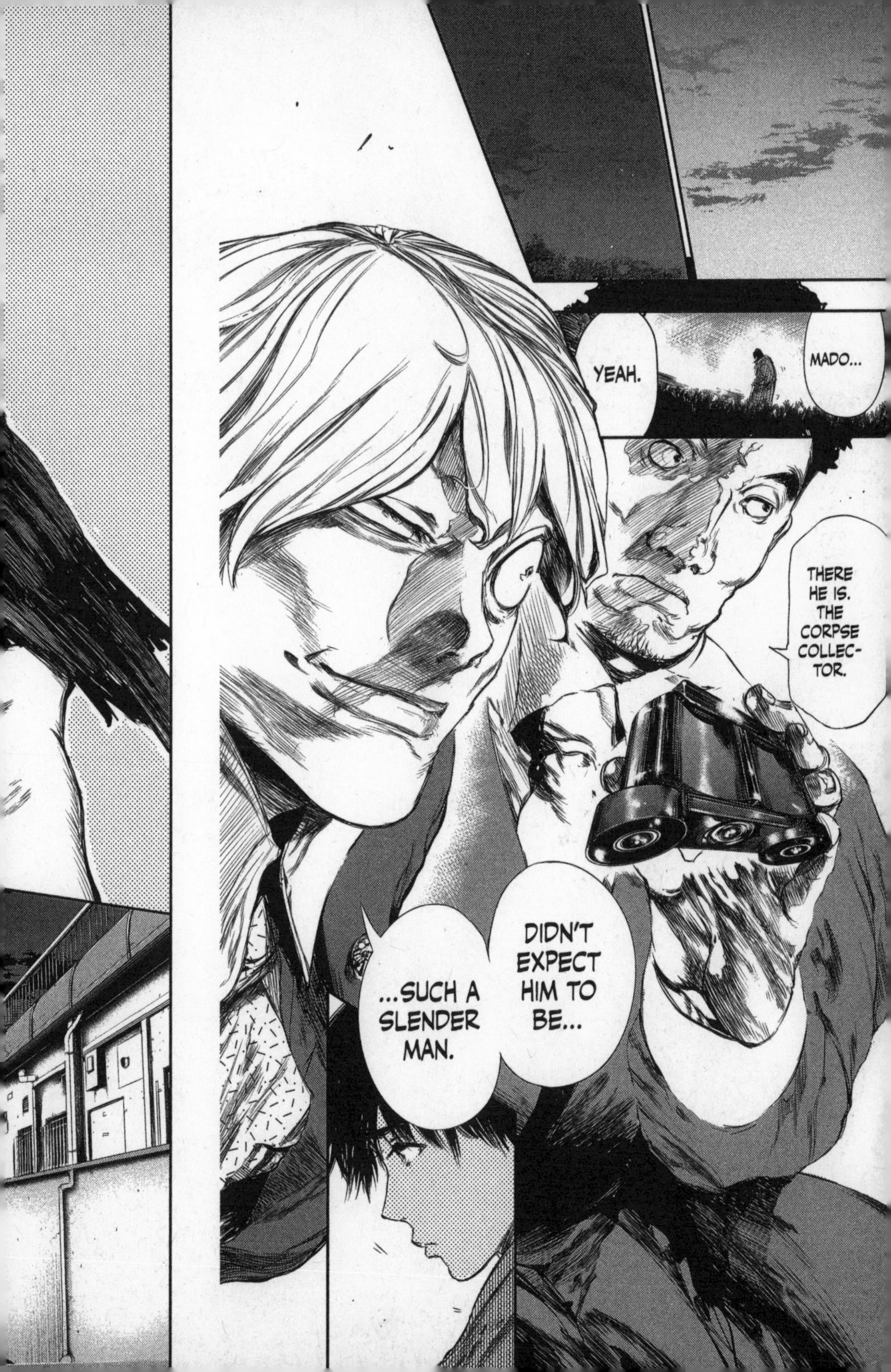
MADO...
YEAH.
THERE HE IS. THE CORPSE COLLECTOR.
DIDN'T EXPECT HIM TO BE...
...SUCH A SLENDER MAN.

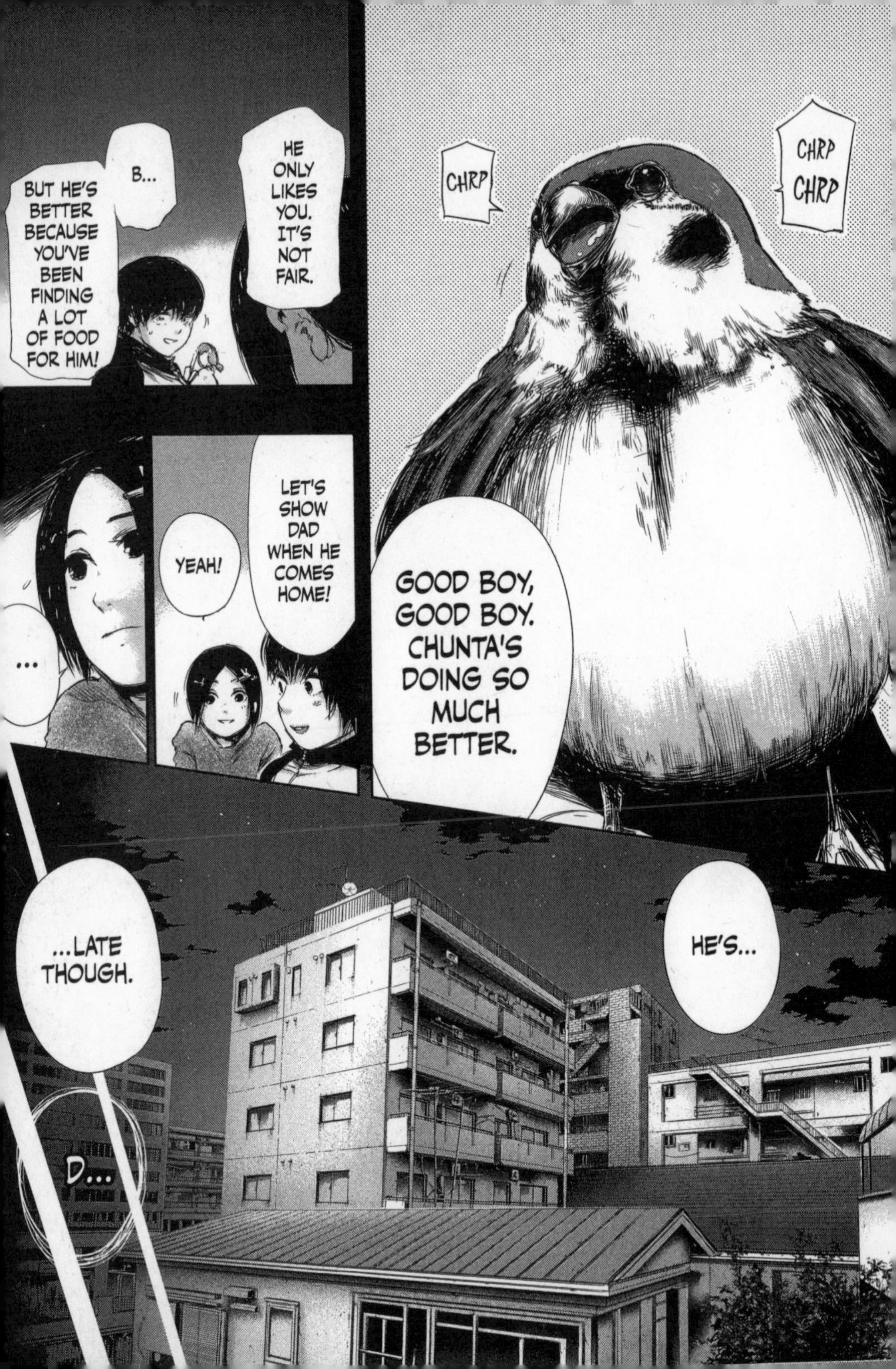
CHRP CHRP
CHRP
GOOD BOY, GOOD BOY. CHUNTA'S DOING SO MUCH BETTER.
HE ONLY LIKES YOU. IT'S NOT FAIR.
B...
BUT HE'S BETTER BECAUSE YOU'VE BEEN FINDING A LOT OF FOOD FOR HIM!
LET'S SHOW DAD WHEN HE COMES HOME!
YEAH!
...
HE'S...
...LATE THOUGH.
D...

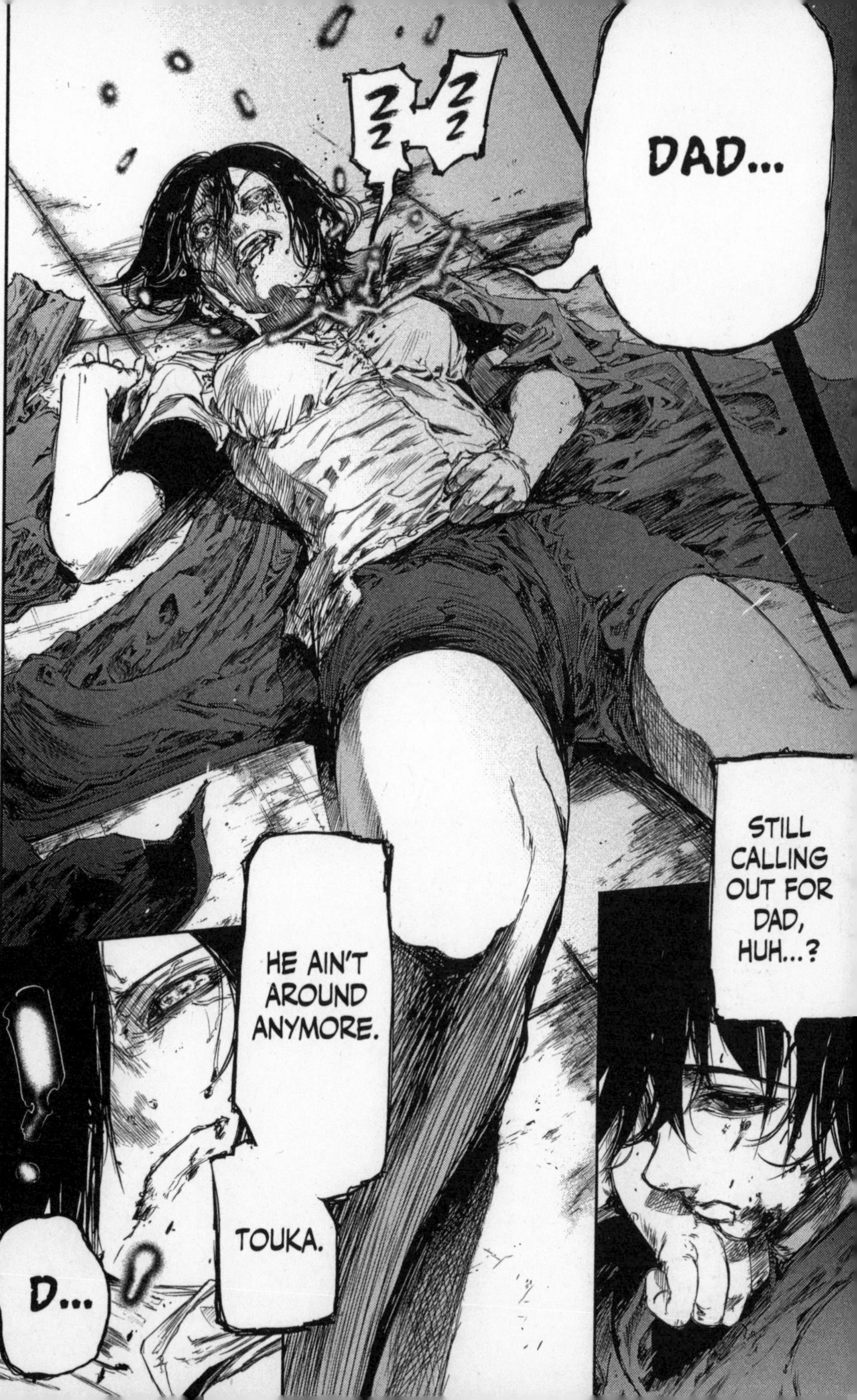
DAD...
ZZZZ
STILL CALLING OUT FOR DAD, HUH...?
HE AIN'T AROUND ANYMORE.
TOUKA.
D...

東京喰種
トーキョーグール
Tokyo
Ghoul

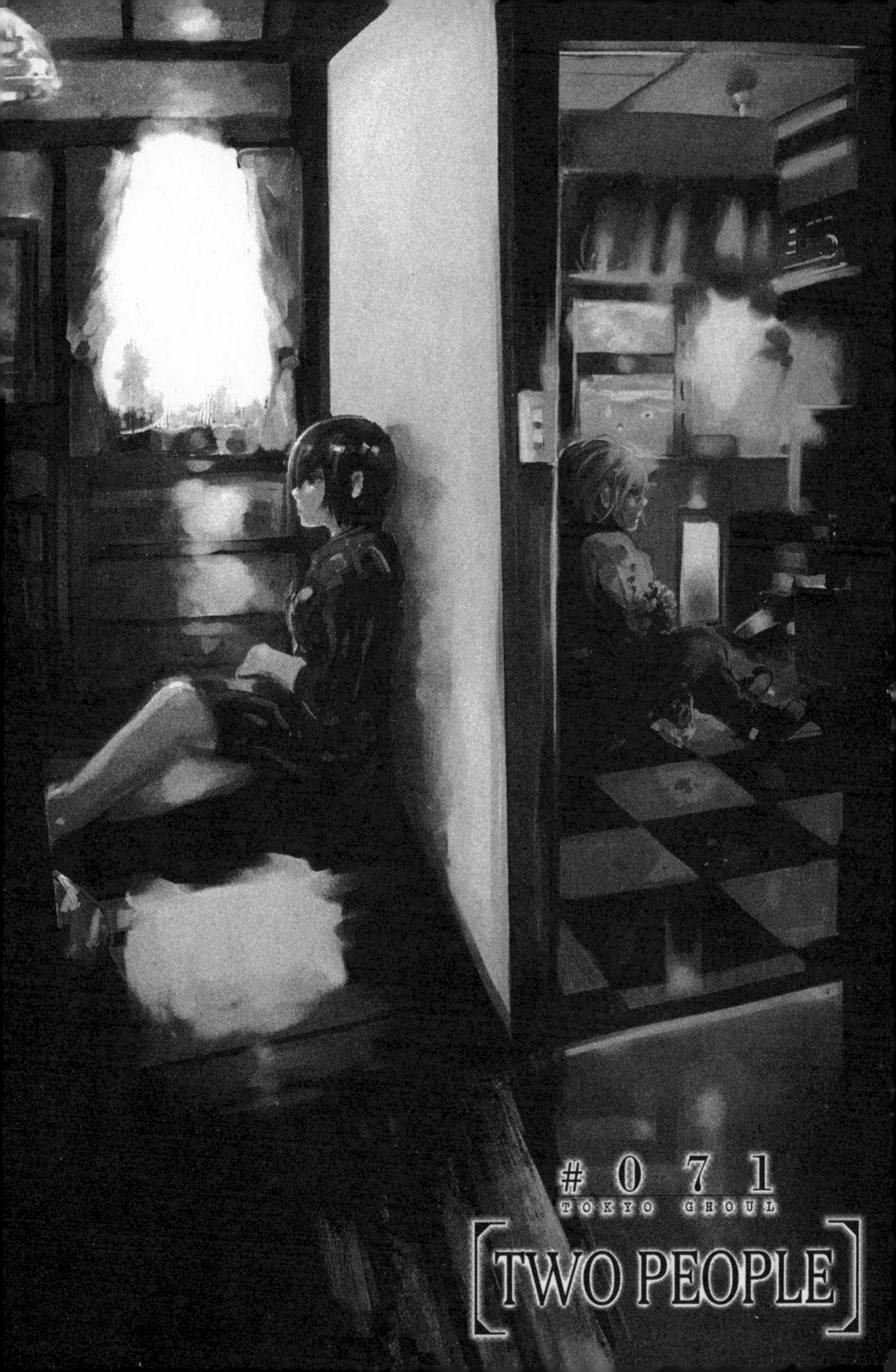
#071
TOKYO GHOUL
[TWO PEOPLE]

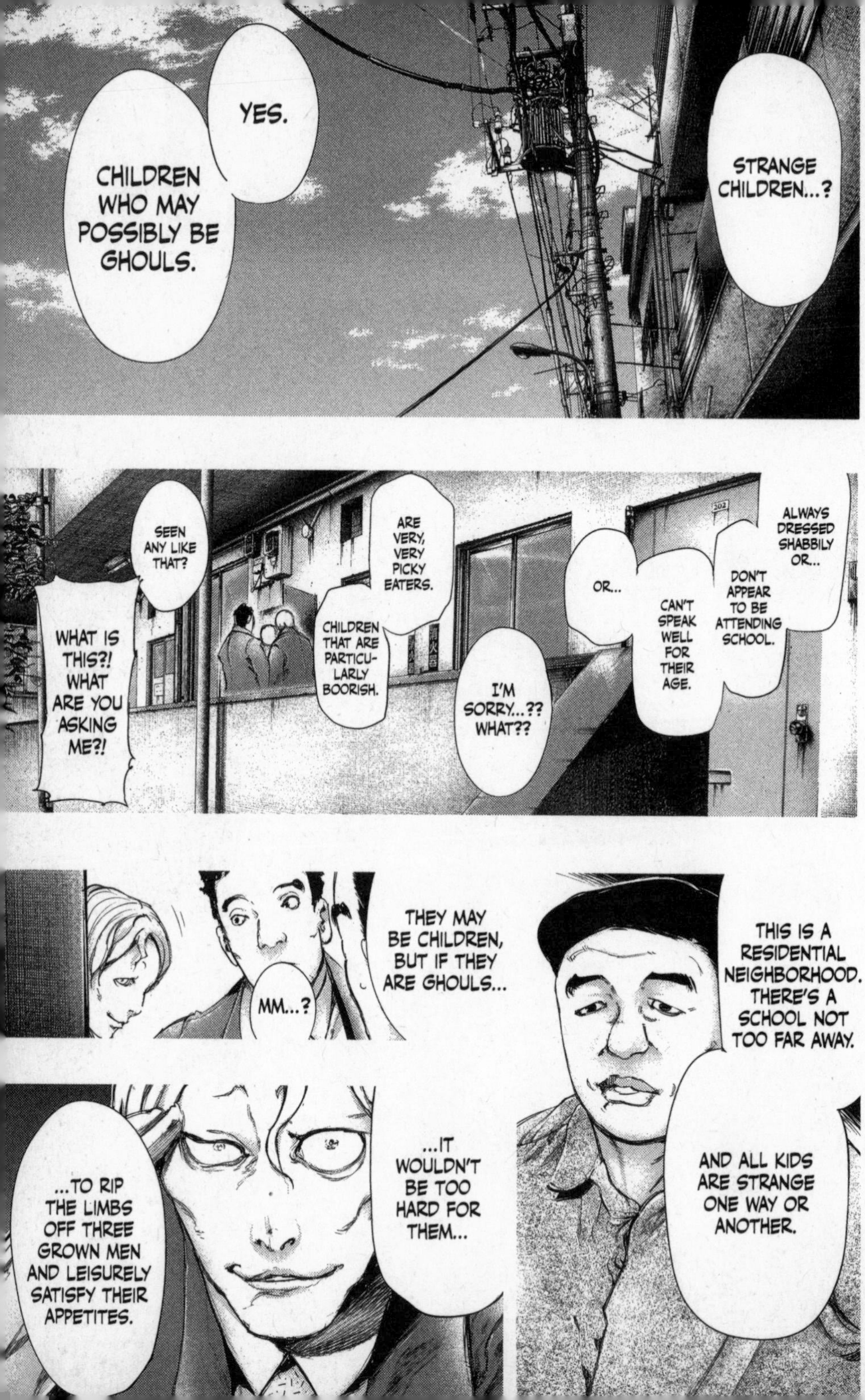
STRANGE CHILDREN...?
YES.
CHILDREN WHO MAY POSSIBLY BE GHOULS.
ALWAYS DRESSED SHABBILY OR...
DON'T APPEAR TO BE ATTENDING SCHOOL.
OR...
CAN'T SPEAK WELL FOR THEIR AGE.
I'M SORRY...?? WHAT??
ARE VERY, VERY PICKY EATERS.
CHILDREN THAT ARE PARTICU-LARLY BOORISH.
SEEN ANY LIKE THAT?
WHAT IS THIS?! WHAT ARE YOU ASKING ME?!
THIS IS A RESIDENTIAL NEIGHBORHOOD. THERE'S A SCHOOL NOT TOO FAR AWAY.
AND ALL KIDS ARE STRANGE ONE WAY OR ANOTHER.
THEY MAY BE CHILDREN, BUT IF THEY ARE GHOULS...
MM...?
...IT WOULDN'T BE TOO HARD FOR THEM...
...TO RIP THE LIMBS OFF THREE GROWN MEN AND LEISURELY SATISFY THEIR APPETITES.

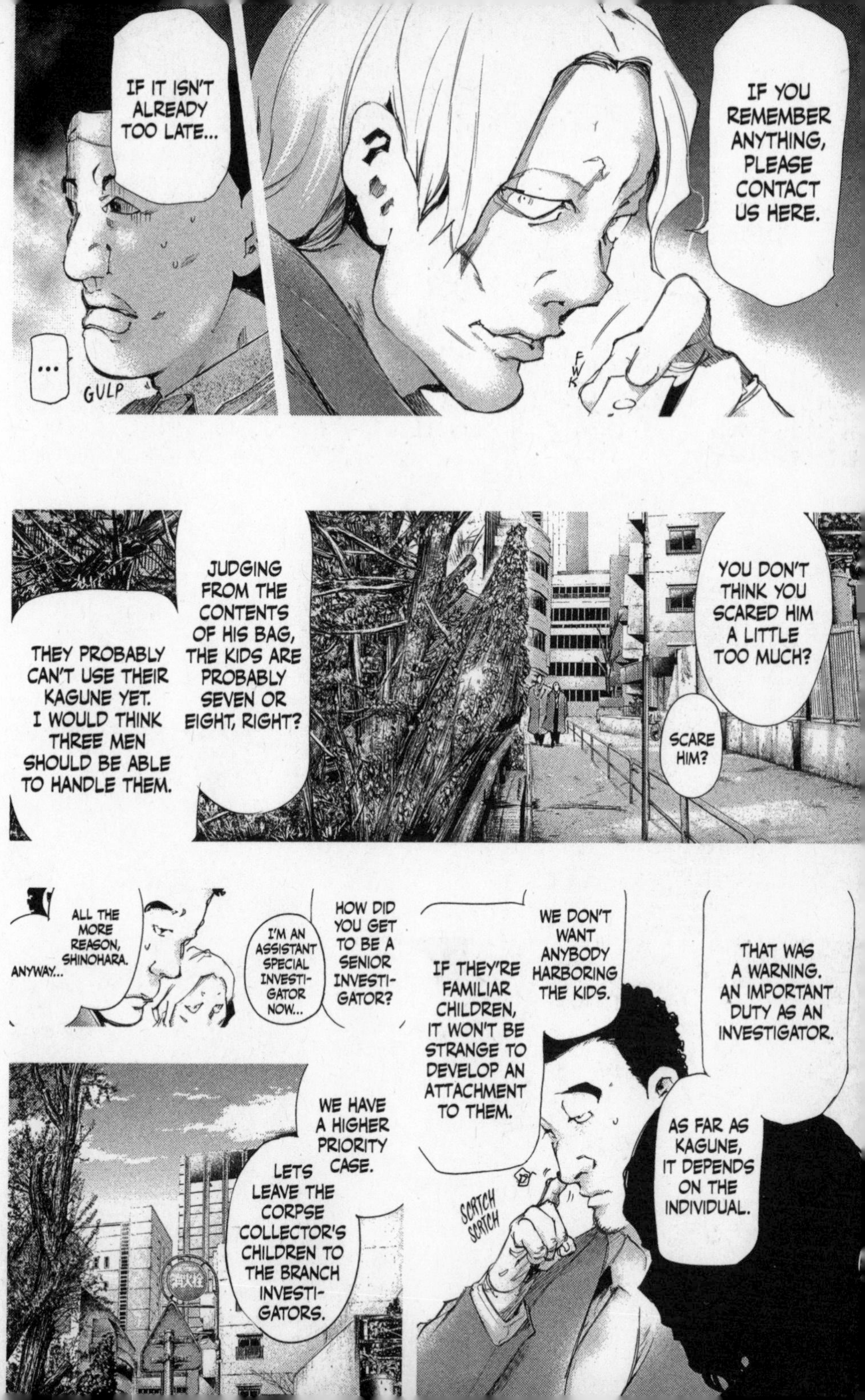
IF YOU REMEMBER ANYTHING, PLEASE CONTACT US HERE.
FWK
IF IT ISN'T ALREADY TOO LATE...
...
GULP
YOU DON'T THINK YOU SCARED HIM A LITTLE TOO MUCH?
SCARE HIM?
JUDGING FROM THE CONTENTS OF HIS BAG, THE KIDS ARE PROBABLY SEVEN OR EIGHT, RIGHT?
THEY PROBABLY CAN'T USE THEIR KAGUNE YET. I WOULD THINK THREE MEN SHOULD BE ABLE TO HANDLE THEM.
THAT WAS A WARNING. AN IMPORTANT DUTY AS AN INVESTIGATOR.
WE DON'T WANT ANYBODY HARBORING THE KIDS.
IF THEY'RE FAMILIAR CHILDREN, IT WON'T BE STRANGE TO DEVELOP AN ATTACHMENT TO THEM.
AS FAR AS KAGUNE, IT DEPENDS ON THE INDIVIDUAL.
SCRTCH SCRTCH
HOW DID YOU GET TO BE A SENIOR INVESTIGATOR?
I'M AN ASSISTANT SPECIAL INVESTIGATOR NOW...
ALL THE MORE REASON, SHINOHARA.
ANYWAY...
WE HAVE A HIGHER PRIORITY CASE.
LETS LEAVE THE CORPSE COLLECTOR'S CHILDREN TO THE BRANCH INVESTIGATORS.

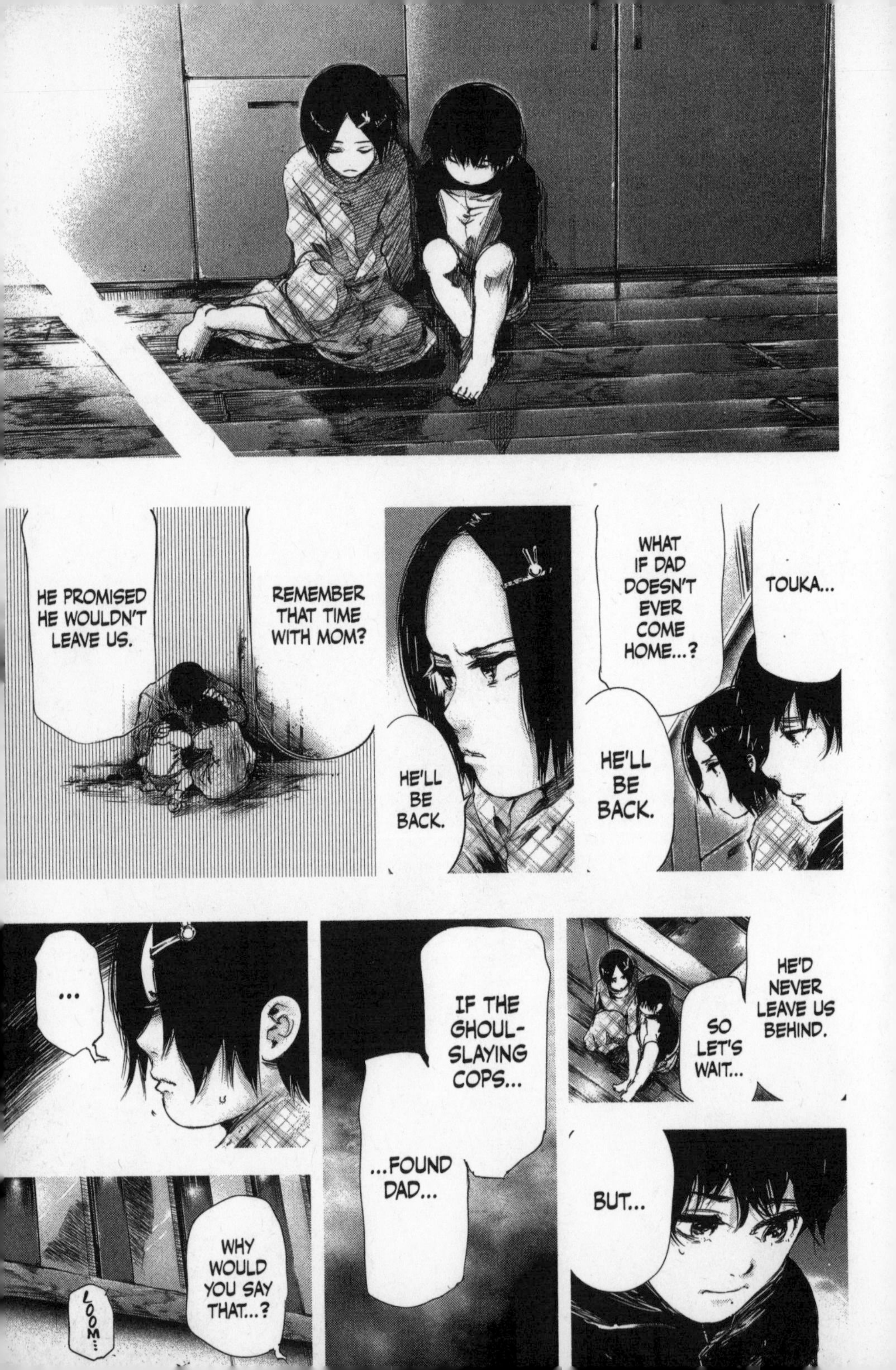
TOUKA...
WHAT IF DAD DOESN'T EVER COME HOME...?
HE'LL BE BACK.
HE'LL BE BACK.
REMEMBER THAT TIME WITH MOM?
HE PROMISED HE WOULDN'T LEAVE US.
HE'D NEVER LEAVE US BEHIND.
SO LET'S WAIT...
BUT...
IF THE GHOUL-SLAYING COPS...
...FOUND DAD...
...
WHY WOULD YOU SAY THAT...?
LOOOM...

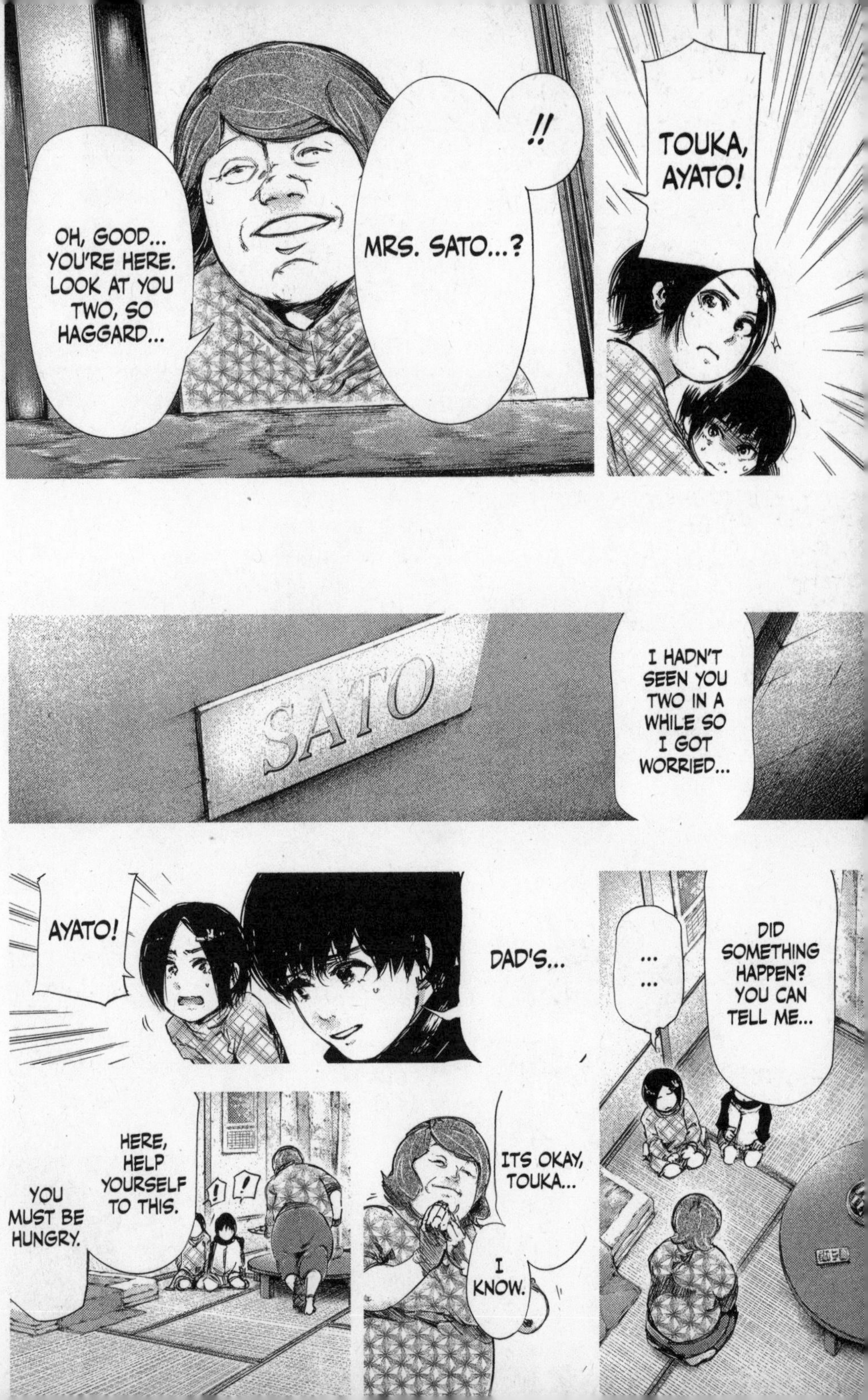
TOUKA, AYATO!
!!
MRS. SATO...?
OH, GOOD... YOU'RE HERE. LOOK AT YOU TWO, SO HAGGARD...
SATO
I HADN'T SEEN YOU TWO IN A WHILE SO I GOT WORRIED...
DID SOMETHING HAPPEN? YOU CAN TELL ME...
... ...
DAD'S...
AYATO!
ITS OKAY, TOUKA...
I KNOW.
! !
HERE, HELP YOURSELF TO THIS.
YOU MUST BE HUNGRY.

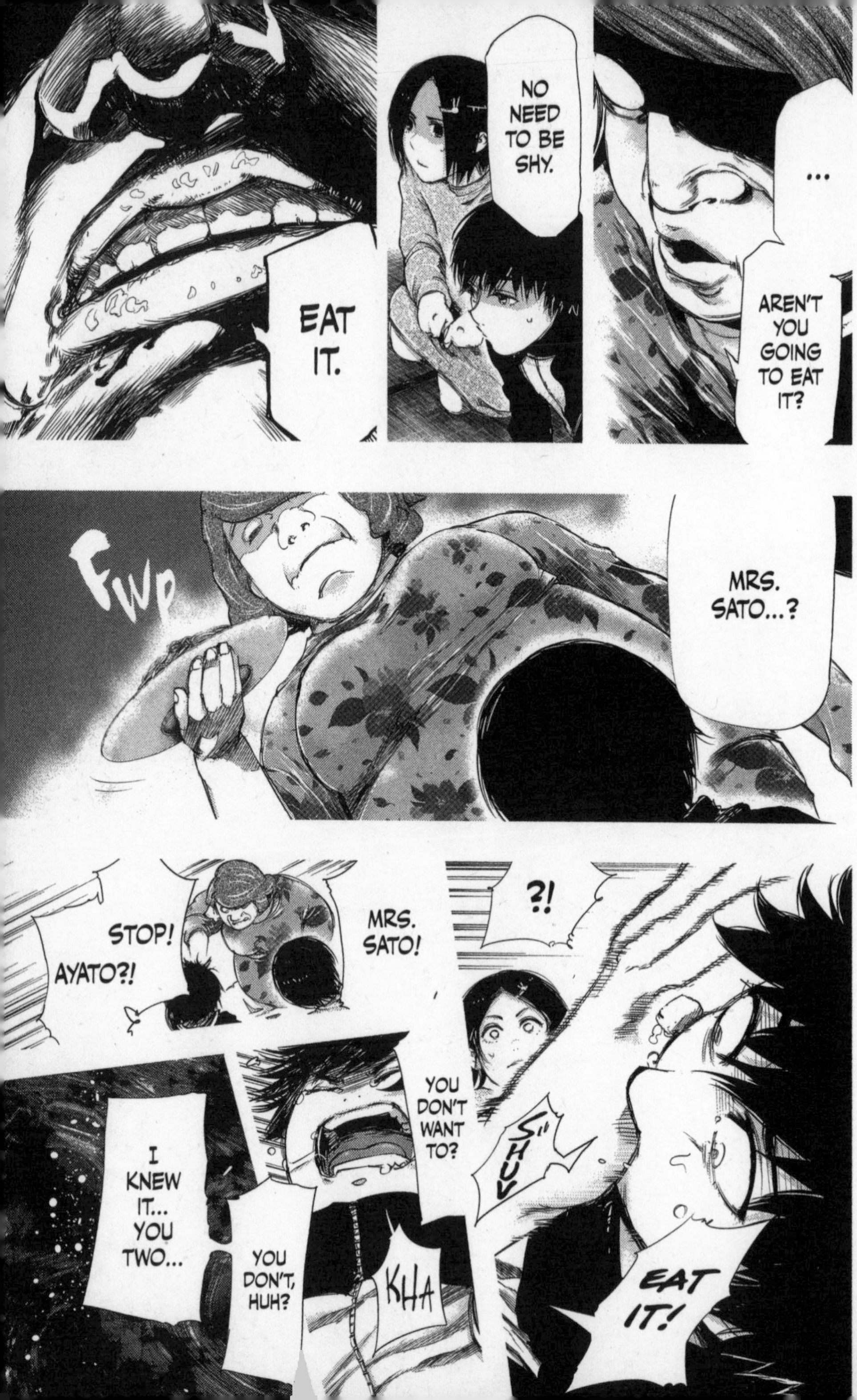
...
AREN'T YOU GOING TO EAT IT?
NO NEED TO BE SHY.
EAT IT.
MRS. SATO...?
FWP
?!
SHUV
EAT IT!
MRS. SATO!
STOP!
AYATO?!
YOU DON'T WANT TO?
KHA
YOU DON'T, HUH?
I KNEW IT... YOU TWO...

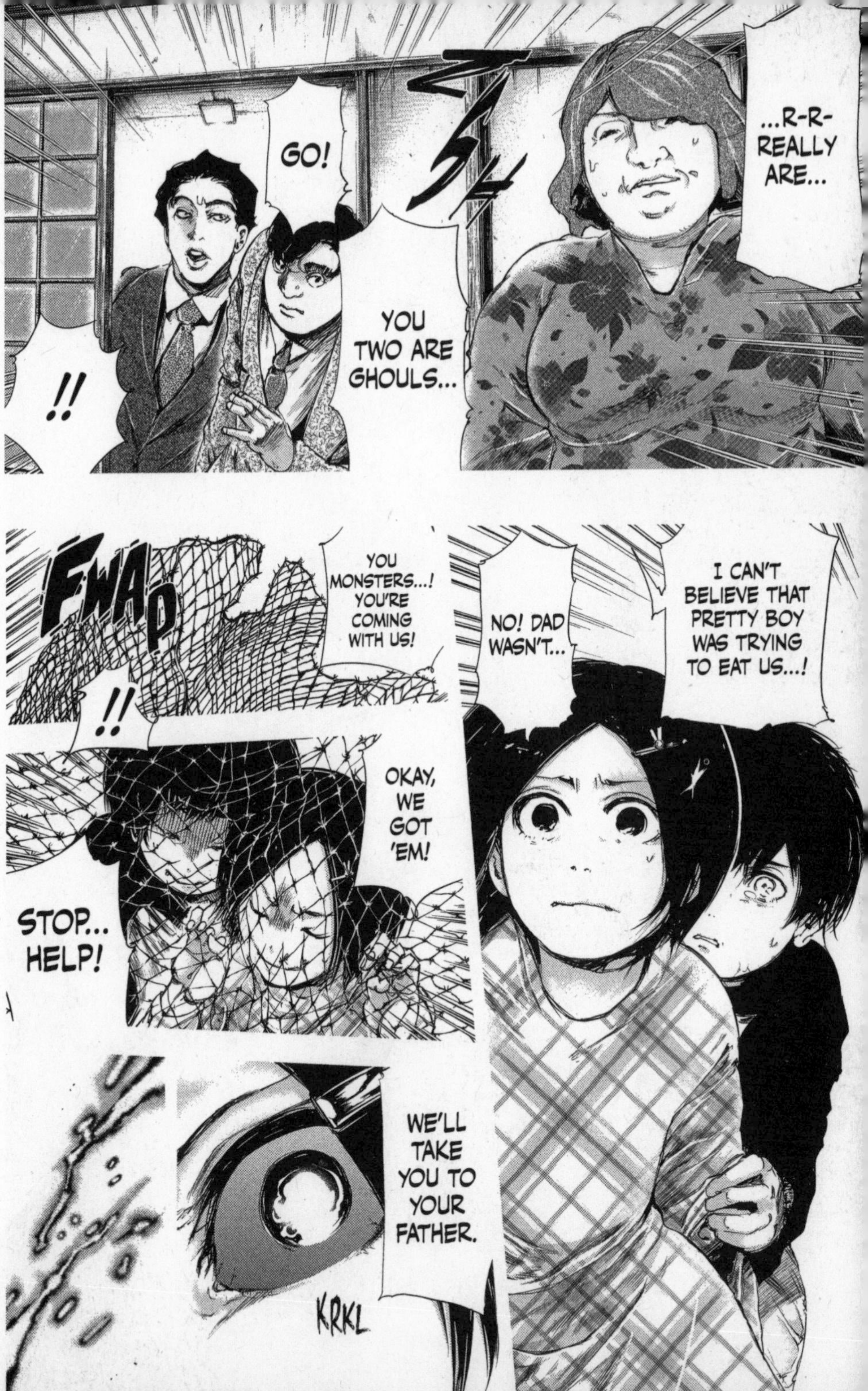
...R-R-REALLY ARE...
GO!
YOU TWO ARE GHOULS...
!!
I CAN'T BELIEVE THAT PRETTY BOY WAS TRYING TO EAT US...!
NO! DAD WASN'T...
YOU MONSTERS...! YOU'RE COMING WITH US!
FWAP
!!
OKAY, WE GOT 'EM!
STOP... HELP!
WE'LL TAKE YOU TO YOUR FATHER.
KRKL

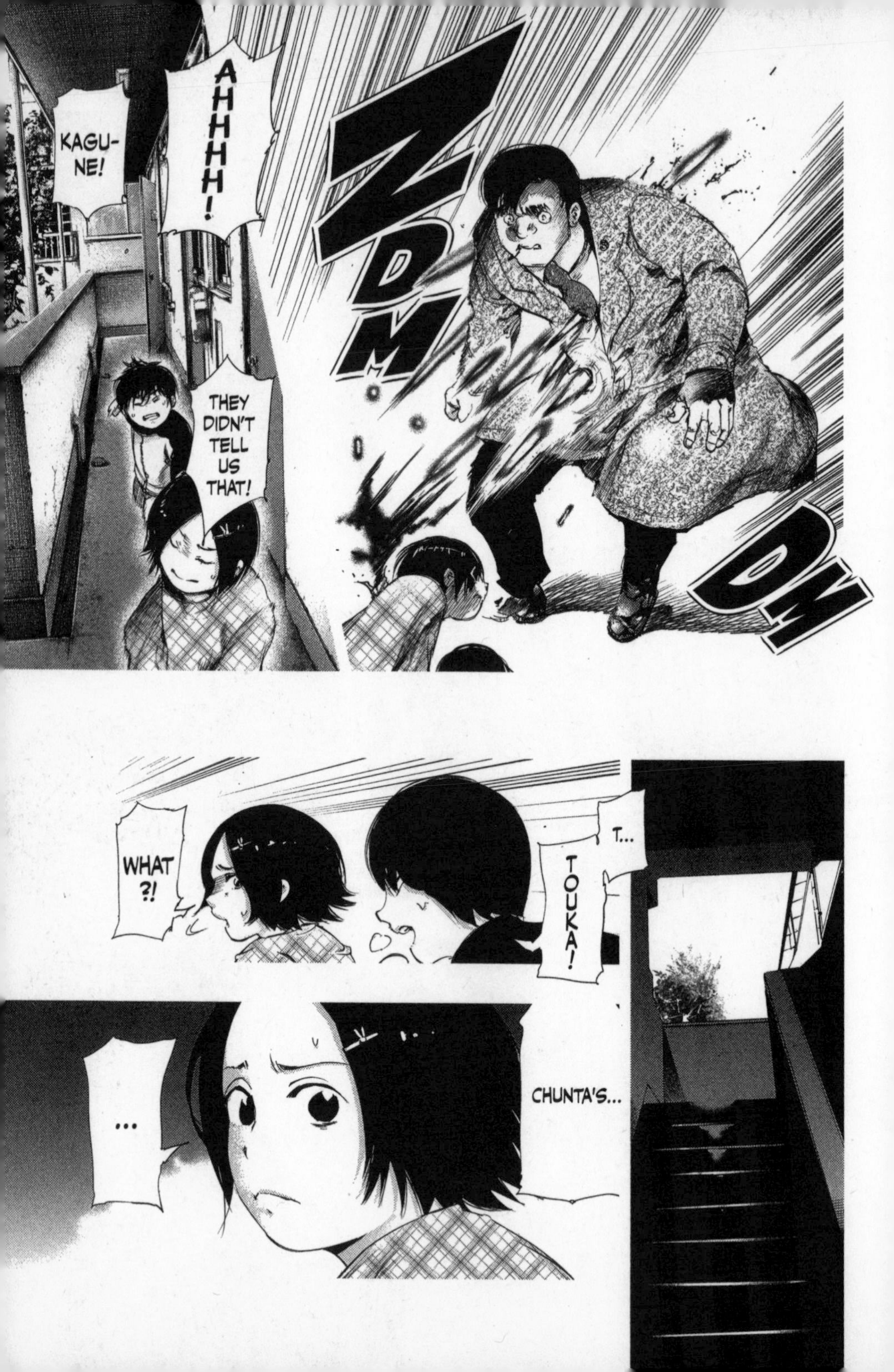
ZDM
DM
AHHHH!
KAGUNE!
THEY DIDN'T TELL US THAT!
T... TOUKA!
WHAT?!
CHUNTA'S...
...

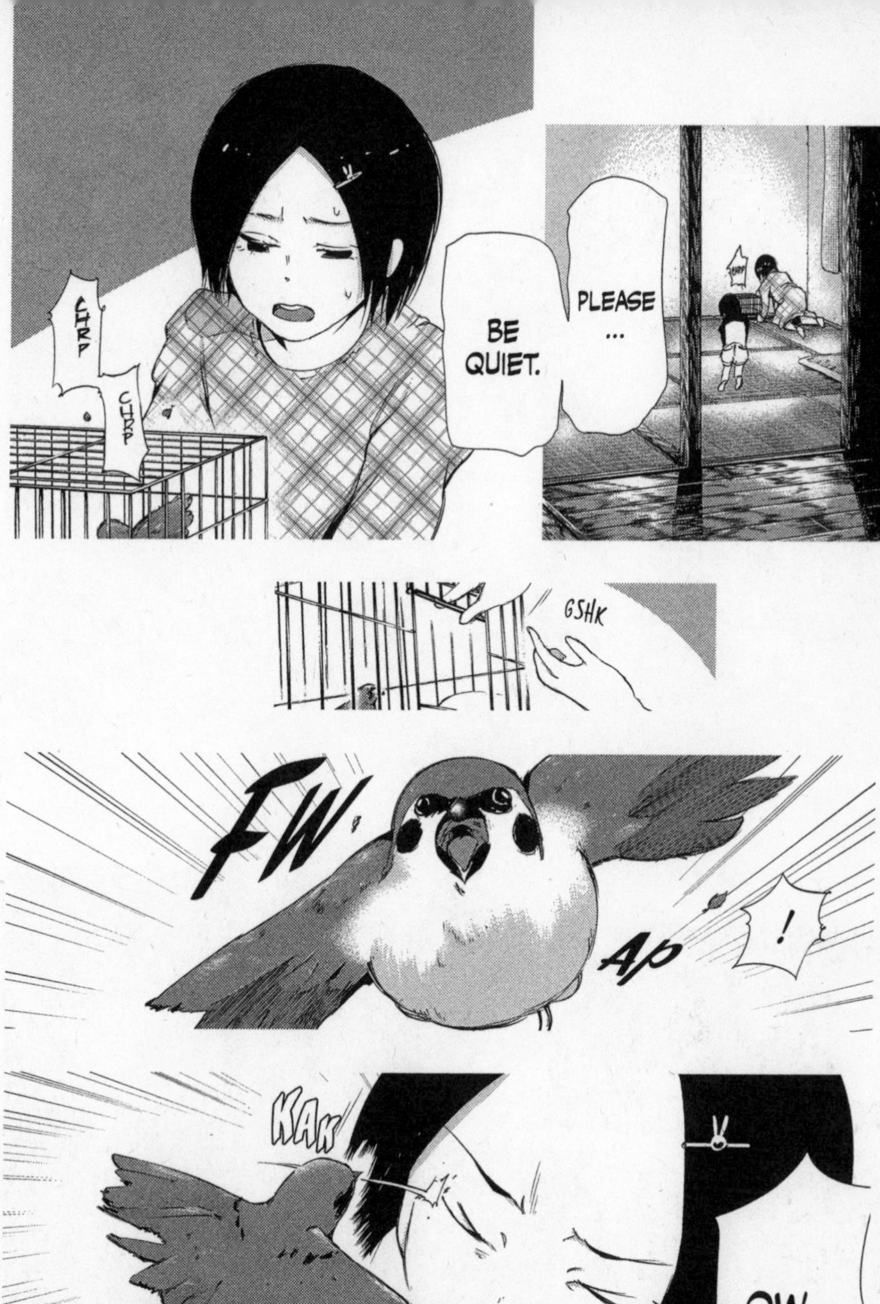
PLEASE ...
BE QUIET.
CHIRP
CHIRP
GSHK
FW
AP
!
KAK
OW...

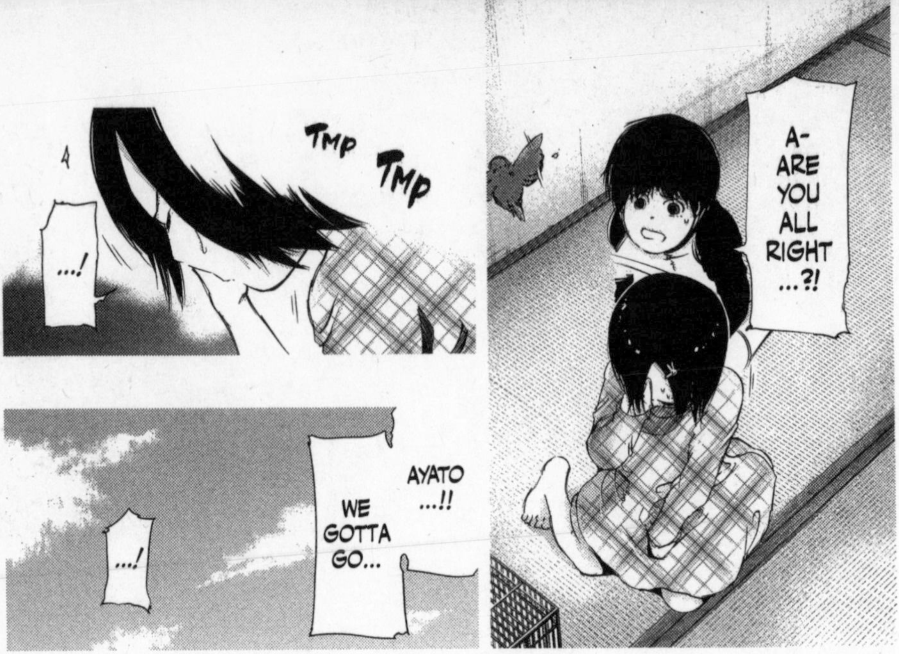
A-
ARE YOU ALL RIGHT ...?!
TMP
TMP
A
...!
AYATO ...!!
WE GOTTA GO...
...!

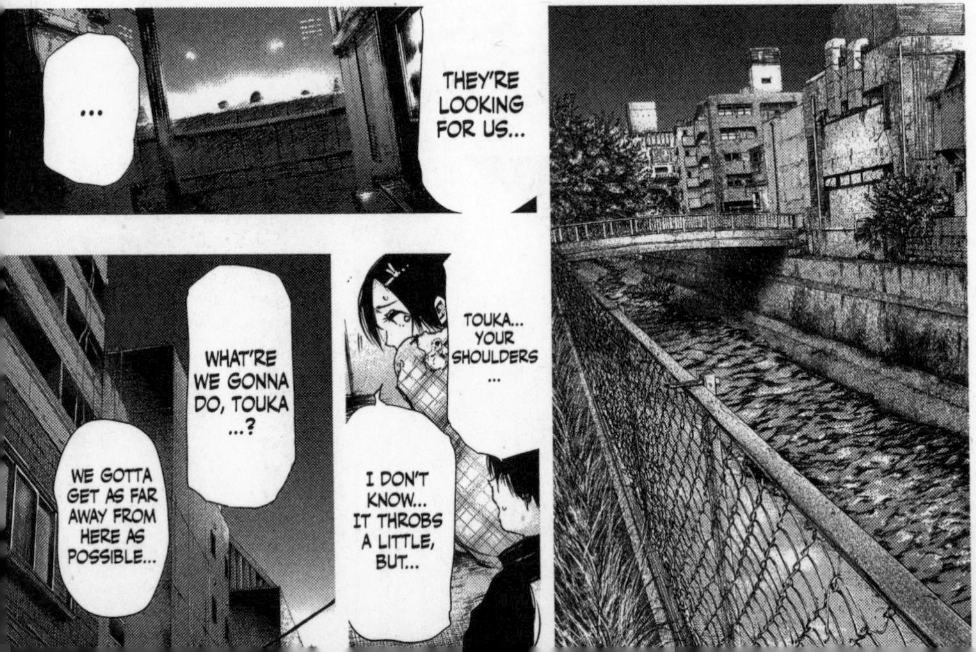
THEY'RE LOOKING FOR US...
...
TOUKA... YOUR SHOULDERS ...
I DON'T KNOW... IT THROBS A LITTLE, BUT...
WHAT'RE WE GONNA DO, TOUKA ...?
WE GOTTA GET AS FAR AWAY FROM HERE AS POSSIBLE...

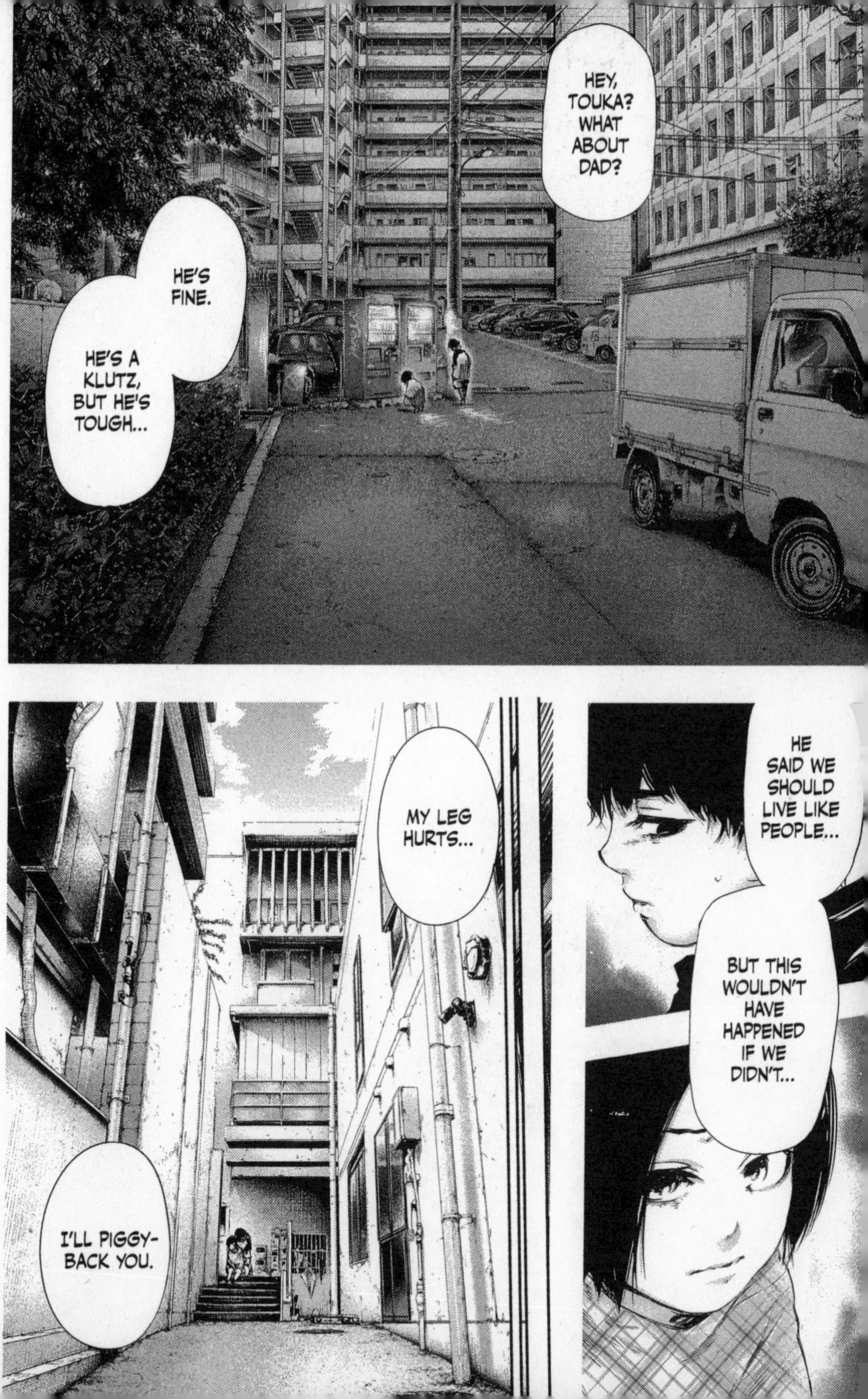
HEY, TOUKA? WHAT ABOUT DAD?
HE'S FINE.
HE'S A KLUTZ, BUT HE'S TOUGH...
HE SAID WE SHOULD LIVE LIKE PEOPLE...
BUT THIS WOULDN'T HAVE HAPPENED IF WE DIDN'T...
MY LEG HURTS...
I'LL PIGGY-BACK YOU.

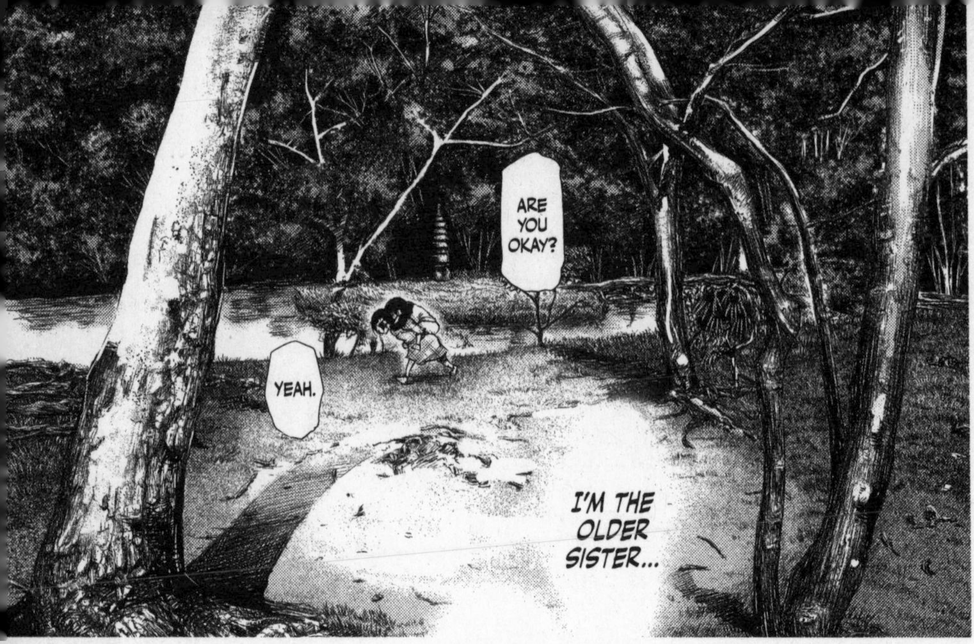
ARE YOU OKAY?
YEAH.
I'M THE OLDER SISTER...
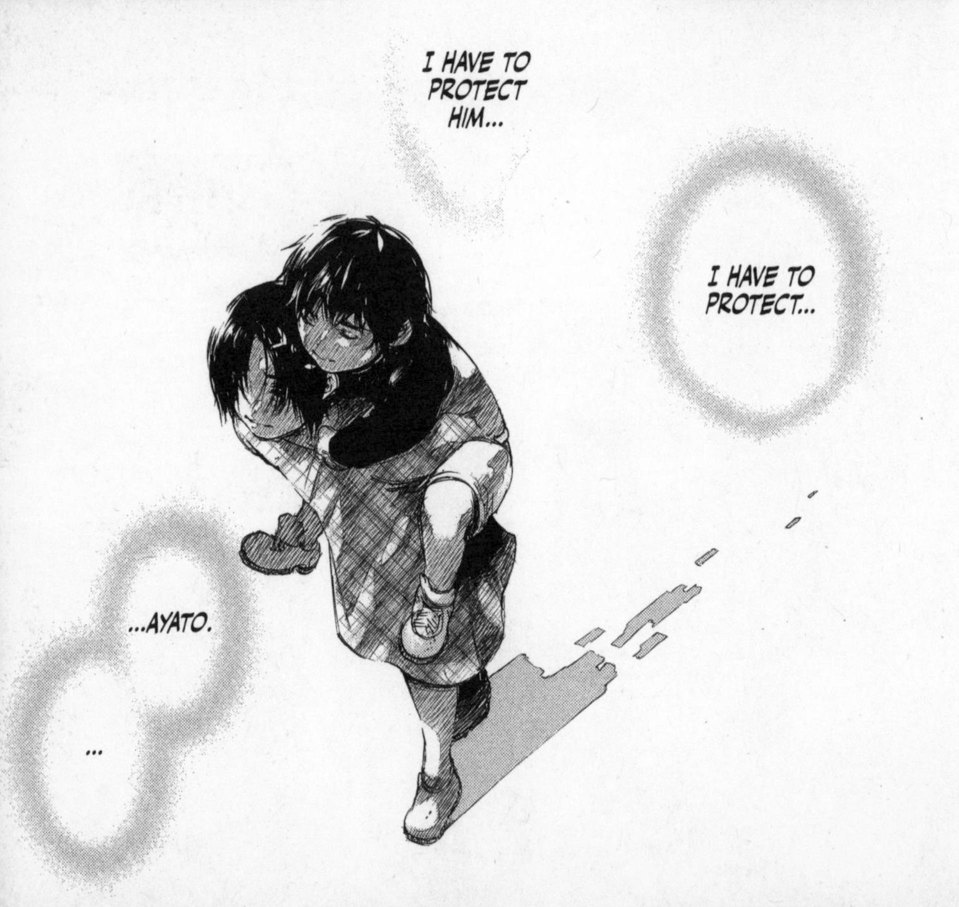
I HAVE TO PROTECT HIM...
I HAVE TO PROTECT...
...AYATO.
...

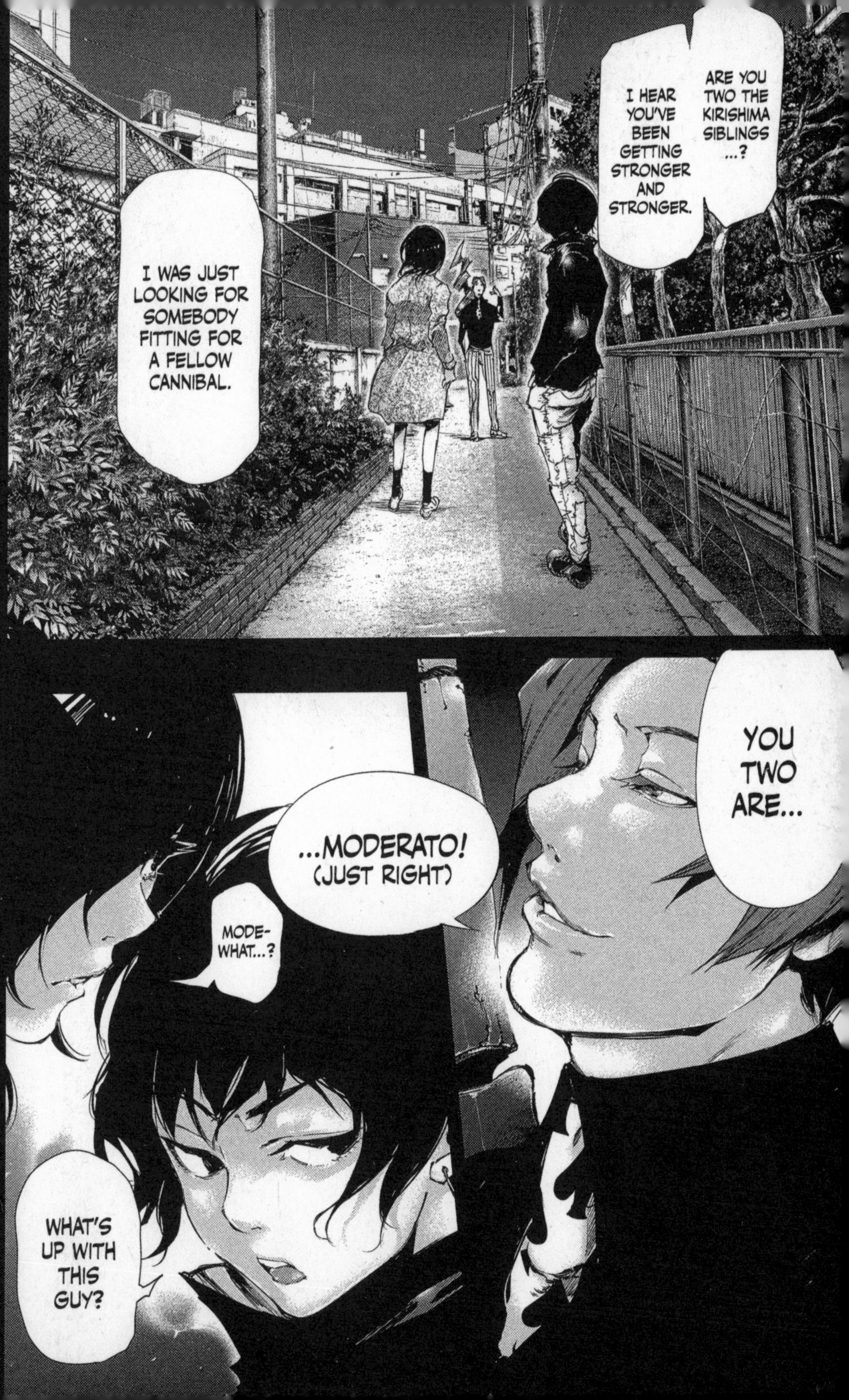
ARE YOU TWO THE KIRISHIMA SIBLINGS ...?
I HEAR YOU'VE BEEN GETTING STRONGER AND STRONGER.
I WAS JUST LOOKING FOR SOMEBODY FITTING FOR A FELLOW CANNIBAL.
YOU TWO ARE...
...MODERATO! (JUST RIGHT)
MODE-WHAT...?
WHAT'S UP WITH THIS GUY?

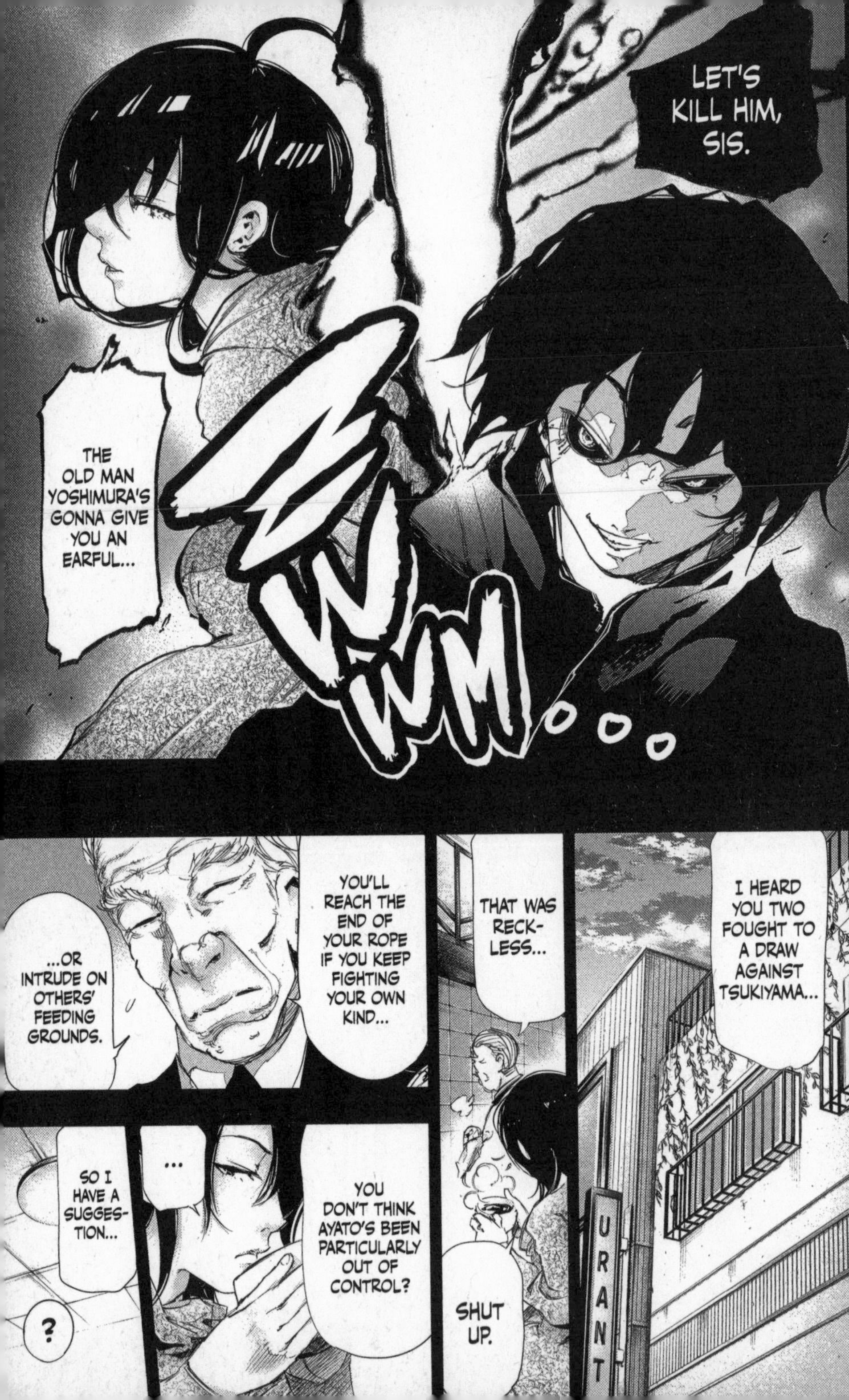
LET'S KILL HIM, SIS.
THE OLD MAN YOSHIMURA'S GONNA GIVE YOU AN EARFUL...
I HEARD YOU TWO FOUGHT TO A DRAW AGAINST TSUKIYAMA...
THAT WAS RECK-LESS...
SHUT UP.
URANT
YOU'LL REACH THE END OF YOUR ROPE IF YOU KEEP FIGHTING YOUR OWN KIND...
...OR INTRUDE ON OTHERS' FEEDING GROUNDS.
YOU DON'T THINK AYATO'S BEEN PARTICULARLY OUT OF CONTROL?
...
SO I HAVE A SUGGES-TION...
?

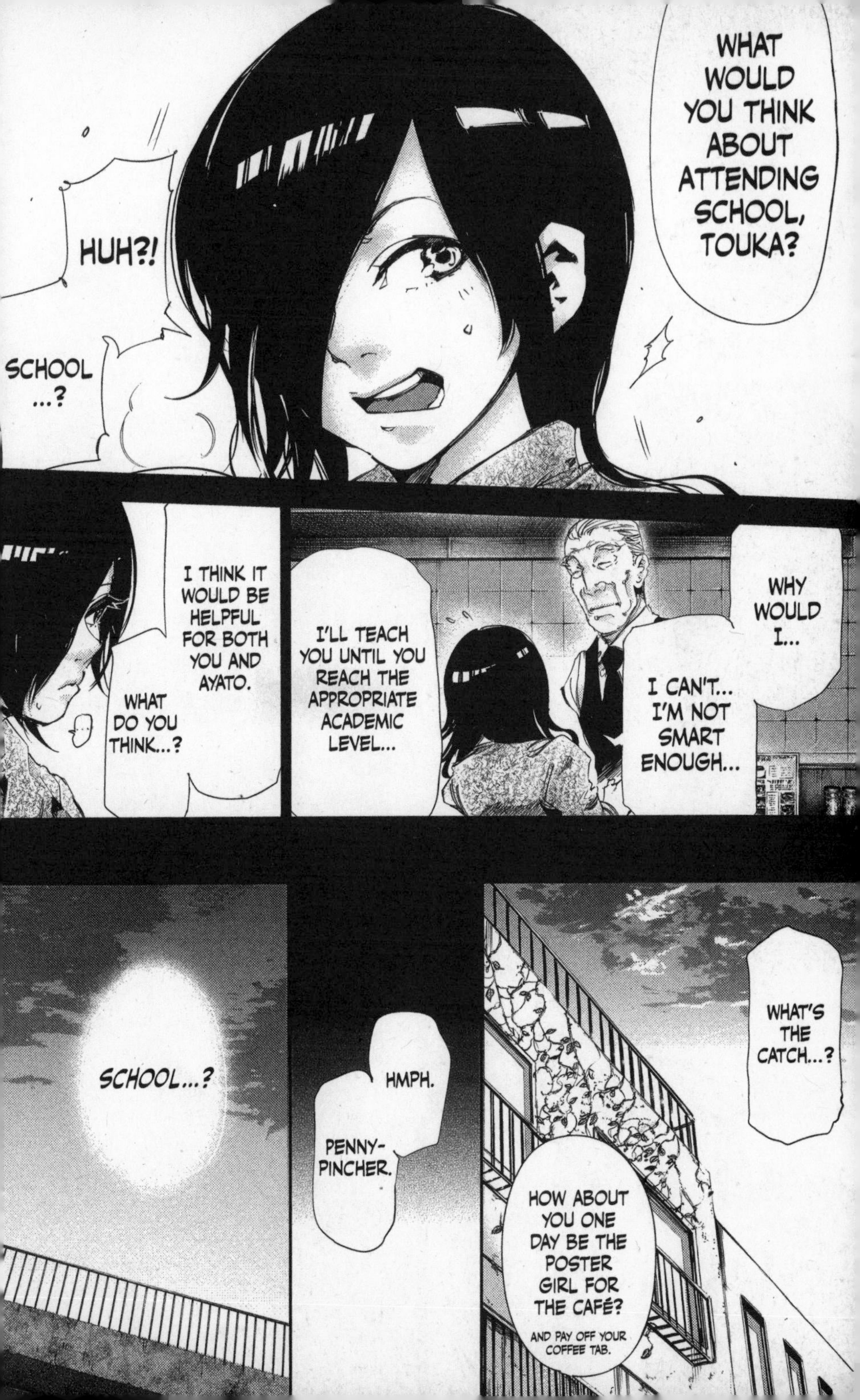
WHAT WOULD YOU THINK ABOUT ATTENDING SCHOOL, TOUKA?
HUH?!
SCHOOL ...?
WHY WOULD I...
I CAN'T... I'M NOT SMART ENOUGH...
I'LL TEACH YOU UNTIL YOU REACH THE APPROPRIATE ACADEMIC LEVEL...
I THINK IT WOULD BE HELPFUL FOR BOTH YOU AND AYATO.
WHAT DO YOU THINK...?
WHAT'S THE CATCH...?
HOW ABOUT YOU ONE DAY BE THE POSTER GIRL FOR THE CAFÉ?
AND PAY OFF YOUR COFFEE TAB.
HMPH.
PENNY-PINCHER.
SCHOOL...?

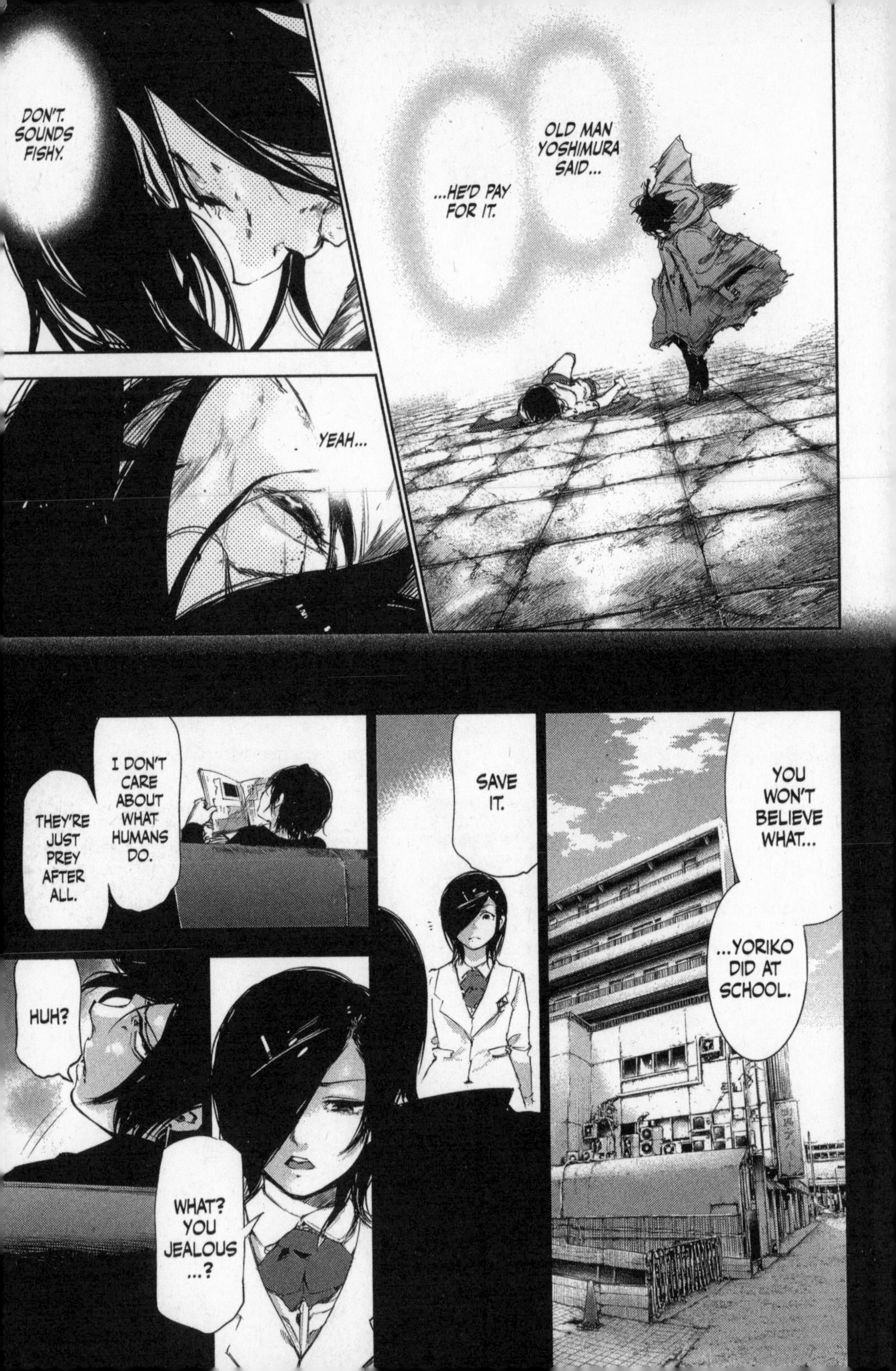
OLD MAN YOSHIMURA SAID...
...HE'D PAY FOR IT.
DON'T. SOUNDS FISHY.
YEAH...
YOU WON'T BELIEVE WHAT...
...YORIKO DID AT SCHOOL.
SAVE IT.
I DON'T CARE ABOUT WHAT HUMANS DO.
THEY'RE JUST PREY AFTER ALL.
WHAT? YOU JEALOUS ...?
HUH?

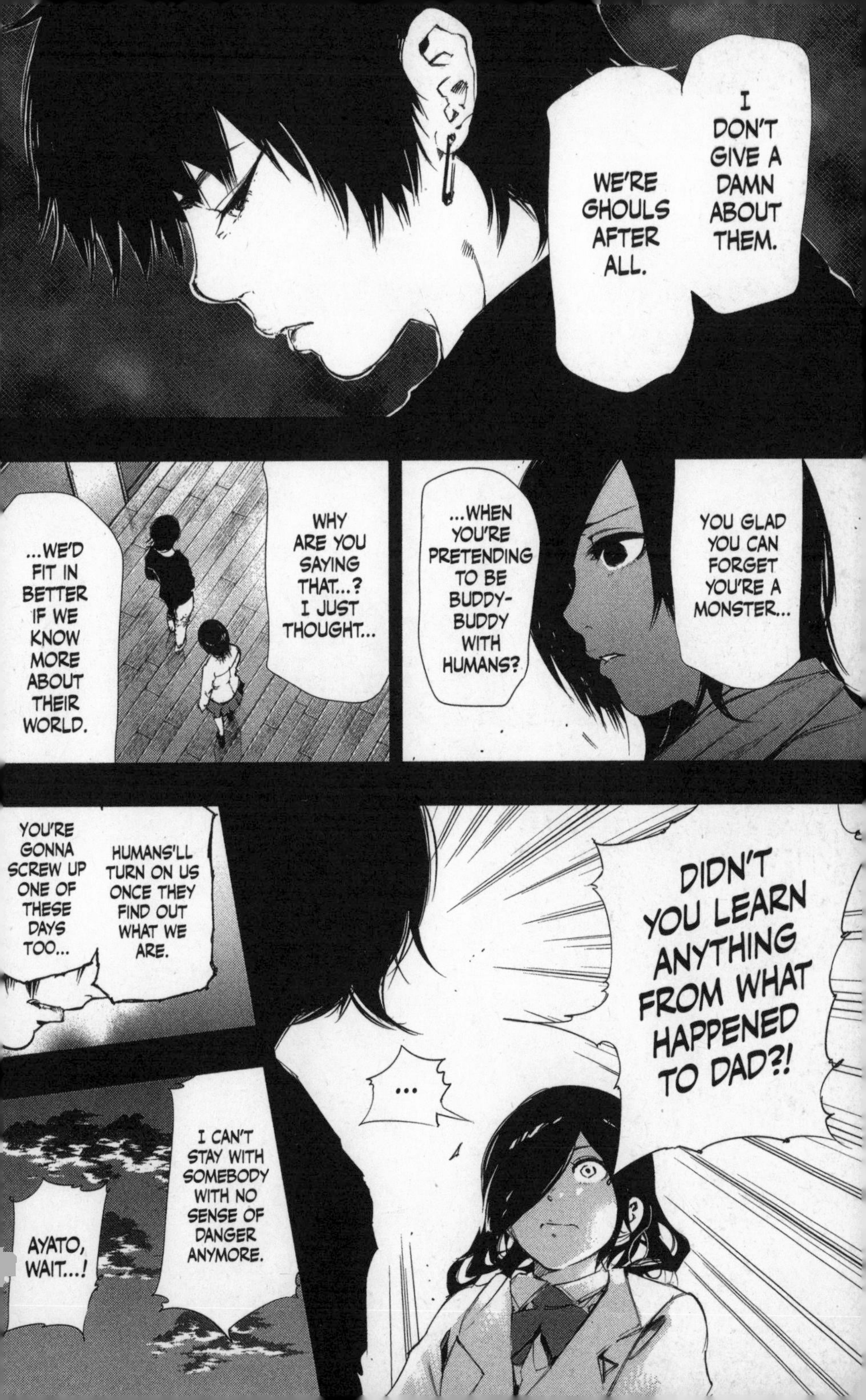
I DON'T GIVE A DAMN ABOUT THEM.
WE'RE GHOULS AFTER ALL.
YOU GLAD YOU CAN FORGET YOU'RE A MONSTER...
...WHEN YOU'RE PRETENDING TO BE BUDDY-BUDDY WITH HUMANS?
WHY ARE YOU SAYING THAT...? I JUST THOUGHT...
...WE'D FIT IN BETTER IF WE KNOW MORE ABOUT THEIR WORLD.
DIDN'T YOU LEARN ANYTHING FROM WHAT HAPPENED TO DAD?!
...
HUMANS'LL TURN ON US ONCE THEY FIND OUT WHAT WE ARE.
YOU'RE GONNA SCREW UP ONE OF THESE DAYS TOO...
I CAN'T STAY WITH SOMEBODY WITH NO SENSE OF DANGER ANYMORE.
AYATO, WAIT...!

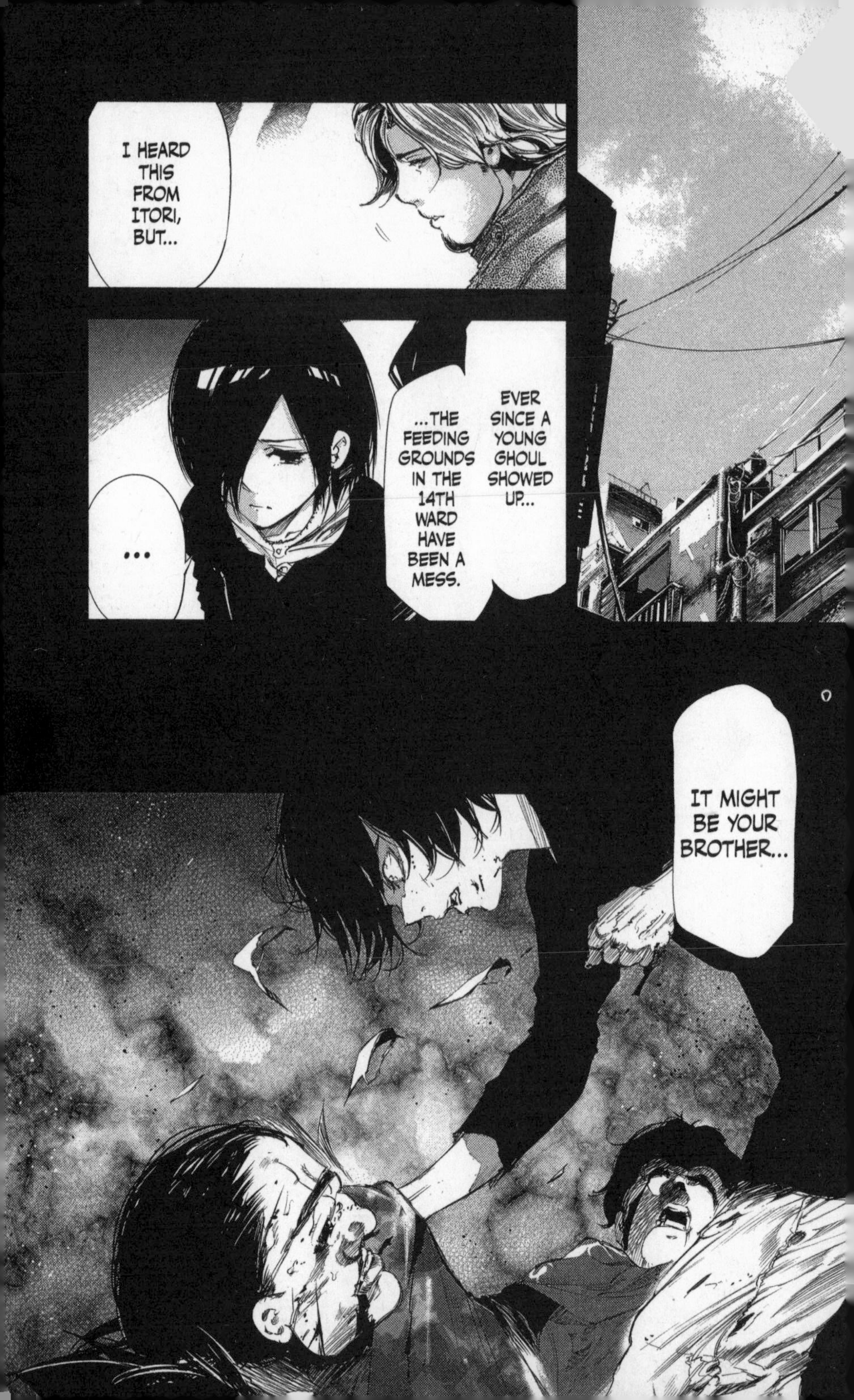
I HEARD THIS FROM ITORI, BUT...
EVER SINCE A YOUNG GHOUL SHOWED UP...
...THE FEEDING GROUNDS IN THE 14TH WARD HAVE BEEN A MESS.
...
IT MIGHT BE YOUR BROTHER...

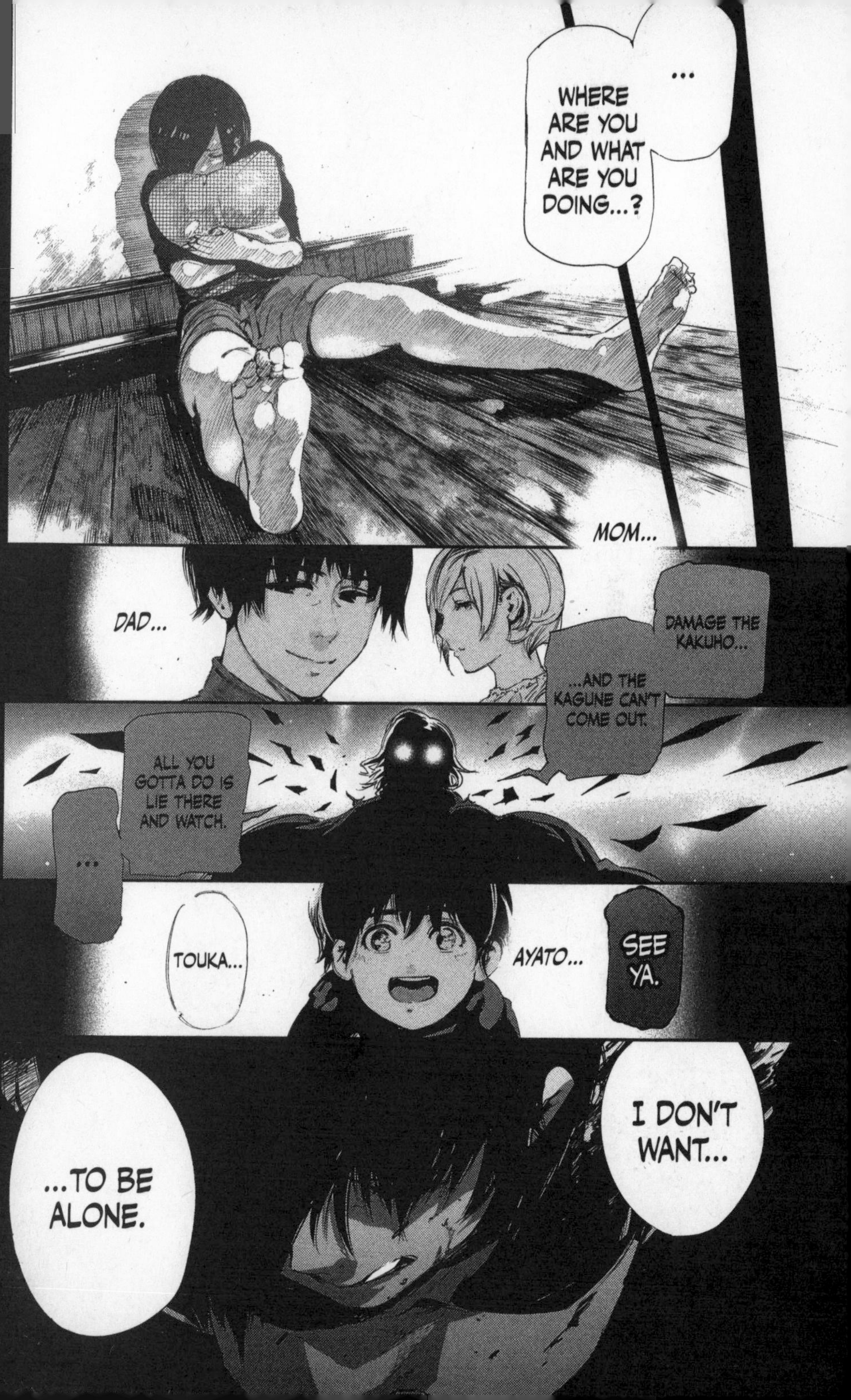
...
WHERE ARE YOU AND WHAT ARE YOU DOING...?
MOM...
DAMAGE THE KAKUHO...
...AND THE KAGUNE CAN'T COME OUT.
DAD...
ALL YOU GOTTA DO IS LIE THERE AND WATCH.
...
SEE YA.
AYATO...
TOUKA...
I DON'T WANT...
...TO BE ALONE.

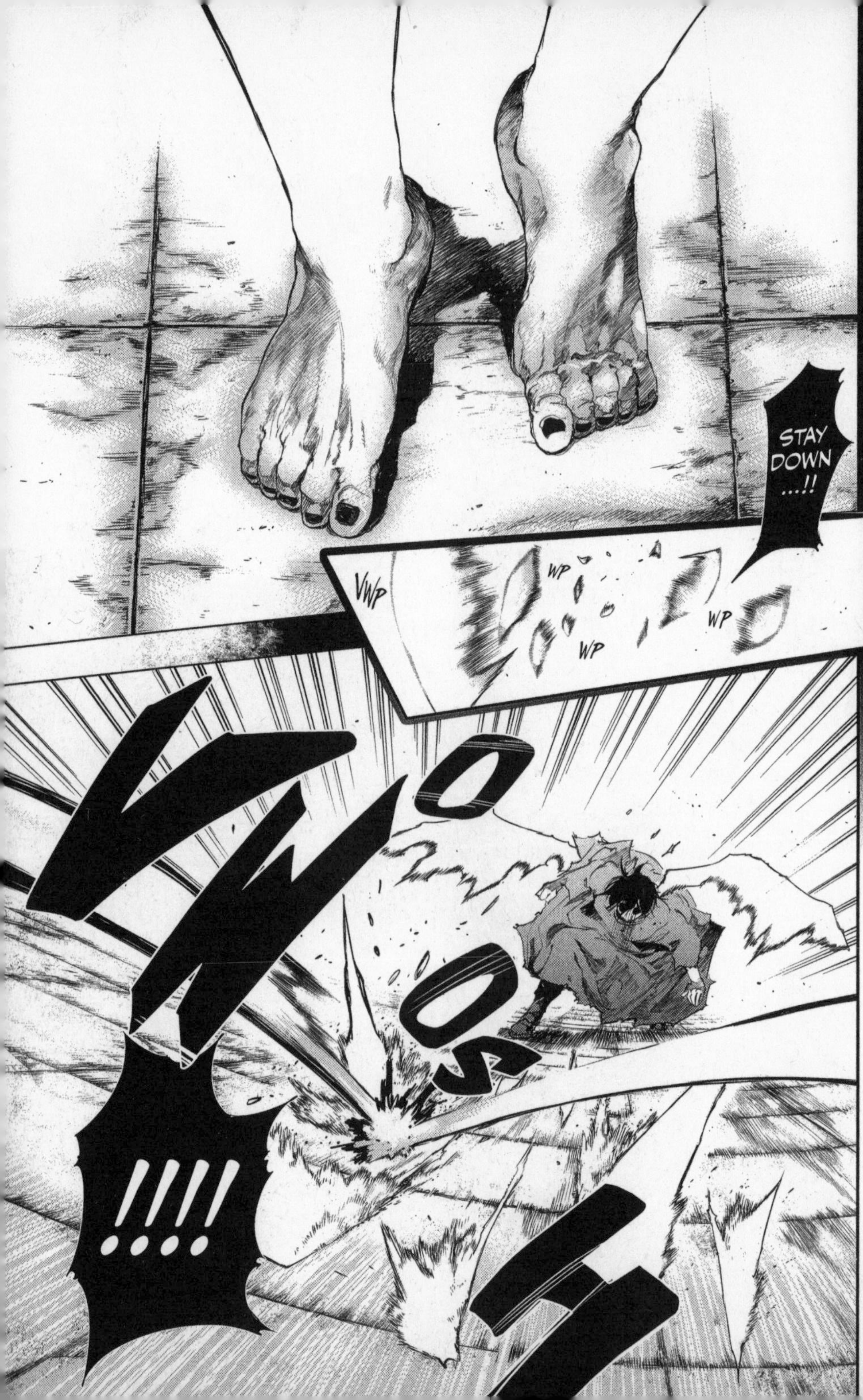

STAY DOWN ...!!
VWP
WP
WP
WP
WOOSH!!!!

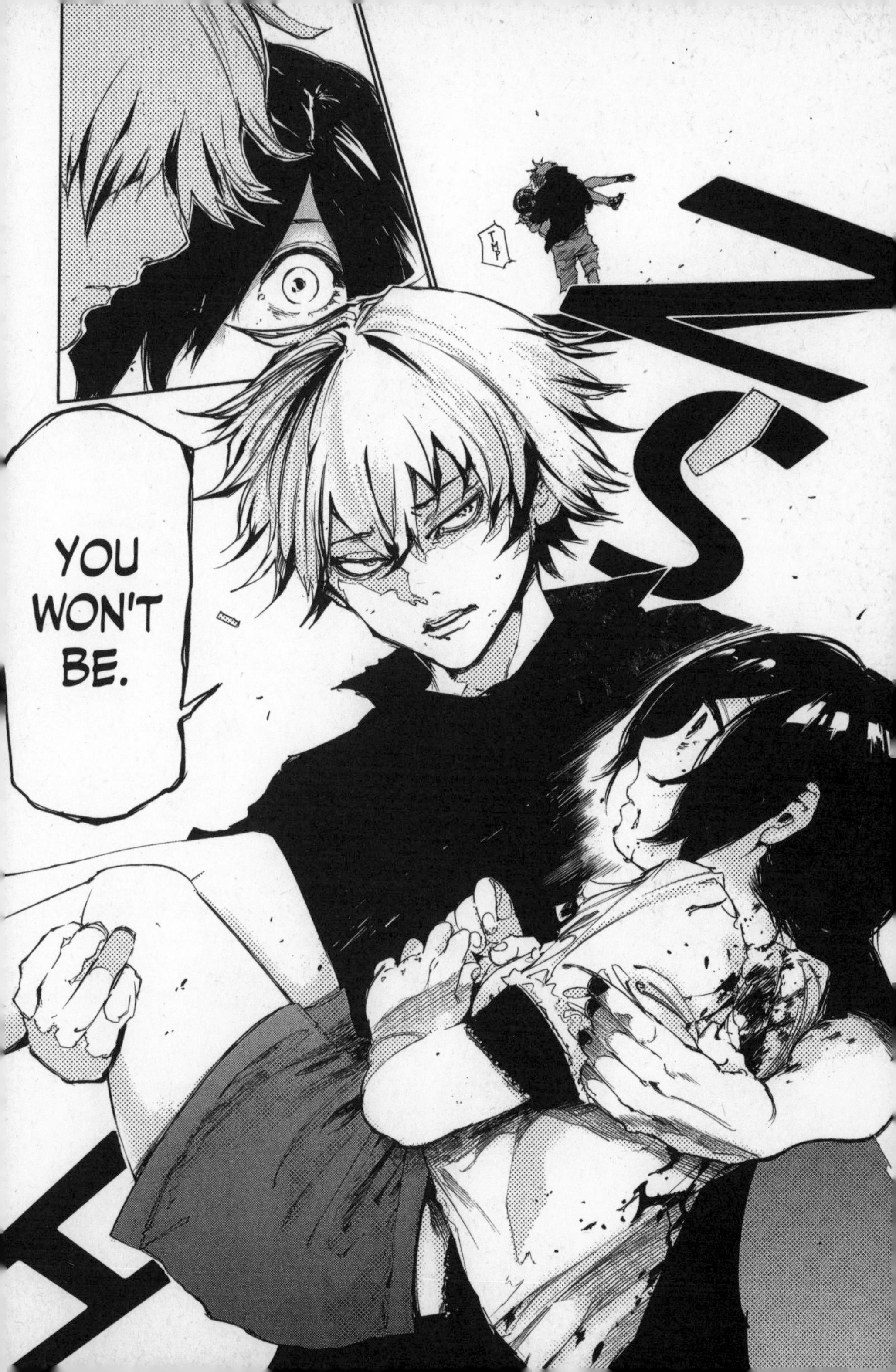
TMP
YOU WON'T BE.

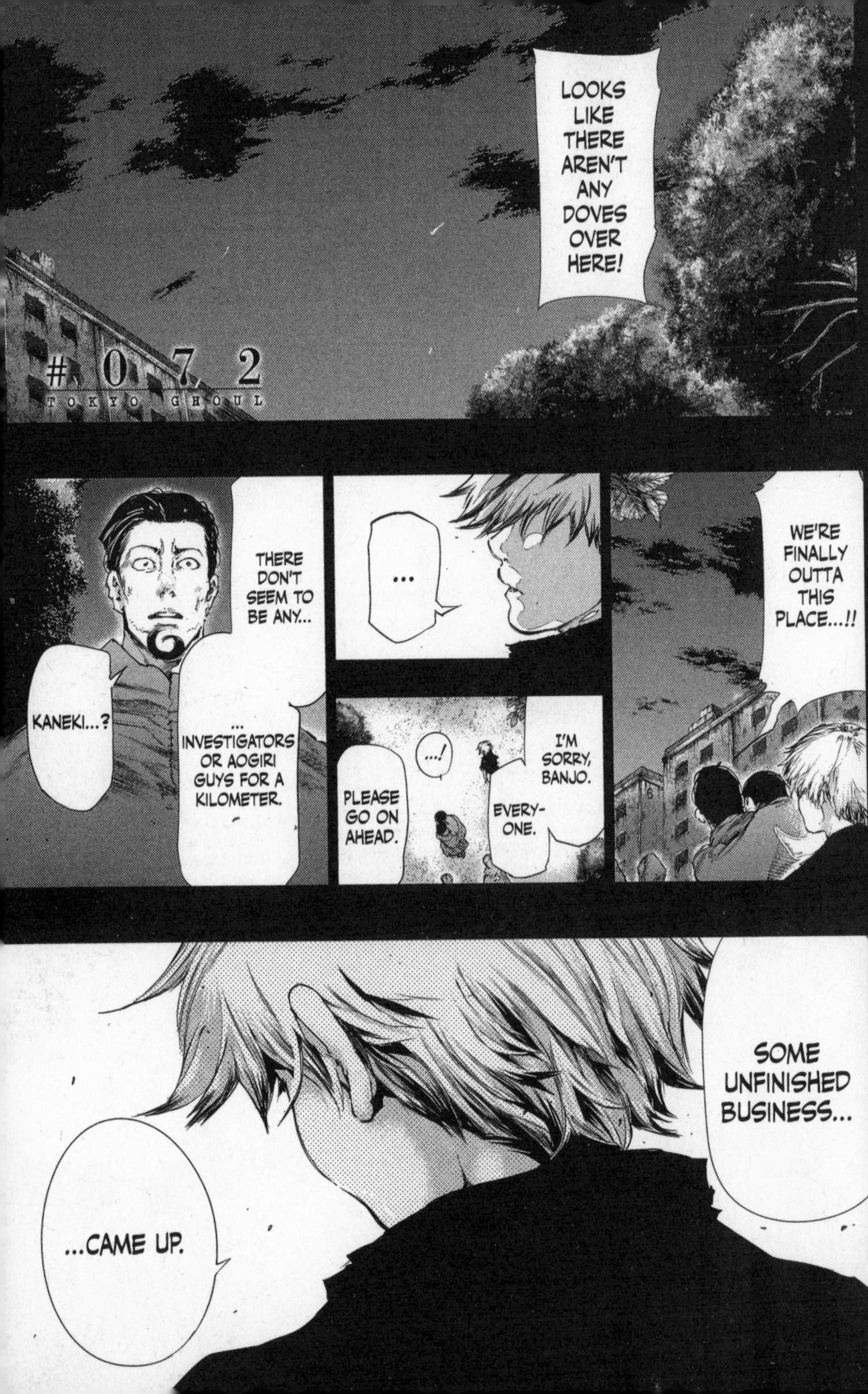
LOOKS LIKE THERE AREN'T ANY DOVES OVER HERE!
#072
TOKYO GHOUL
WE'RE FINALLY OUTTA THIS PLACE...!!
...
I'M SORRY, BANJO.
EVERY-ONE.
...!
PLEASE GO ON AHEAD.
THERE DON'T SEEM TO BE ANY...
...INVESTIGATORS OR AOGIRI GUYS FOR A KILOMETER.
KANEKI...?
SOME UNFINISHED BUSINESS...
...CAME UP.

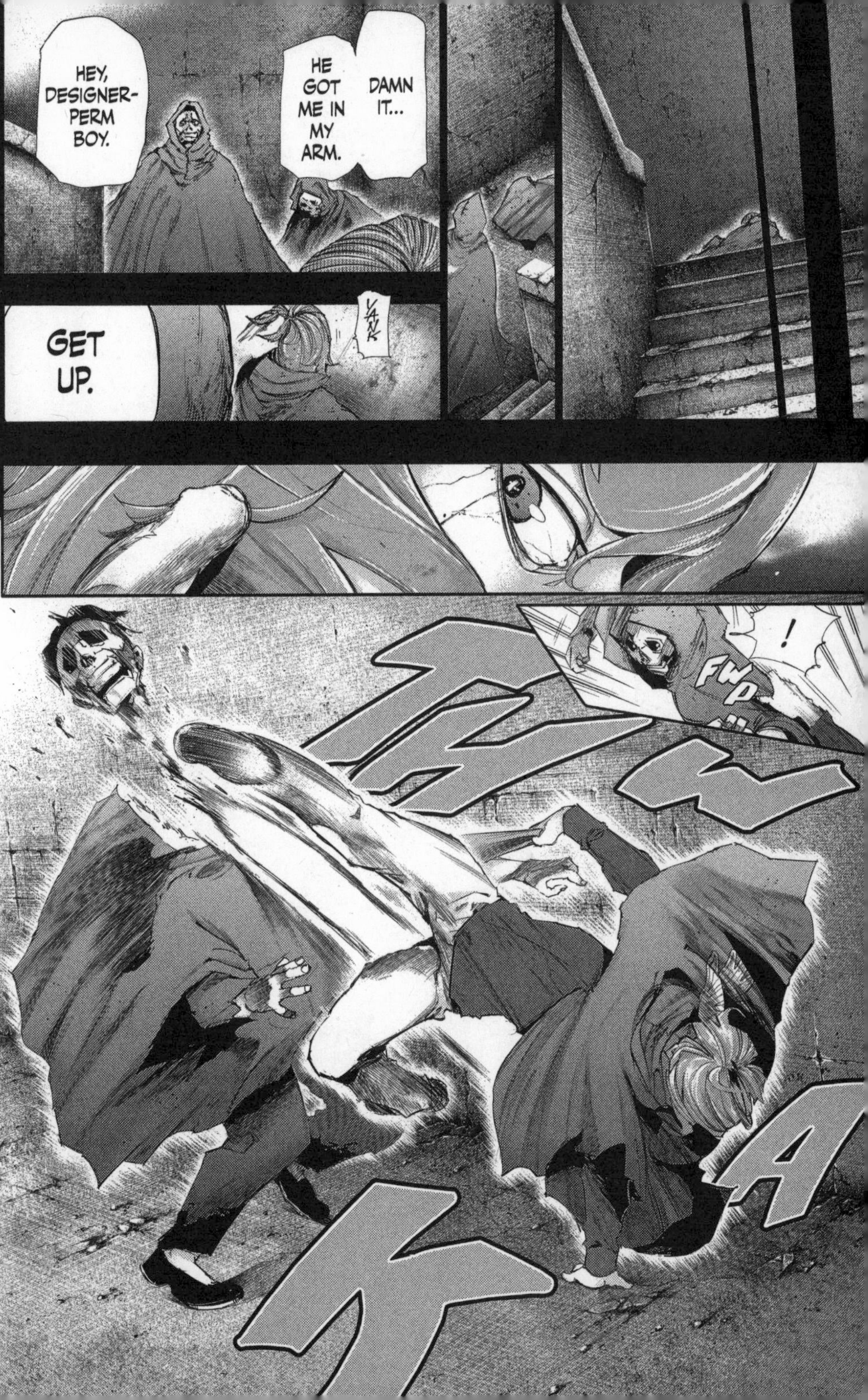
DAMN IT...
HE GOT ME IN MY ARM.
HEY, DESIGNER-PERM BOY.
YANK
GET UP.
!
FWP

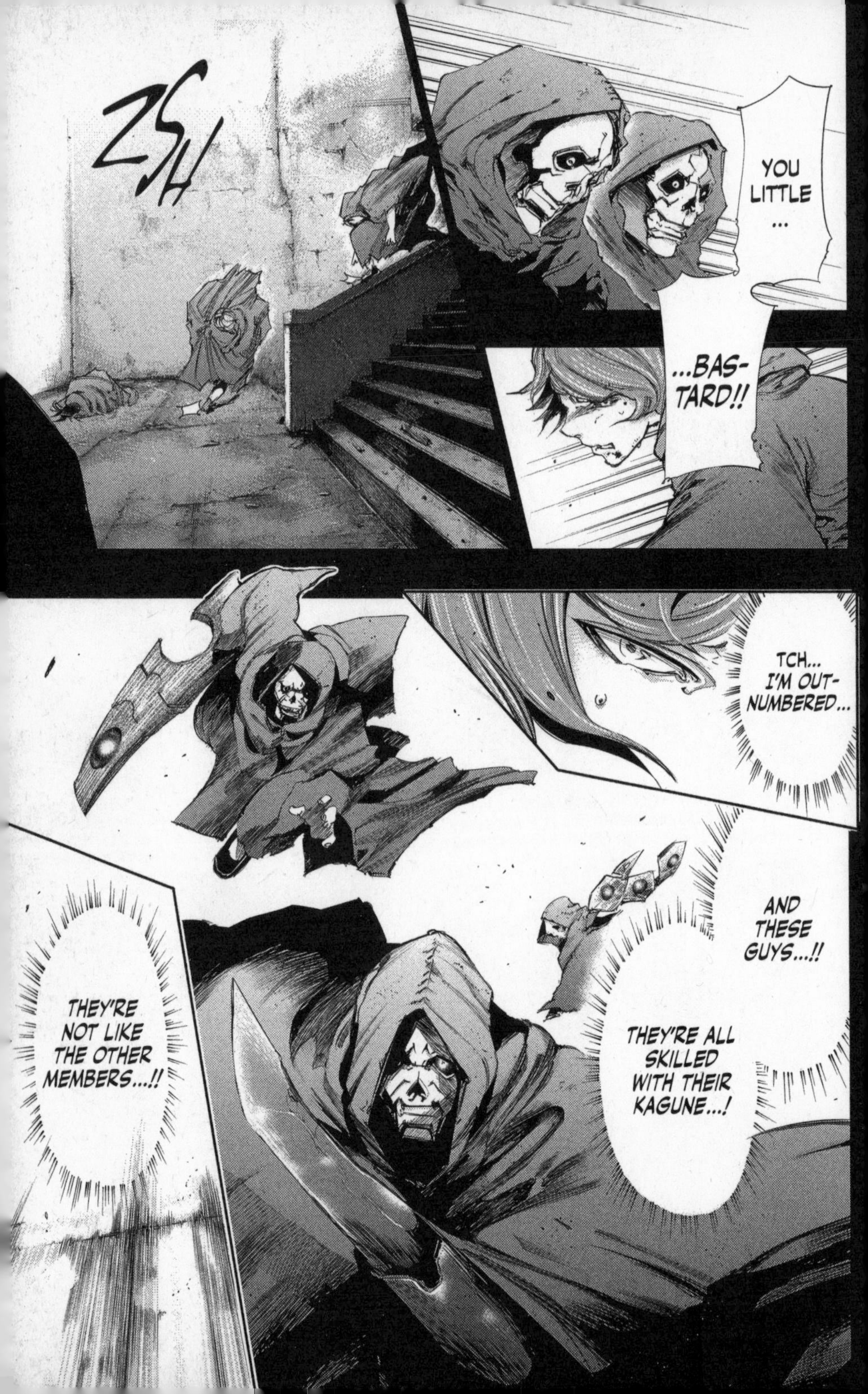
YOU LITTLE ...
...BAS-TARD!!
ZSH
TCH... I'M OUT-NUMBERED...
AND THESE GUYS...!!
THEY'RE ALL SKILLED WITH THEIR KAGUNE...!
THEY'RE NOT LIKE THE OTHER MEMBERS...!!

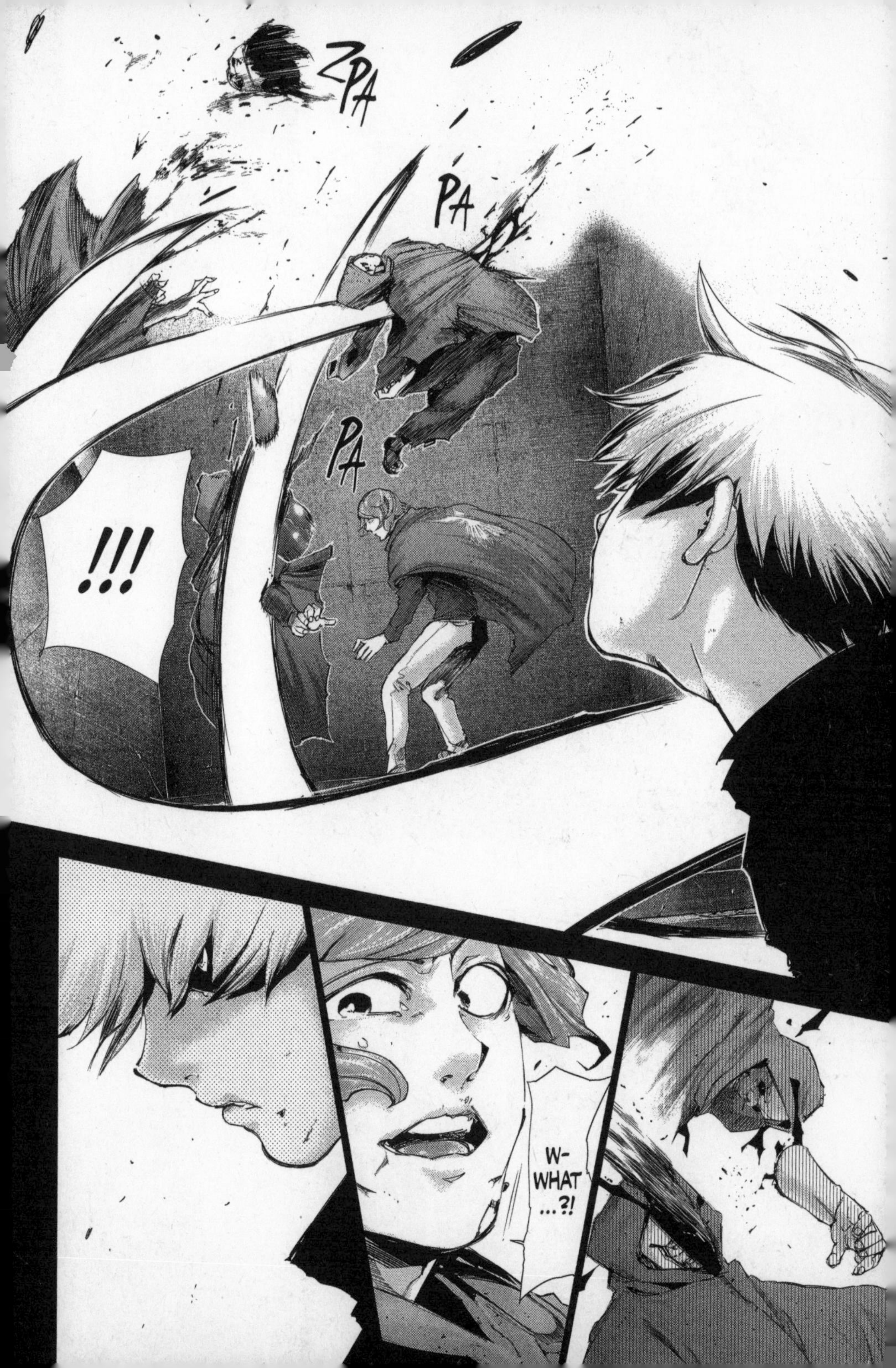
ZPA
PA
PA
!!!
W-
WHAT
...?!

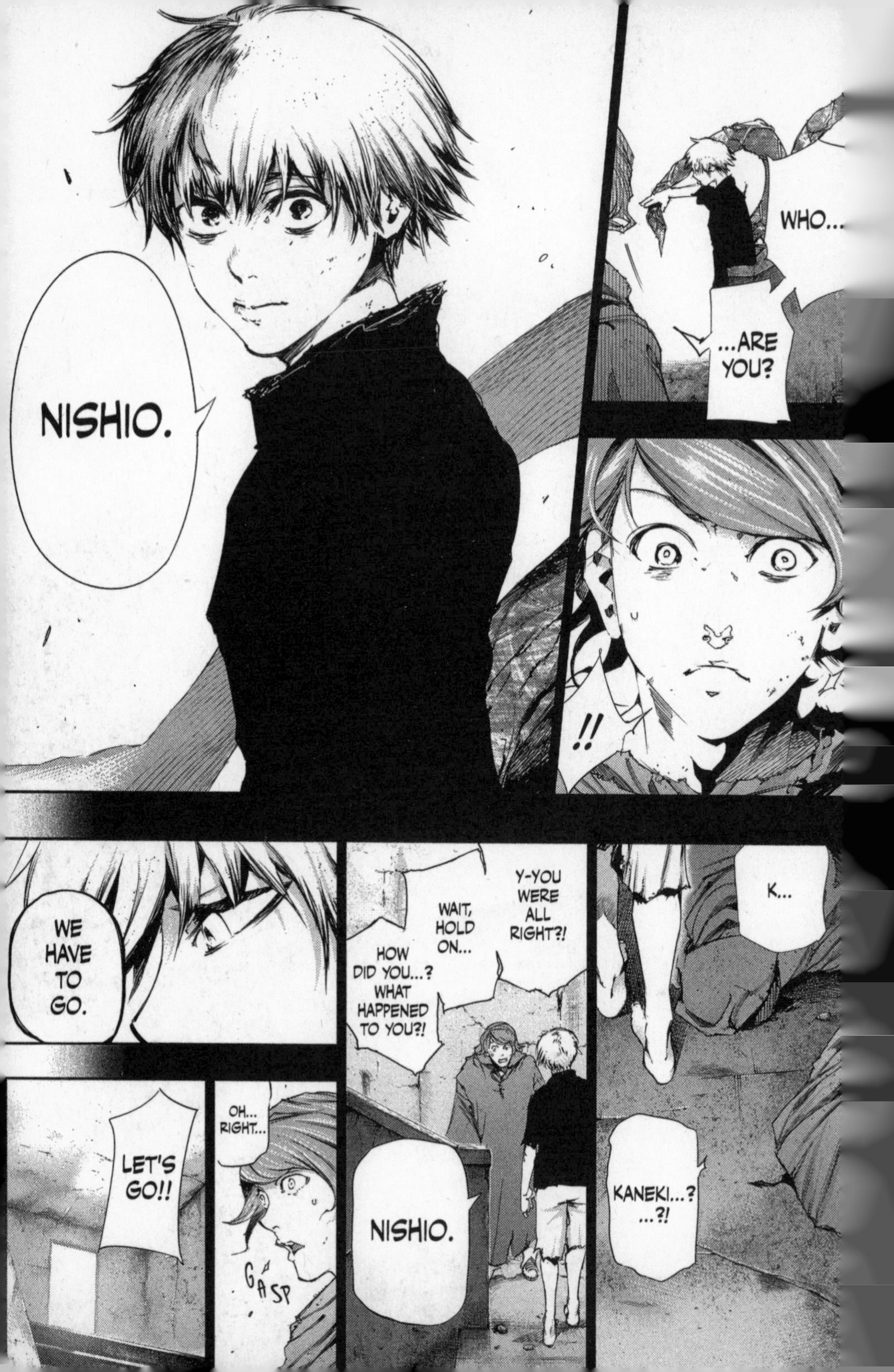
WHO...
...ARE YOU?
!!
NISHIO.
K...
KANEKI...? ...?!
Y-YOU WERE ALL RIGHT?!
WAIT, HOLD ON...
HOW DID YOU...? WHAT HAPPENED TO YOU?!
NISHIO.
WE HAVE TO GO.
OH... RIGHT...
GASP
LET'S GO!!

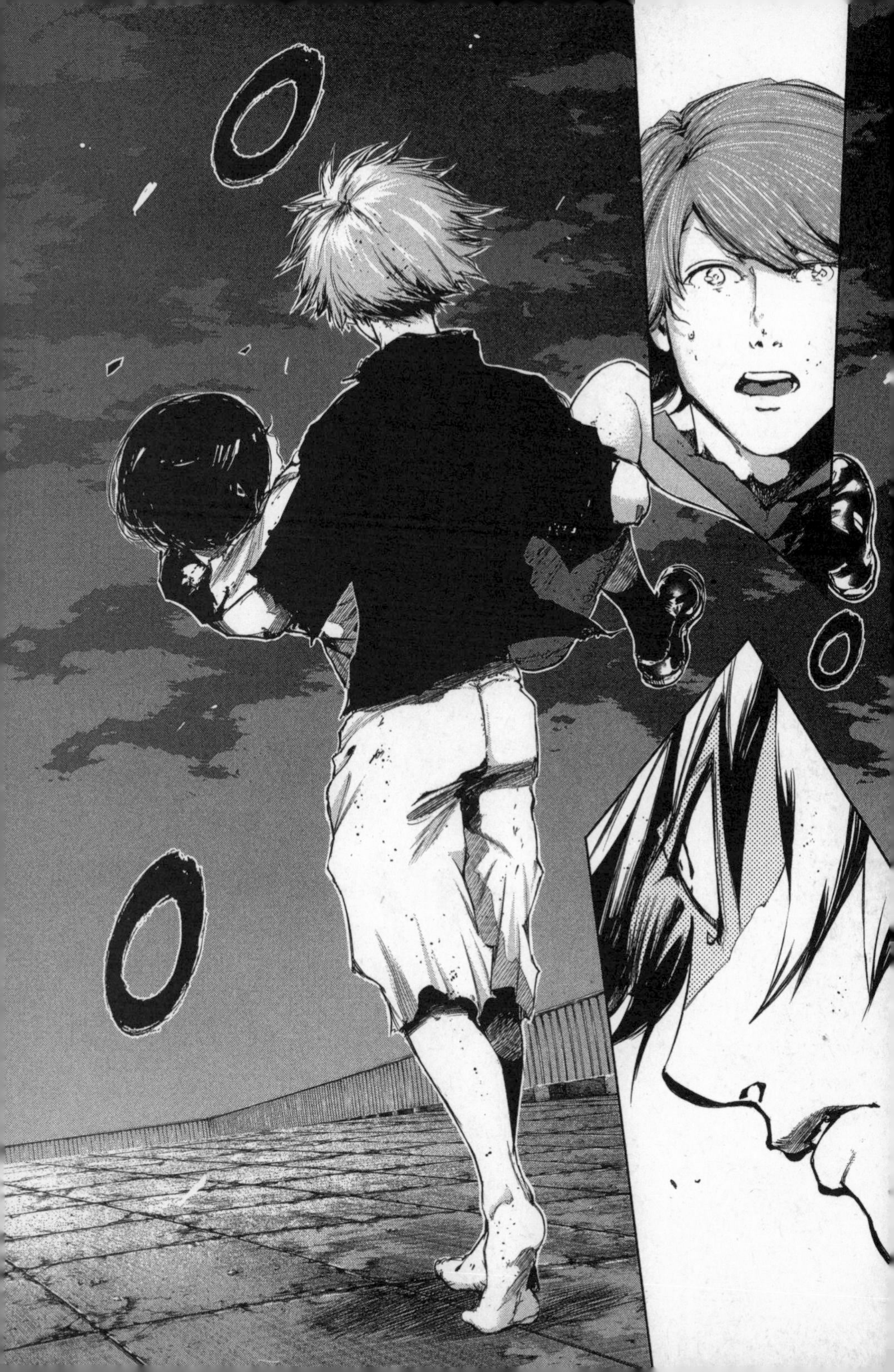

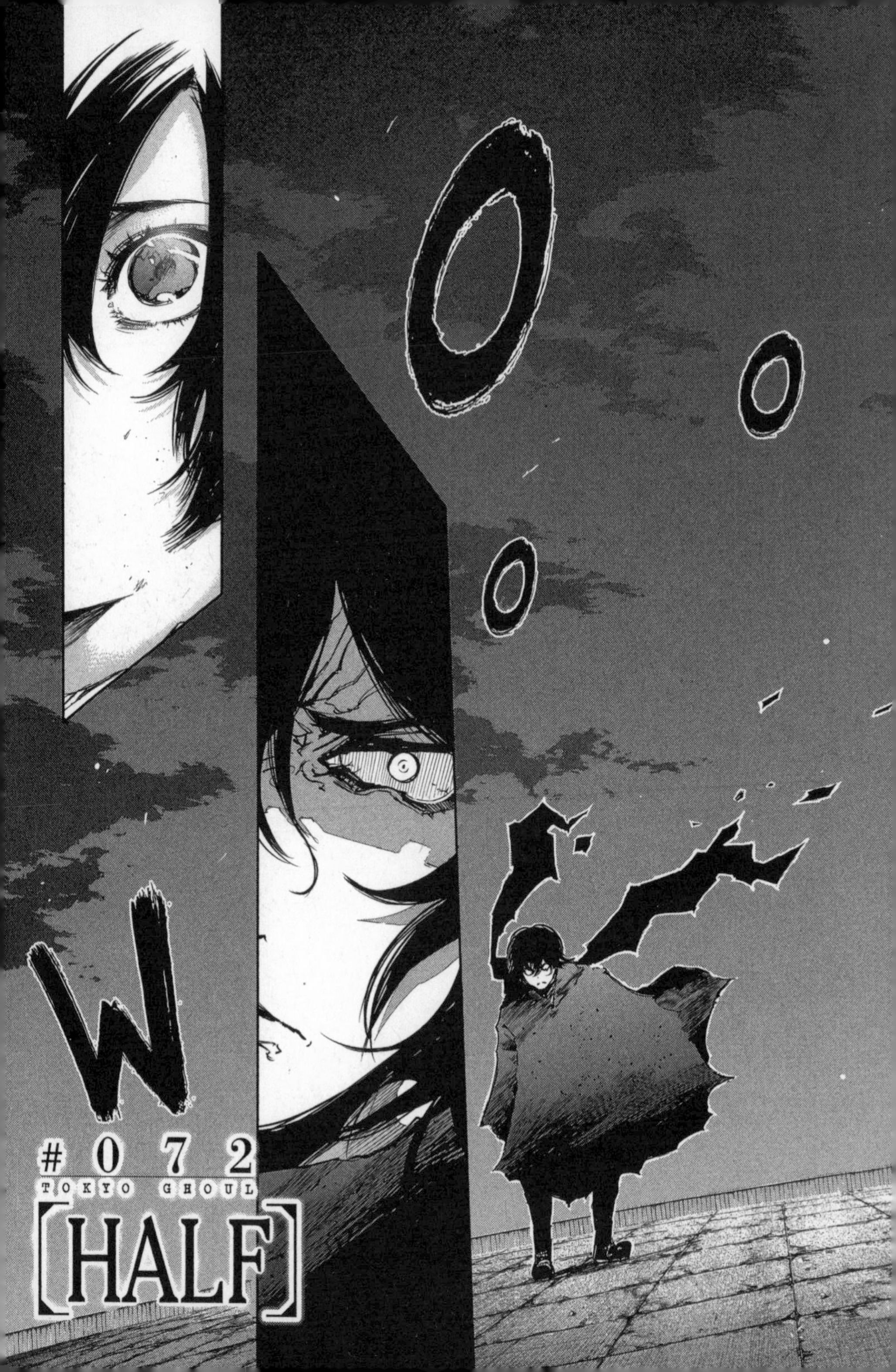

W
#072
TOKYO GHOUL
[HALF]

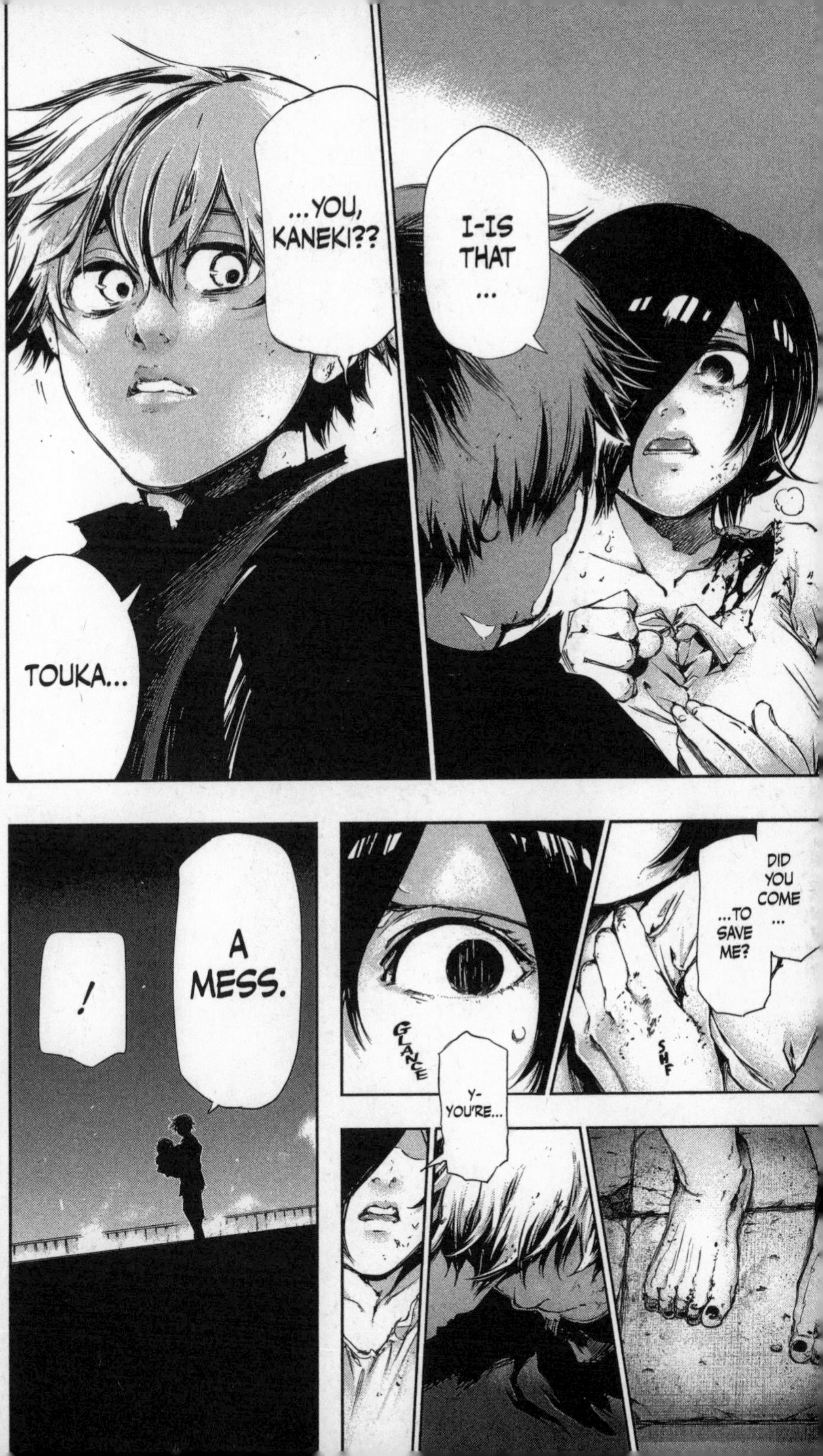
I-IS THAT ...
...YOU, KANEKI??
TOUKA...
DID YOU COME ...
...TO SAVE ME?
SHF
GLANCE
Y- YOU'RE...
A MESS.
!

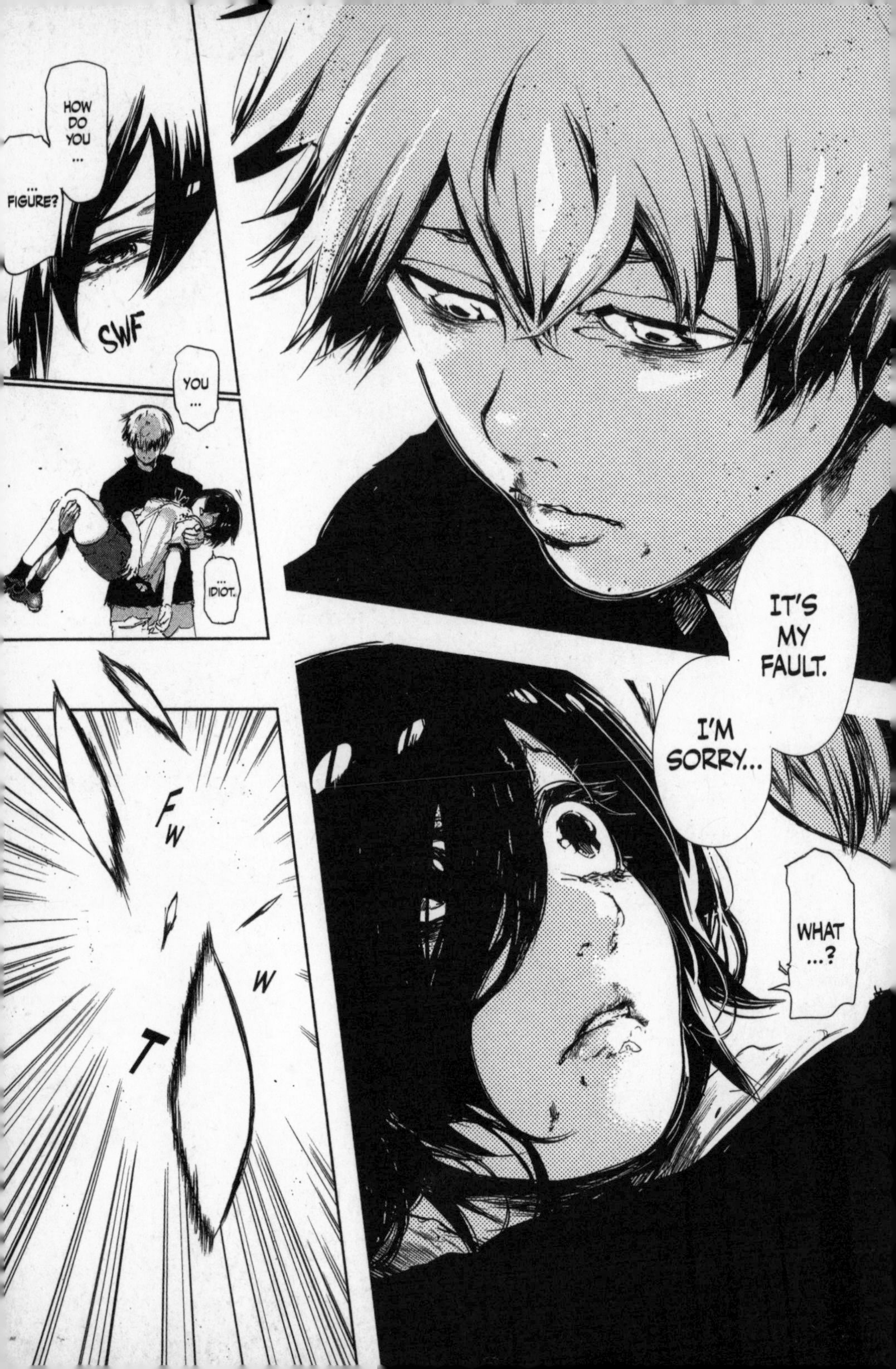
HOW DO YOU ... ... FIGURE?
SWF
YOU ...
... IDIOT.
IT'S MY FAULT.
I'M SORRY...
WHAT ...?
FWWT

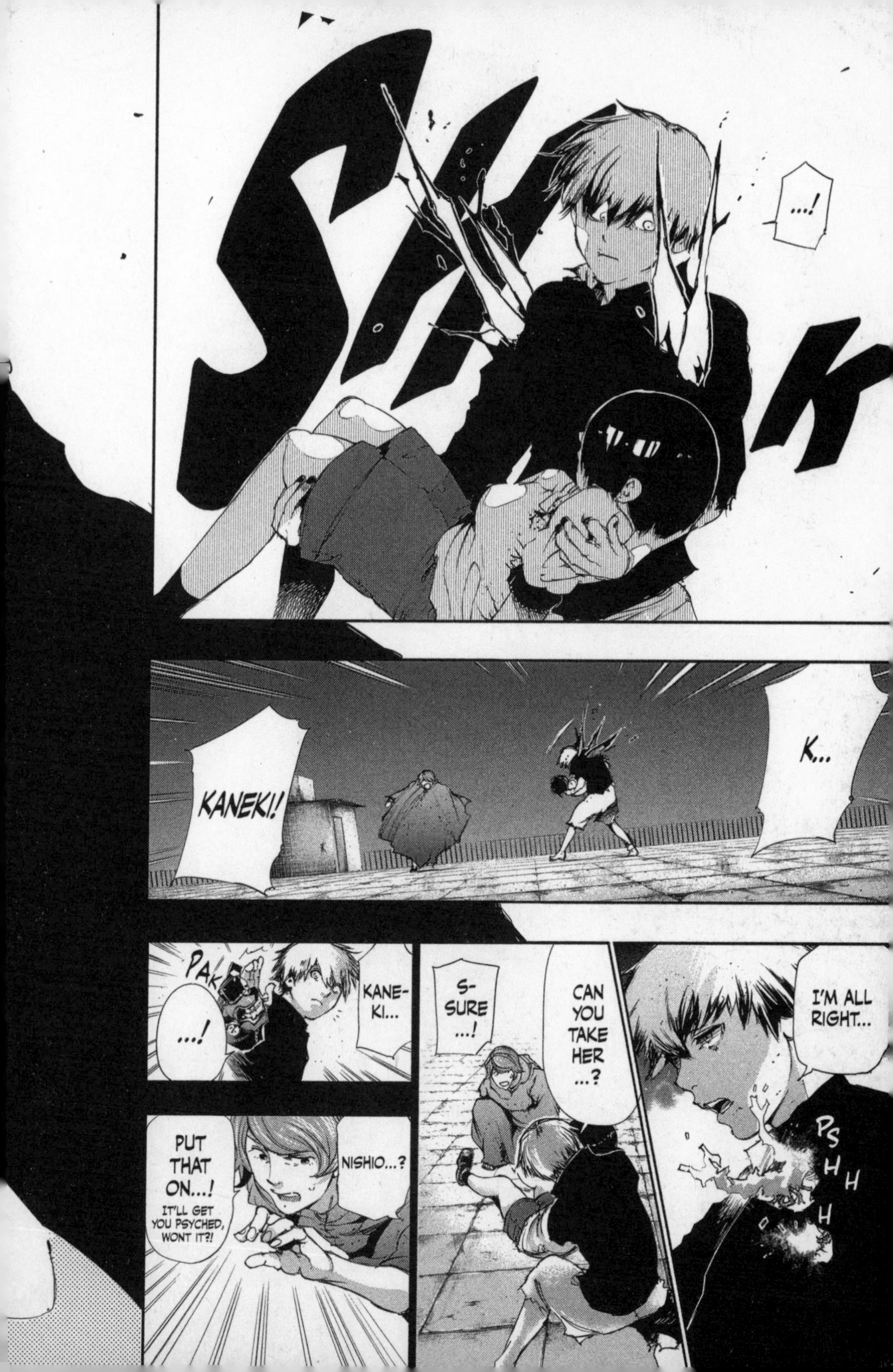
...!
K...
KANEKI!
I'M ALL RIGHT...
PSHHH
CAN YOU TAKE HER ...?
S-SURE ...!
KANE-KI...
...!
PAK
NISHIO...?
PUT THAT ON...!
IT'LL GET YOU PSYCHED, WONT IT?!

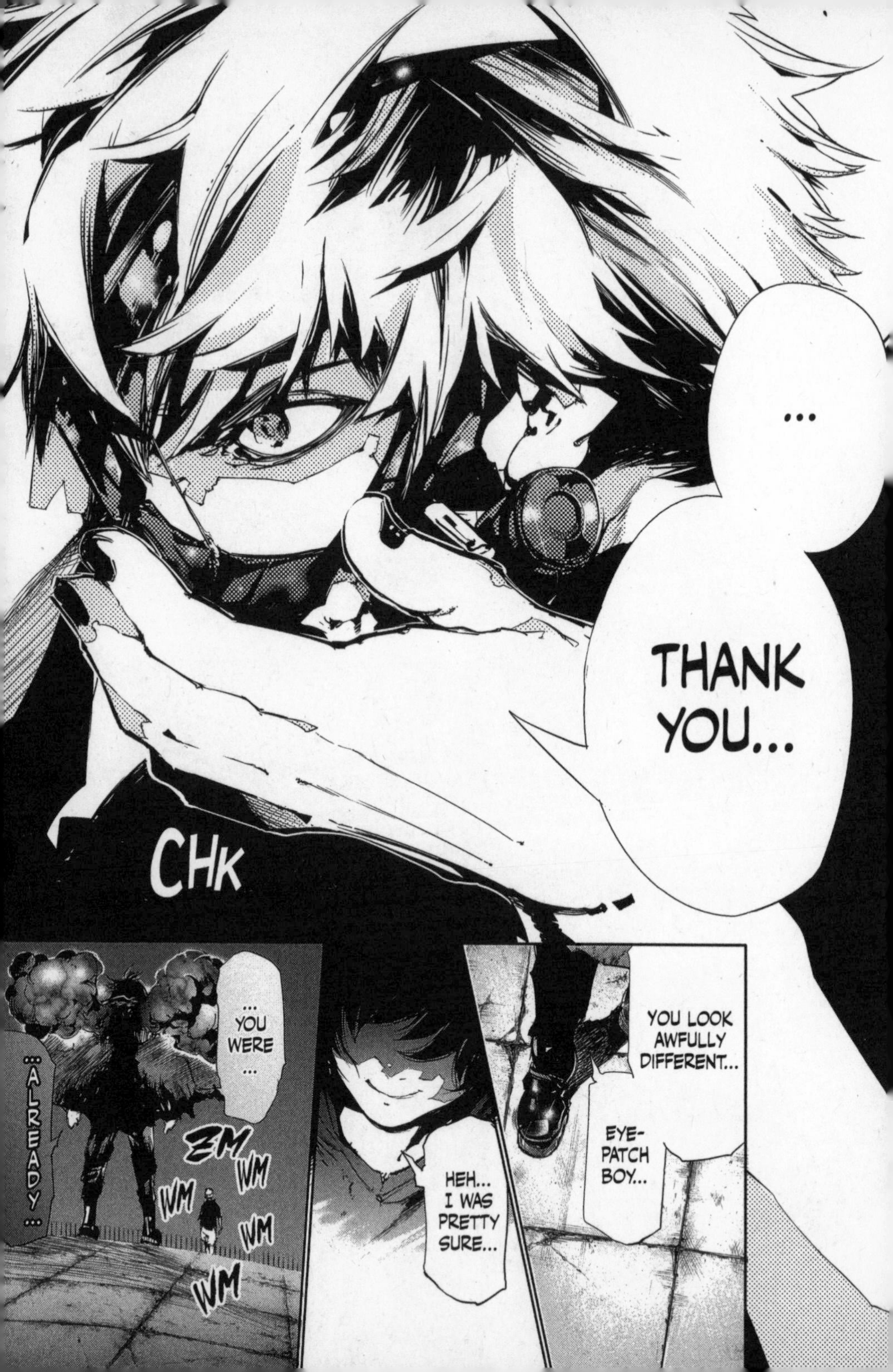
...
THANK YOU...
CHK
YOU LOOK AWFULLY DIFFERENT...
EYE-PATCH BOY...
HEH... I WAS PRETTY SURE...
... YOU WERE ...
...ALREADY...
ZM WM WM WM WM WM

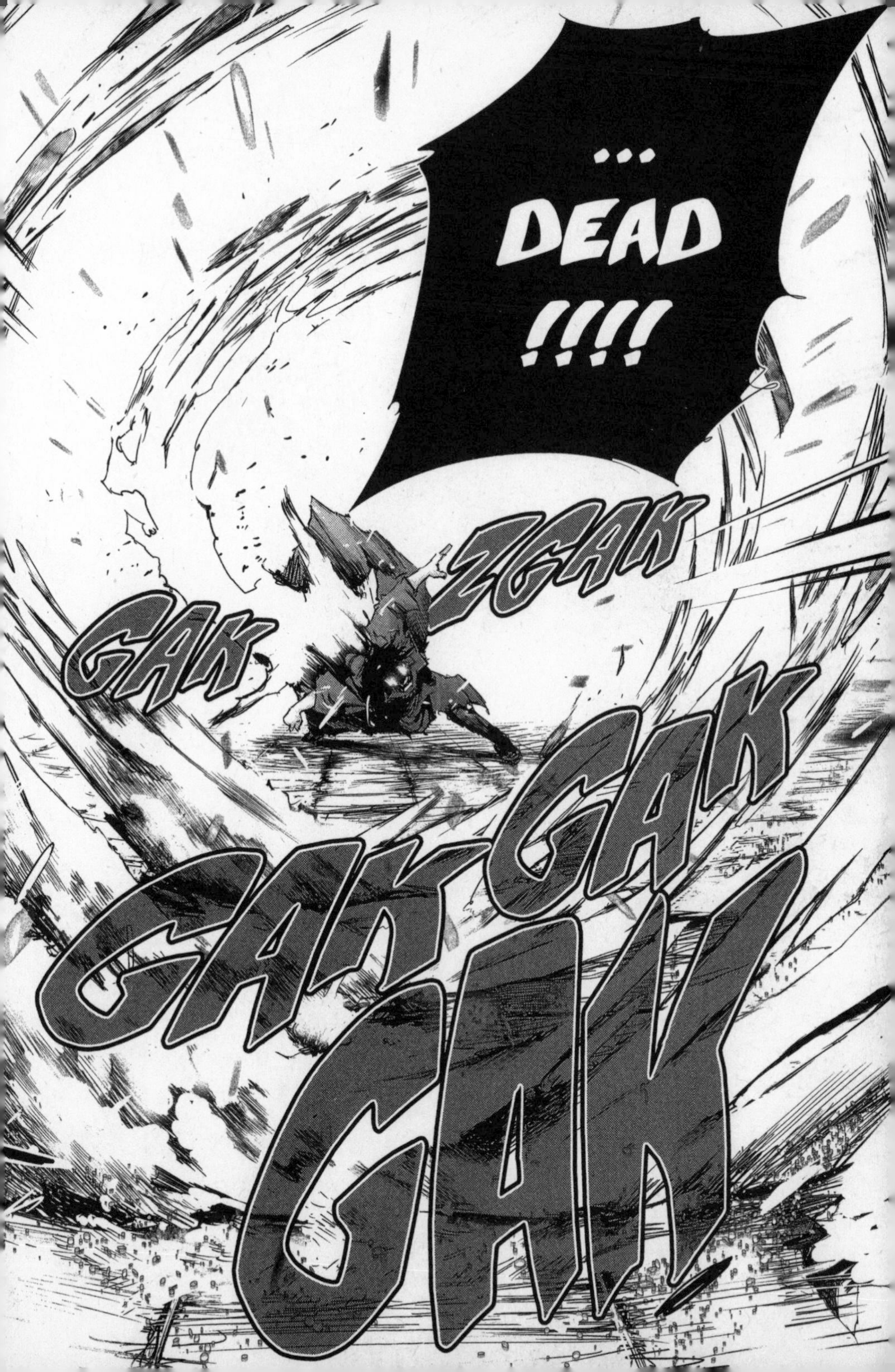

...DEAD!!!!
ZGAK
GAK
GAK
GAK
GAK

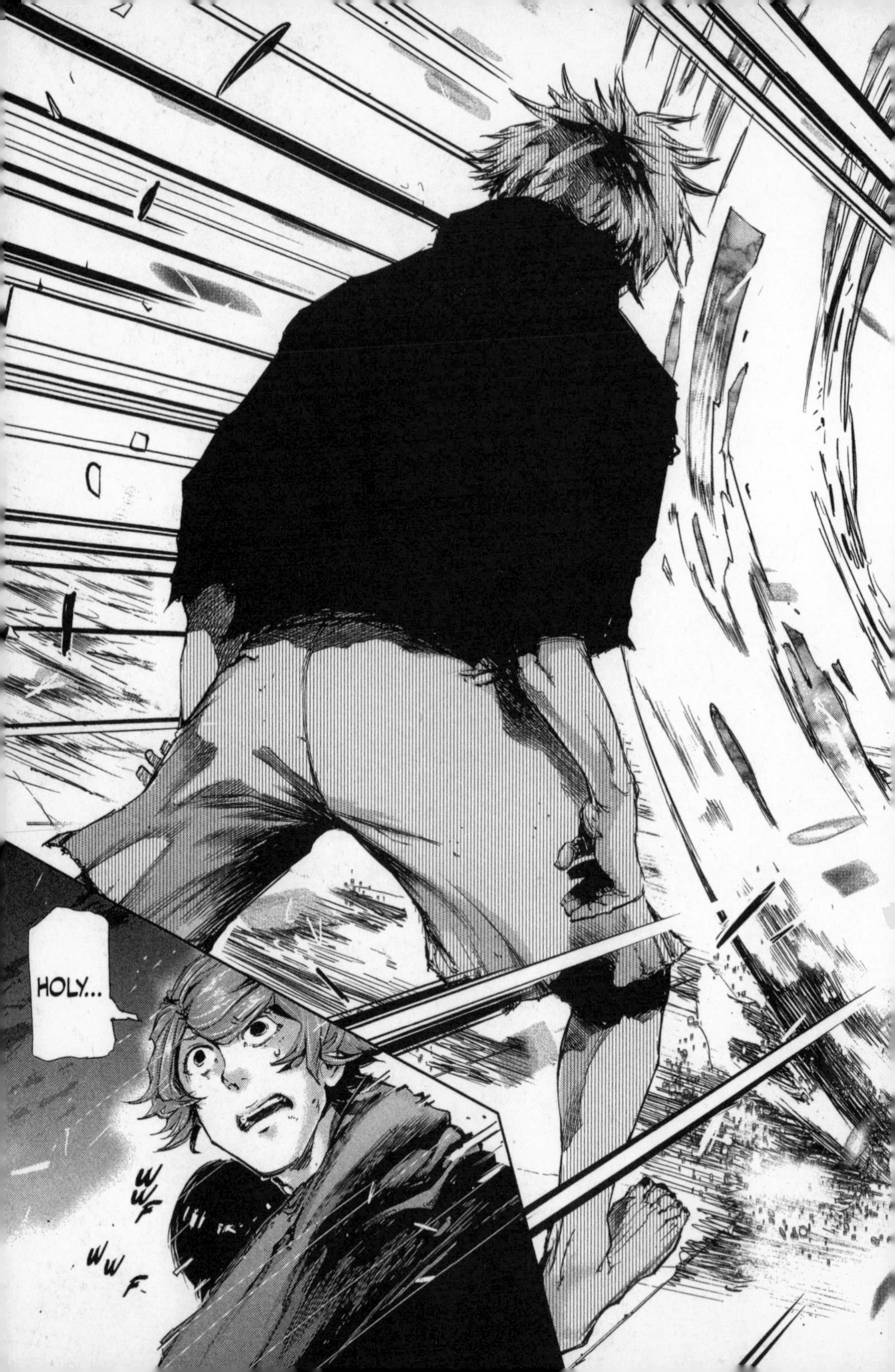
HOLY...
WUF
WWF-

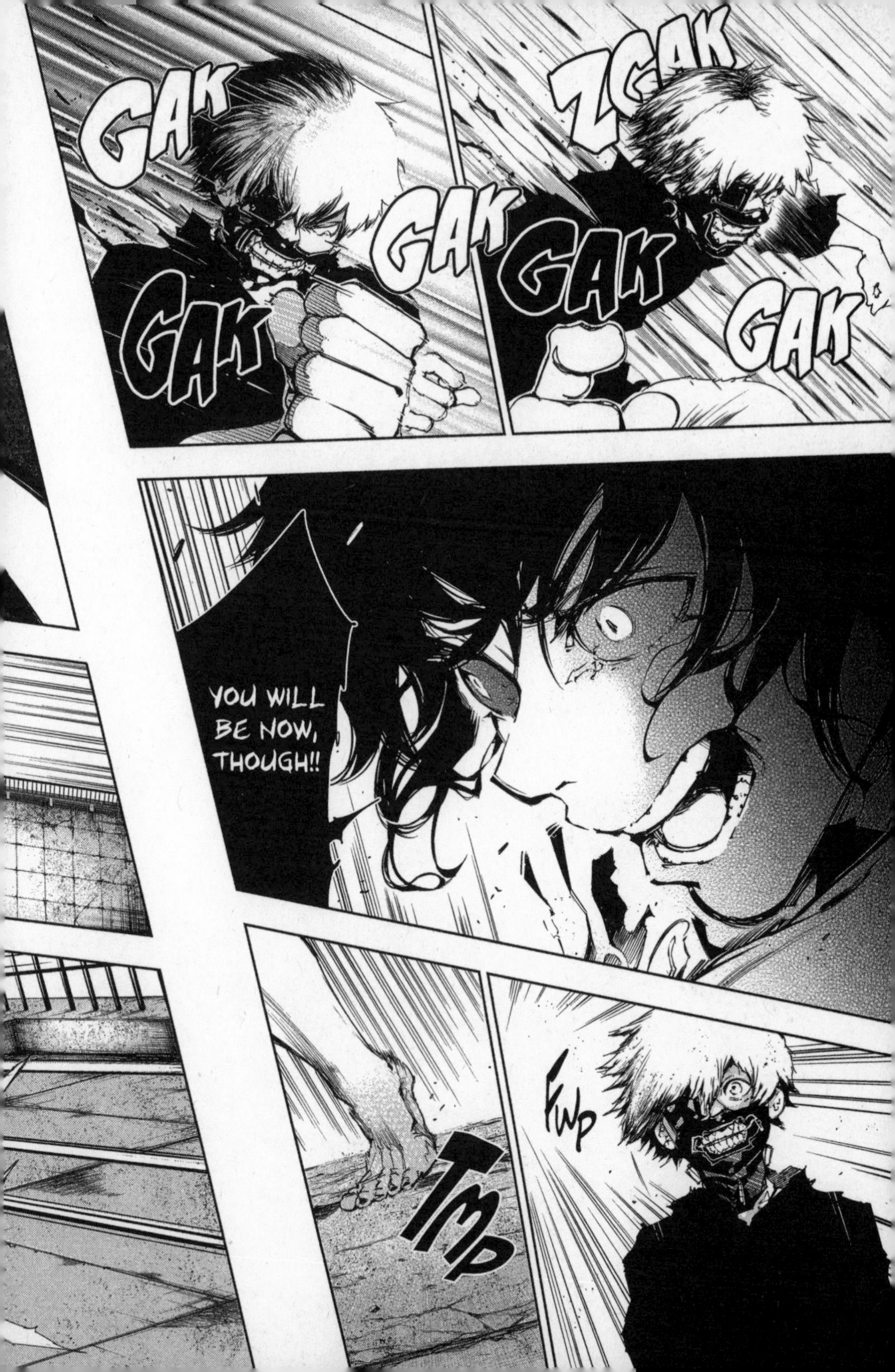
ZGAK
GAK
GAK
GAK
GAK
GAK
YOU WILL BE NOW, THOUGH!!
FWP
TMP

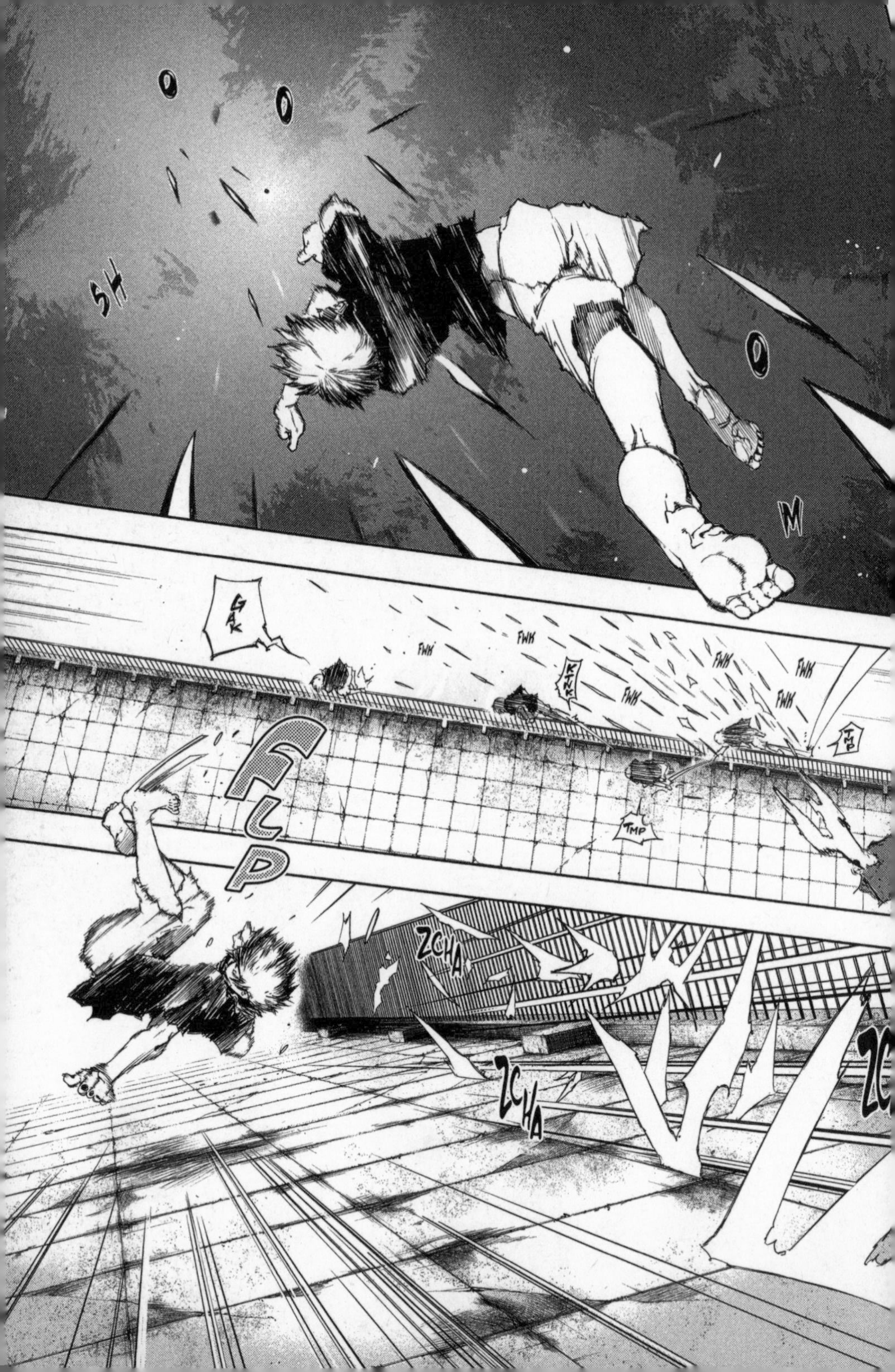
SHOOOM
FWK
FWK
FWK
TMP
FWK
KTNK
FWK
FWK
GAK
TMP
FLP
ZCHA
ZCHA

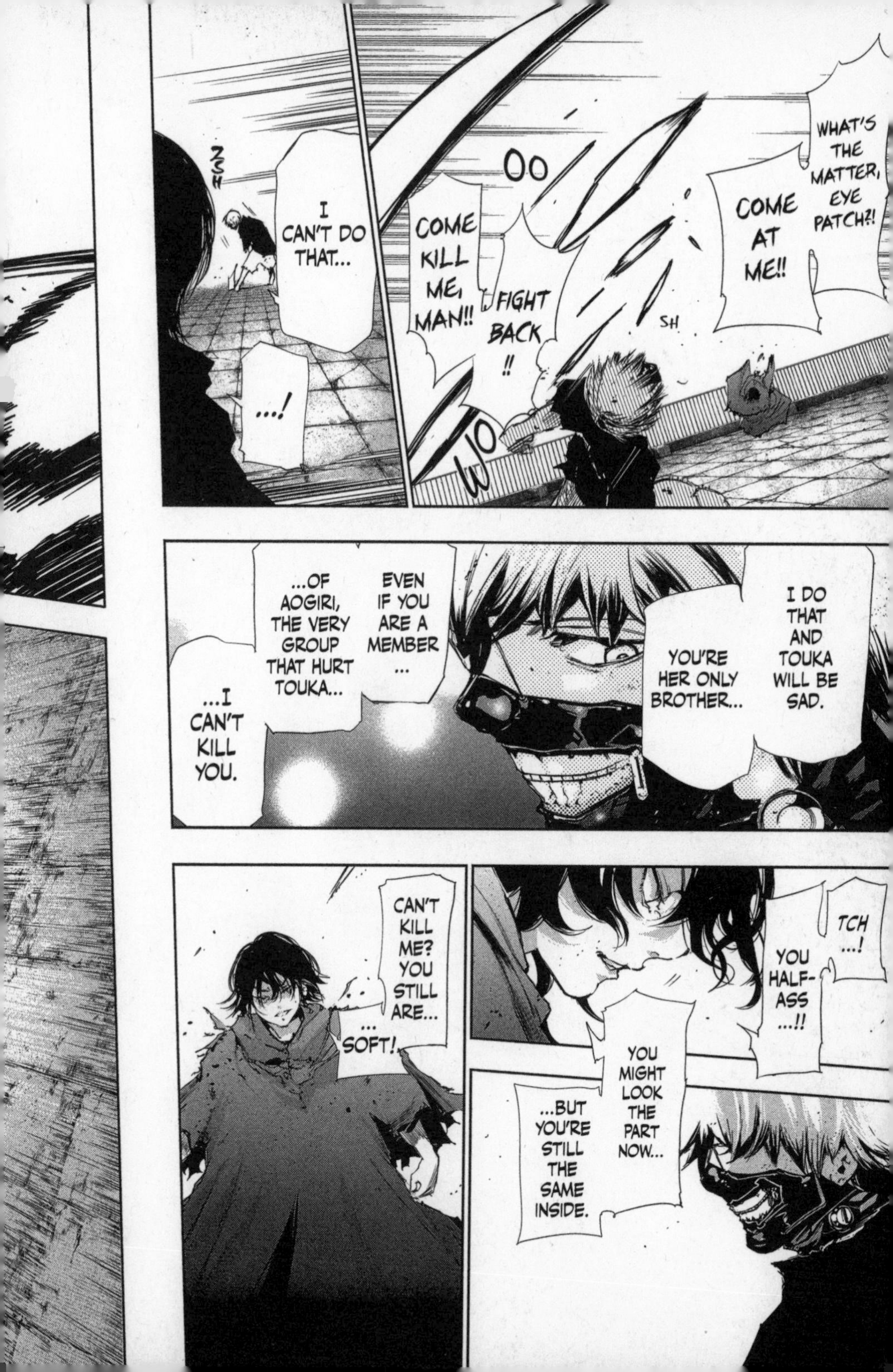
WHAT'S THE MATTER, EYE PATCH?!
COME AT ME!!
SH
FIGHT BACK!!
COME KILL ME, MAN!!
OO
WO
ZSH
I CAN'T DO THAT...
...!
I DO THAT AND TOUKA WILL BE SAD.
YOU'RE HER ONLY BROTHER...
EVEN IF YOU ARE A MEMBER...
...OF AOGIRI, THE VERY GROUP THAT HURT TOUKA...
...I CAN'T KILL YOU.
TCH...!
YOU HALF-ASS...!!
YOU MIGHT LOOK THE PART NOW...
...BUT YOU'RE STILL THE SAME INSIDE.
CAN'T KILL ME? YOU STILL ARE...
...SOFT!

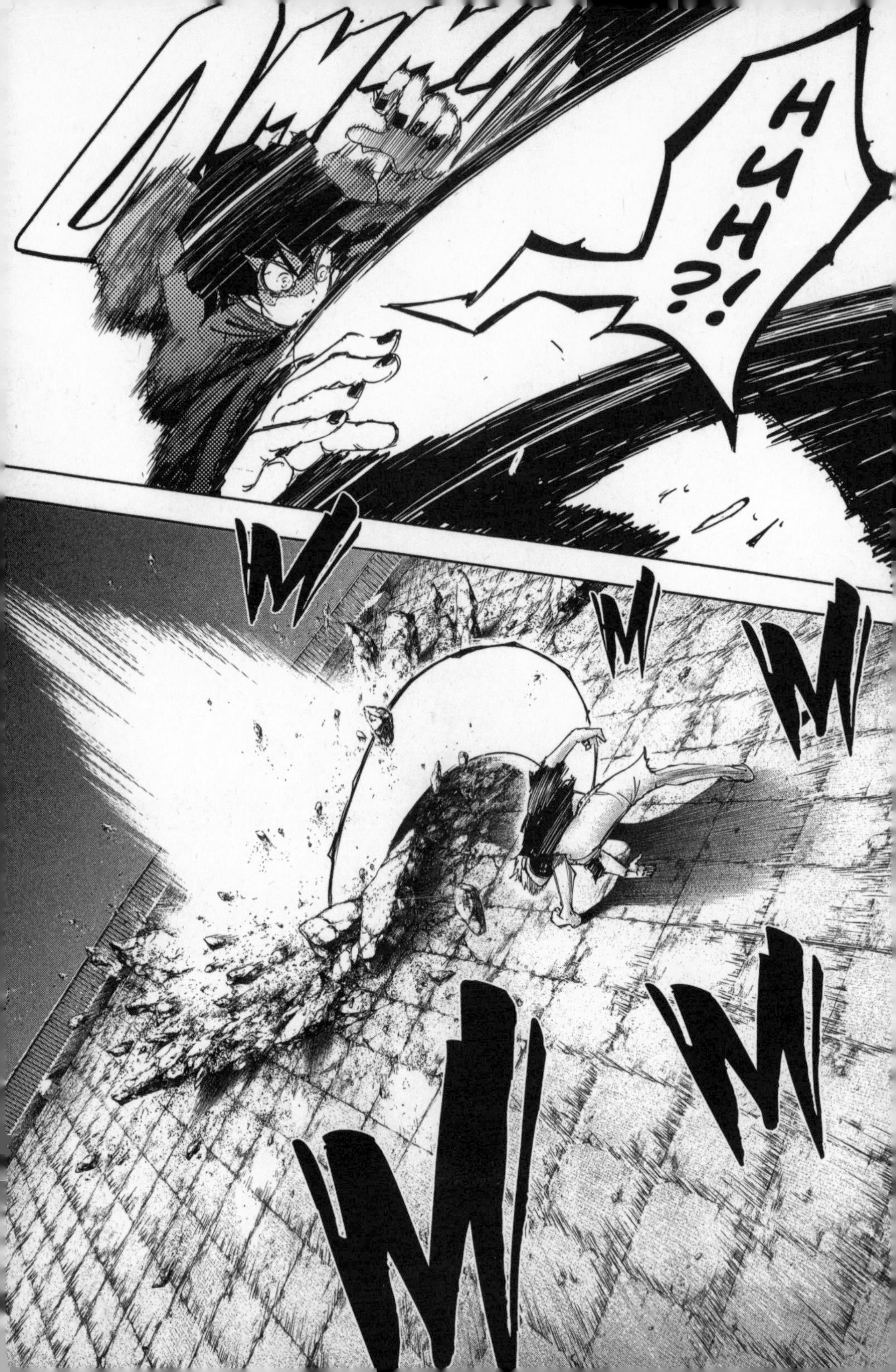
HUH?!

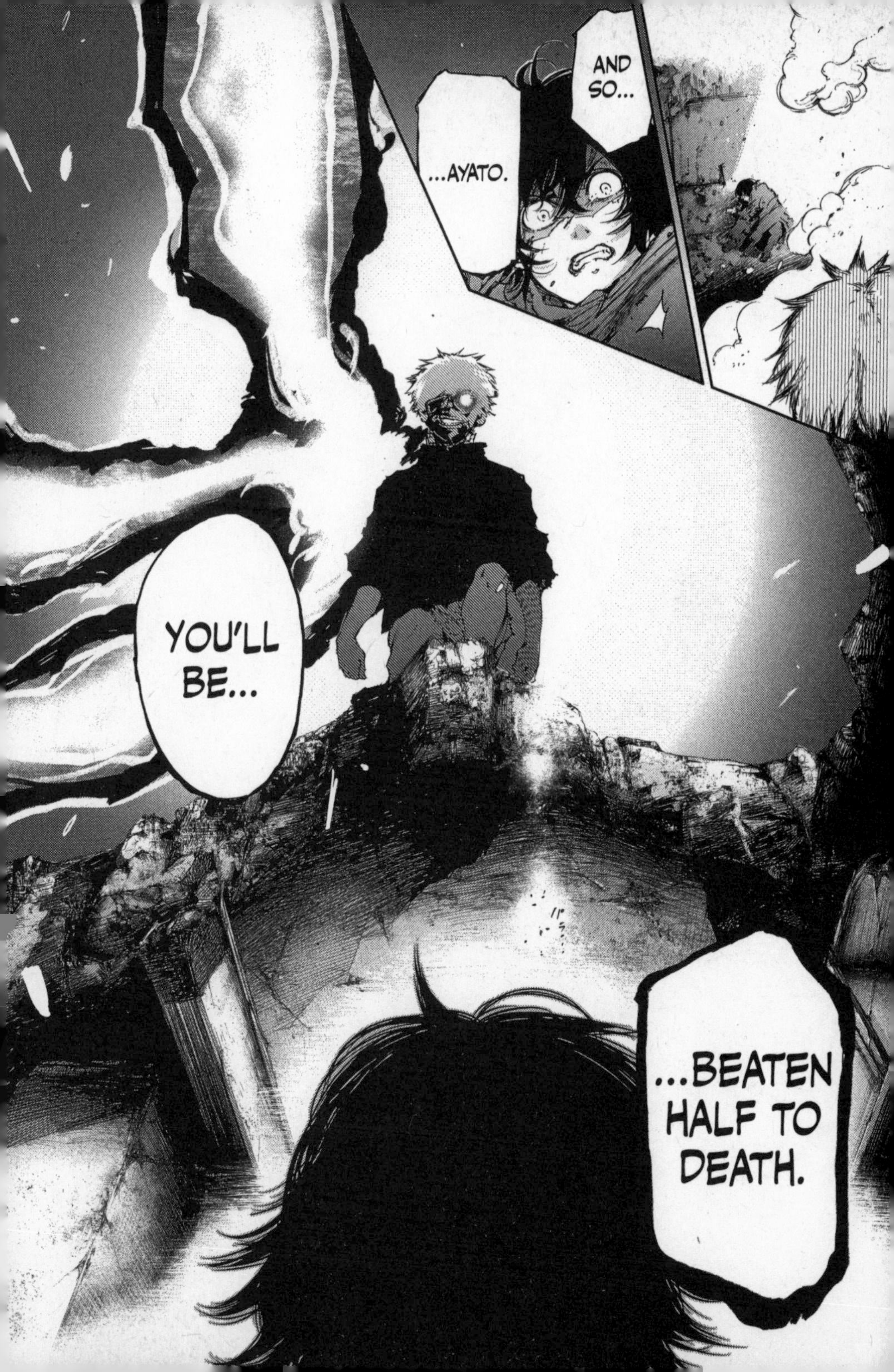
AND SO...
...AYATO.
YOU'LL BE...
...BEATEN HALF TO DEATH.

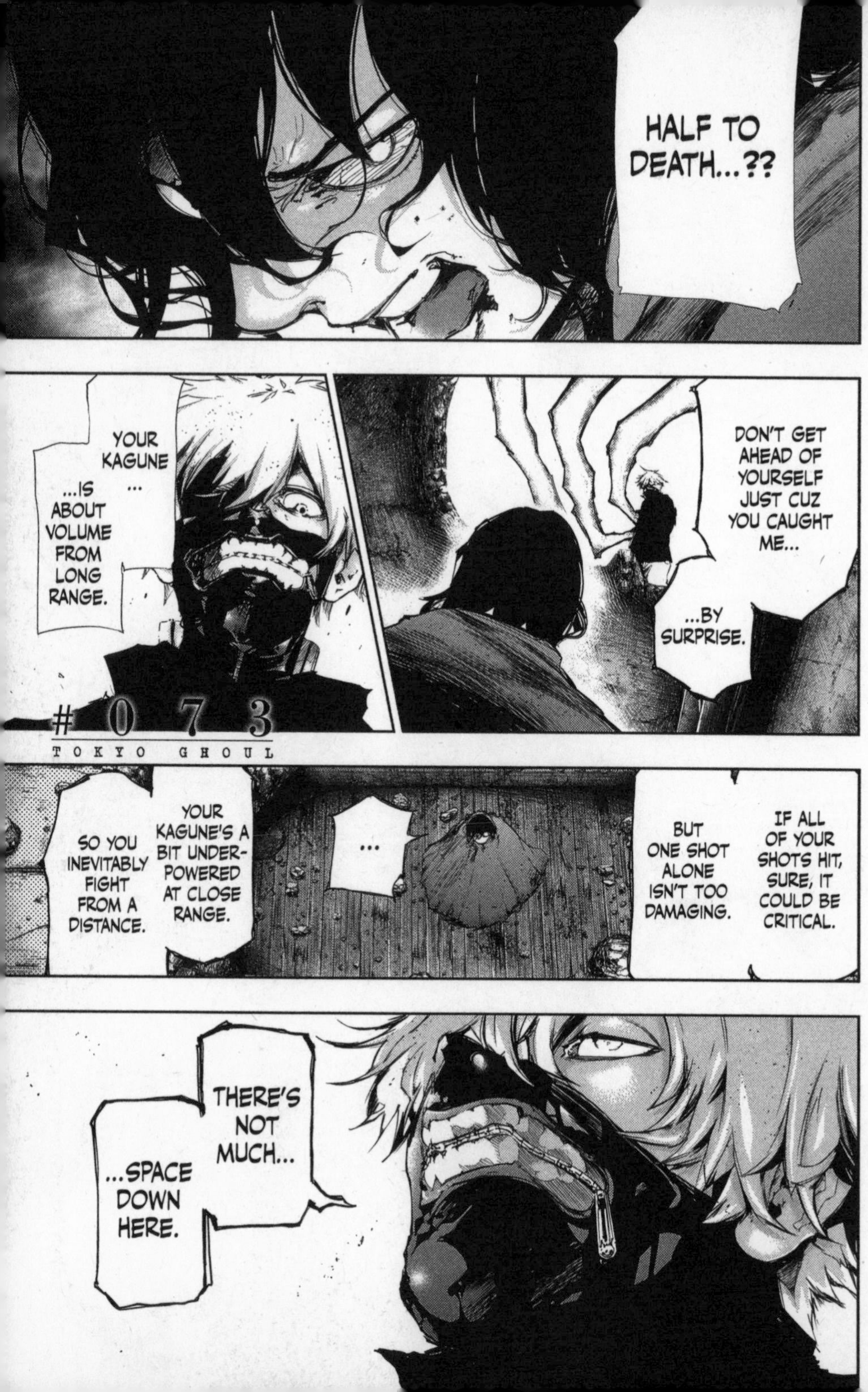
HALF TO DEATH...??
DON'T GET AHEAD OF YOURSELF JUST CUZ YOU CAUGHT ME...
...BY SURPRISE.
YOUR KAGUNE ...
...IS ABOUT VOLUME FROM LONG RANGE.
#073
TOKYO GHOUL
IF ALL OF YOUR SHOTS HIT, SURE, IT COULD BE CRITICAL.
BUT ONE SHOT ALONE ISN'T TOO DAMAGING.
...
YOUR KAGUNE'S A BIT UNDER-POWERED AT CLOSE RANGE.
SO YOU INEVITABLY FIGHT FROM A DISTANCE.
THERE'S NOT MUCH...
...SPACE DOWN HERE.

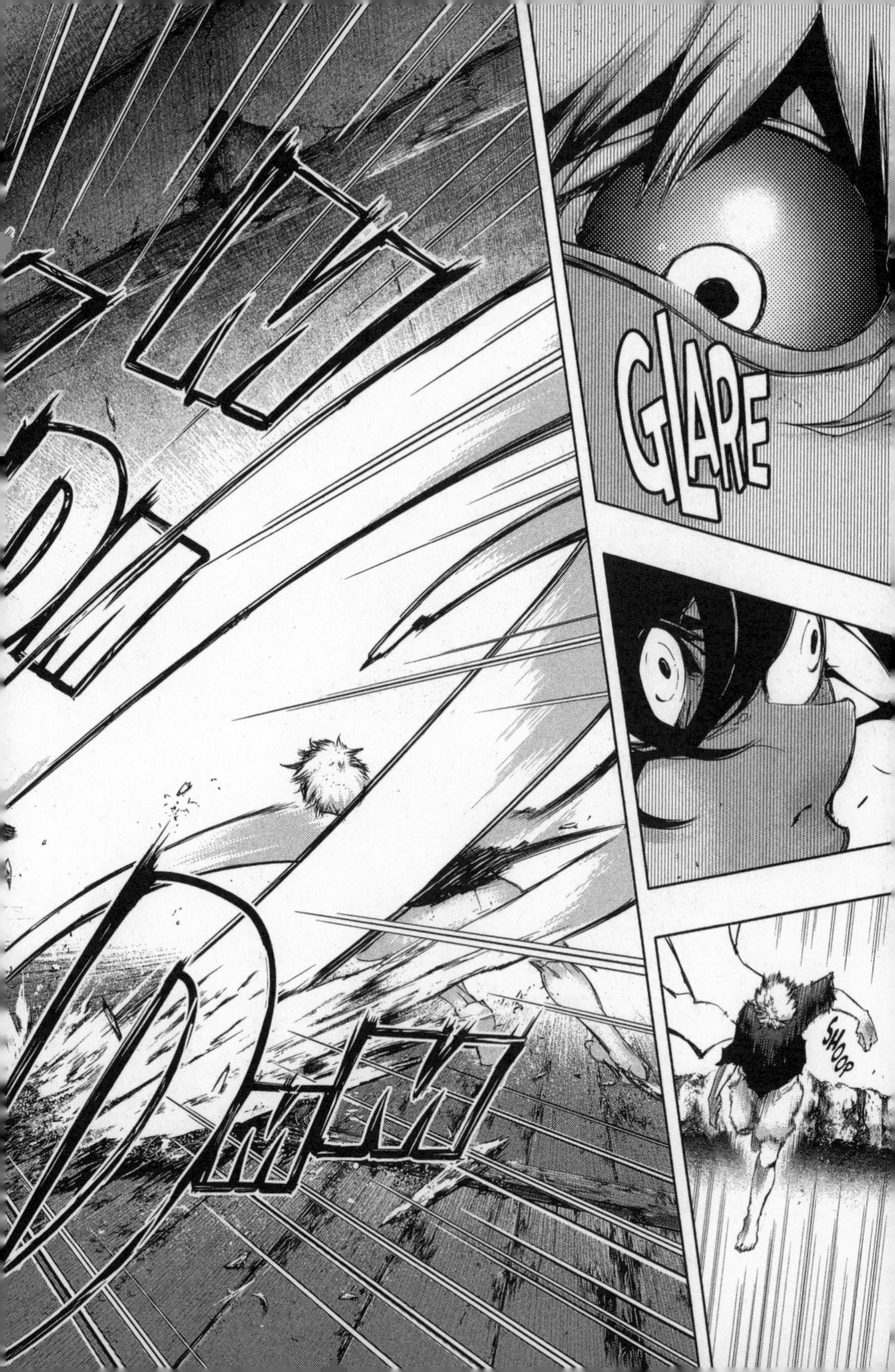
GLARE
SHOOP

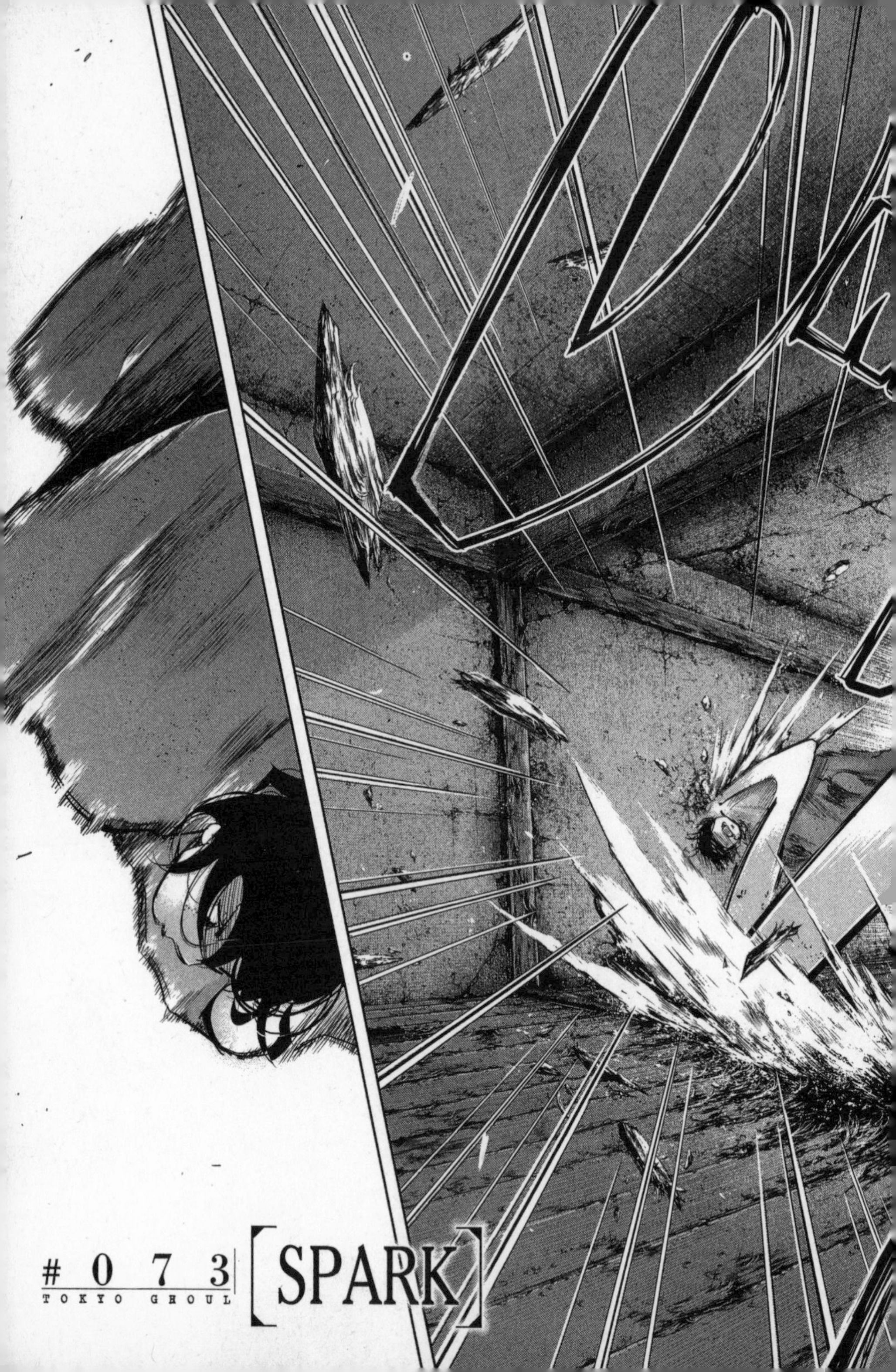

#073
TOKYO GHOUL
[SPARK]

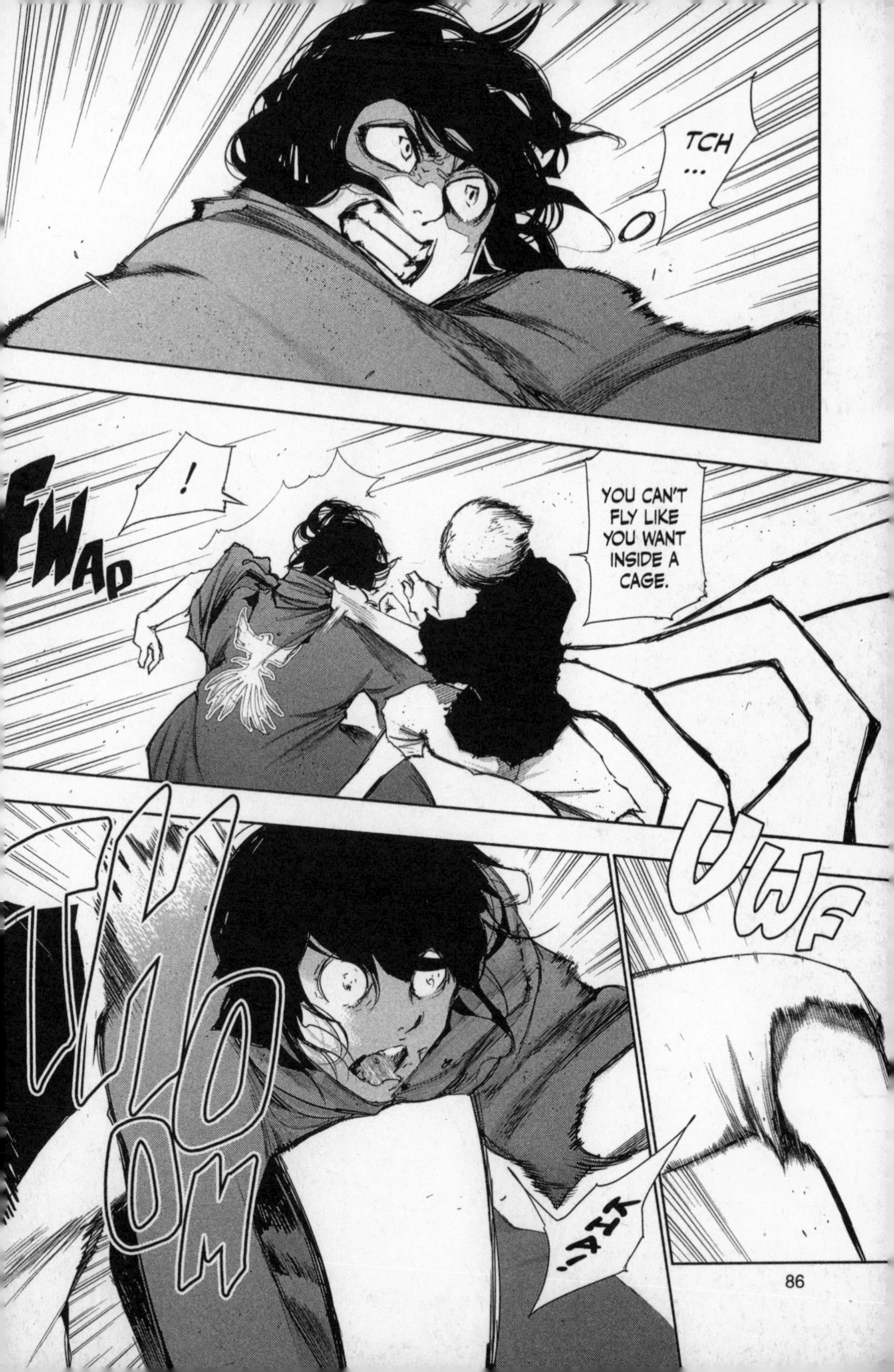
TCH ...
YOU CAN'T FLY LIKE YOU WANT INSIDE A CAGE.
!
FWAP
UWF
KHA!
WHOOM

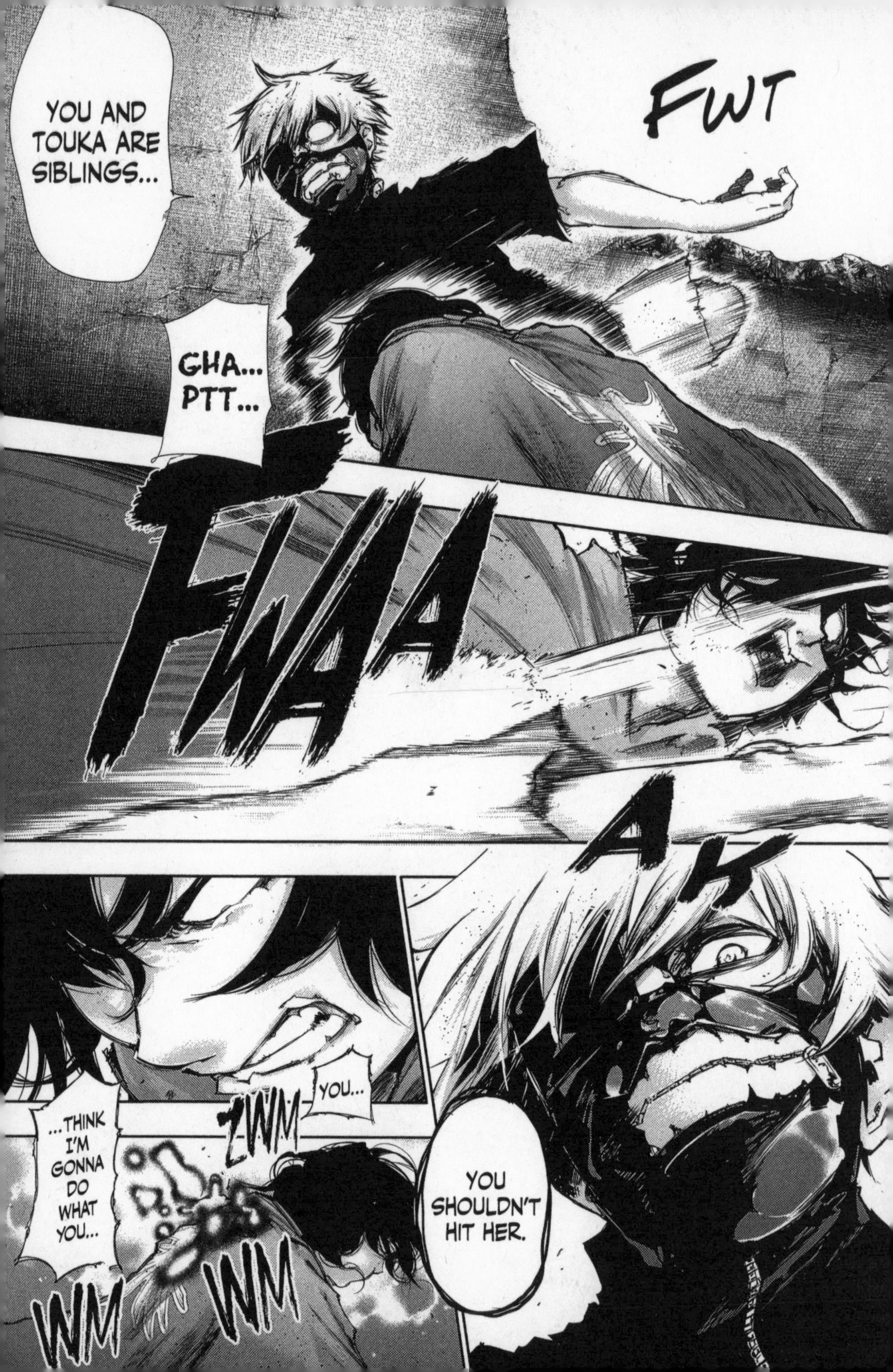
FWT
YOU AND TOUKA ARE SIBLINGS...
GHA... PTT...
FWA
AH
YOU SHOULDN'T HIT HER.
YOU...
ZWM
...THINK I'M GONNA DO WHAT YOU...
WM
WM

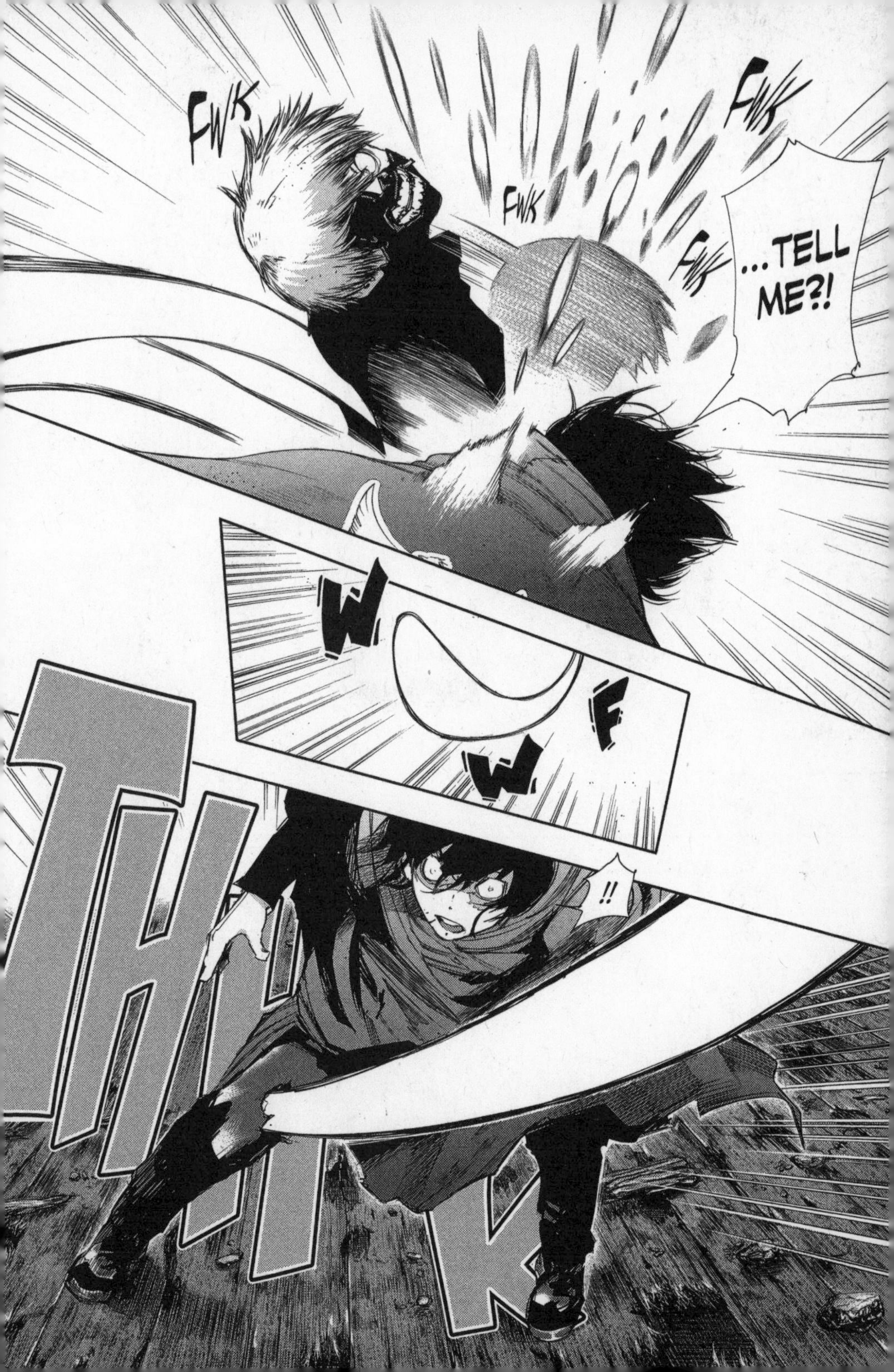
FWK
...TELL ME?!
FWK
FWK
FWK
!!

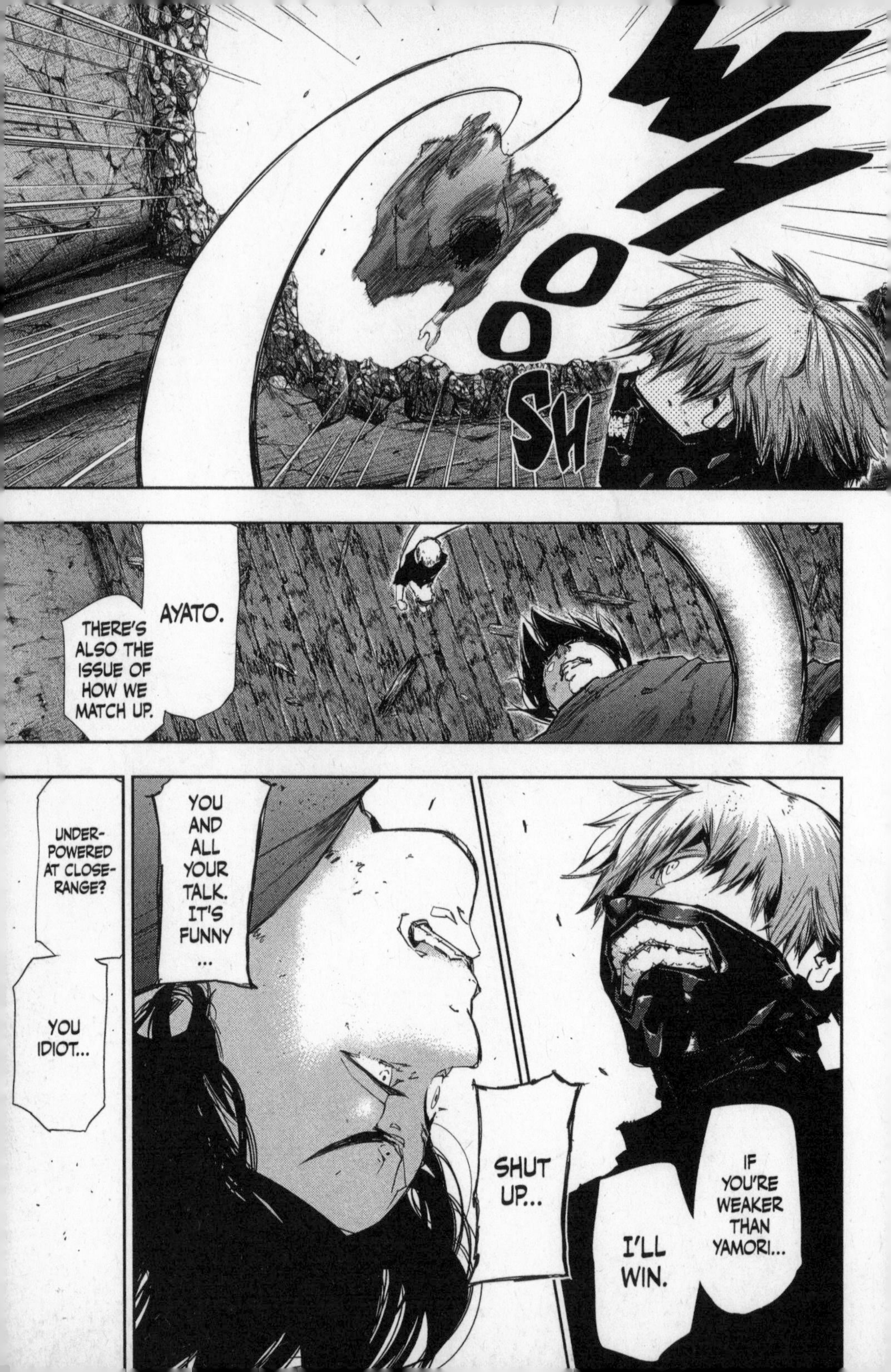
WHOOSH
AYATO.
THERE'S ALSO THE ISSUE OF HOW WE MATCH UP.
IF YOU'RE WEAKER THAN YAMORI...
I'LL WIN.
SHUT UP...
YOU AND ALL YOUR TALK. IT'S FUNNY ...
UNDER-POWERED AT CLOSE-RANGE?
YOU IDIOT...

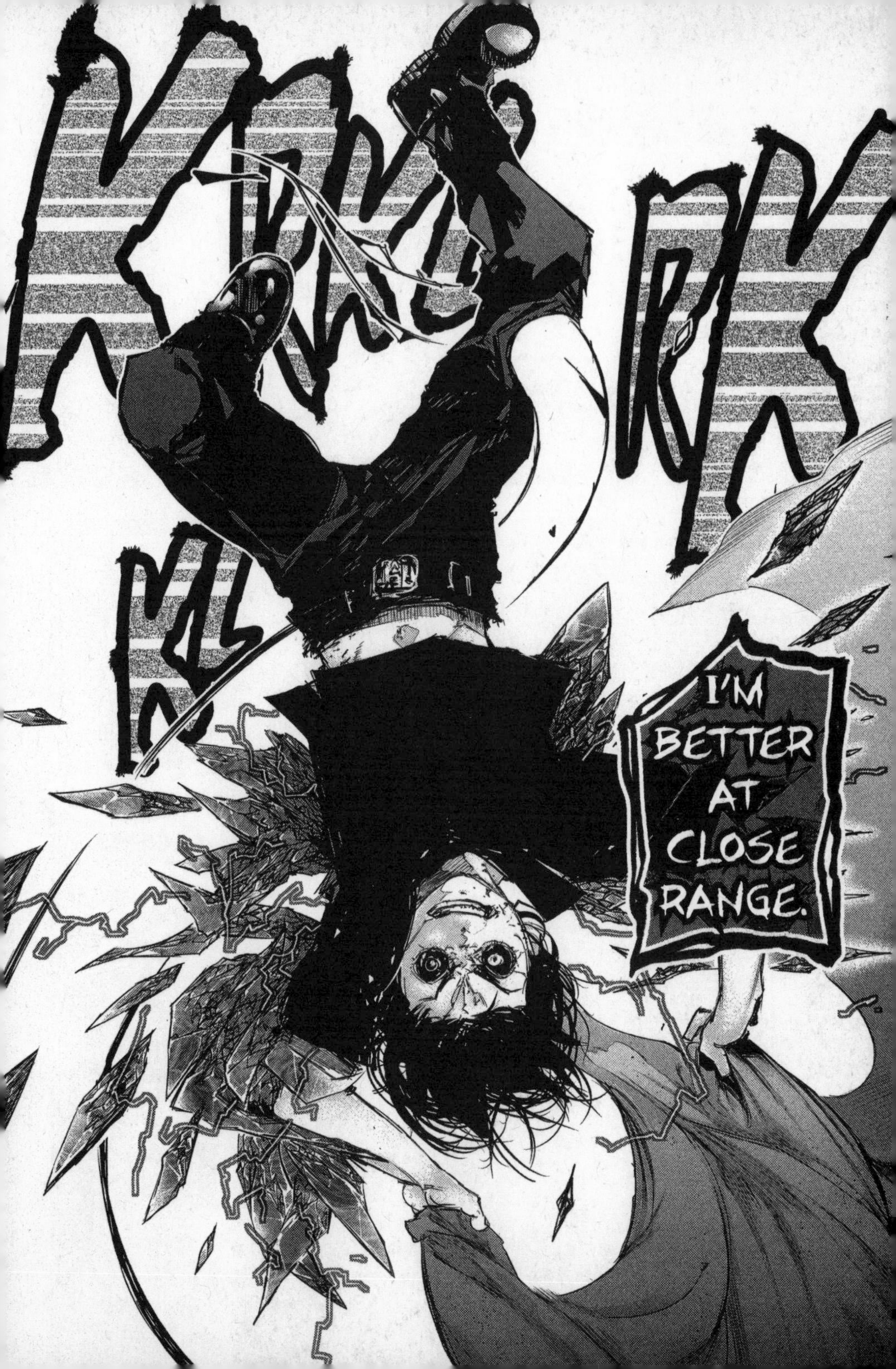
I'M BETTER AT CLOSE RANGE.

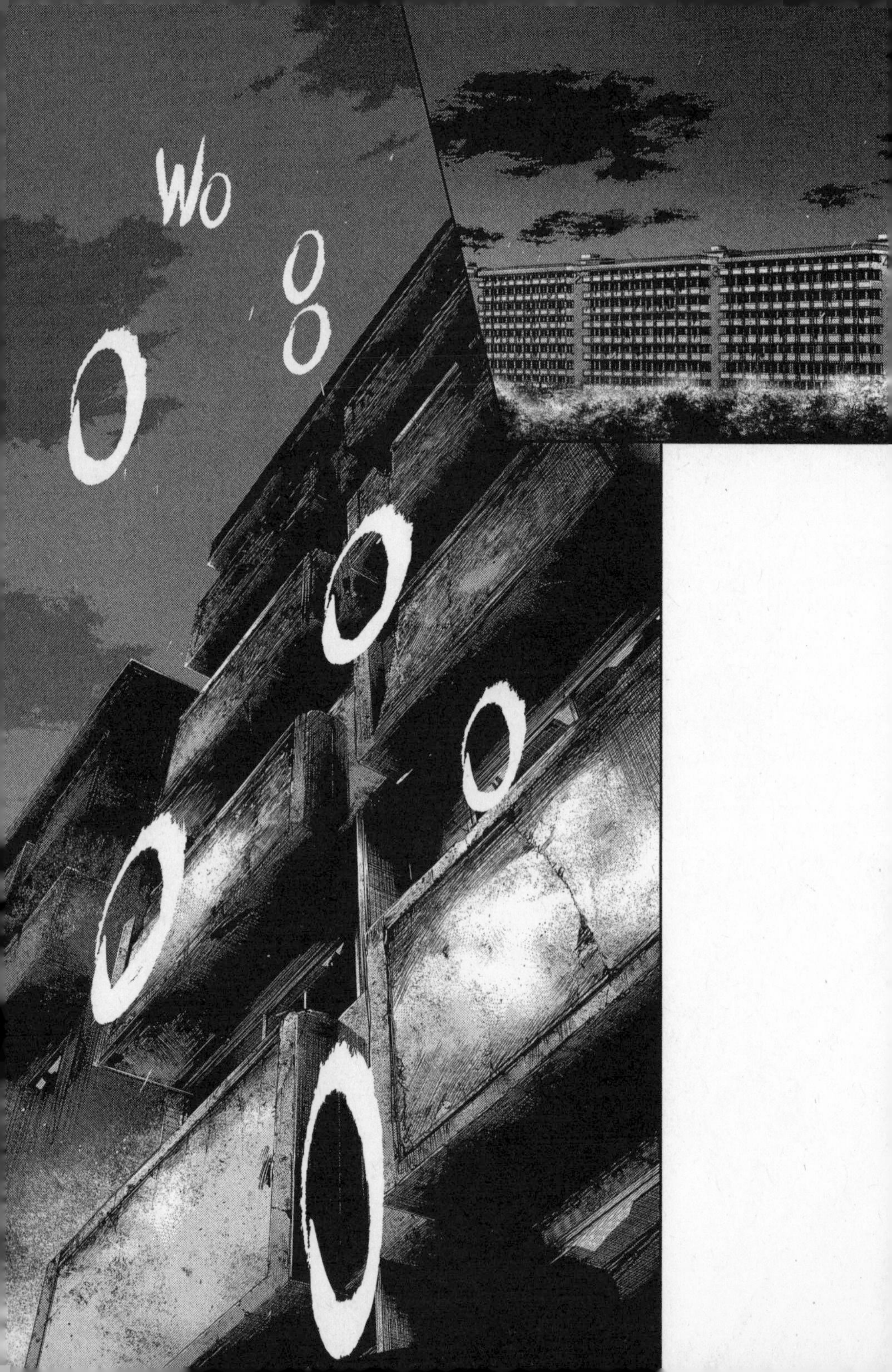
WoooOOOOO

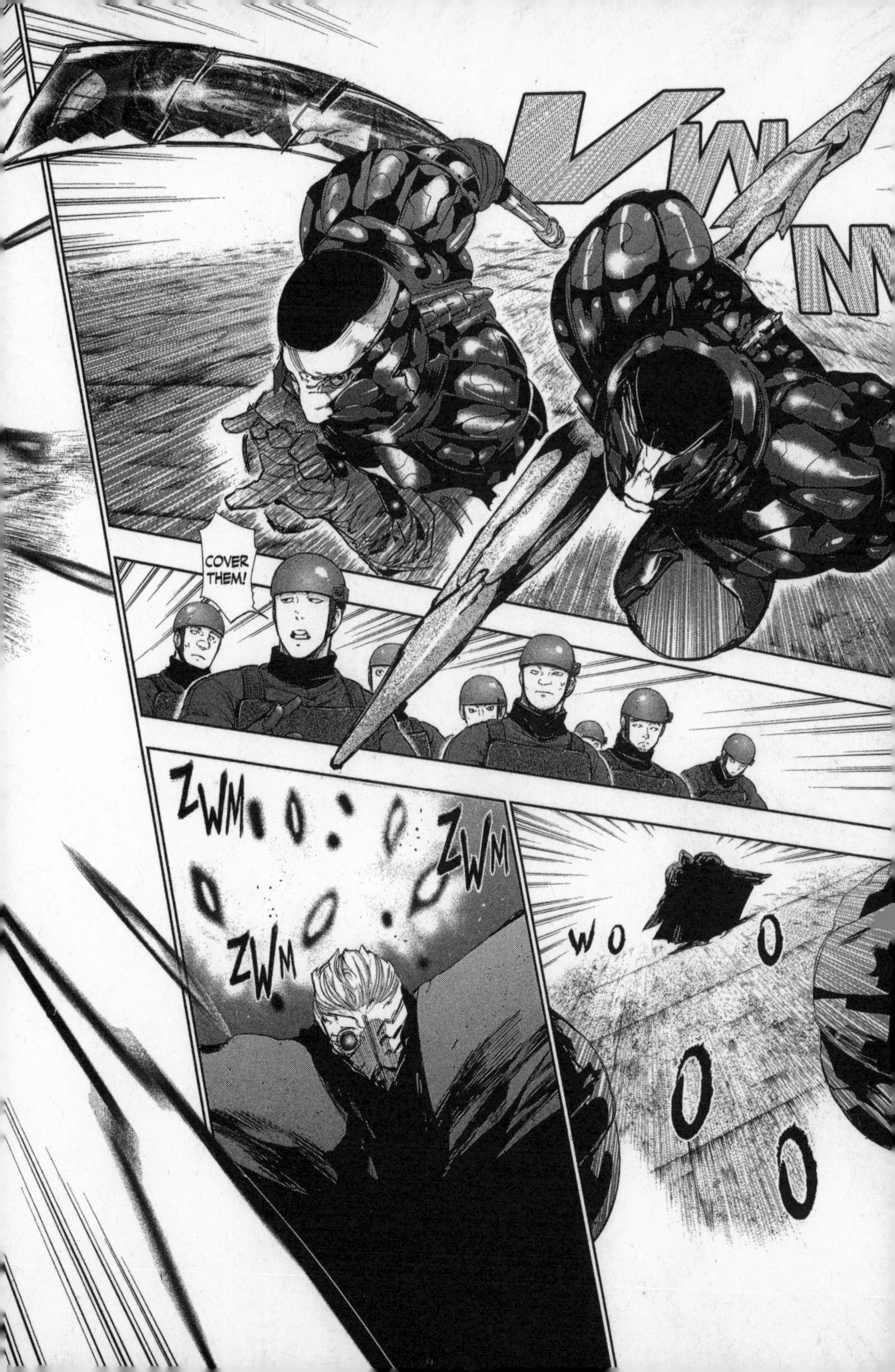
VWM
COVER THEM!
WOOOOOO
ZWM
ZWM
ZWM

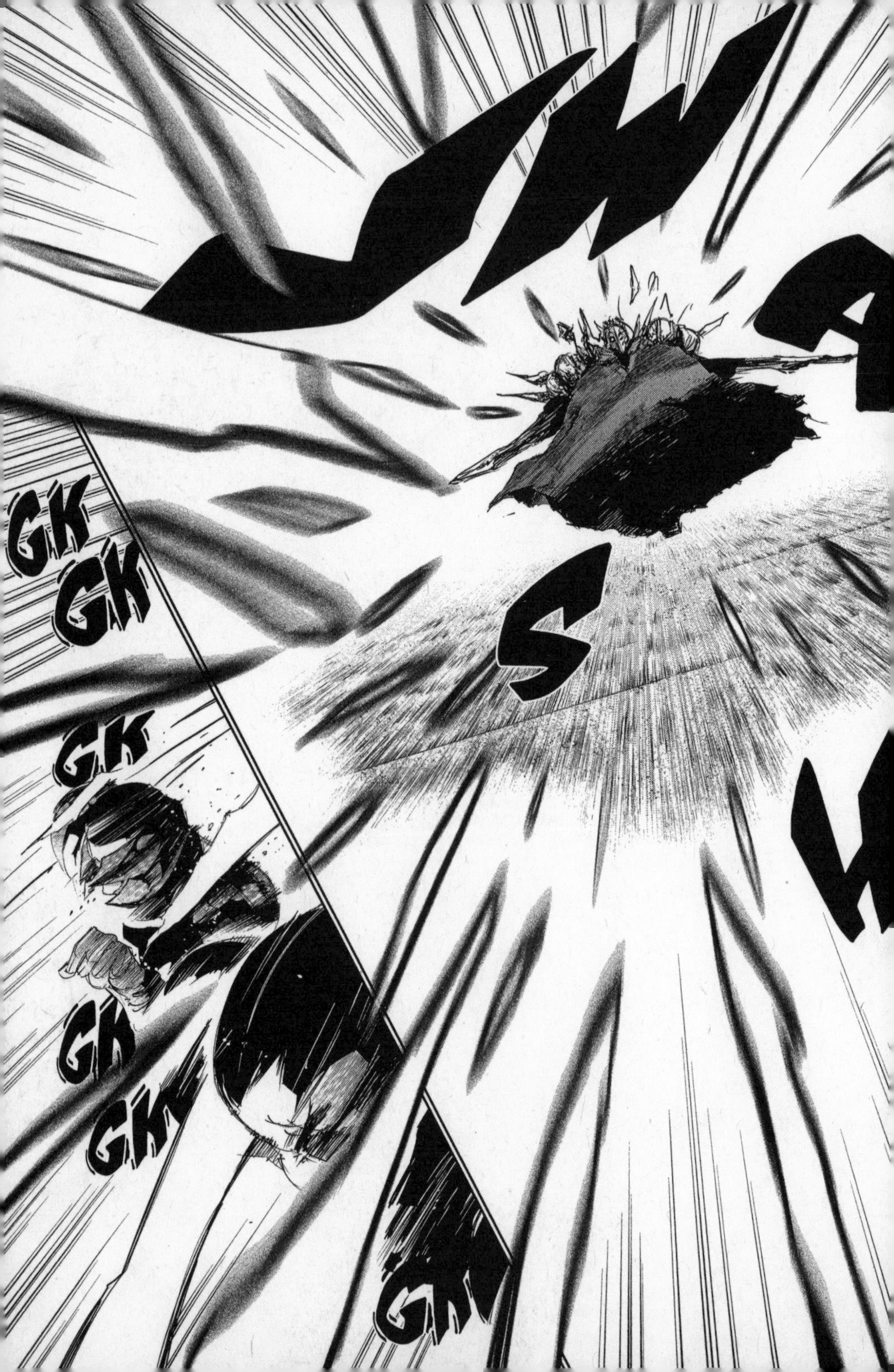
GK GK
GK
GK
GK
GK

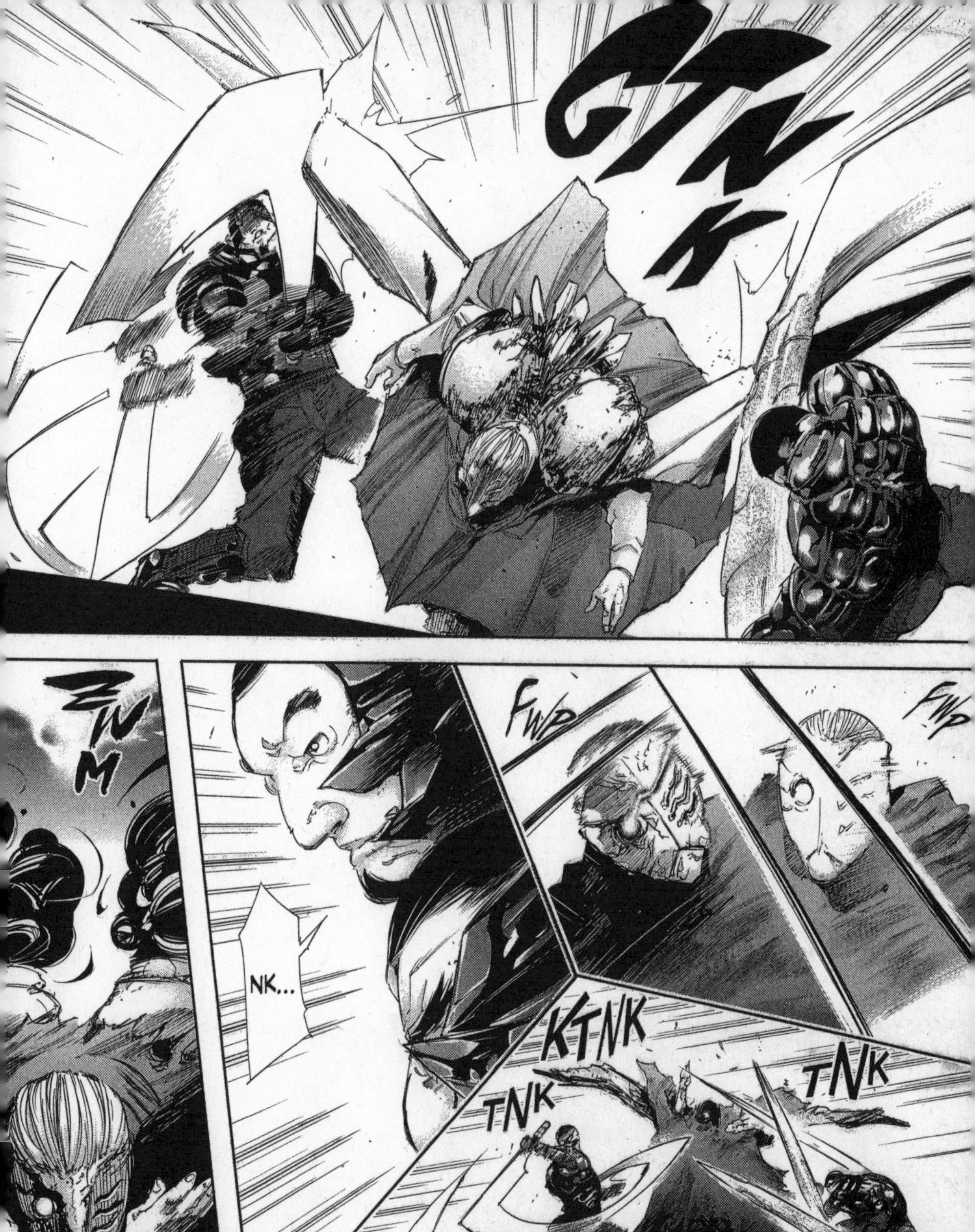
GTNK
FWP
FWP
TNK
KTNK
TNK
NK...
ZWM

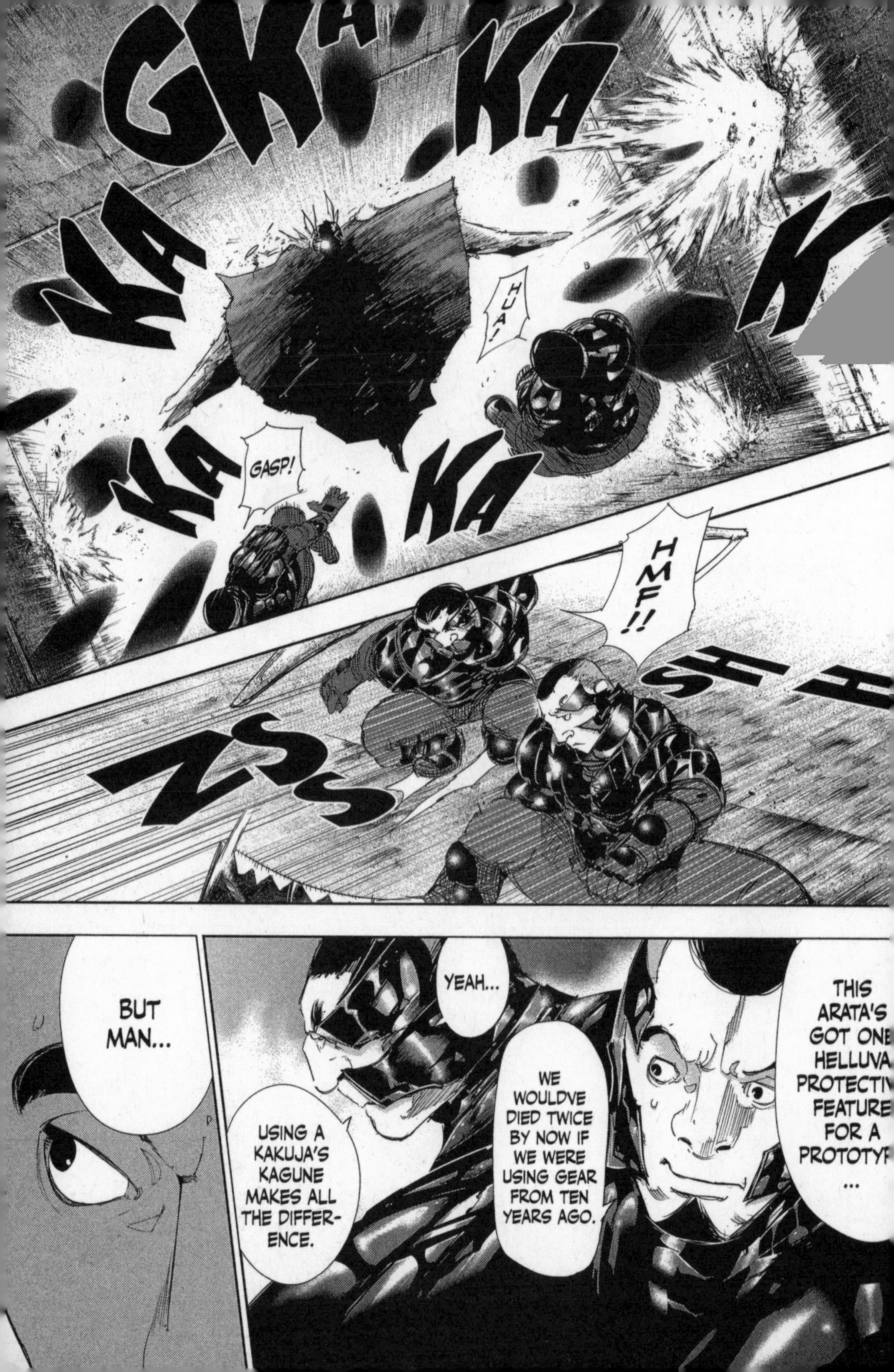
GKA KA
KA
HUA!
KA KA
KA
GASP!
HMF!!
THIS ARATA'S GOT ONE HELLUVA PROTECTIV FEATURE FOR A PROTOTYP...
WE WOULDVE DIED TWICE BY NOW IF WE WERE USING GEAR FROM TEN YEARS AGO.
YEAH...
USING A KAKUJA'S KAGUNE MAKES ALL THE DIFFER-ENCE.
BUT MAN...

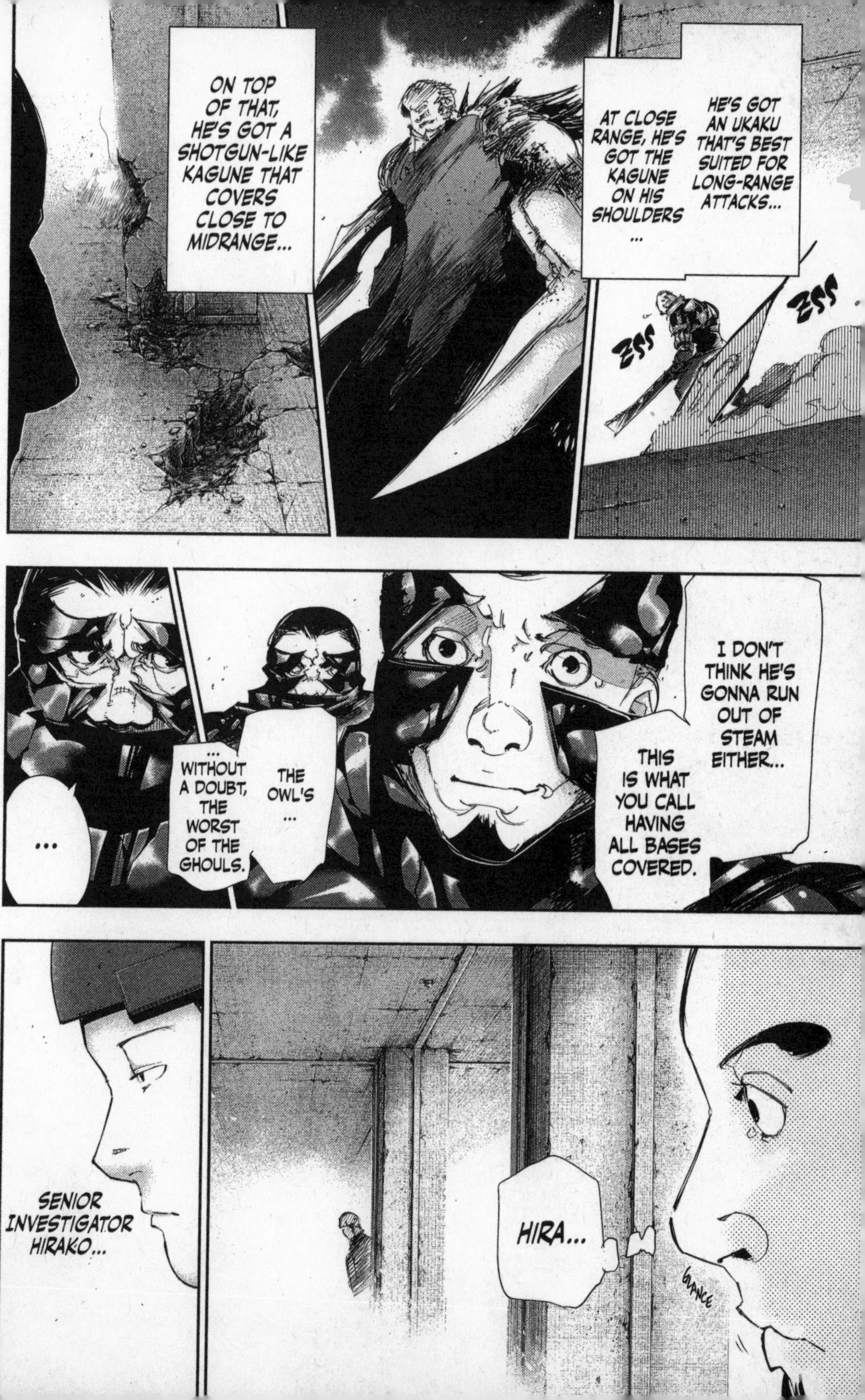
HE'S GOT AN UKAKU THAT'S BEST SUITED FOR LONG-RANGE ATTACKS...
AT CLOSE RANGE, HE'S GOT THE KAGUNE ON HIS SHOULDERS ...
ZSS
ZSS
ON TOP OF THAT, HE'S GOT A SHOTGUN-LIKE KAGUNE THAT COVERS CLOSE TO MIDRANGE...
I DON'T THINK HE'S GONNA RUN OUT OF STEAM EITHER...
THIS IS WHAT YOU CALL HAVING ALL BASES COVERED.
THE OWL'S ...
... WITHOUT A DOUBT, THE WORST OF THE GHOULS.
...
HIRA...
GLANCE
SENIOR INVESTIGATOR HIRAKO...

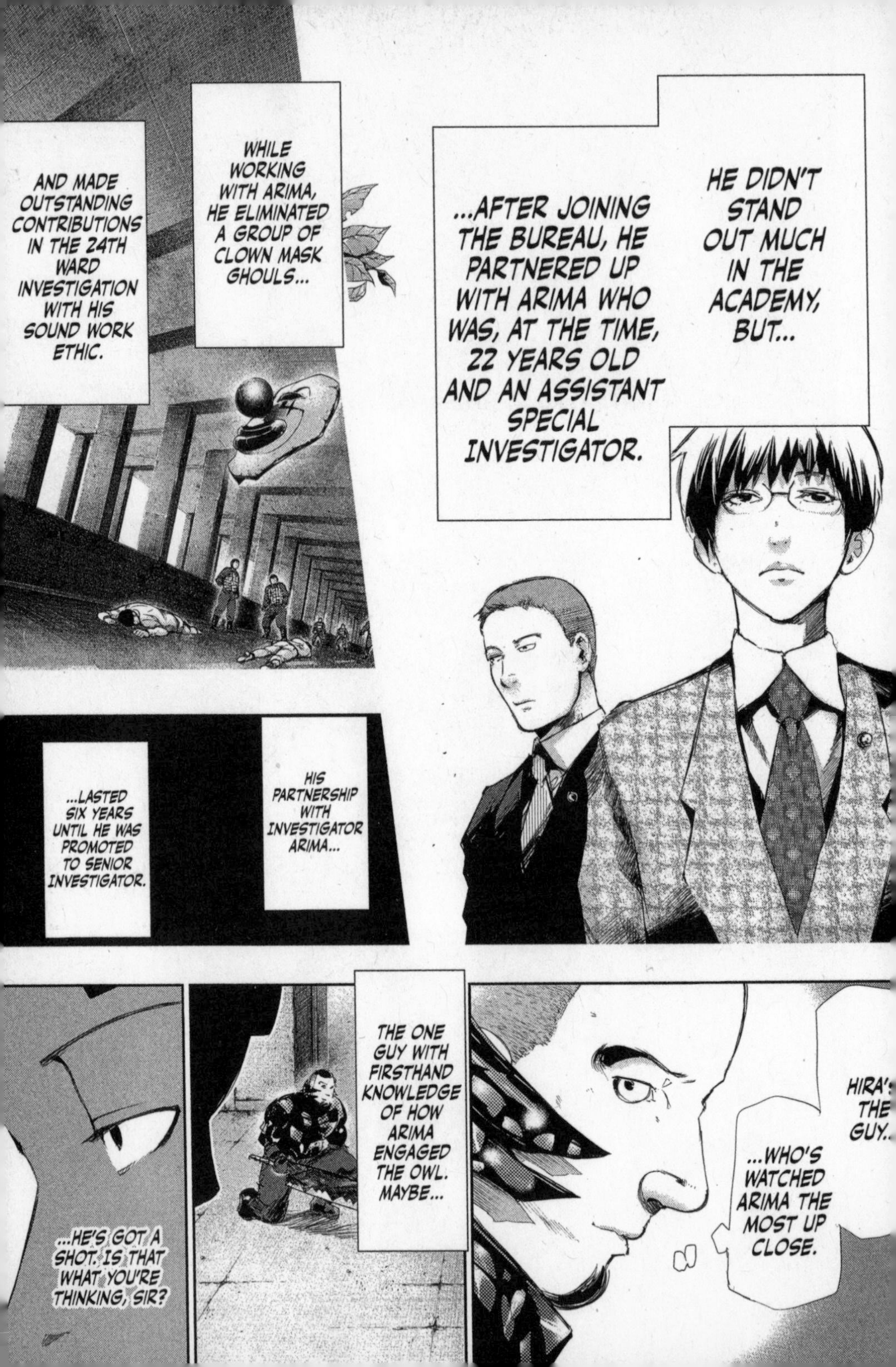
HE DIDN'T STAND OUT MUCH IN THE ACADEMY, BUT...
...AFTER JOINING THE BUREAU, HE PARTNERED UP WITH ARIMA WHO WAS, AT THE TIME, 22 YEARS OLD AND AN ASSISTANT SPECIAL INVESTIGATOR.
WHILE WORKING WITH ARIMA, HE ELIMINATED A GROUP OF CLOWN MASK GHOULS...
AND MADE OUTSTANDING CONTRIBUTIONS IN THE 24TH WARD INVESTIGATION WITH HIS SOUND WORK ETHIC.
HIS PARTNERSHIP WITH INVESTIGATOR ARIMA...
...LASTED SIX YEARS UNTIL HE WAS PROMOTED TO SENIOR INVESTIGATOR.
HIRA'S THE GUY...
...WHO'S WATCHED ARIMA THE MOST UP CLOSE.
THE ONE GUY WITH FIRSTHAND KNOWLEDGE OF HOW ARIMA ENGAGED THE OWL. MAYBE...
...HE'S GOT A SHOT. IS THAT WHAT YOU'RE THINKING, SIR?

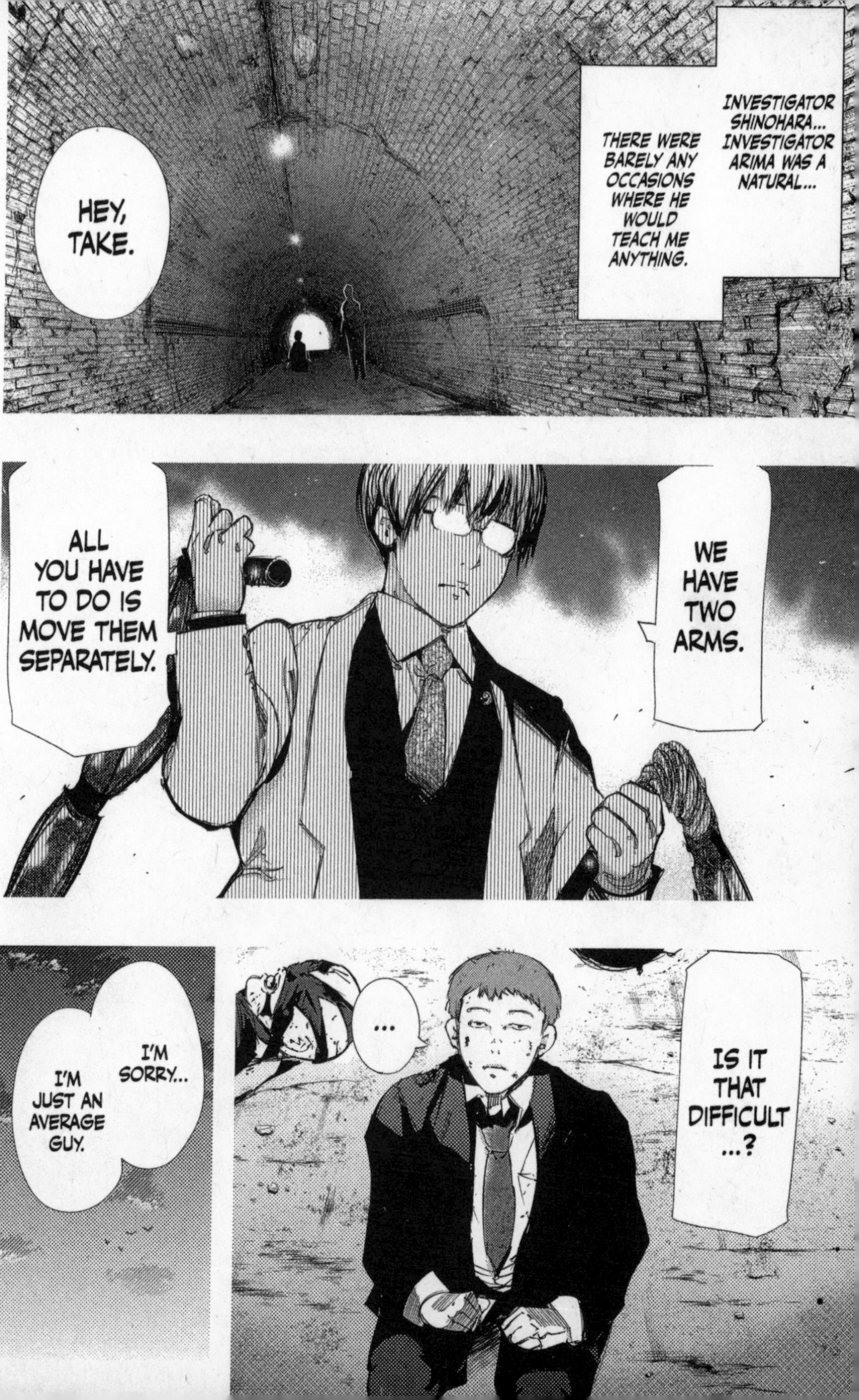
INVESTIGATOR SHINOHARA... INVESTIGATOR ARIMA WAS A NATURAL...
THERE WERE BARELY ANY OCCASIONS WHERE HE WOULD TEACH ME ANYTHING.
HEY, TAKE.
WE HAVE TWO ARMS.
ALL YOU HAVE TO DO IS MOVE THEM SEPARATELY.
IS IT THAT DIFFICULT ...?
...
I'M SORRY...
I'M JUST AN AVERAGE GUY.

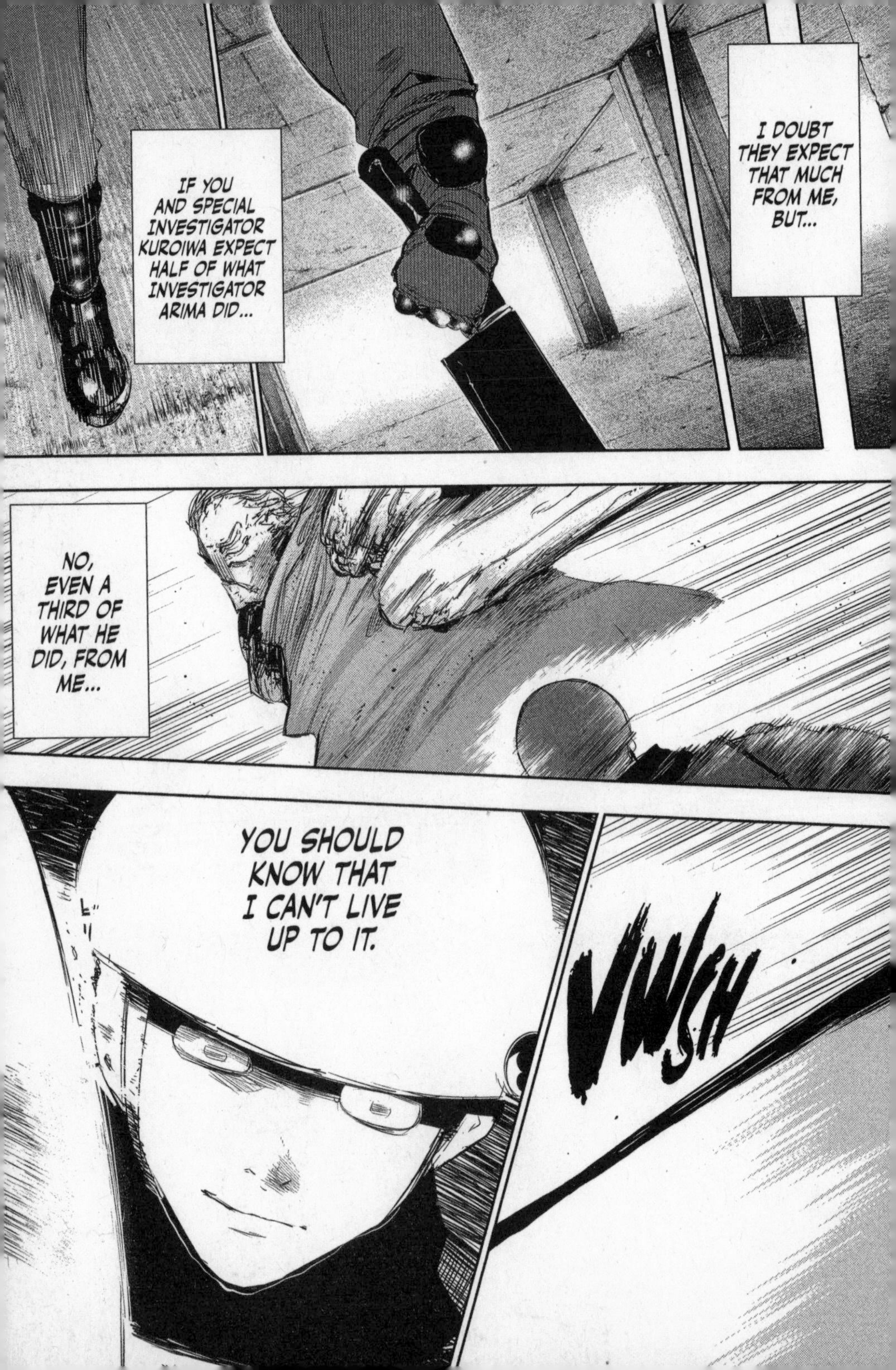
I DOUBT THEY EXPECT THAT MUCH FROM ME, BUT...
IF YOU AND SPECIAL INVESTIGATOR KUROIWA EXPECT HALF OF WHAT INVESTIGATOR ARIMA DID...
NO, EVEN A THIRD OF WHAT HE DID, FROM ME...
VWSH
YOU SHOULD KNOW THAT I CAN'T LIVE UP TO IT.

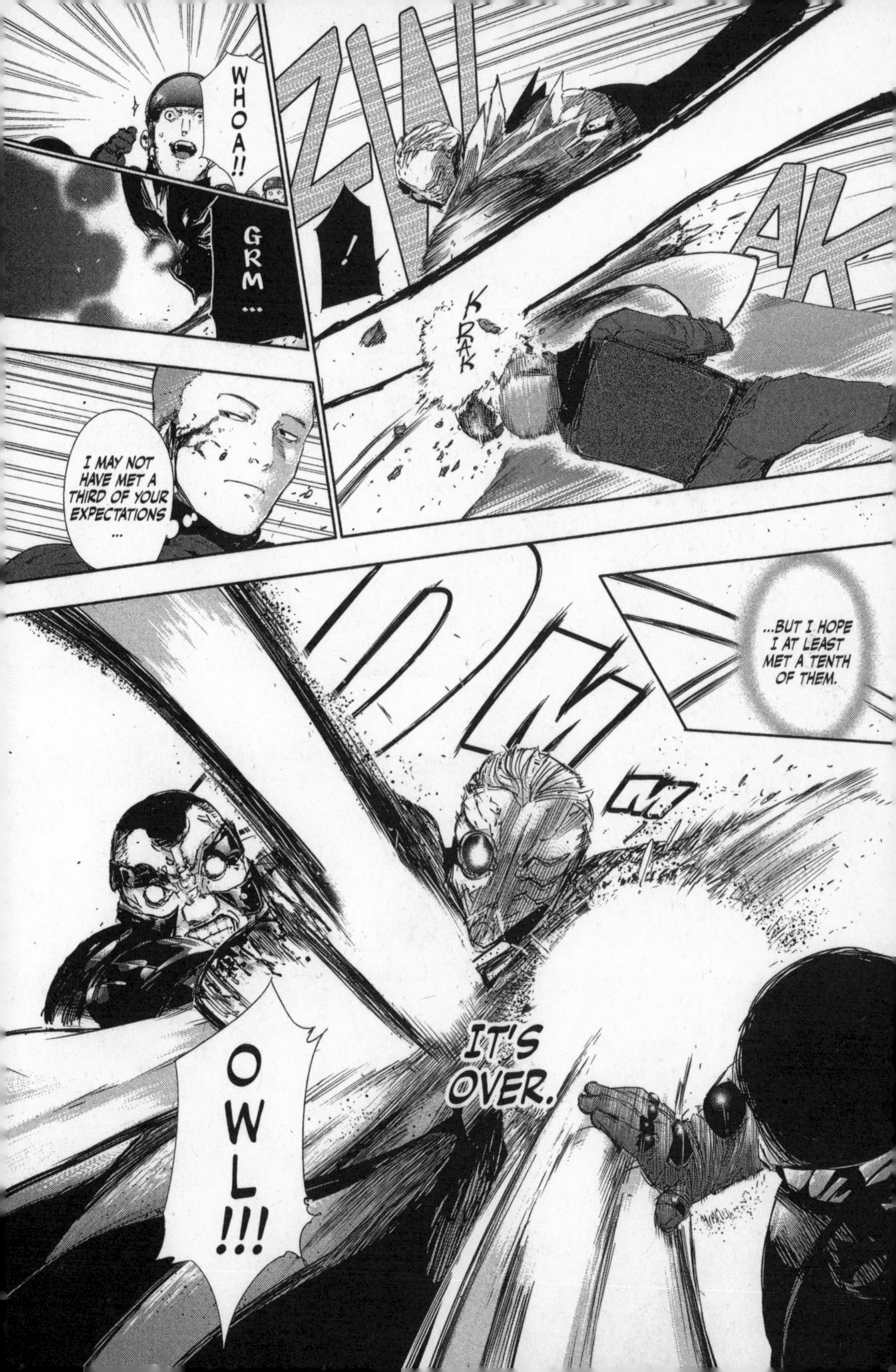
ZWAK
!
KRAK
WHOA!!
GRM...
I MAY NOT HAVE MET A THIRD OF YOUR EXPECTATIONS...
...BUT I HOPE I AT LEAST MET A TENTH OF THEM.
IT'S OVER.
OWL!!!

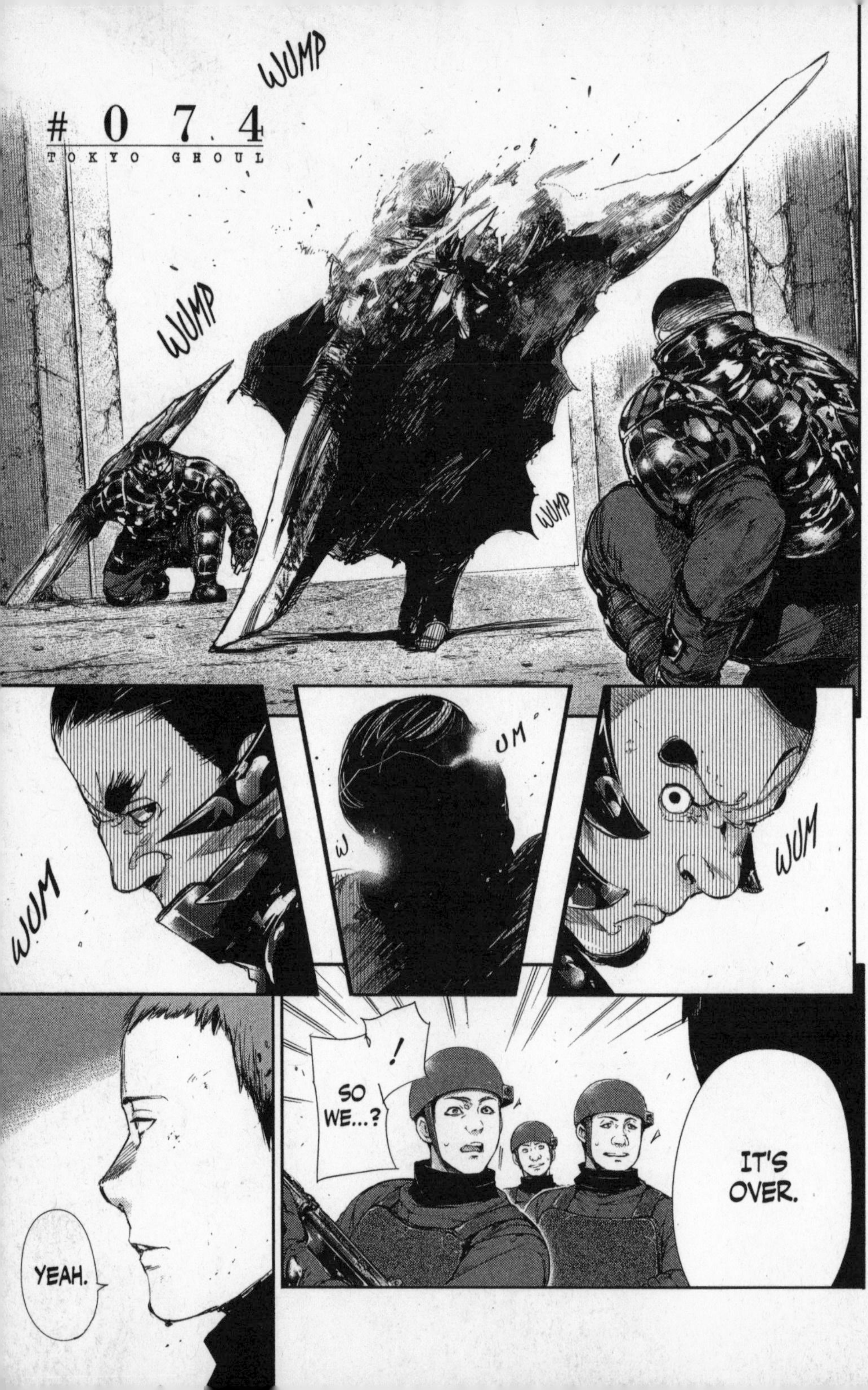

#074
TOKYO GHOUL
WUMP
WUMP
WUMP
WUM
UM
W
WUM
IT'S OVER.
!
SO WE...?
YEAH.

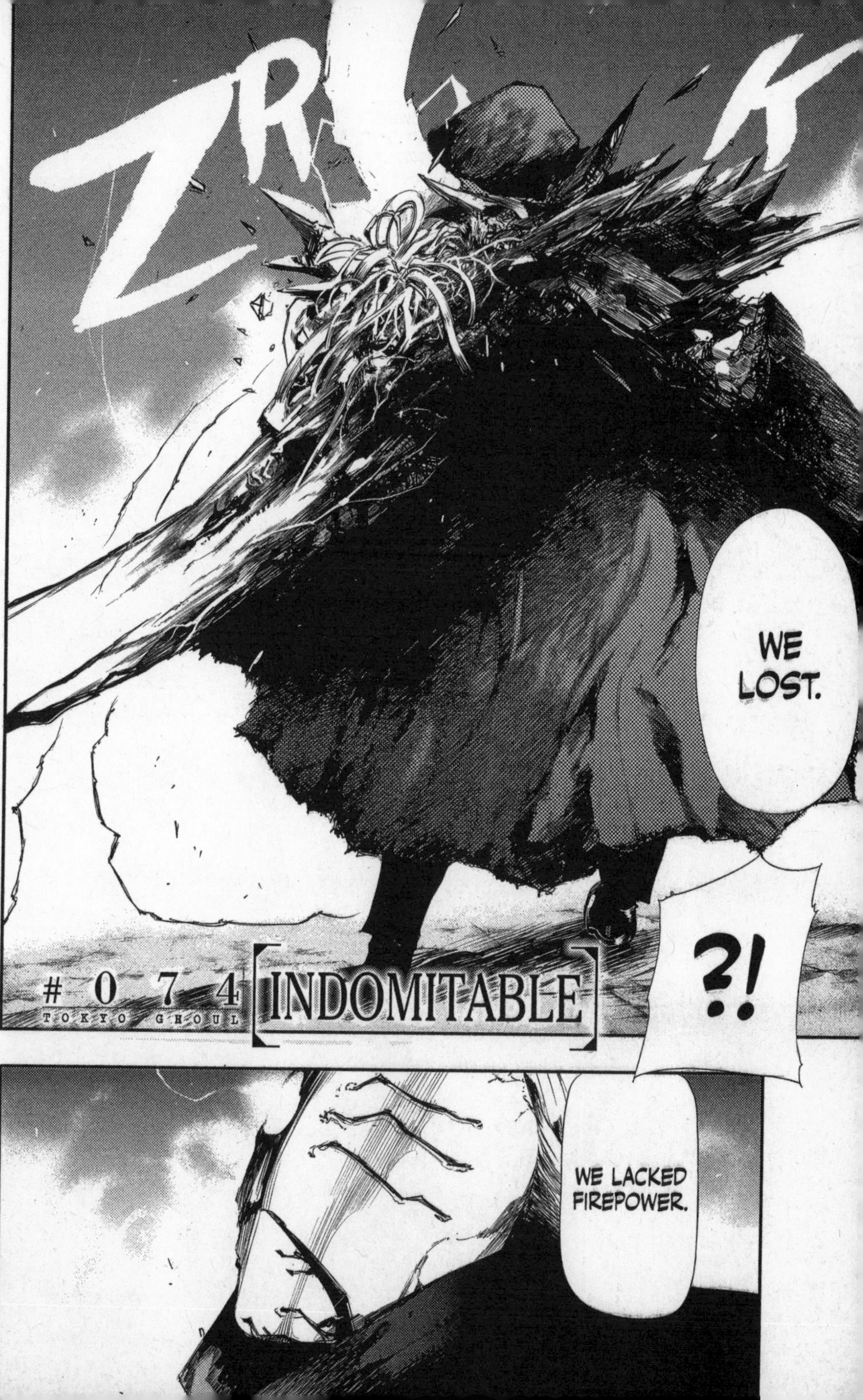
WE LOST.
?!
#074 INDOMITABLE
TOKYO GHOUL
WE LACKED FIREPOWER.

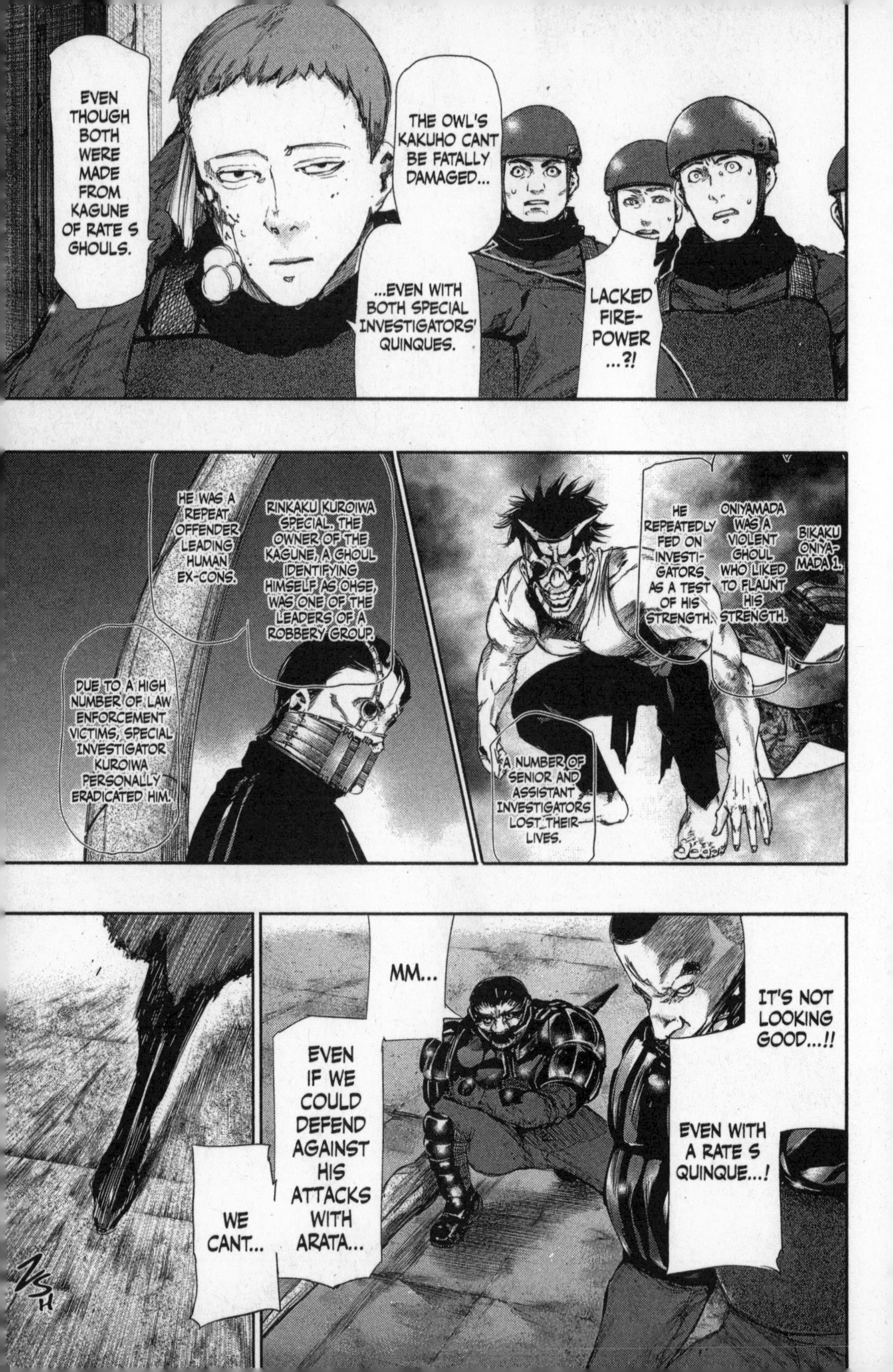
LACKED FIRE-POWER ...?!
THE OWL'S KAKUHO CANT BE FATALLY DAMAGED...
...EVEN WITH BOTH SPECIAL INVESTIGATORS' QUINQUES.
EVEN THOUGH BOTH WERE MADE FROM KAGUNE OF RATE S GHOULS.
BIKAKU ONIYAMADA 1.
ONIYAMADA WAS A VIOLENT GHOUL WHO LIKED TO FLAUNT HIS STRENGTH.
HE REPEATEDLY FED ON INVESTIGATORS AS A TEST OF HIS STRENGTH.
A NUMBER OF SENIOR AND ASSISTANT INVESTIGATORS LOST THEIR LIVES.
RINKAKU KUROIWA SPECIAL. THE OWNER OF THE KAGUNE, A GHOUL IDENTIFYING HIMSELF AS OHSE, WAS ONE OF THE LEADERS OF A ROBBERY GROUP.
HE WAS A REPEAT OFFENDER LEADING HUMAN EX-CONS.
DUE TO A HIGH NUMBER OF LAW ENFORCEMENT VICTIMS, SPECIAL INVESTIGATOR KUROIWA PERSONALLY ERADICATED HIM.
IT'S NOT LOOKING GOOD...!!
EVEN WITH A RATE S QUINQUE...!
MM...
EVEN IF WE COULD DEFEND AGAINST HIS ATTACKS WITH ARATA...
WE CANT...
ZSH

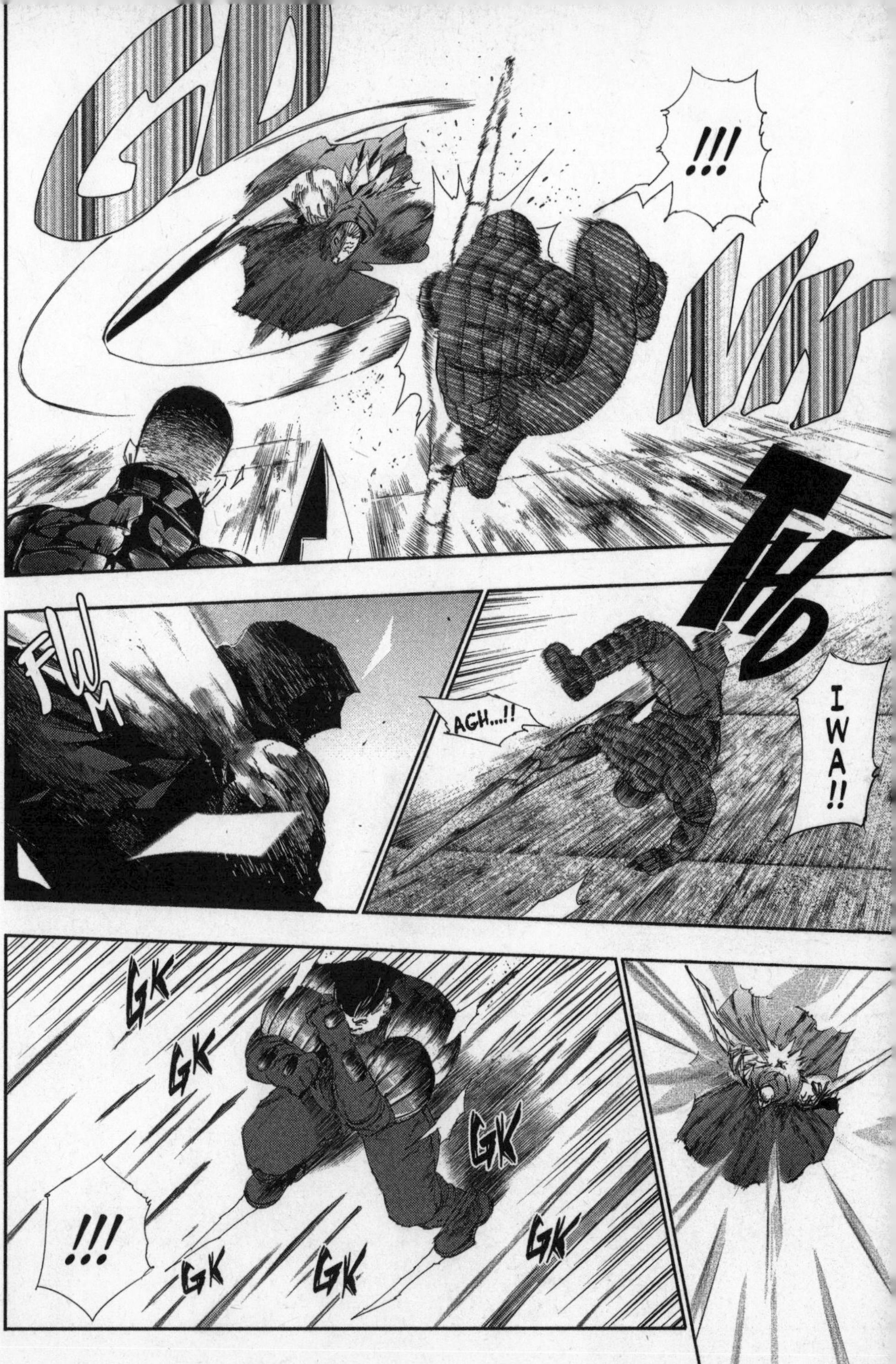
!!!
GD
THD
IWA!!
AGH...!!
FWM
GK
GK
GK
GK
GK
GK
!!!

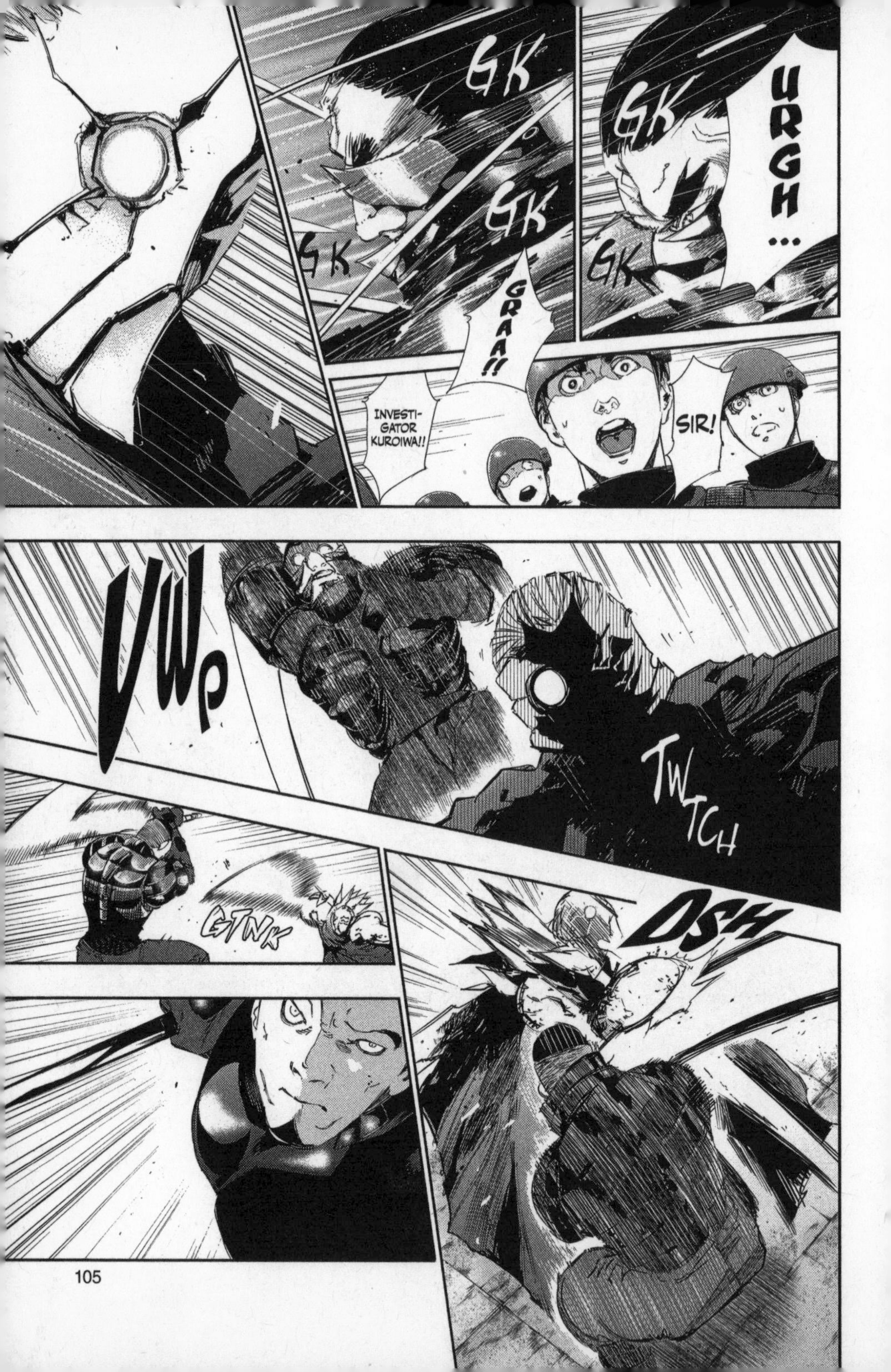
GK
GK
URGH...
GK
GK
GK
GRAAA!!
SIR!
INVESTI-
GATOR
KUROIWA!!
VWP
TWITCH
DSH
GTNK

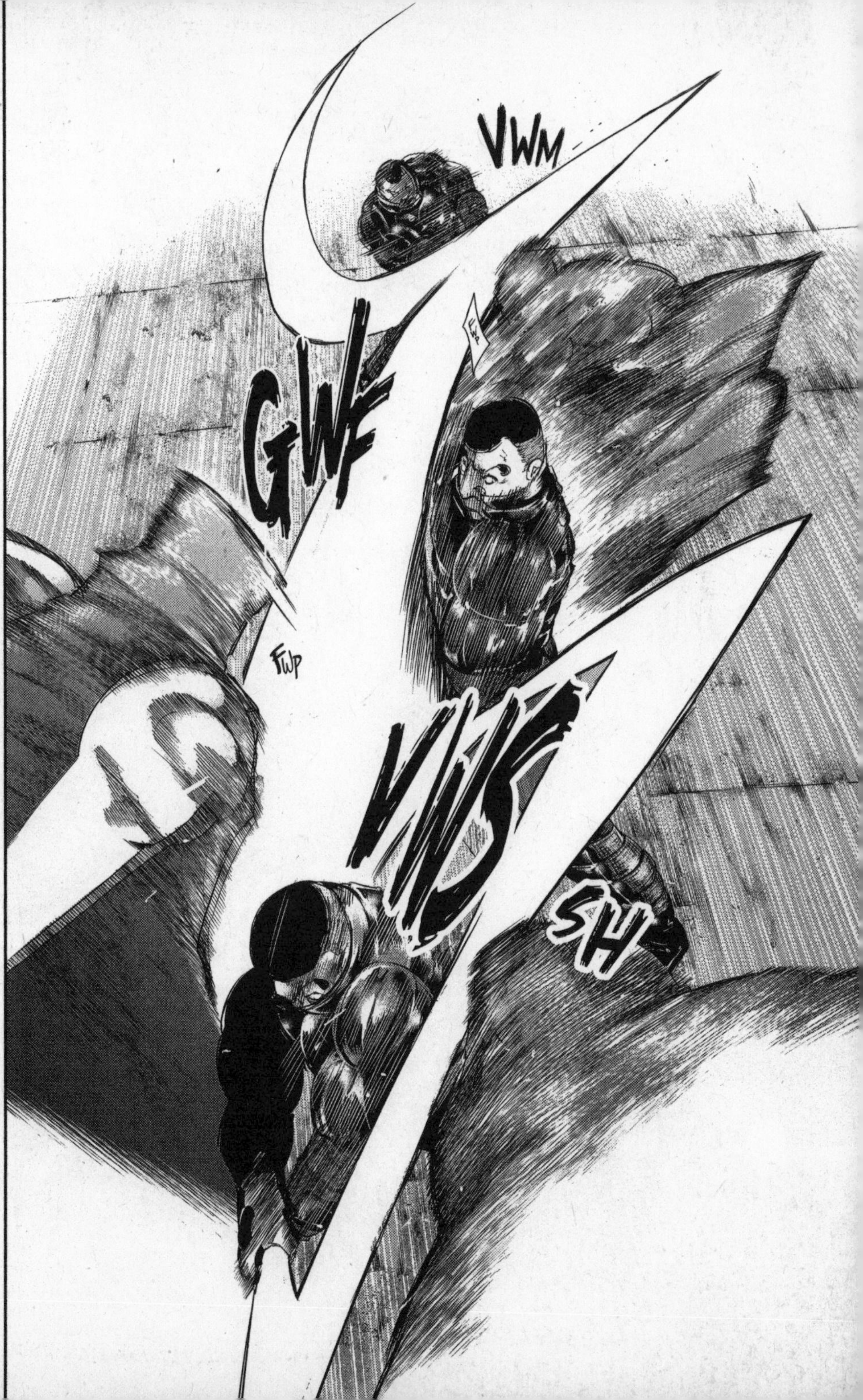
VWM
FWP
GWF
FWP
VWS
SH

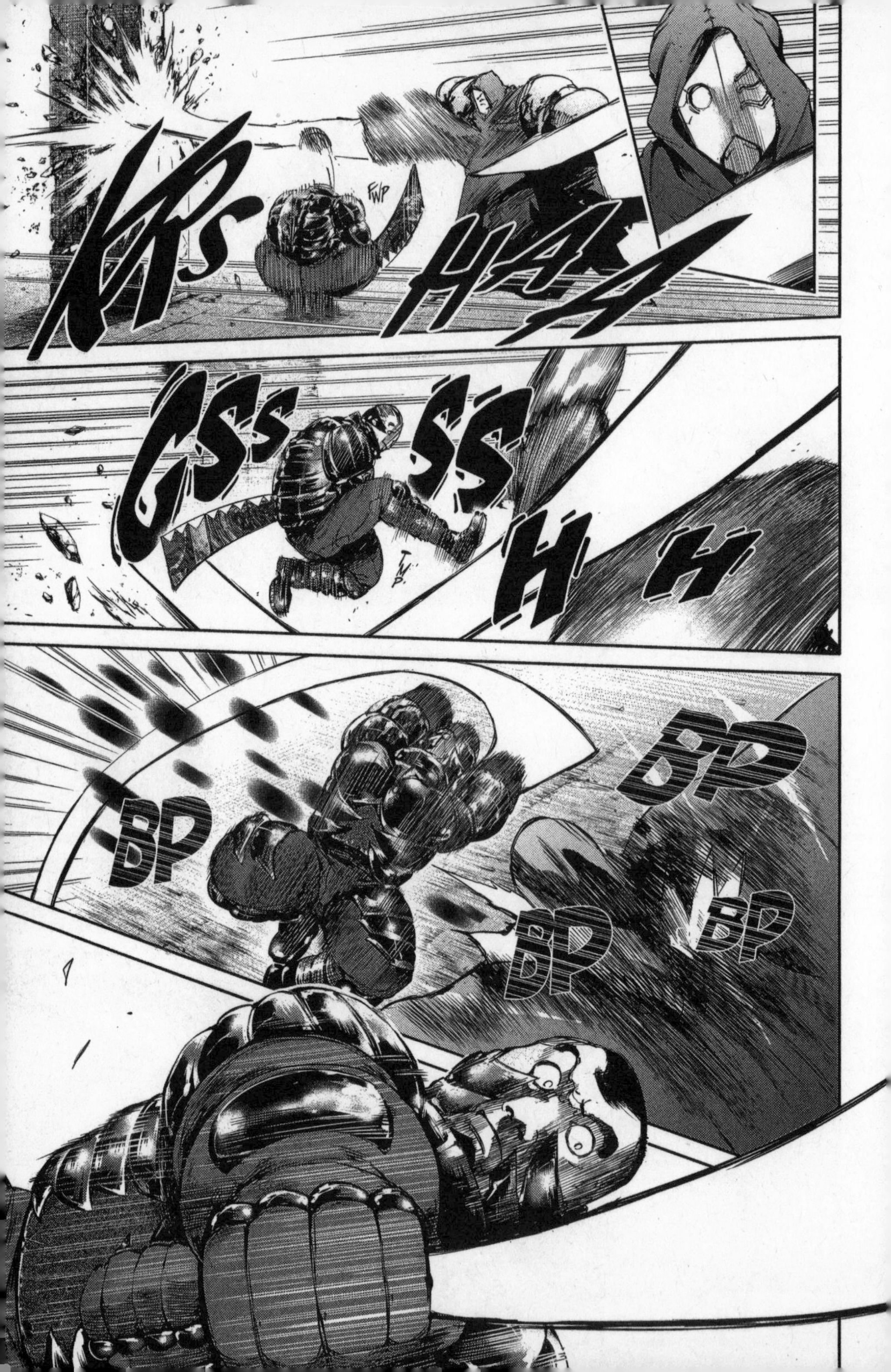
KRS
FWP
HAA
CSSS
SSH H
TMP
BP
BP
BP
BP

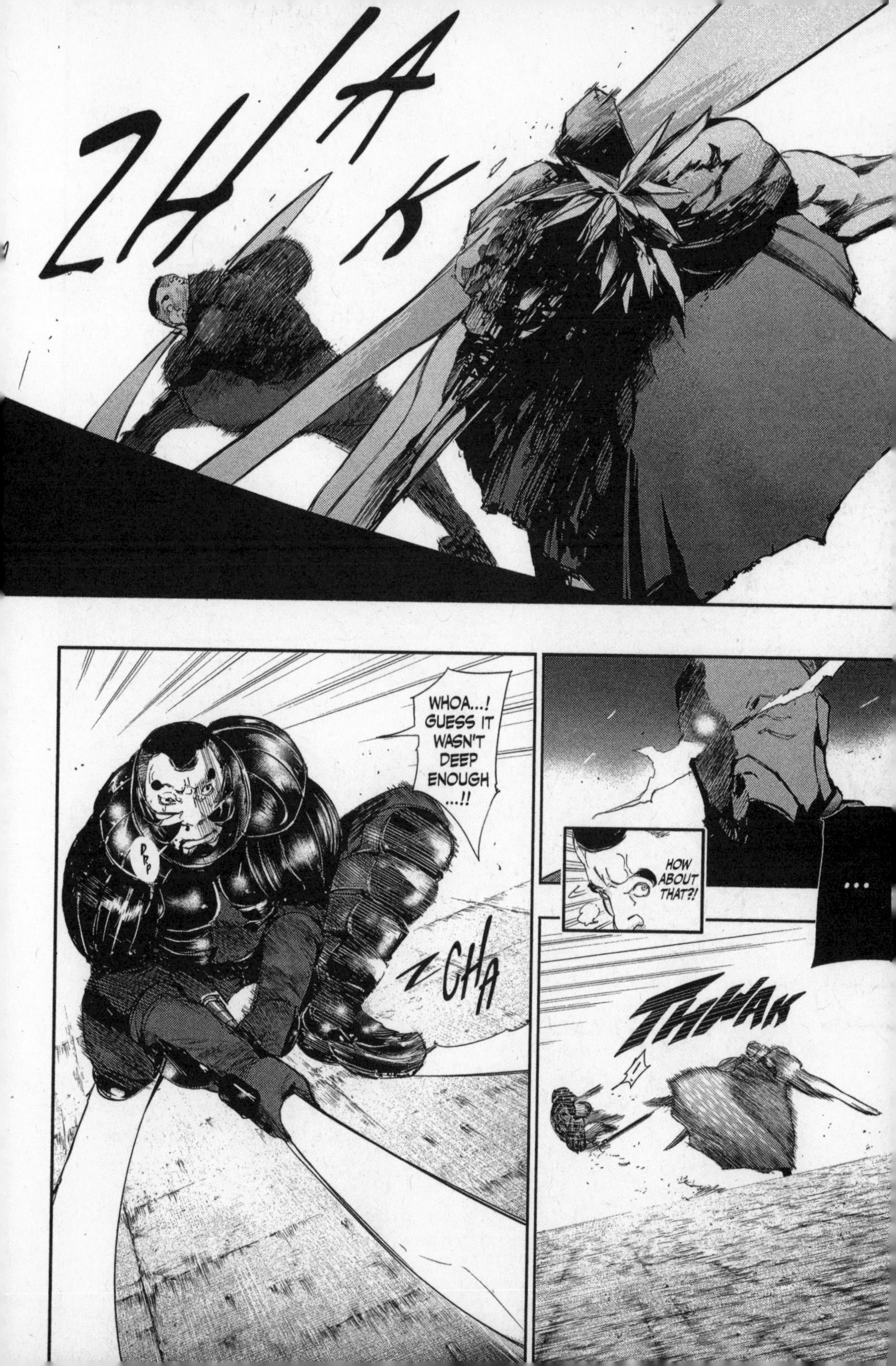
ZHAK
...
HOW ABOUT THAT?!
THWAK
WHOA...! GUESS IT WASN'T DEEP ENOUGH ...!!
ppp
ZCHA

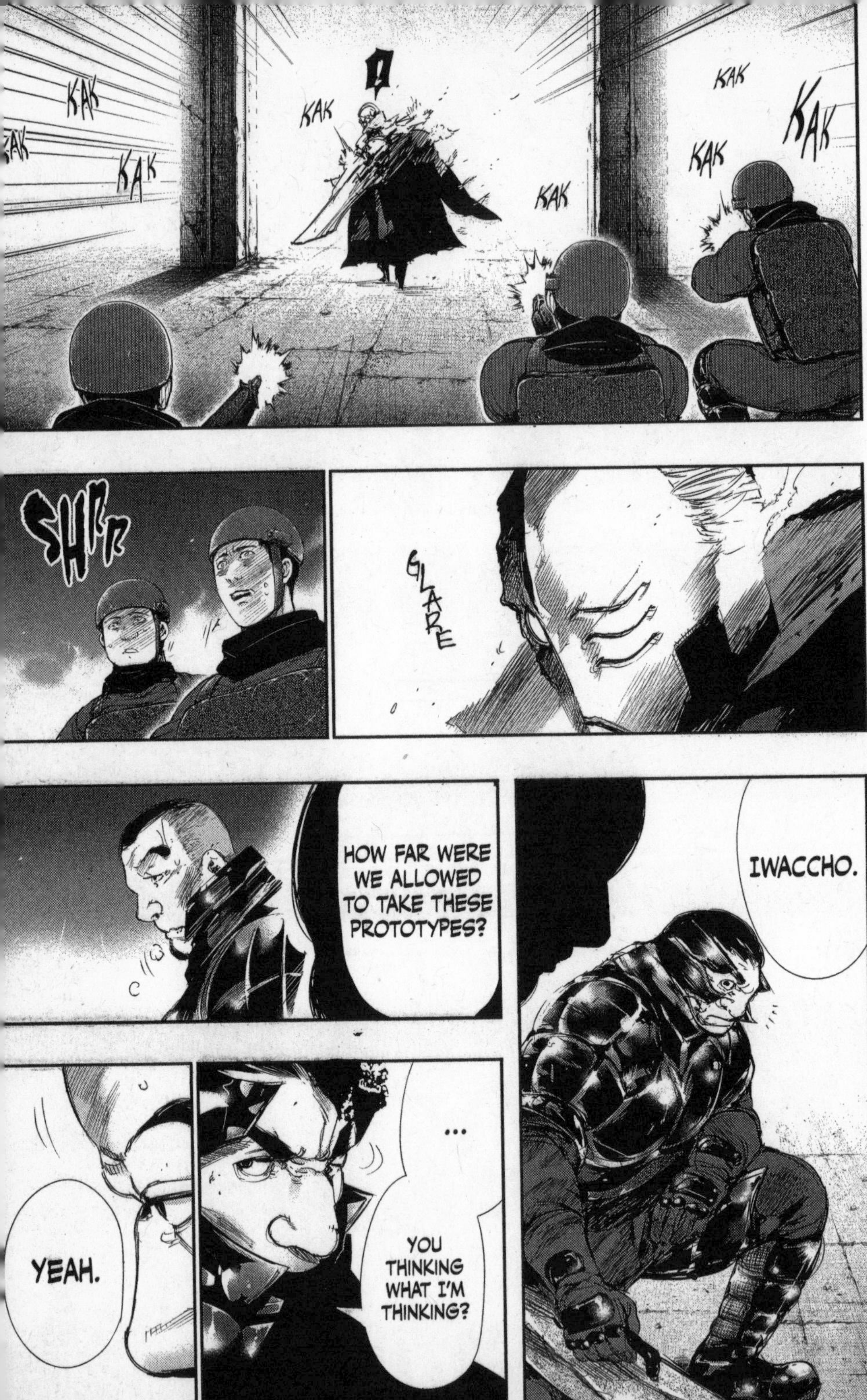
KAK
KAK
KAK
KAK
!
KAK
KAK
KAK
KAK
GLARE
SHRR
IWACCHO.
HOW FAR WERE WE ALLOWED TO TAKE THESE PROTOTYPES?
...
YOU THINKING WHAT I'M THINKING?
YEAH.

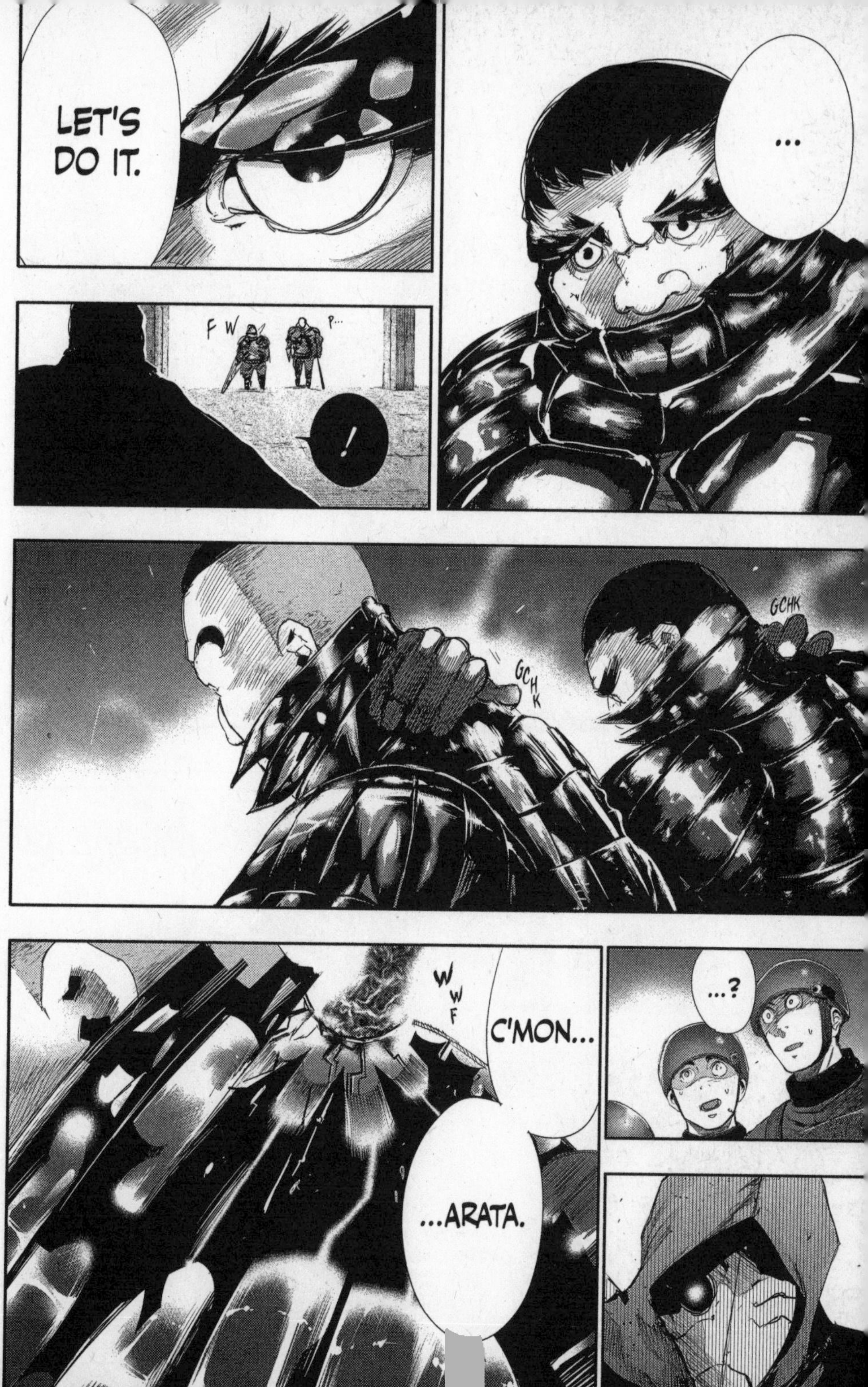
...
LET'S DO IT.
F W
P...
!
GCHK
GCHK
...?
W W F
C'MON...
...ARATA.

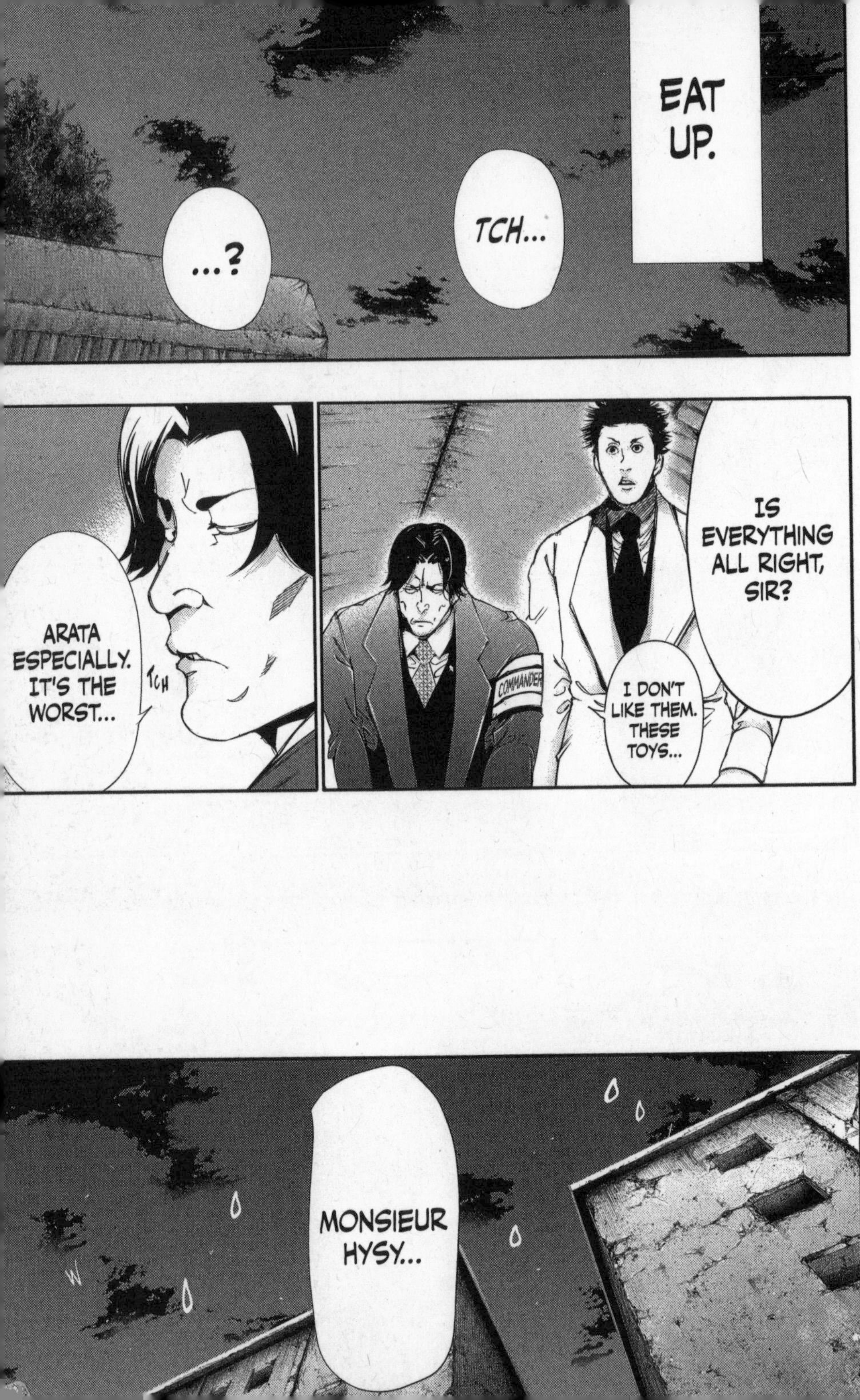
EAT UP.
TCH...
...?
IS EVERYTHING ALL RIGHT, SIR?
I DON'T LIKE THEM. THESE TOYS...
COMMANDER
TCH
ARATA ESPECIALLY. IT'S THE WORST...
MONSIEUR HYSY...

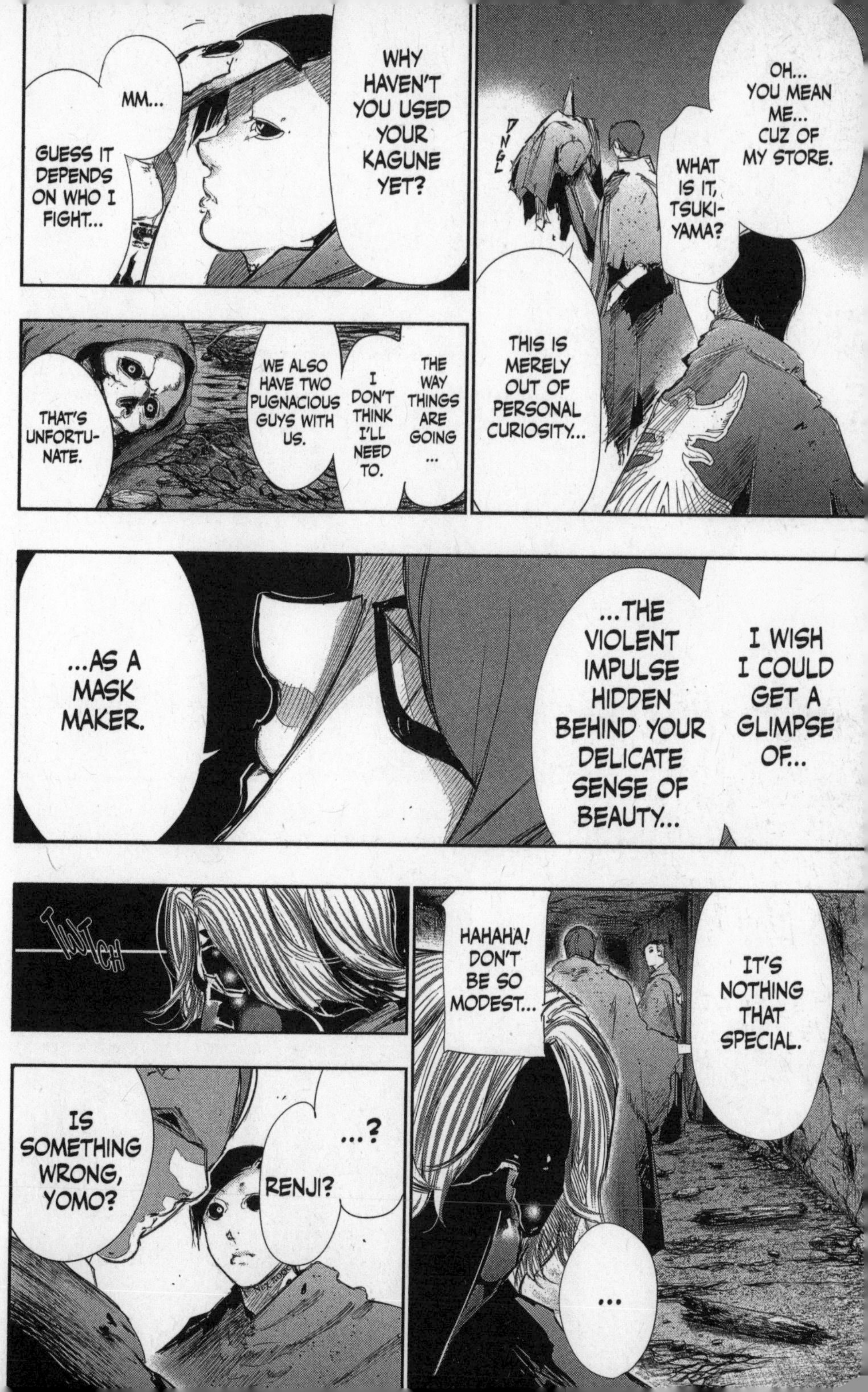
OH... YOU MEAN ME... CUZ OF MY STORE.
WHAT IS IT, TSUKI-YAMA?
DNGL
THIS IS MERELY OUT OF PERSONAL CURIOSITY...
WHY HAVEN'T YOU USED YOUR KAGUNE YET?
MM...
GUESS IT DEPENDS ON WHO I FIGHT...
THE WAY THINGS ARE GOING...
I DON'T THINK I'LL NEED TO.
WE ALSO HAVE TWO PUGNACIOUS GUYS WITH US.
THAT'S UNFORTU-NATE.
I WISH I COULD GET A GLIMPSE OF...
...THE VIOLENT IMPULSE HIDDEN BEHIND YOUR DELICATE SENSE OF BEAUTY...
...AS A MASK MAKER.
IT'S NOTHING THAT SPECIAL.
HAHAHA! DON'T BE SO MODEST...
...
TWITCH
...?
RENJI?
IS SOMETHING WRONG, YOMO?

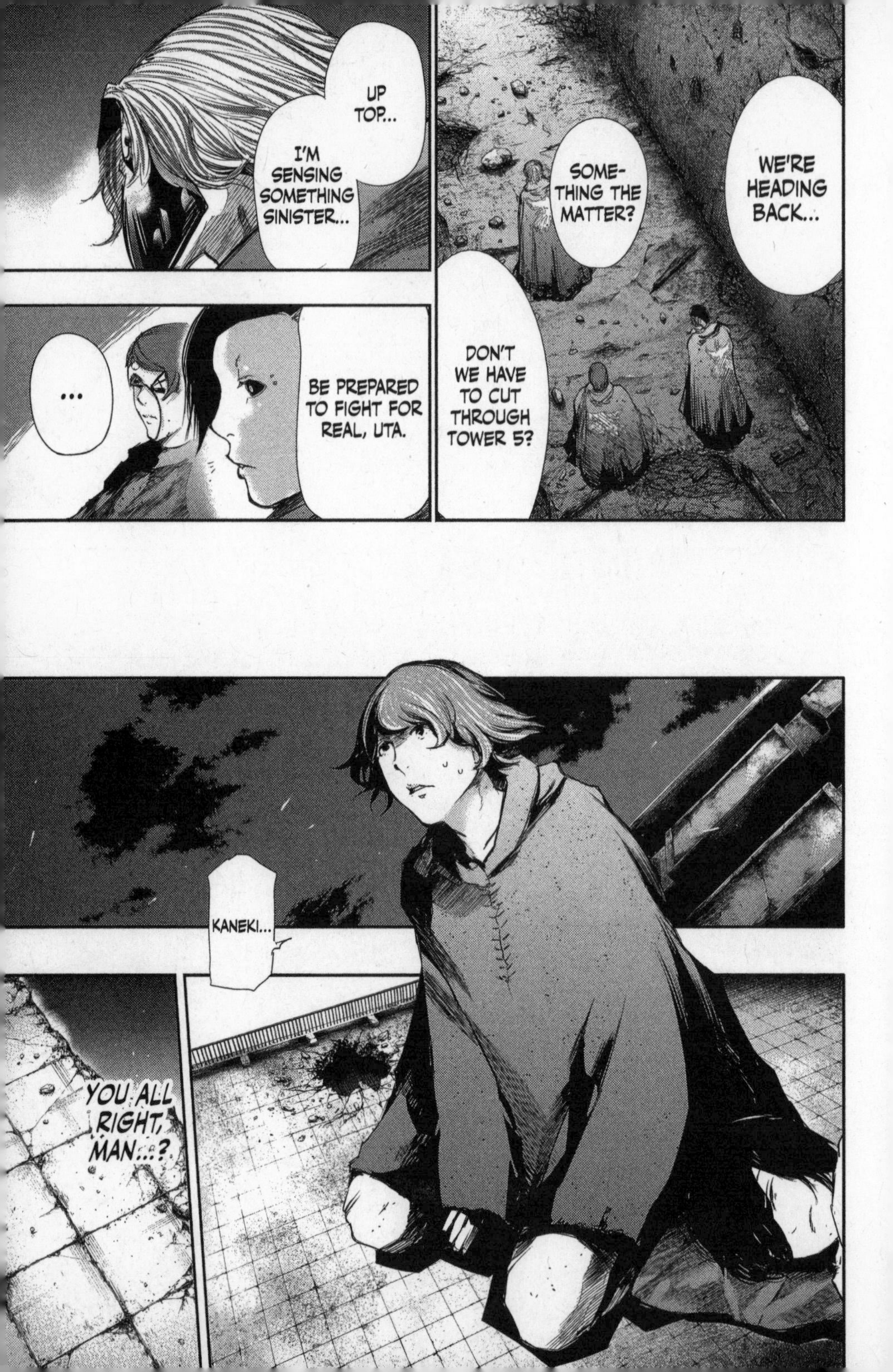
WE'RE HEADING BACK...
SOME-THING THE MATTER?
DON'T WE HAVE TO CUT THROUGH TOWER 5?
UP TOP...
I'M SENSING SOMETHING SINISTER...
BE PREPARED TO FIGHT FOR REAL, UTA.
...
KANEKI...
YOU ALL RIGHT, MAN...?

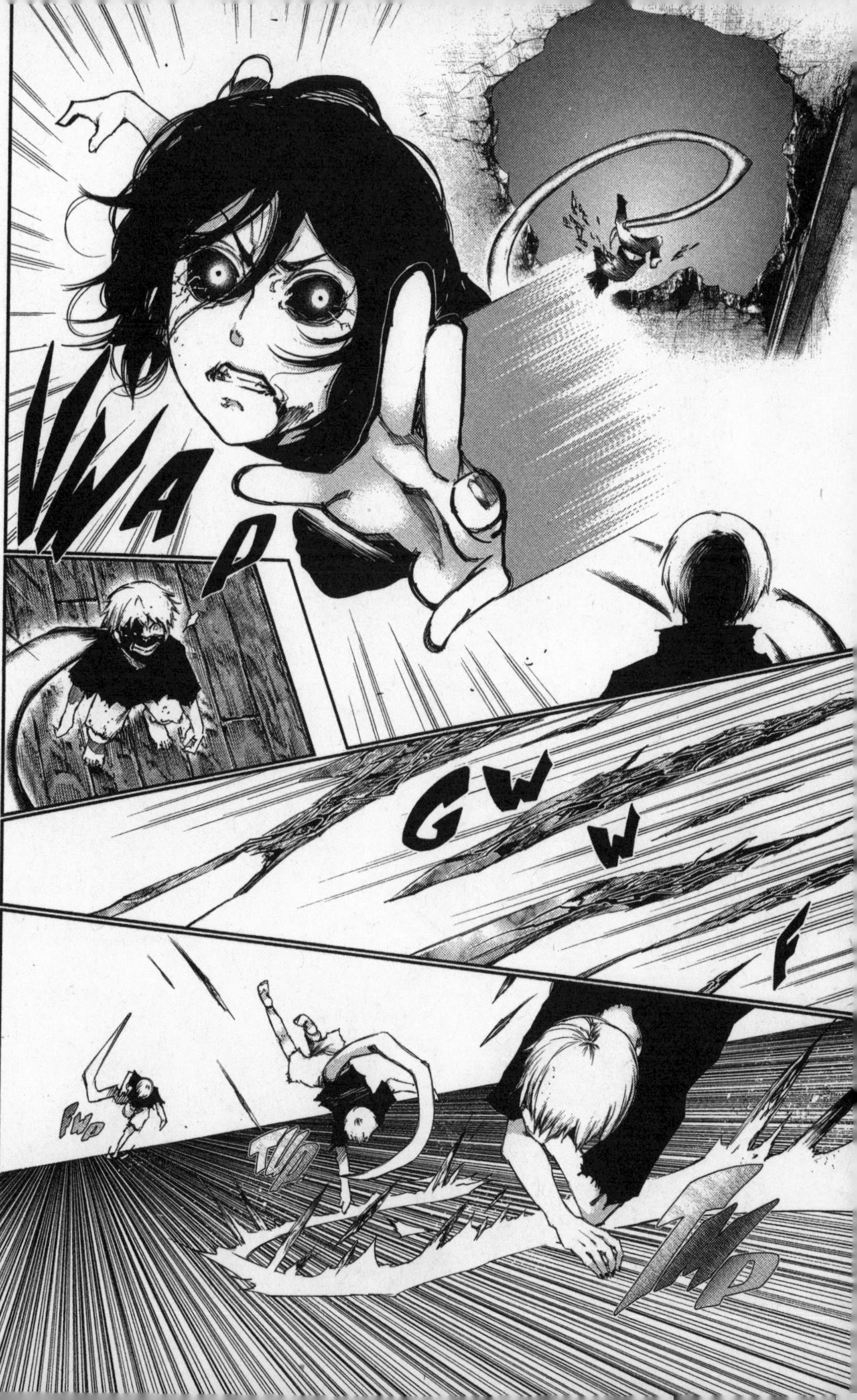
WAD
GWWF
TMP
TUP
FWP

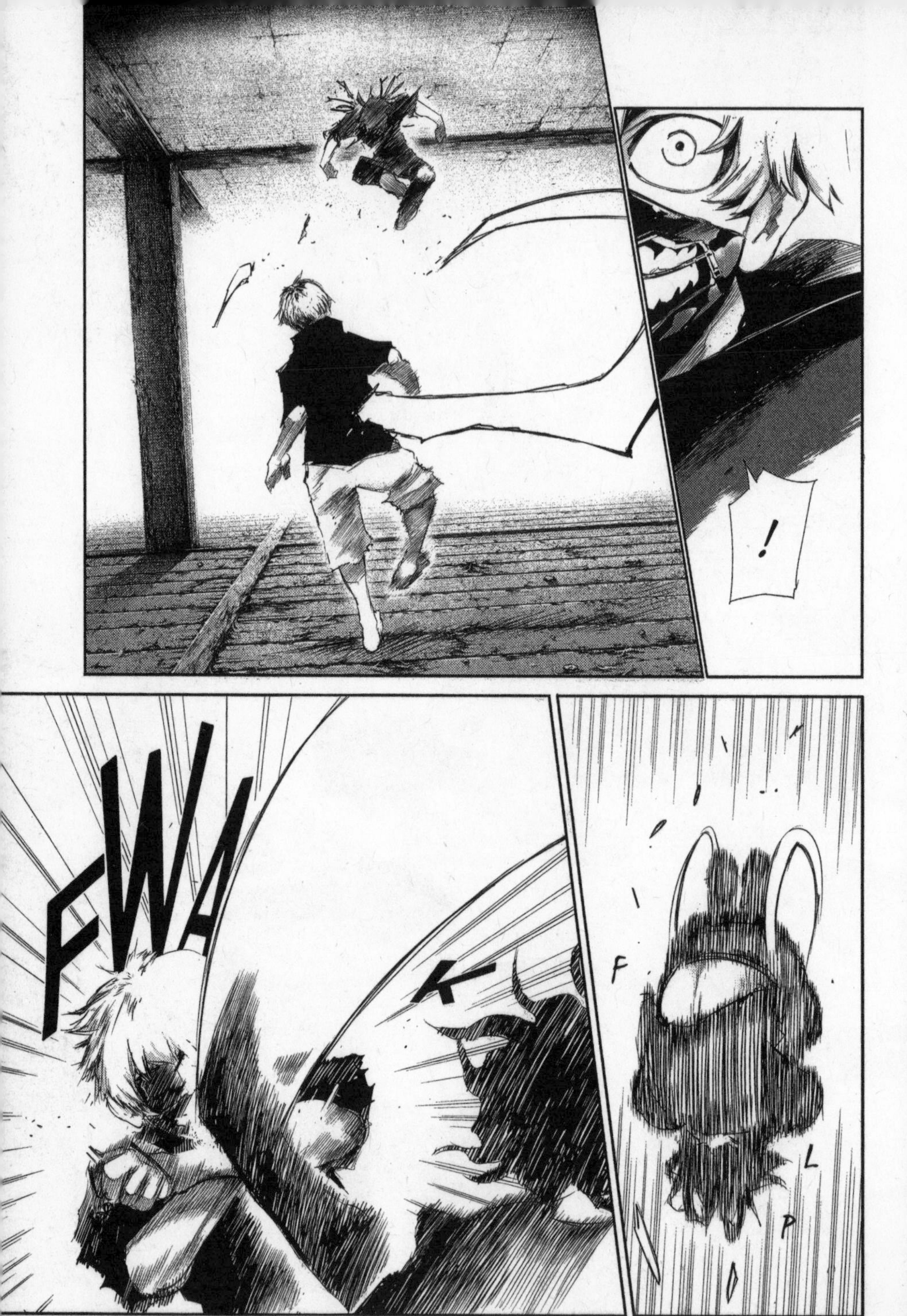
!
F L P
FWAK

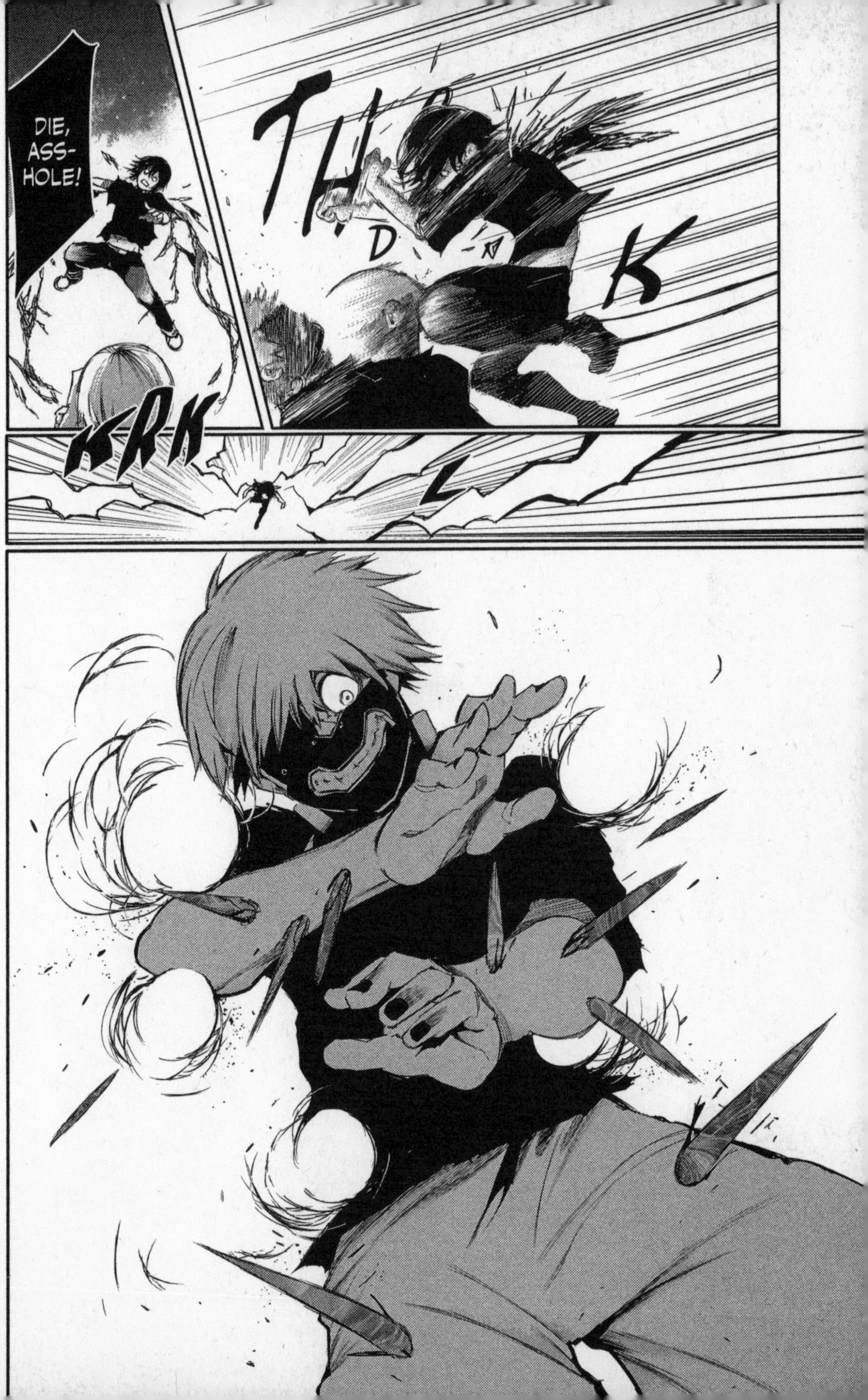
THDK
DIE, ASS-HOLE!
KRK
L

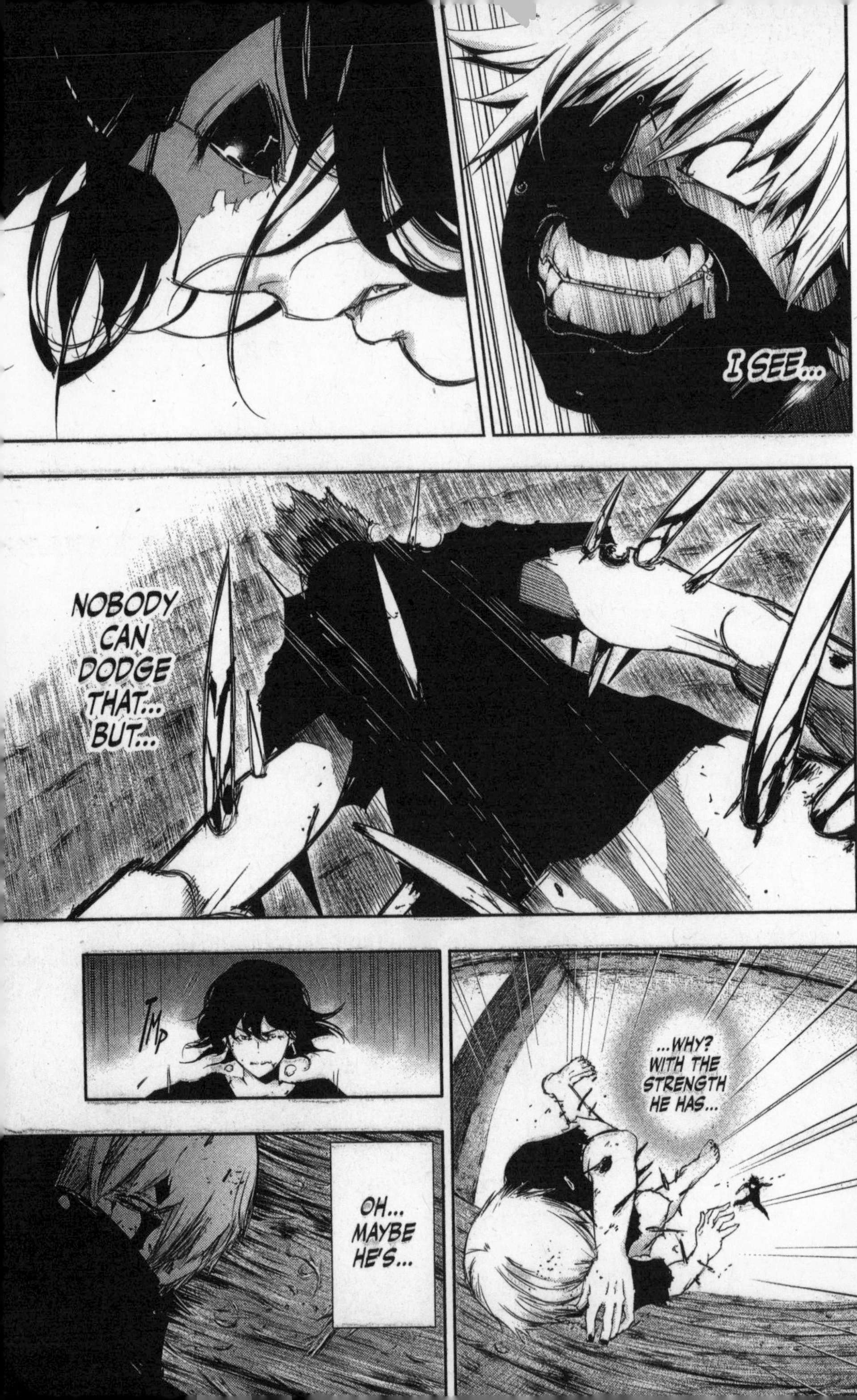
I SEE...
NOBODY CAN DODGE THAT... BUT...
...WHY? WITH THE STRENGTH HE HAS...
TMP
OH... MAYBE HE'S...

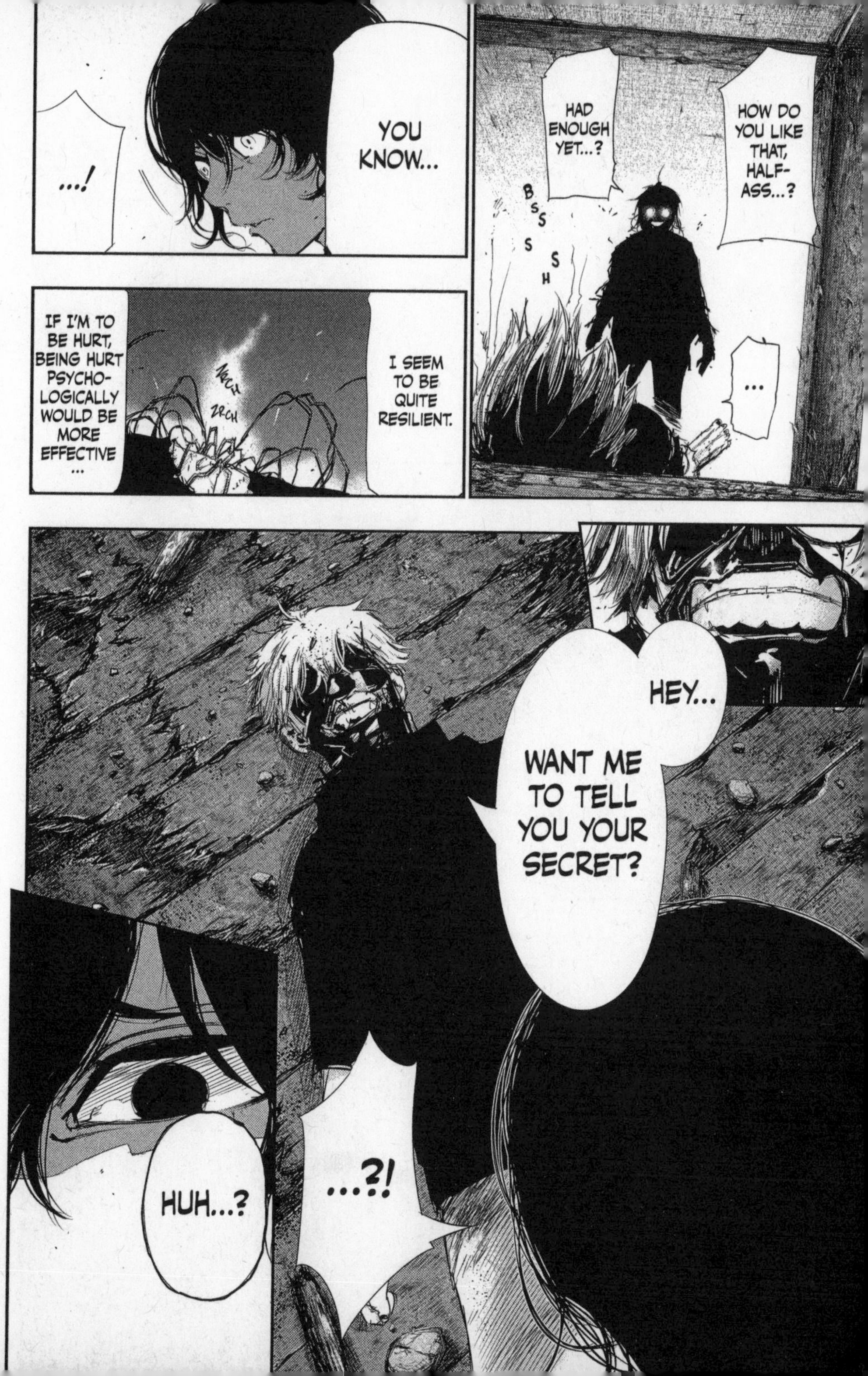
HOW DO YOU LIKE THAT, HALF-ASS...?
HAD ENOUGH YET...?
BSSSSH
...
YOU KNOW...
...!
I SEEM TO BE QUITE RESILIENT.
IF I'M TO BE HURT, BEING HURT PSYCHOLOGICALLY WOULD BE MORE EFFECTIVE...
ZRCH
HEY...
WANT ME TO TELL YOU YOUR SECRET?
...?!
HUH...?

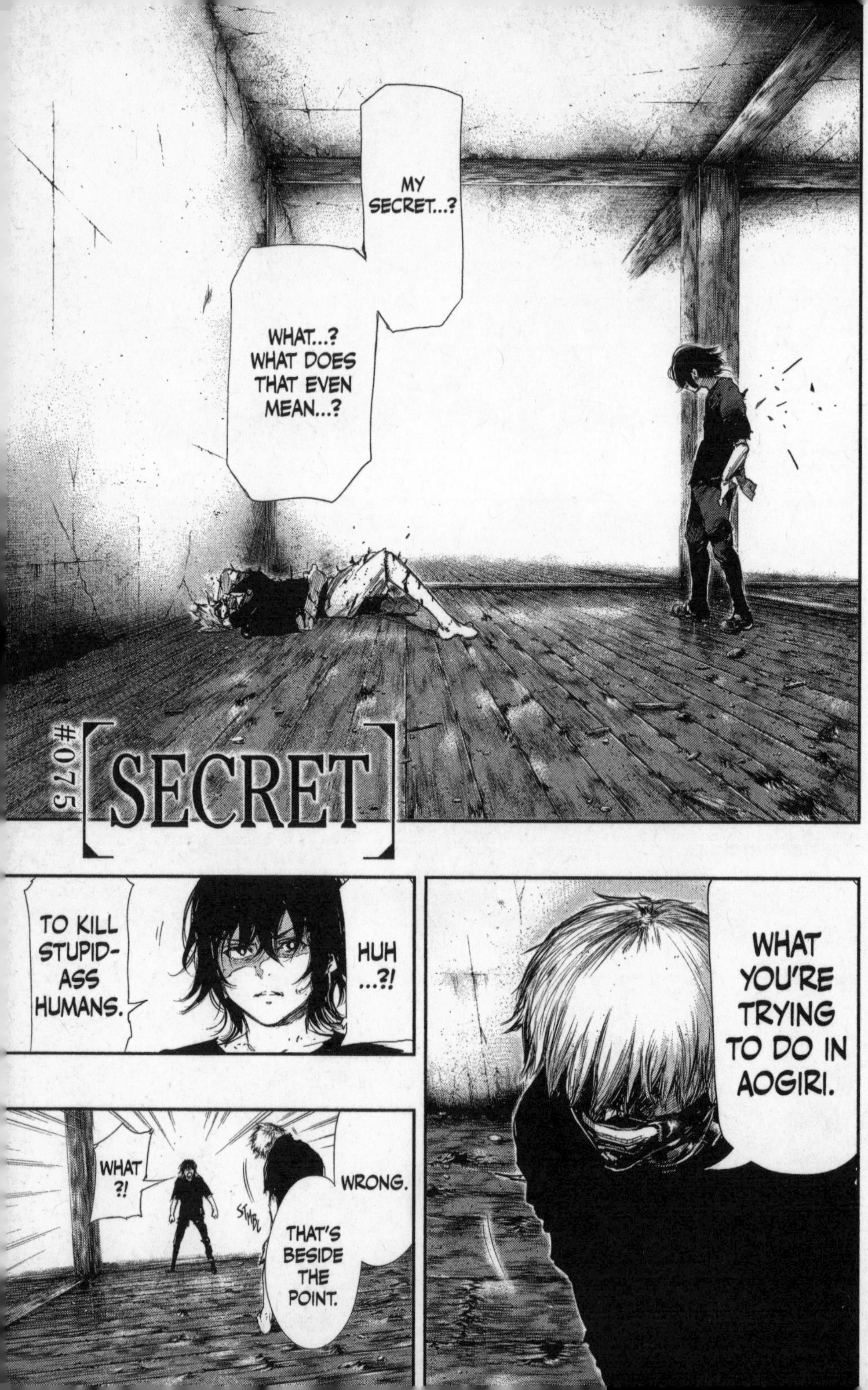
MY SECRET...?
WHAT...? WHAT DOES THAT EVEN MEAN...?
#075 SECRET
WHAT YOU'RE TRYING TO DO IN AOGIRI.
HUH...?!
TO KILL STUPID-ASS HUMANS.
WRONG.
THAT'S BESIDE THE POINT.
STMBL
WHAT?!

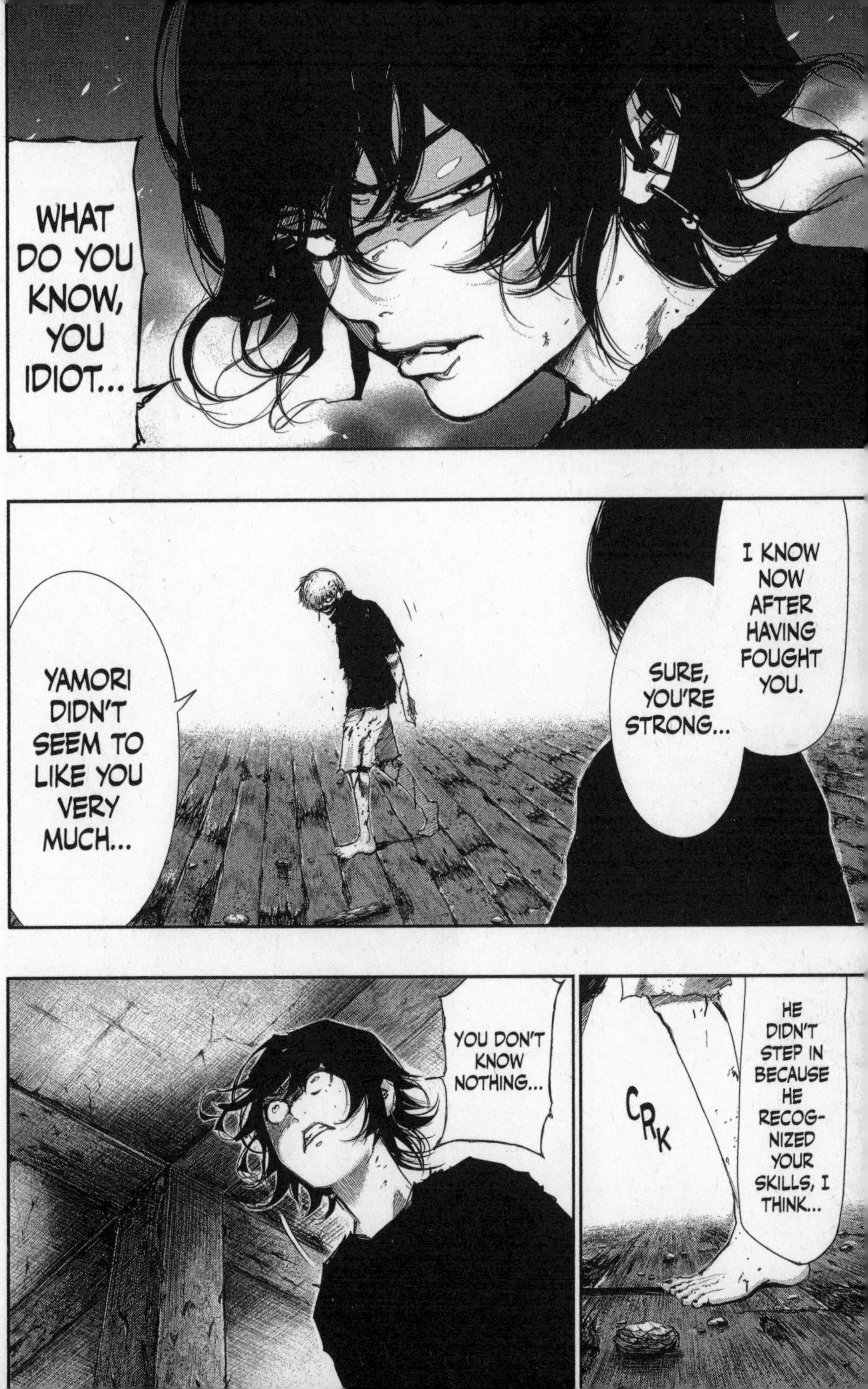
WHAT DO YOU KNOW, YOU IDIOT...
I KNOW NOW AFTER HAVING FOUGHT YOU.
SURE, YOU'RE STRONG...
YAMORI DIDN'T SEEM TO LIKE YOU VERY MUCH...
HE DIDN'T STEP IN BECAUSE HE RECOG-NIZED YOUR SKILLS, I THINK...
CRK
YOU DON'T KNOW NOTHING...

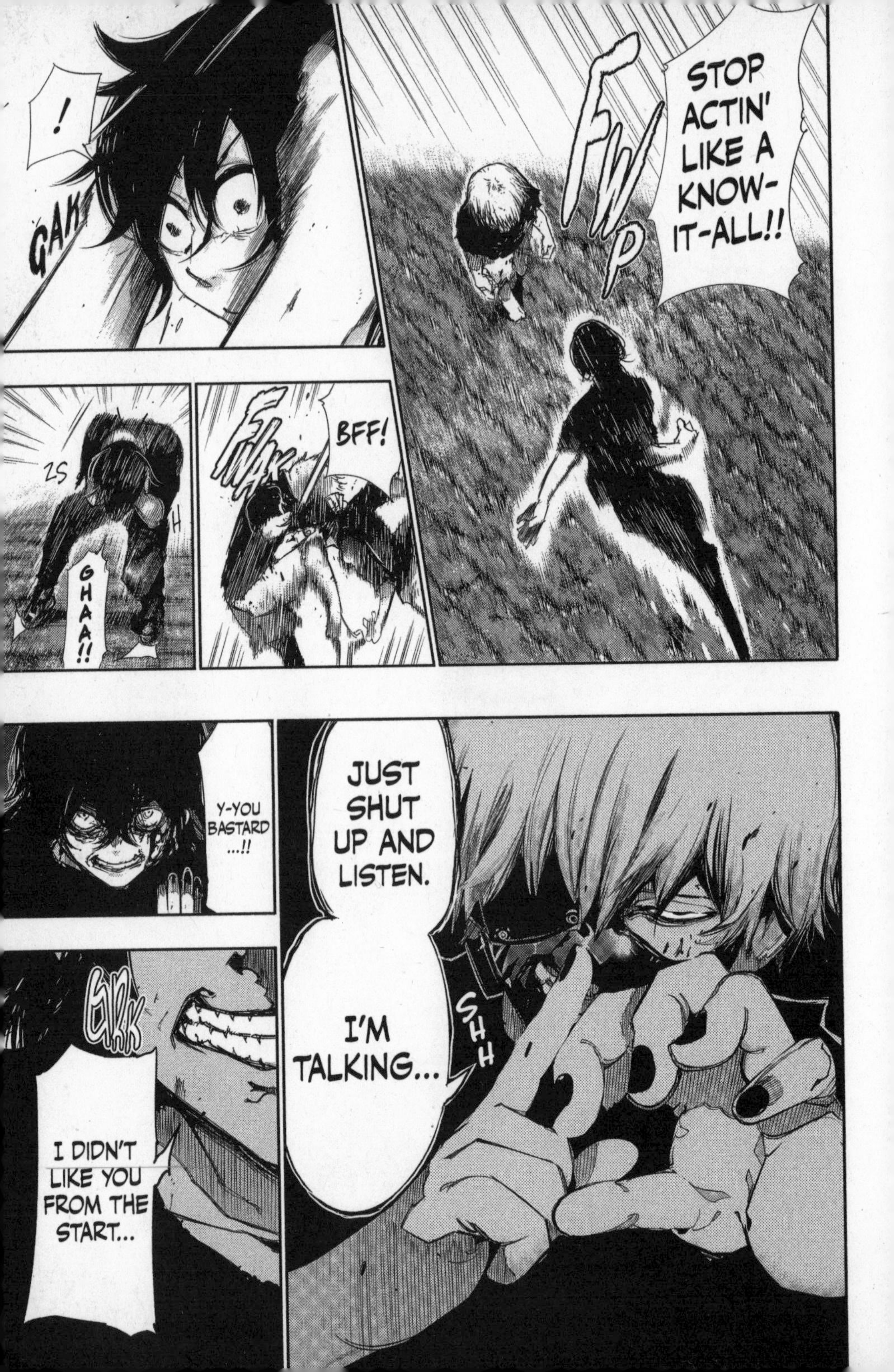
FWP
STOP ACTIN' LIKE A KNOW-IT-ALL!!
!
GAK
BFF!
GHAA!!
JUST SHUT UP AND LISTEN.
I'M TALKING...
SHH
Y-YOU BASTARD ...!!
I DIDN'T LIKE YOU FROM THE START...

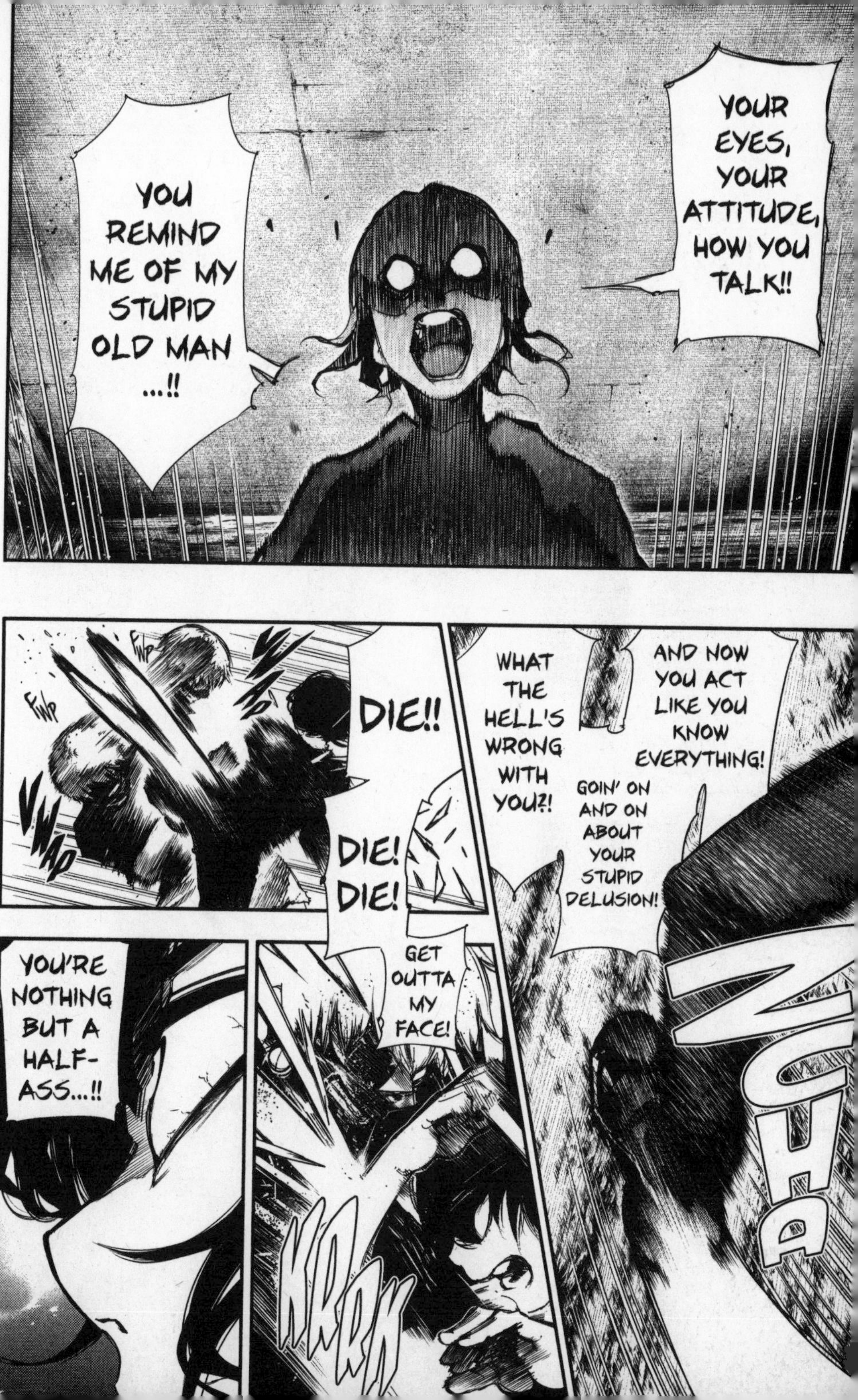
YOUR EYES, YOUR ATTITUDE, HOW YOU TALK!!
YOU REMIND ME OF MY STUPID OLD MAN ...!!
AND NOW YOU ACT LIKE YOU KNOW EVERYTHING!
WHAT THE HELL'S WRONG WITH YOU?!
GOIN' ON AND ON ABOUT YOUR STUPID DELUSION!
NUGHA
DIE!!
DIE! DIE!
VWAP
FWP
FWP
VWAP
GET OUTTA MY FACE!
HRRK
YOU'RE NOTHING BUT A HALF-ASS...!!

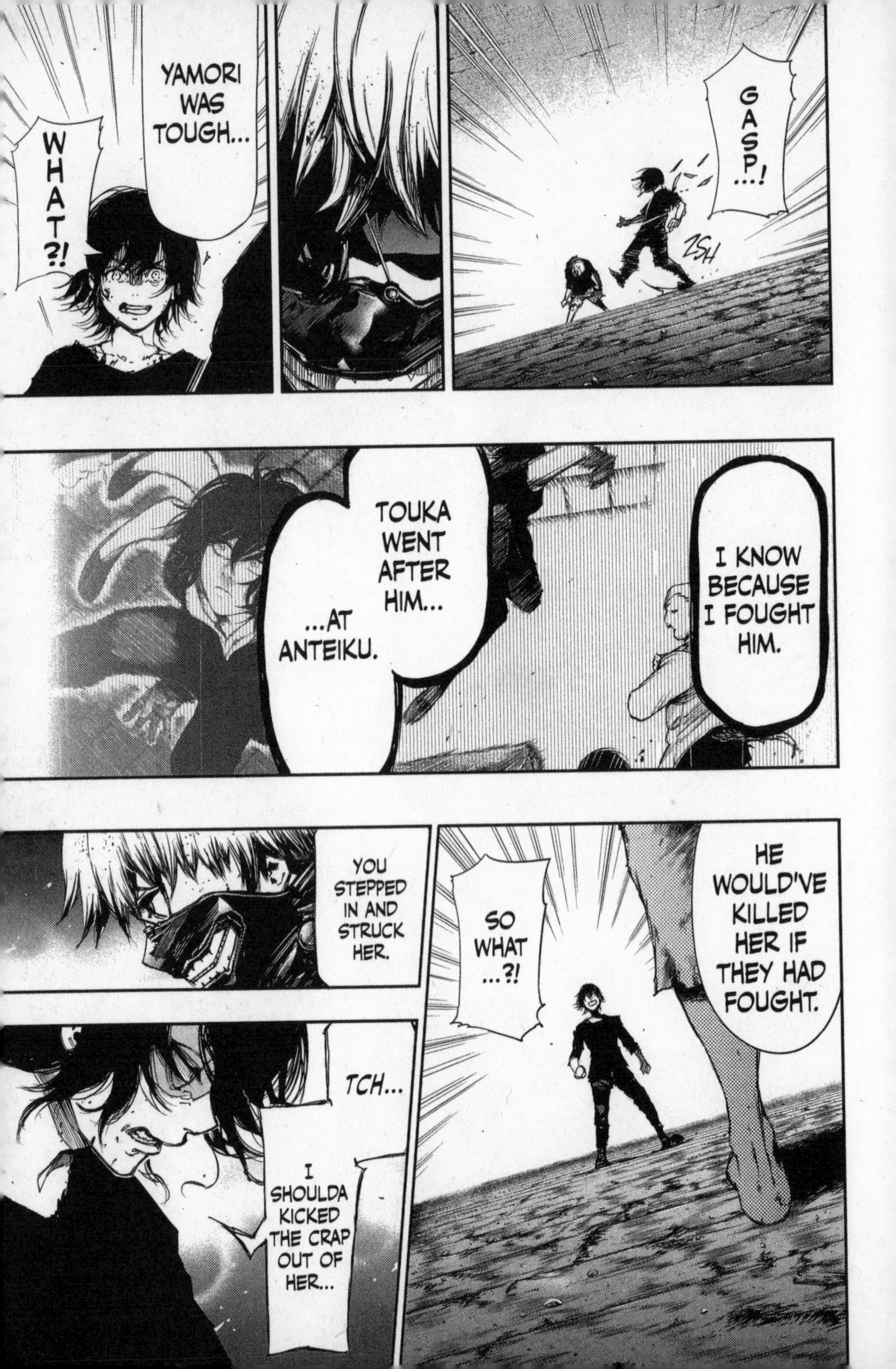
GASP...!
ZSH
YAMORI WAS TOUGH...
WHAT?!
I KNOW BECAUSE I FOUGHT HIM.
TOUKA WENT AFTER HIM...
...AT ANTEIKU.
HE WOULD'VE KILLED HER IF THEY HAD FOUGHT.
SO WHAT...?!
YOU STEPPED IN AND STRUCK HER.
TCH...
I SHOULDA KICKED THE CRAP OUT OF HER...

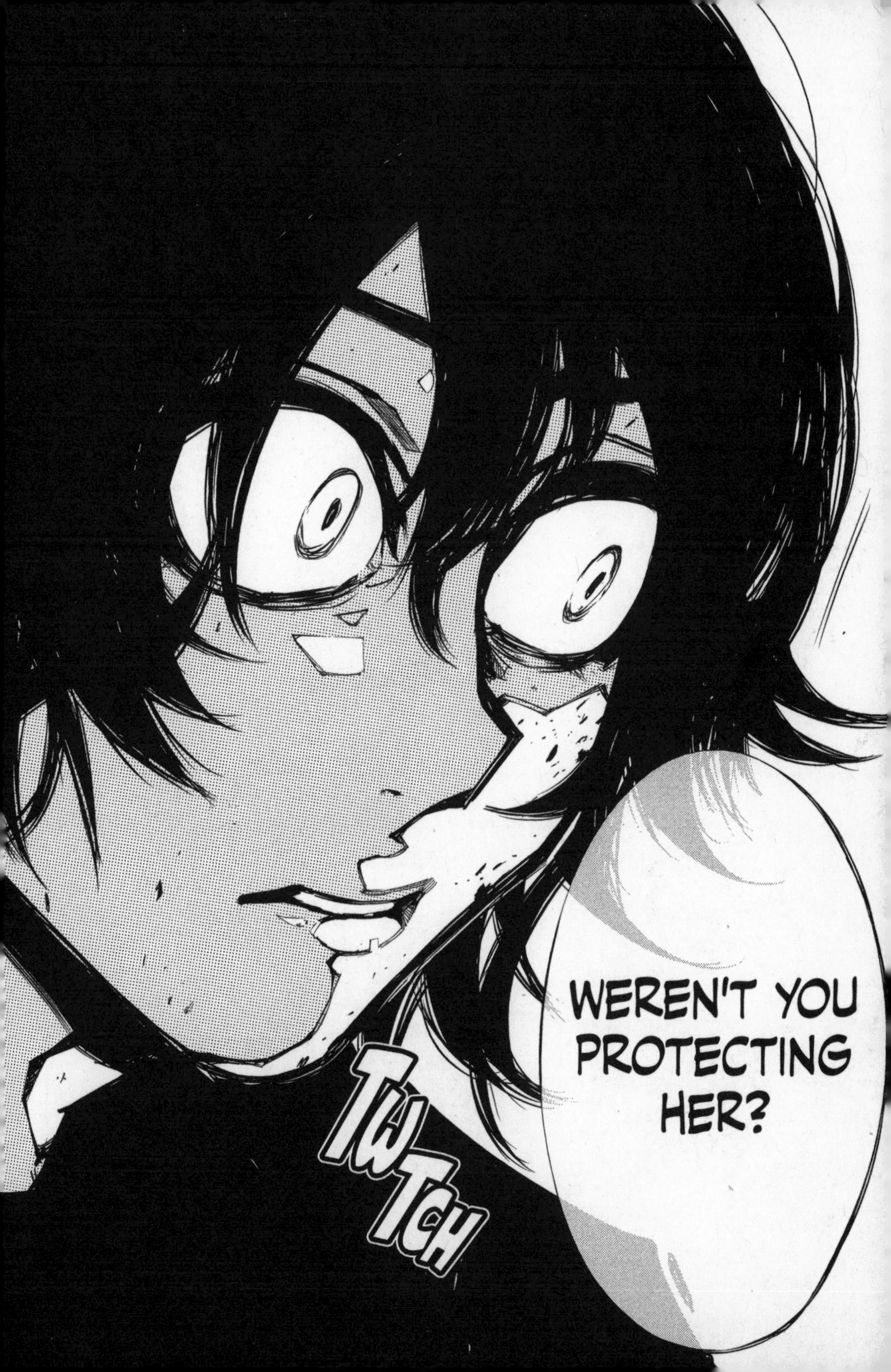
WEREN'T YOU PROTECTING HER?
TWTCH

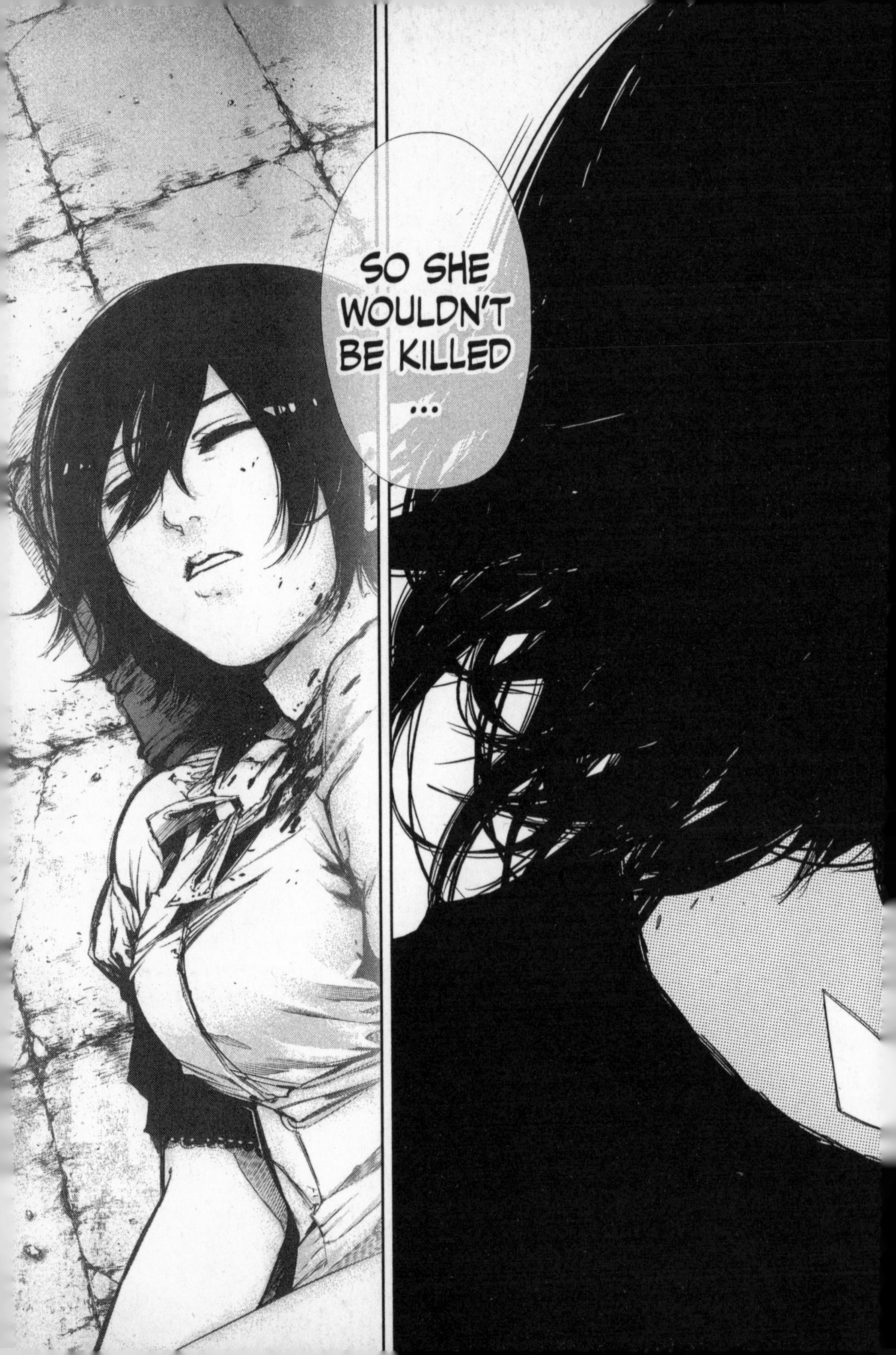
SO SHE WOULDN'T BE KILLED ...

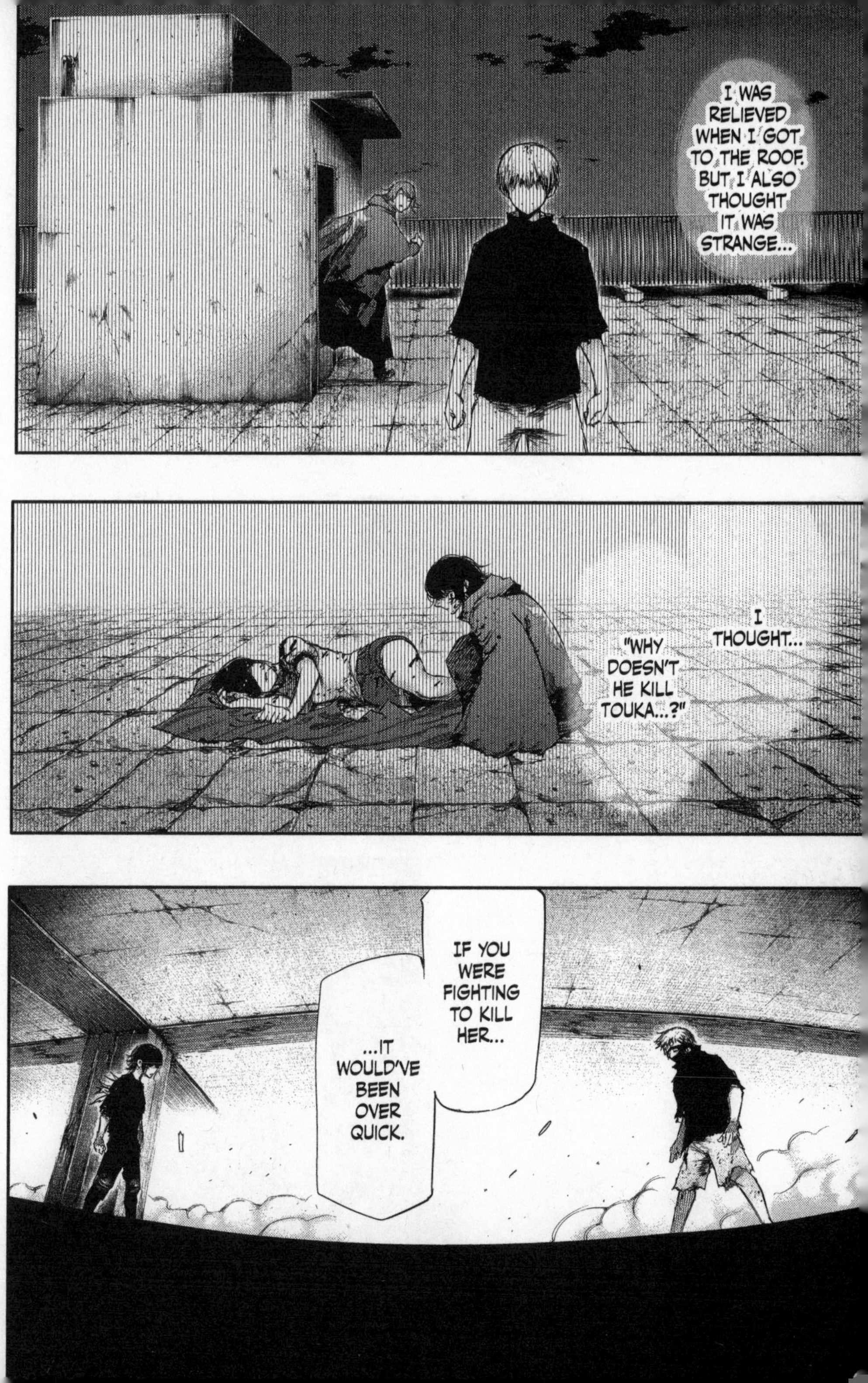
I WAS RELIEVED WHEN I GOT TO THE ROOF. BUT I ALSO THOUGHT IT WAS STRANGE...
I THOUGHT...
"WHY DOESN'T HE KILL TOUKA...?"
IF YOU WERE FIGHTING TO KILL HER...
...IT WOULD'VE BEEN OVER QUICK.

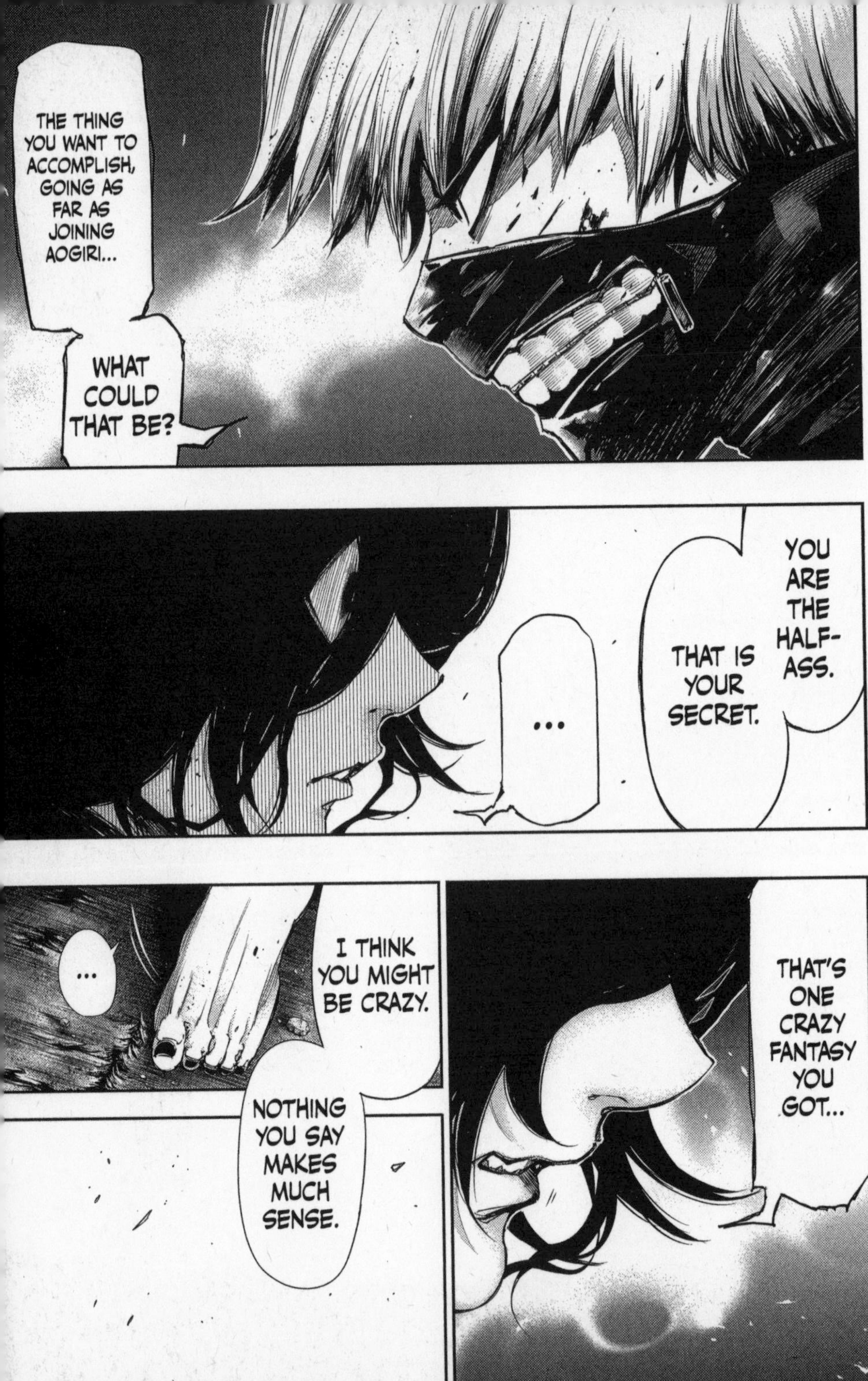
THE THING YOU WANT TO ACCOMPLISH, GOING AS FAR AS JOINING AOGIRI...
WHAT COULD THAT BE?
YOU ARE THE HALF-ASS.
THAT IS YOUR SECRET.
...
THAT'S ONE CRAZY FANTASY YOU GOT...
I THINK YOU MIGHT BE CRAZY.
...
NOTHING YOU SAY MAKES MUCH SENSE.

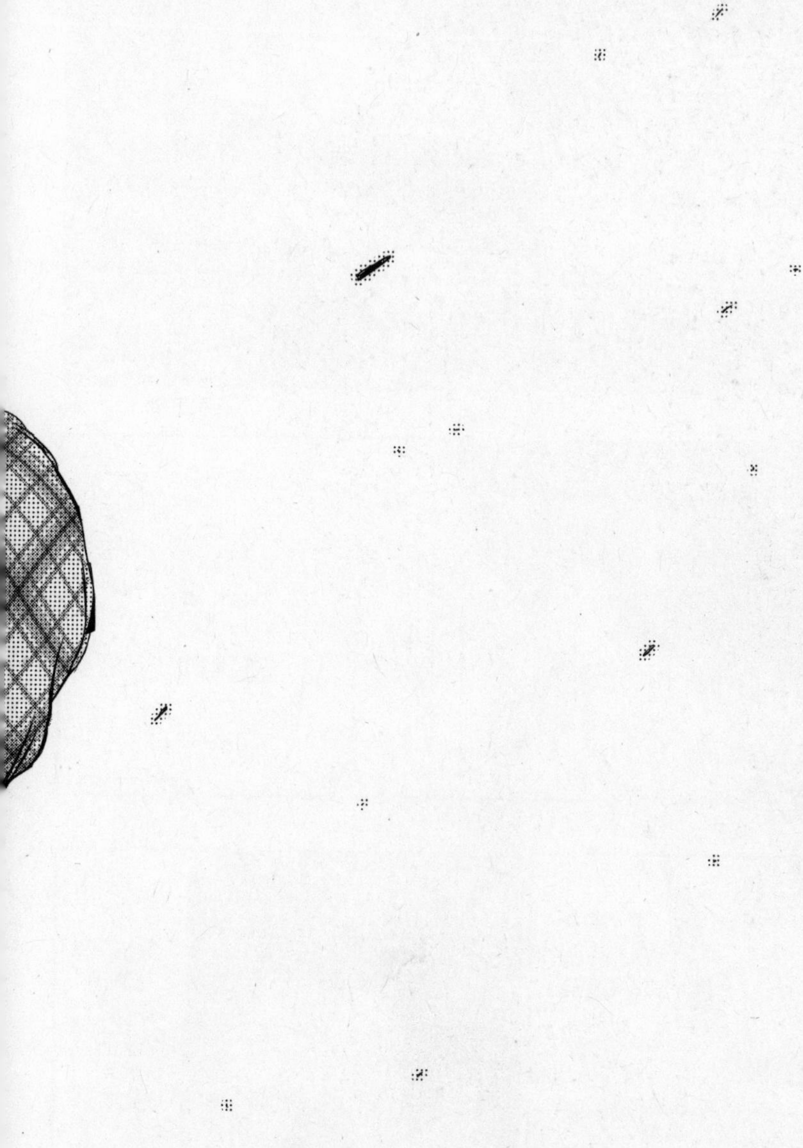

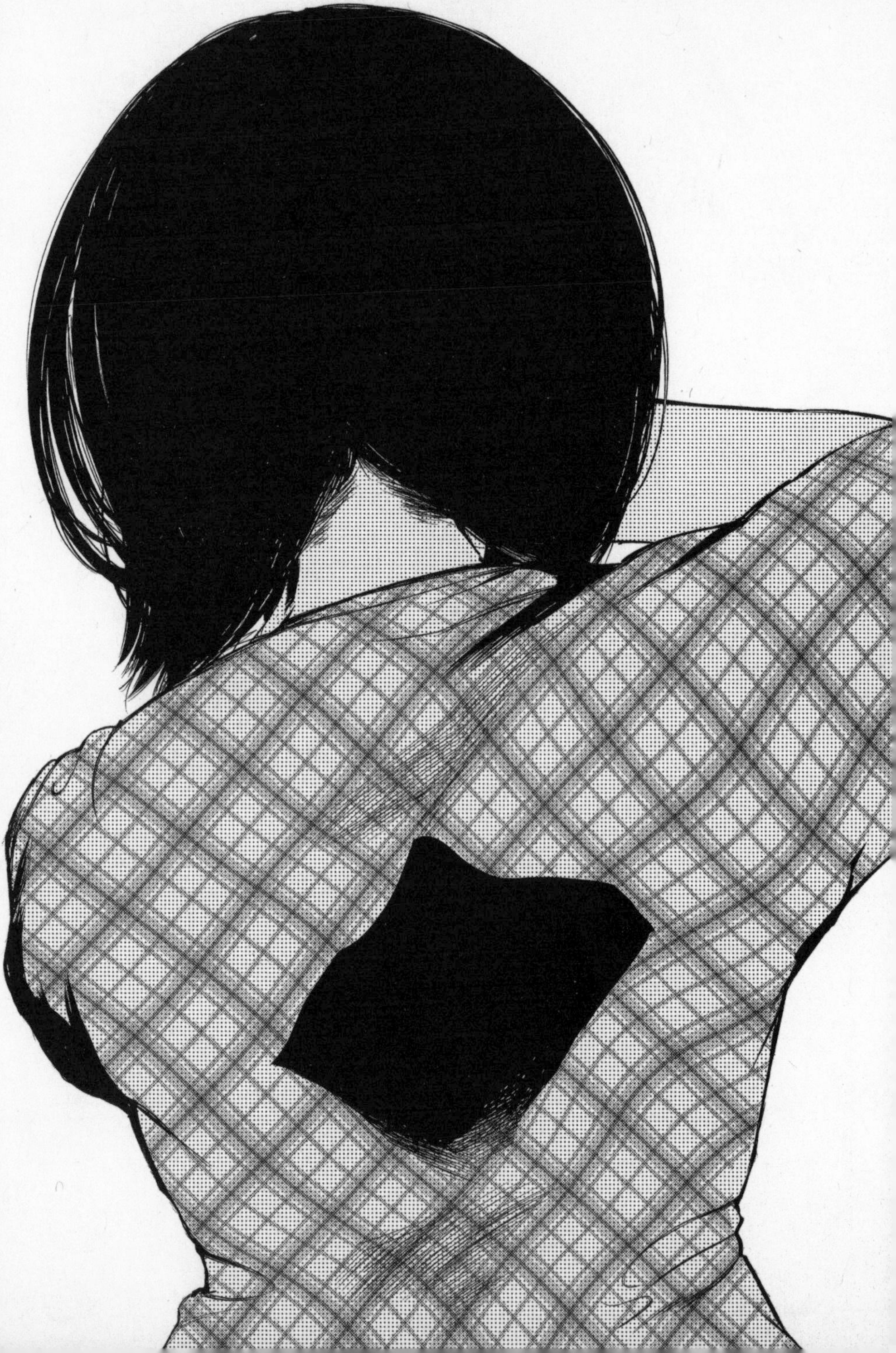

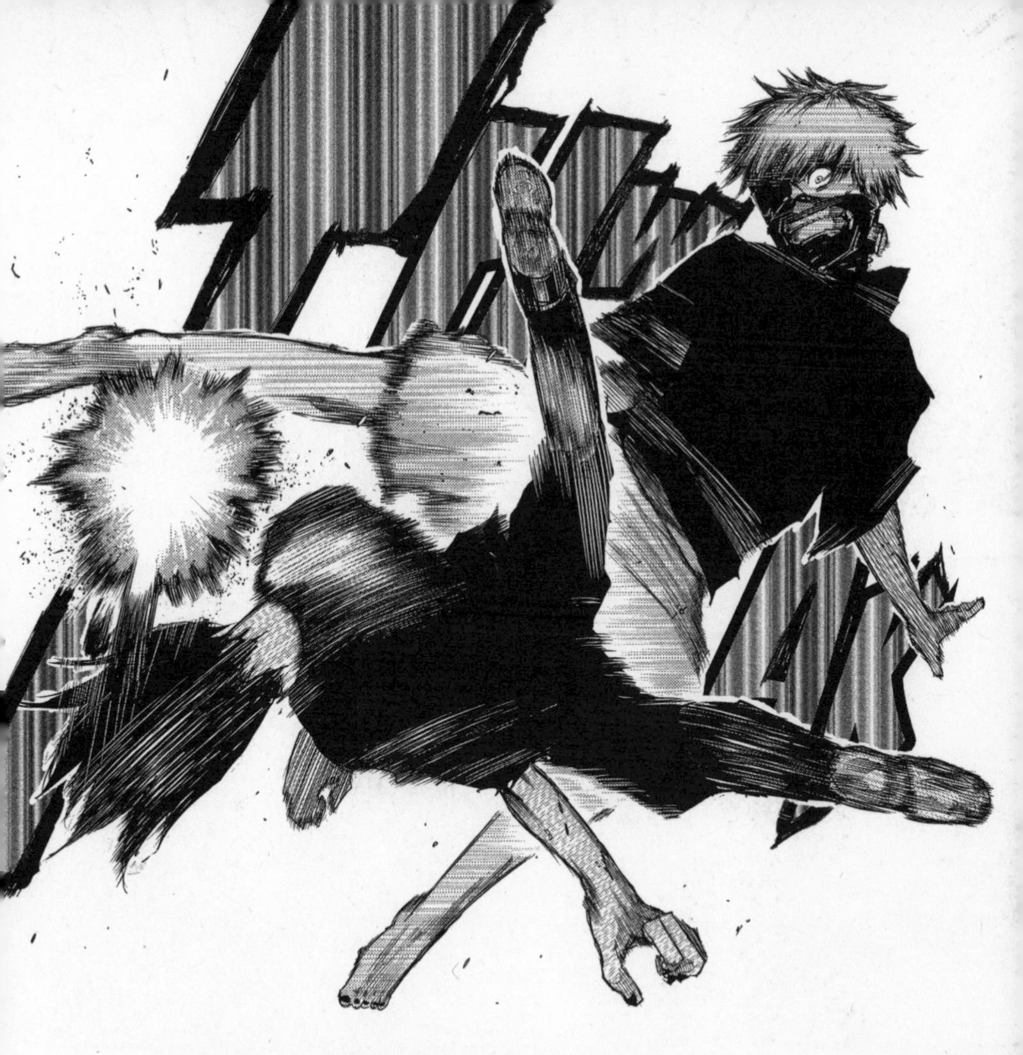

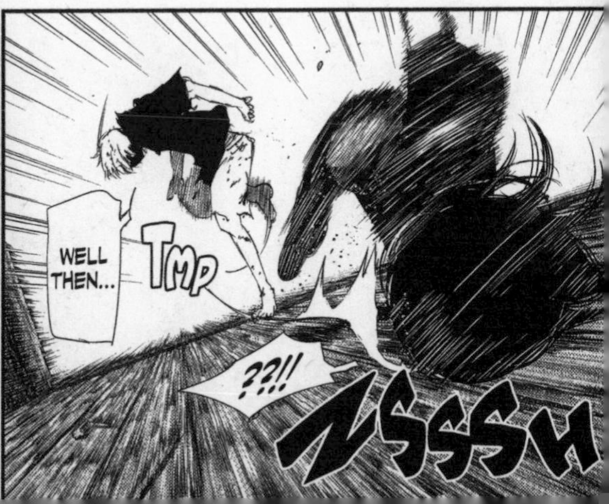
WELL THEN...
TMP
??!!
ZSSSH

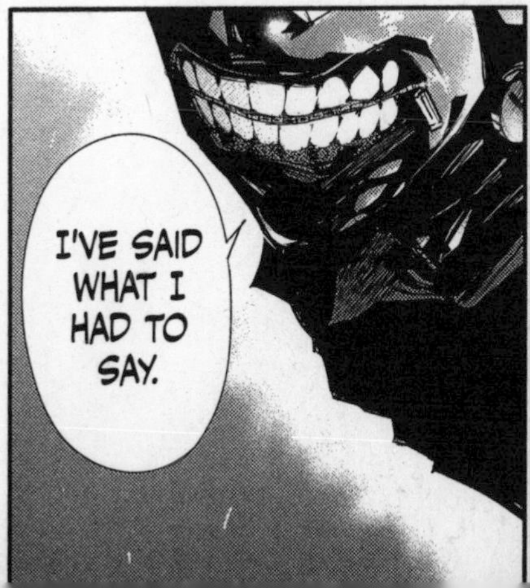
I'VE SAID WHAT I HAD TO SAY.

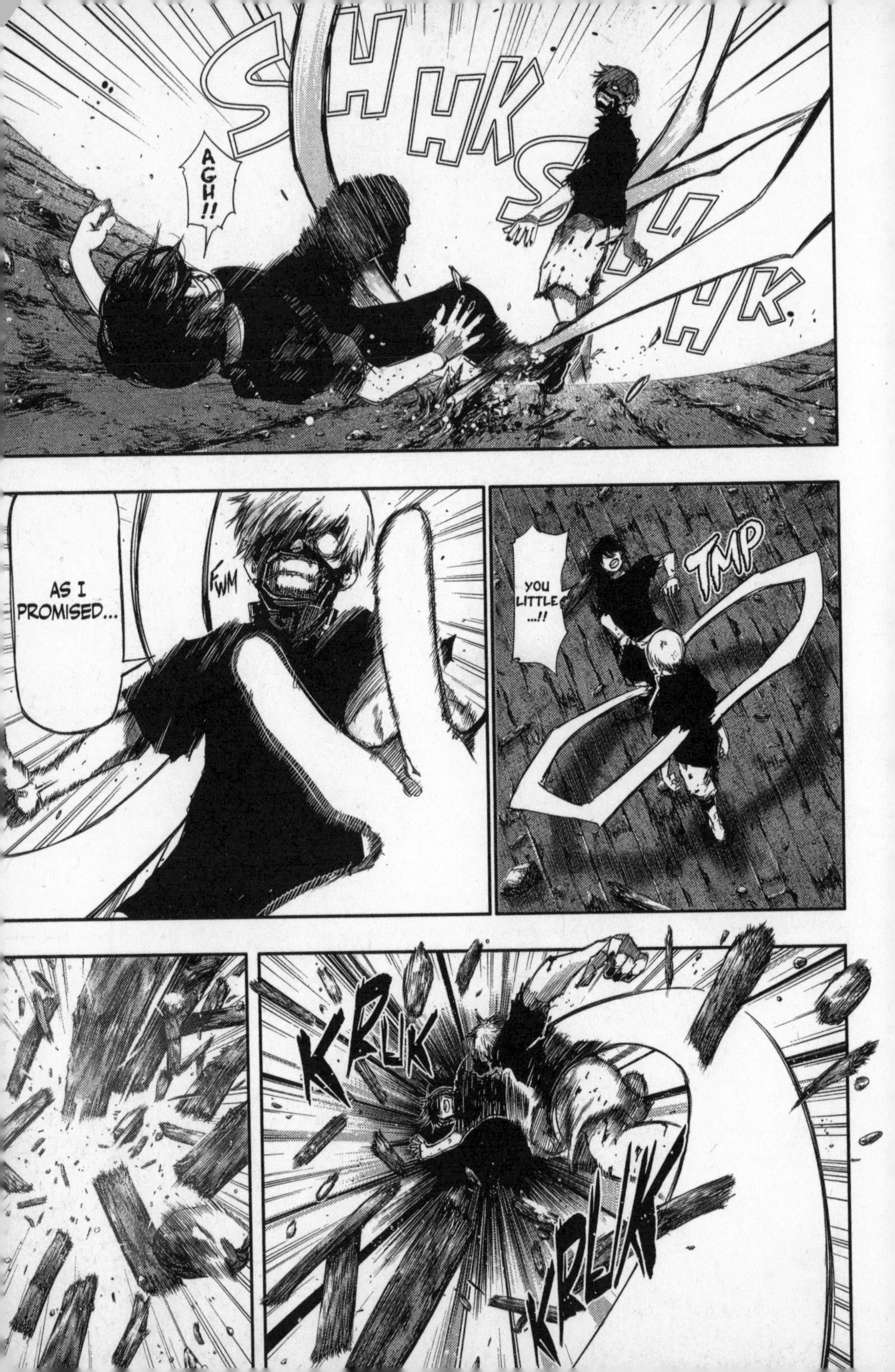
SHHK
AGH!!
SHHK
TMP
YOU LITTLE ...!!
FWM
AS I PROMISED...
KRLK
KRLK

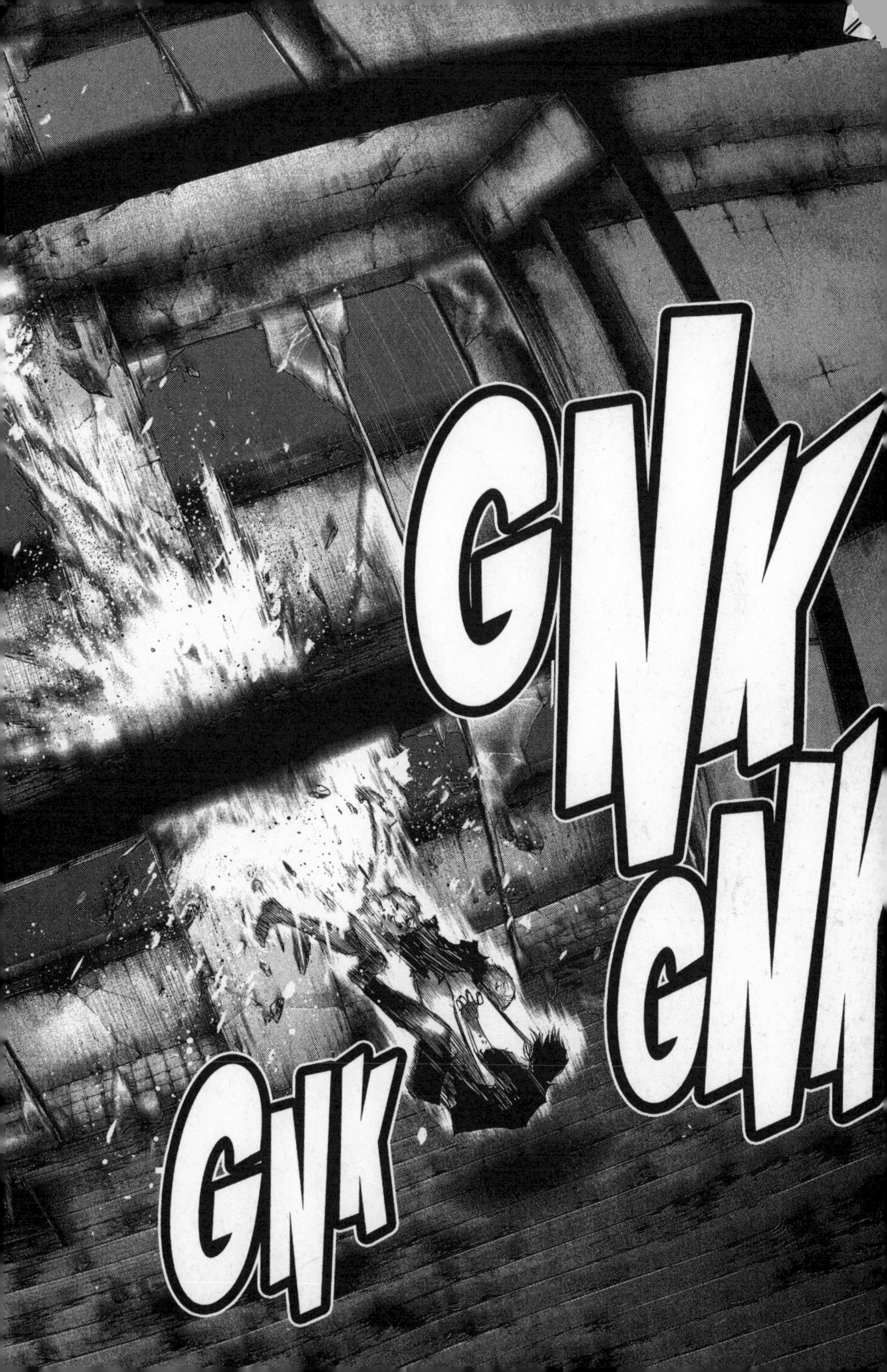
GNK
GNK
GNK

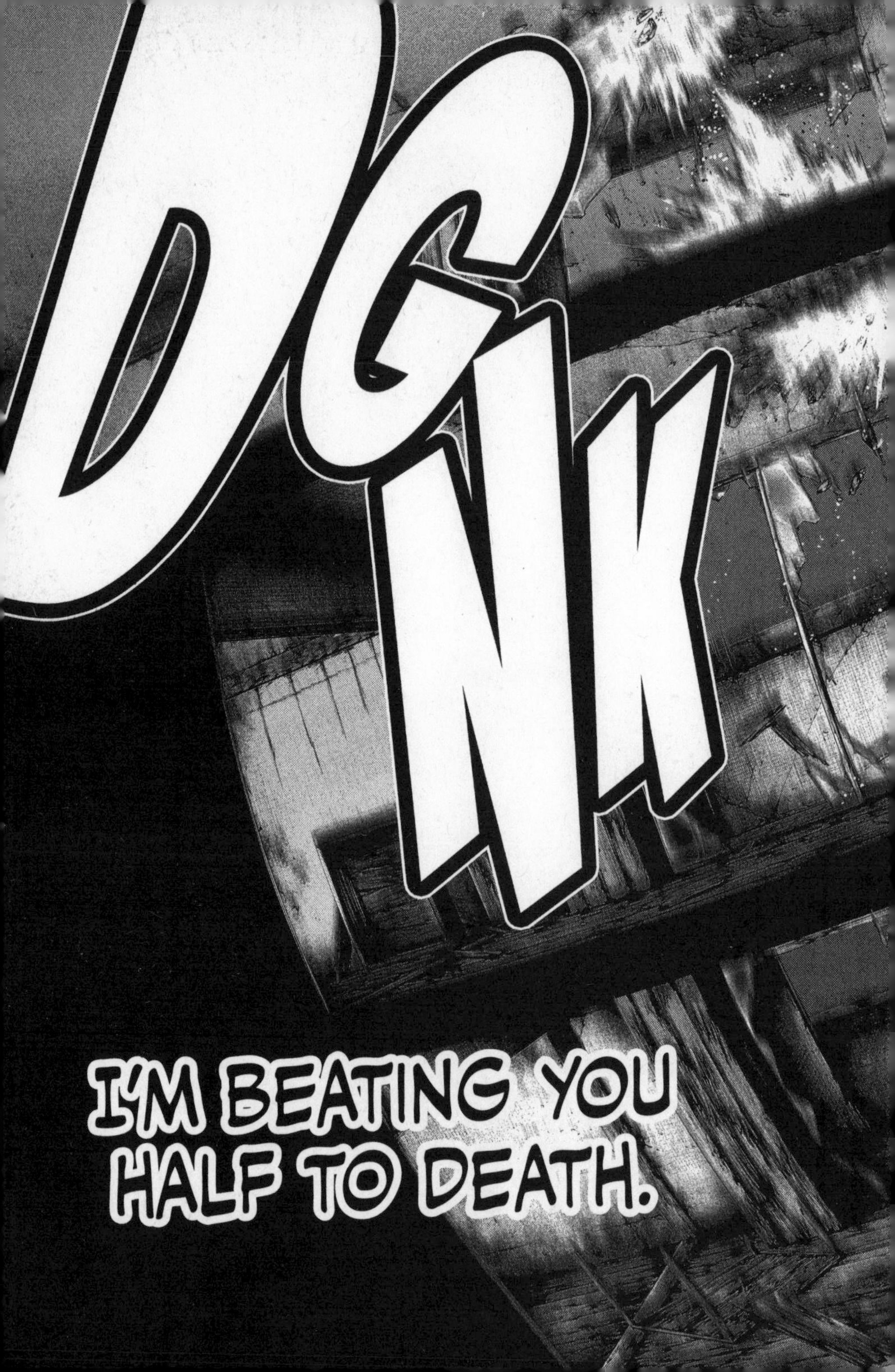
DGNK
I'M BEATING YOU HALF TO DEATH.

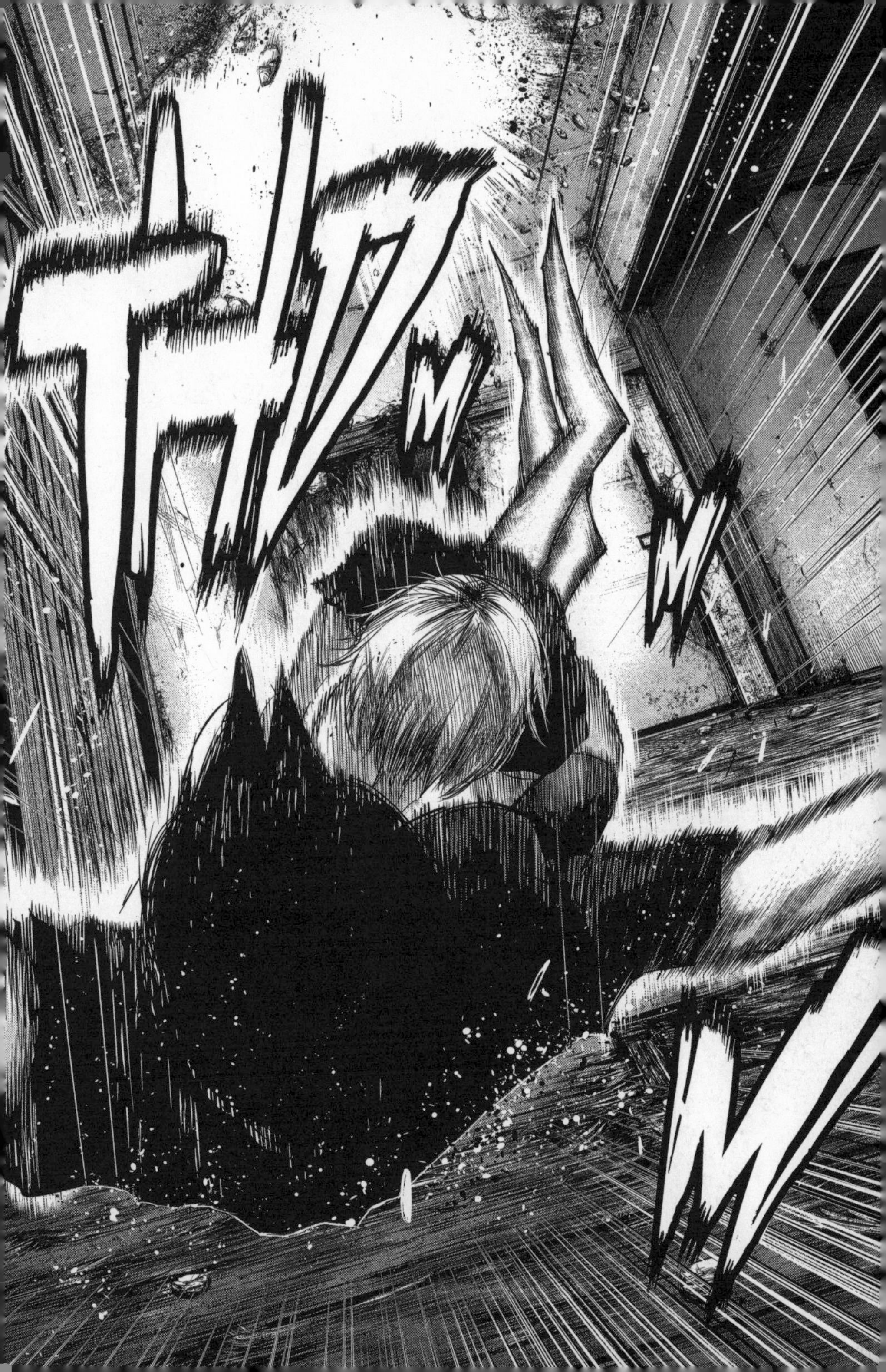
THUMMM

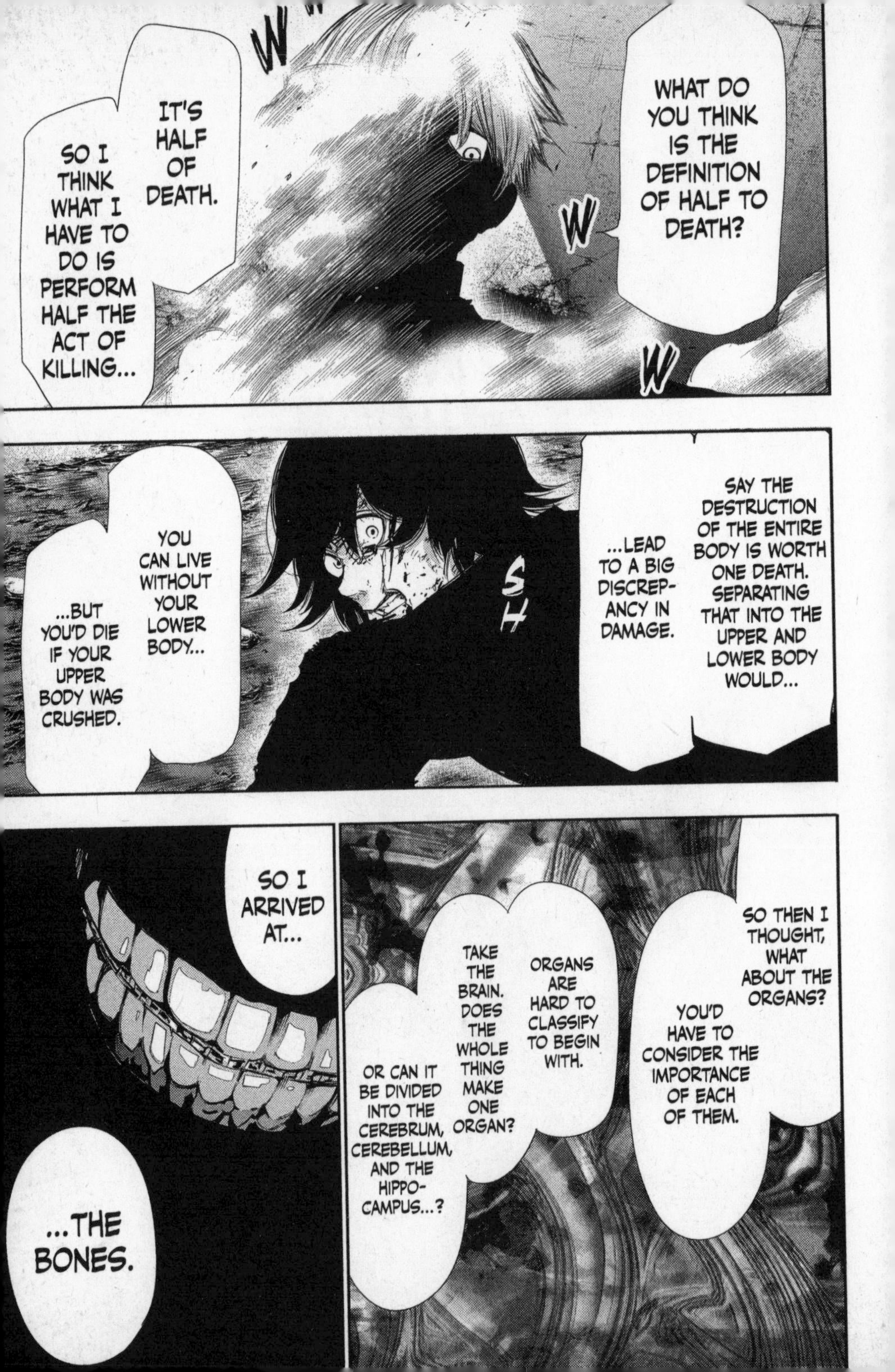
WHAT DO YOU THINK IS THE DEFINITION OF HALF TO DEATH?
W
W
W
W
IT'S HALF OF DEATH.
SO I THINK WHAT I HAVE TO DO IS PERFORM HALF THE ACT OF KILLING...
SAY THE DESTRUCTION OF THE ENTIRE BODY IS WORTH ONE DEATH. SEPARATING THAT INTO THE UPPER AND LOWER BODY WOULD...
...LEAD TO A BIG DISCREP-ANCY IN DAMAGE.
YOU CAN LIVE WITHOUT YOUR LOWER BODY...
...BUT YOU'D DIE IF YOUR UPPER BODY WAS CRUSHED.
SO THEN I THOUGHT, WHAT ABOUT THE ORGANS?
YOU'D HAVE TO CONSIDER THE IMPORTANCE OF EACH OF THEM.
ORGANS ARE HARD TO CLASSIFY TO BEGIN WITH.
TAKE THE BRAIN. DOES THE WHOLE THING MAKE ONE ORGAN?
OR CAN IT BE DIVIDED INTO THE CEREBRUM, CEREBELLUM, AND THE HIPPO-CAMPUS...?
SO I ARRIVED AT...
...THE BONES.

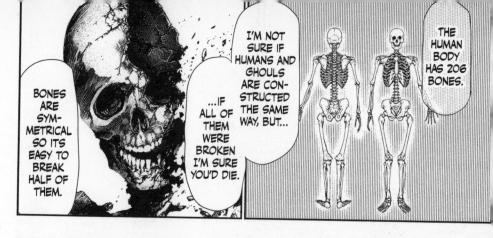

THE HUMAN BODY HAS 206 BONES.

I'M NOT SURE IF HUMANS AND GHOULS ARE CONSTRUCTED THE SAME WAY, BUT...

...IF ALL OF THEM WERE BROKEN I'M SURE YOU'D DIE.

BONES ARE SYMMETRICAL SO ITS EASY TO BREAK HALF OF THEM.

SNAP!

AND SO I'M GOING TO BREAK...

...103 OF YOUR BONES.

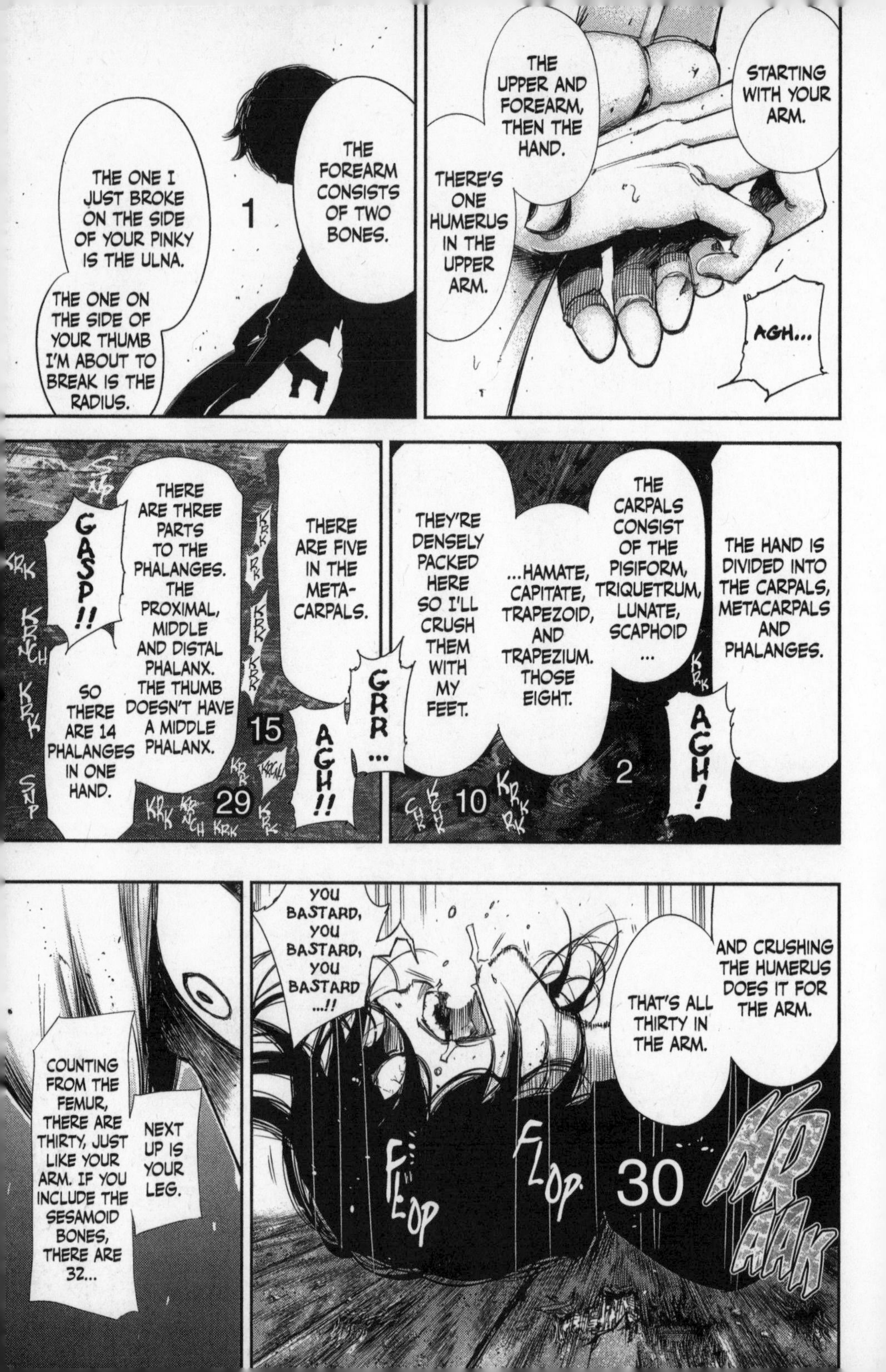
STARTING WITH YOUR ARM.
AGH...
THE UPPER AND FOREARM, THEN THE HAND.
THERE'S ONE HUMERUS IN THE UPPER ARM.
THE FOREARM CONSISTS OF TWO BONES.
1
THE ONE I JUST BROKE ON THE SIDE OF YOUR PINKY IS THE ULNA.
THE ONE ON THE SIDE OF YOUR THUMB I'M ABOUT TO BREAK IS THE RADIUS.
THE HAND IS DIVIDED INTO THE CARPALS, METACARPALS AND PHALANGES.
THE CARPALS CONSIST OF THE PISIFORM, TRIQUETRUM, LUNATE, SCAPHOID ...
KRK
AGH!
...HAMATE, CAPITATE, TRAPEZOID, AND TRAPEZIUM. THOSE EIGHT.
THEY'RE DENSELY PACKED HERE SO I'LL CRUSH THEM WITH MY FEET.
2
KRK
10
THERE ARE FIVE IN THE METACARPALS.
GRR...
AGH!!
THERE ARE THREE PARTS TO THE PHALANGES. THE PROXIMAL, MIDDLE AND DISTAL PHALANX. THE THUMB DOESN'T HAVE A MIDDLE PHALANX.
15
29
GASP!!
SO THERE ARE 14 PHALANGES IN ONE HAND.
KRK
KRNCH
AND CRUSHING THE HUMERUS DOES IT FOR THE ARM.
THAT'S ALL THIRTY IN THE ARM.
YOU BASTARD, YOU BASTARD, YOU BASTARD ...!!
30
FLOP
FLOP
NEXT UP IS YOUR LEG.
COUNTING FROM THE FEMUR, THERE ARE THIRTY, JUST LIKE YOUR ARM. IF YOU INCLUDE THE SESAMOID BONES, THERE ARE 32...

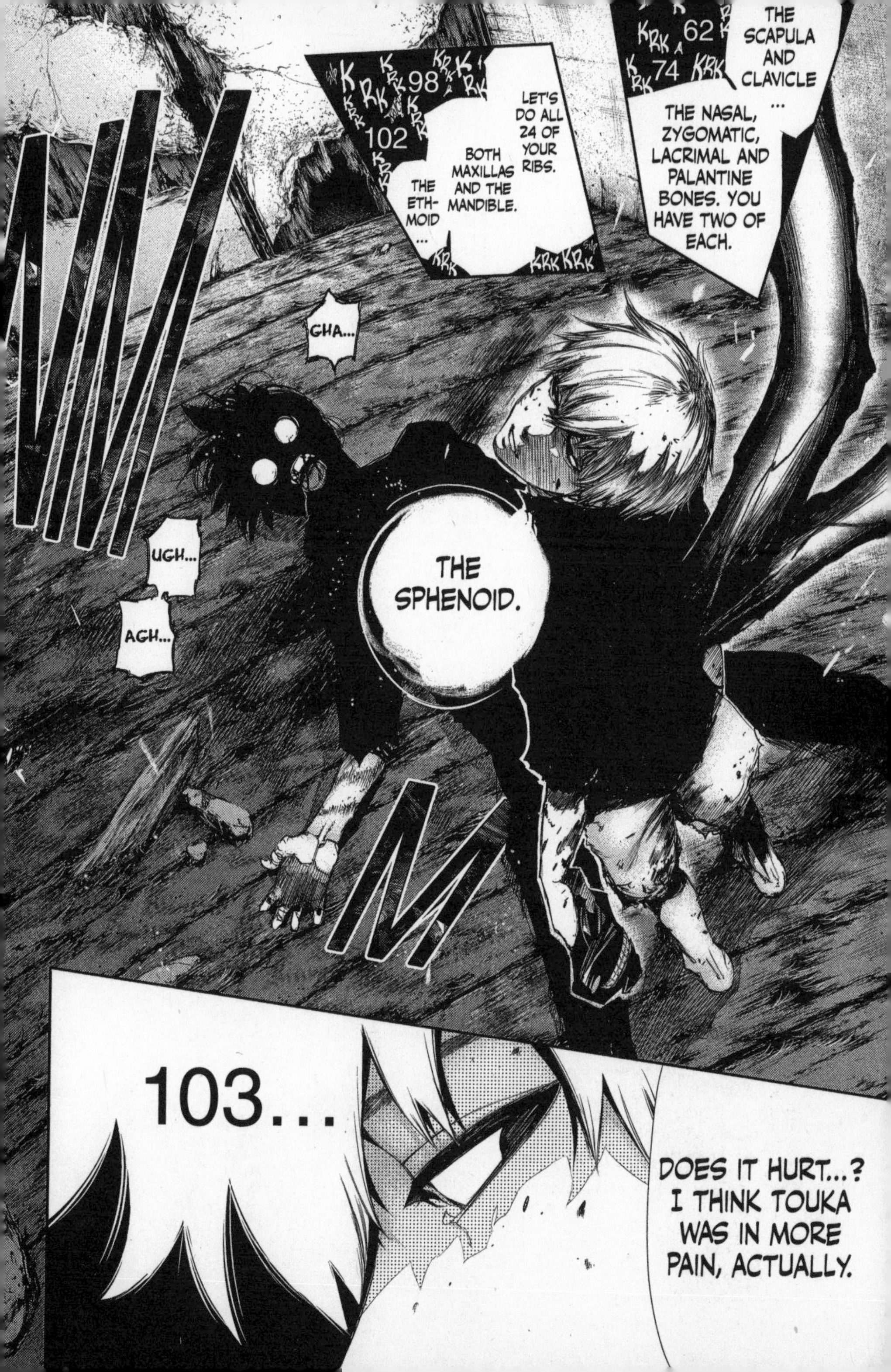

THE SCAPULA AND CLAVICLE ...
62
74
THE NASAL, ZYGOMATIC, LACRIMAL AND PALANTINE BONES. YOU HAVE TWO OF EACH.
LET'S DO ALL 24 OF YOUR RIBS.
98
102
BOTH MAXILLAS AND THE MANDIBLE.
THE ETH-MOID ...
KRK KRK
GHA...
THE SPHENOID.
UGH...
AGH...
DOES IT HURT...? I THINK TOUKA WAS IN MORE PAIN, ACTUALLY.
103...

東京喰種
トーキョーグール
Tokyo
Ghoul

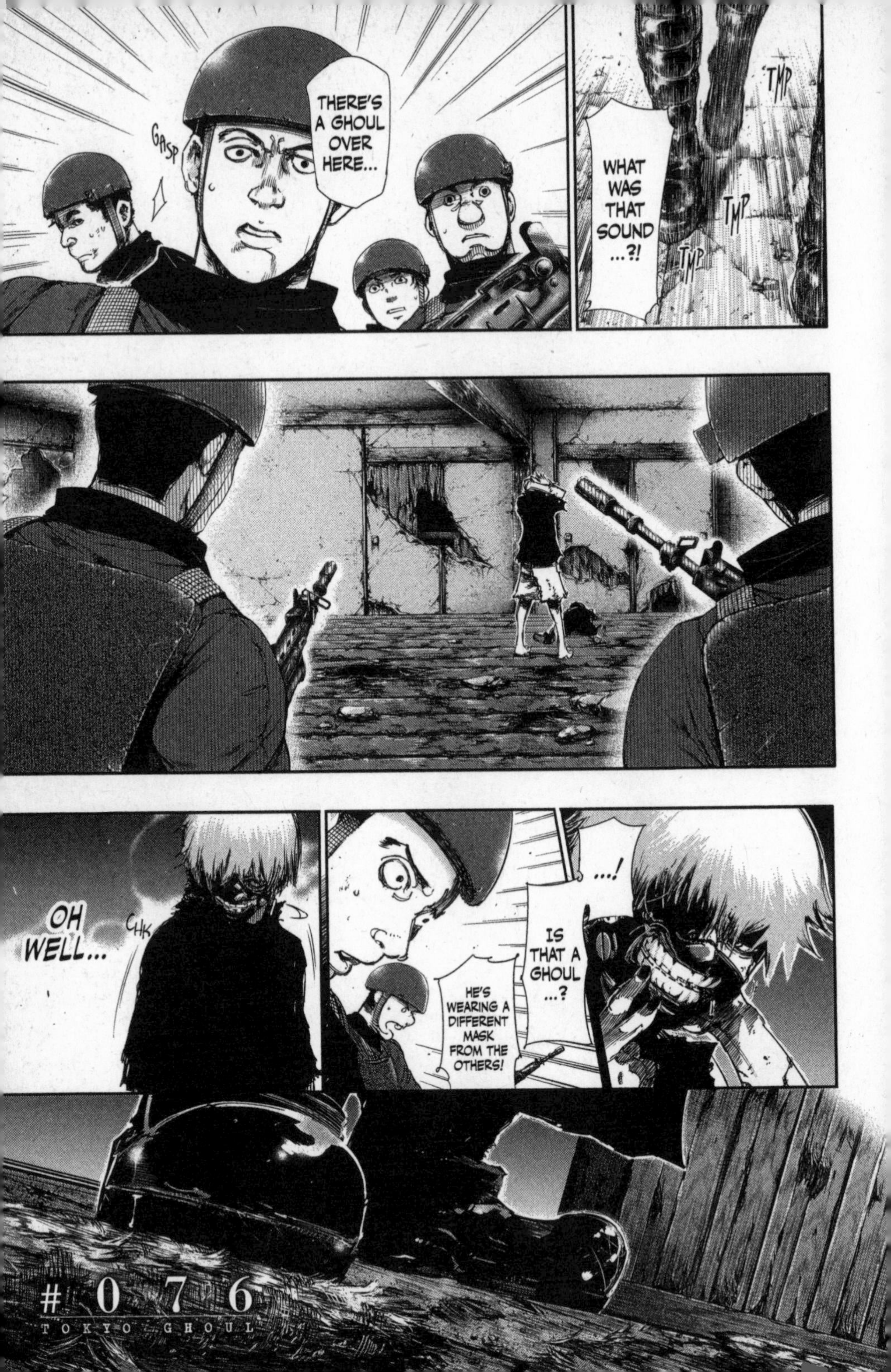
TMP
TMP
TMP
WHAT WAS THAT SOUND ...?!
GASP
THERE'S A GHOUL OVER HERE...
...!
IS THAT A GHOUL ...?
HE'S WEARING A DIFFERENT MASK FROM THE OTHERS!
CHK
OH WELL...
#076
TOKYO GHOUL

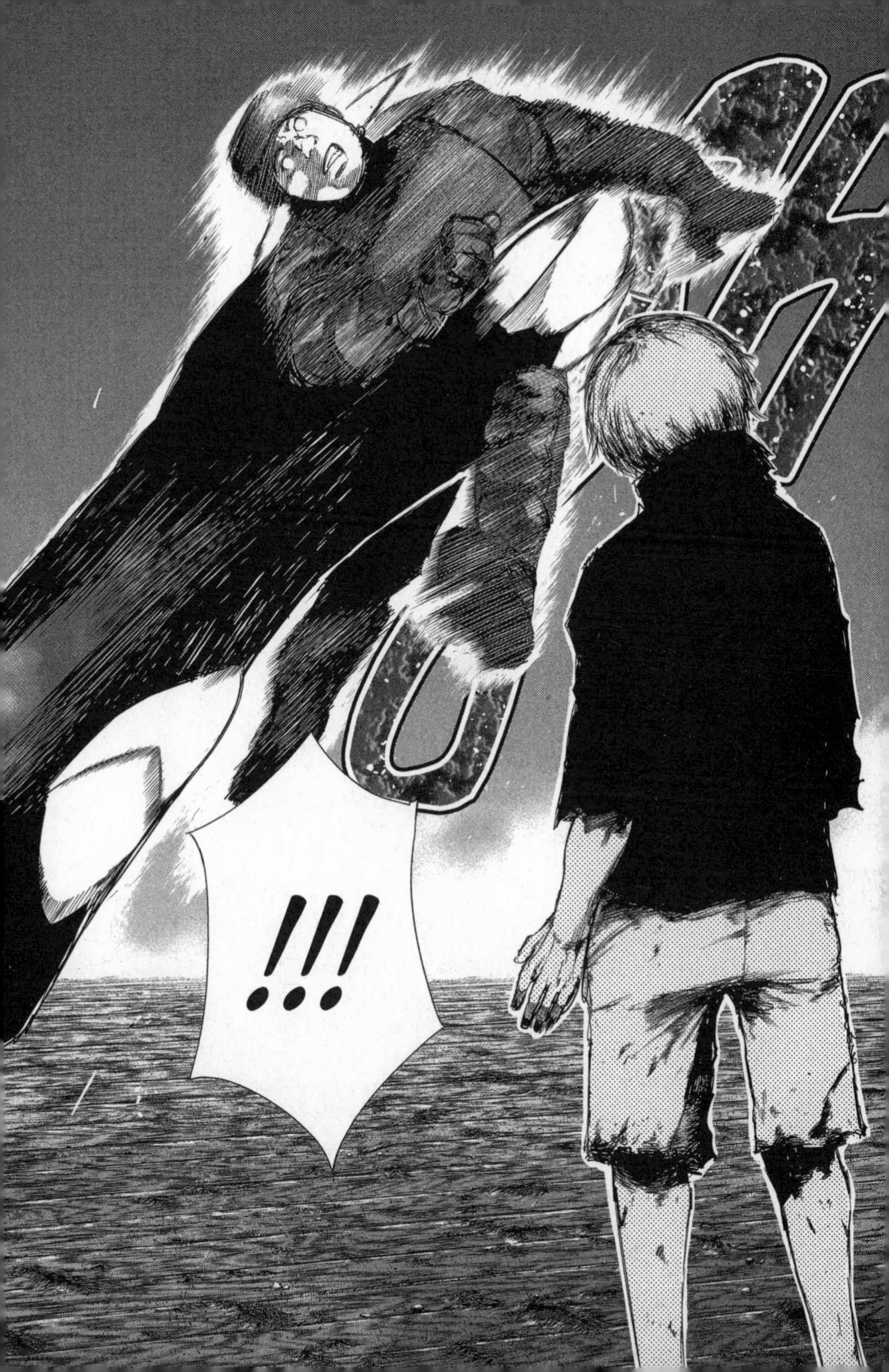
!!!

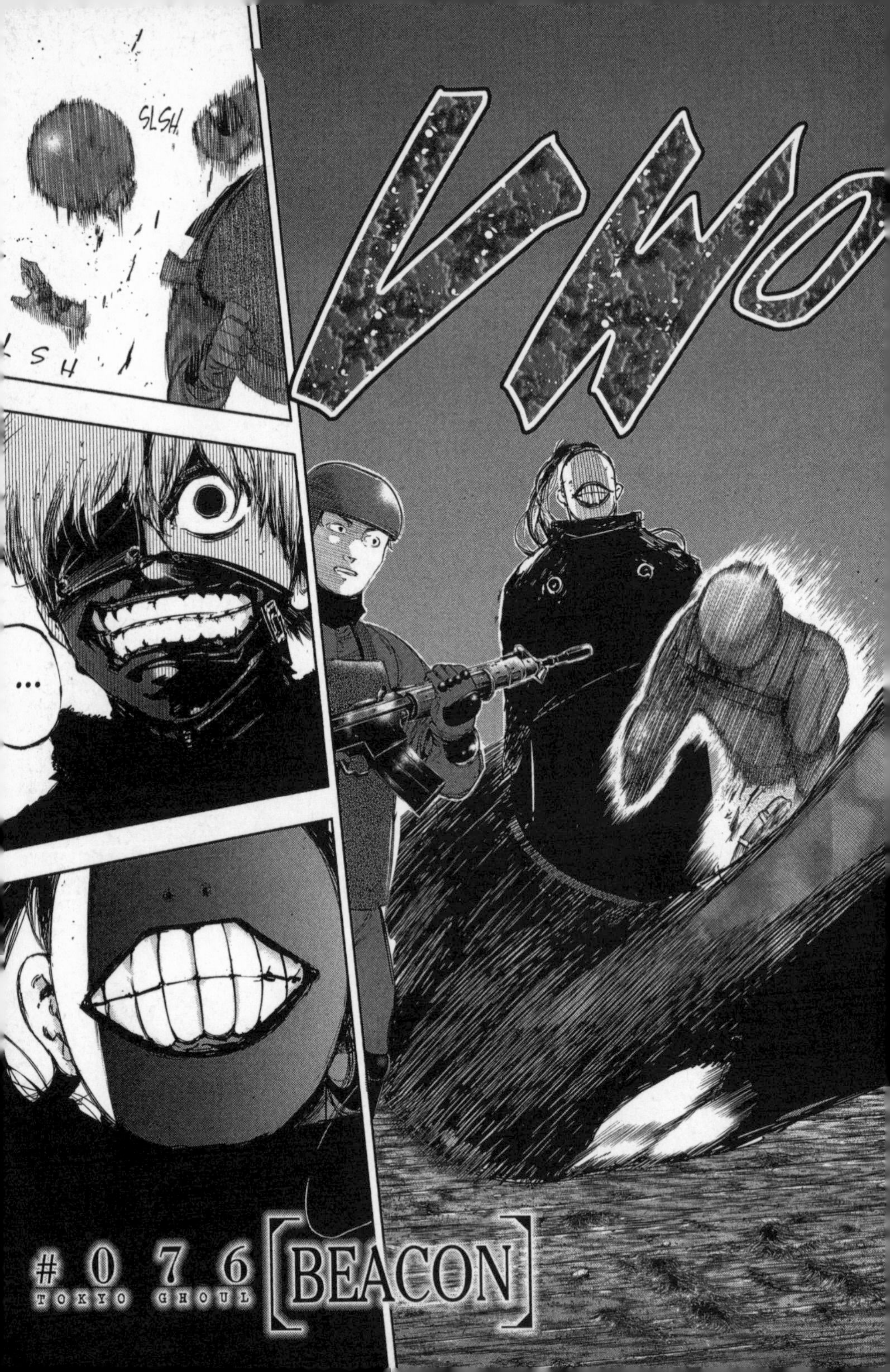
VWO
SLSH
LSH
...
#076 [BEACON]
TOKYO GHOUL

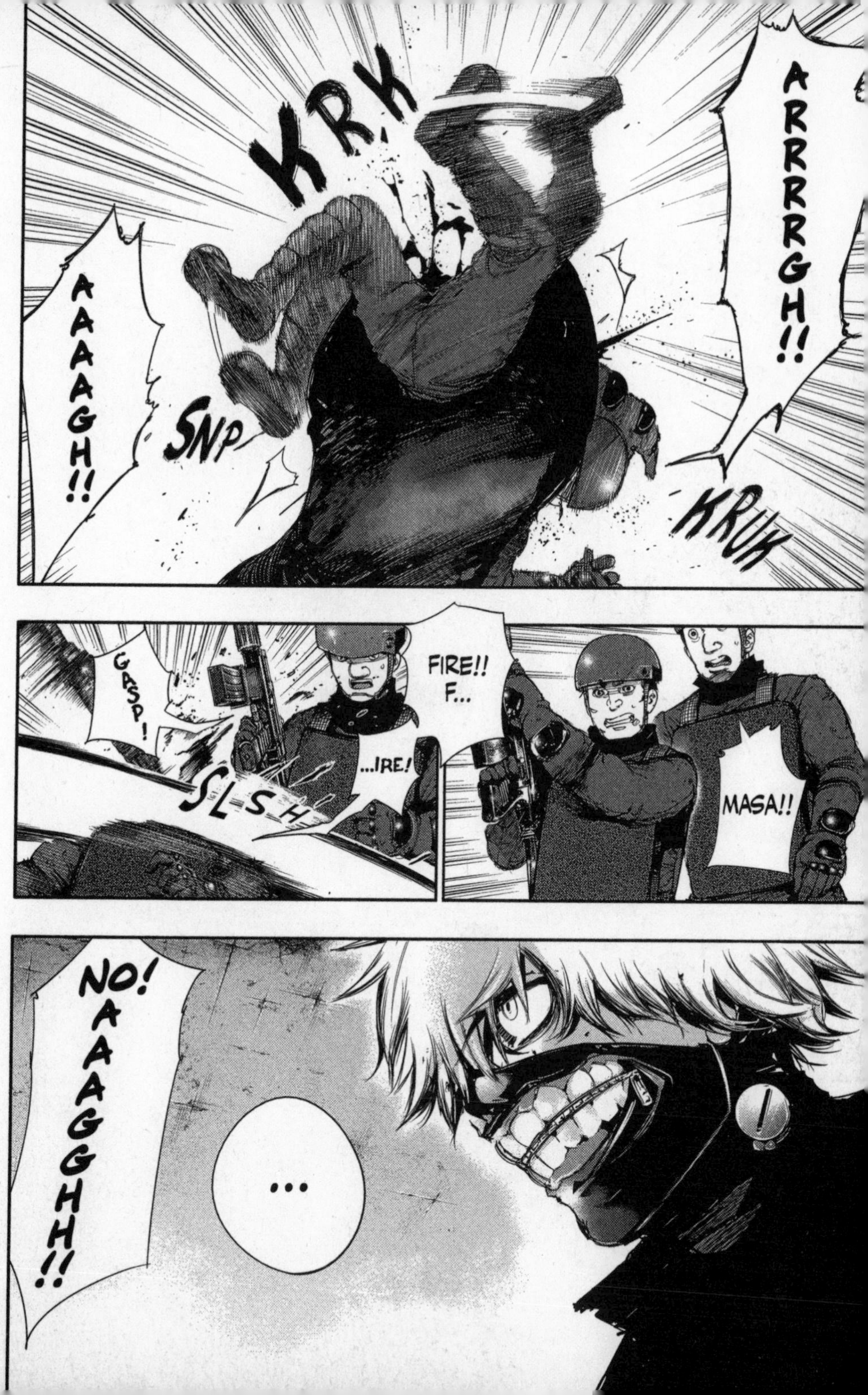
ARRRRGH!!
KRK
KRUK
SNP
AAAAAGH!!
MASA!!
FIRE!! F...
...IRE!
SLSH
GASP!
...
NO! AAAAGGHH!!

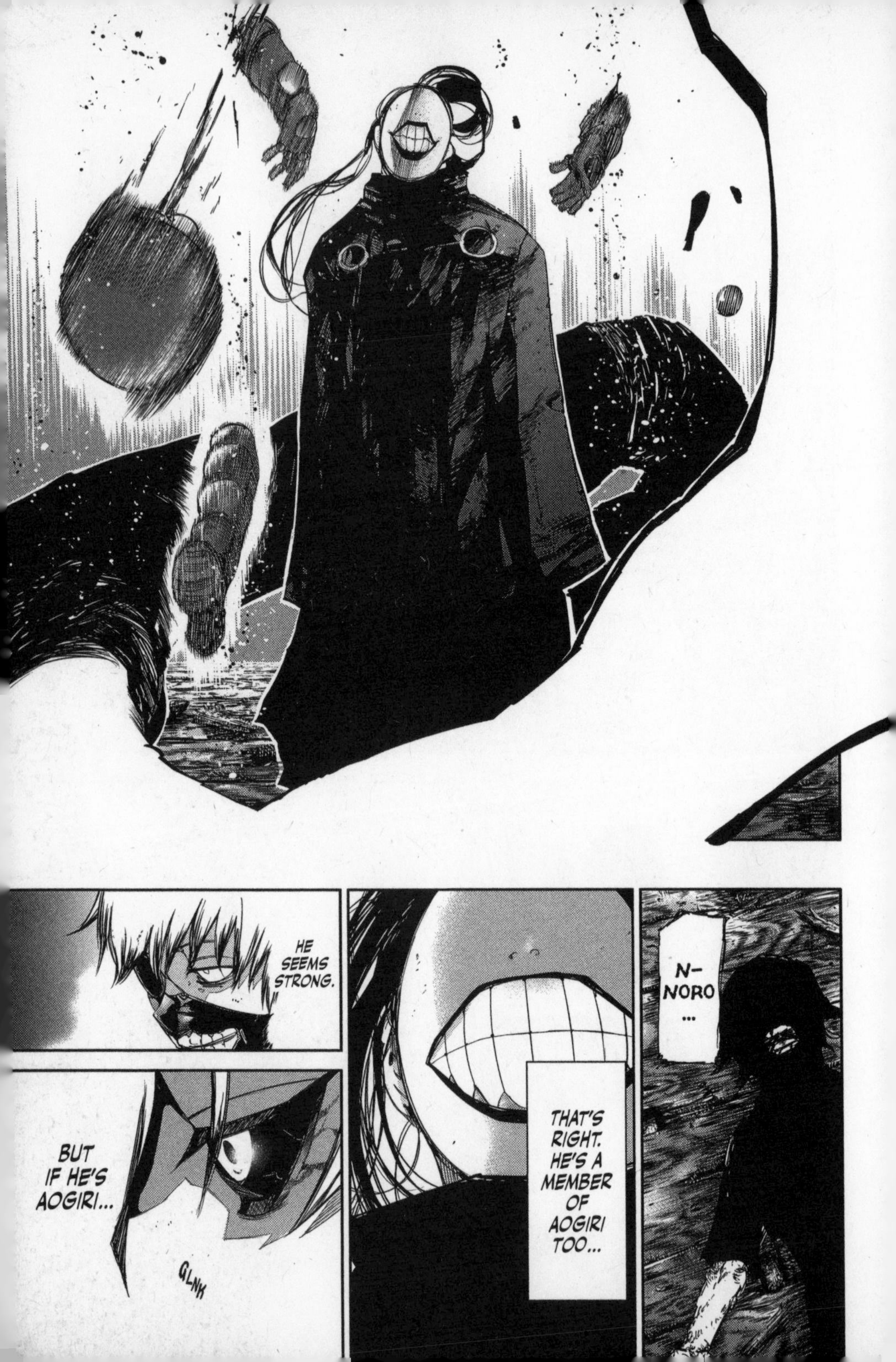

N-NORO...
THAT'S RIGHT. HE'S A MEMBER OF AOGIRI TOO...
HE SEEMS STRONG.
BUT IF HE'S AOGIRI...
GLNK

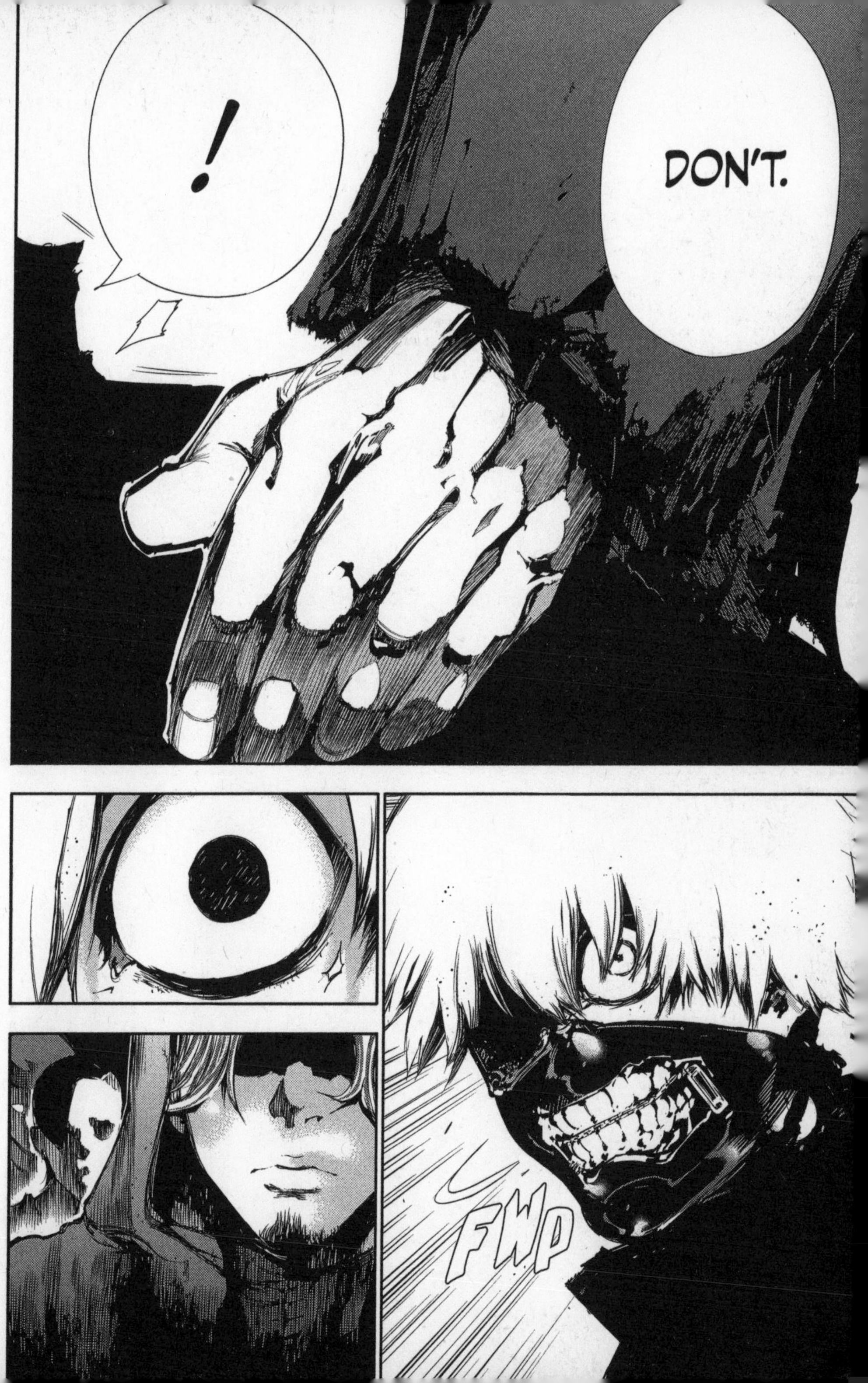
DON'T.
!
FWP

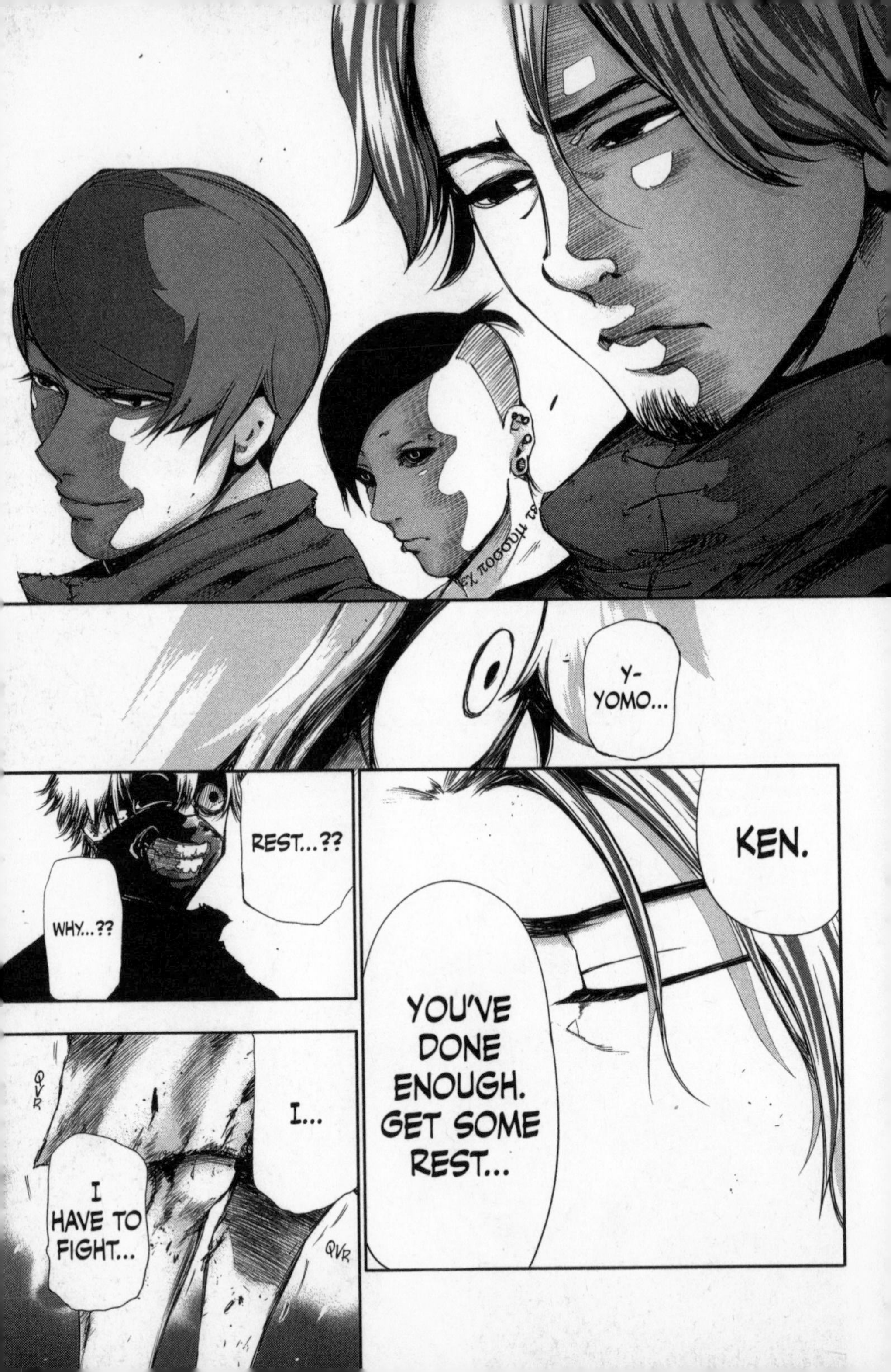
Y-
YOMO...
KEN.
YOU'VE DONE ENOUGH. GET SOME REST...
REST...??
WHY...??
I...
I HAVE TO FIGHT...
QVR
QVR

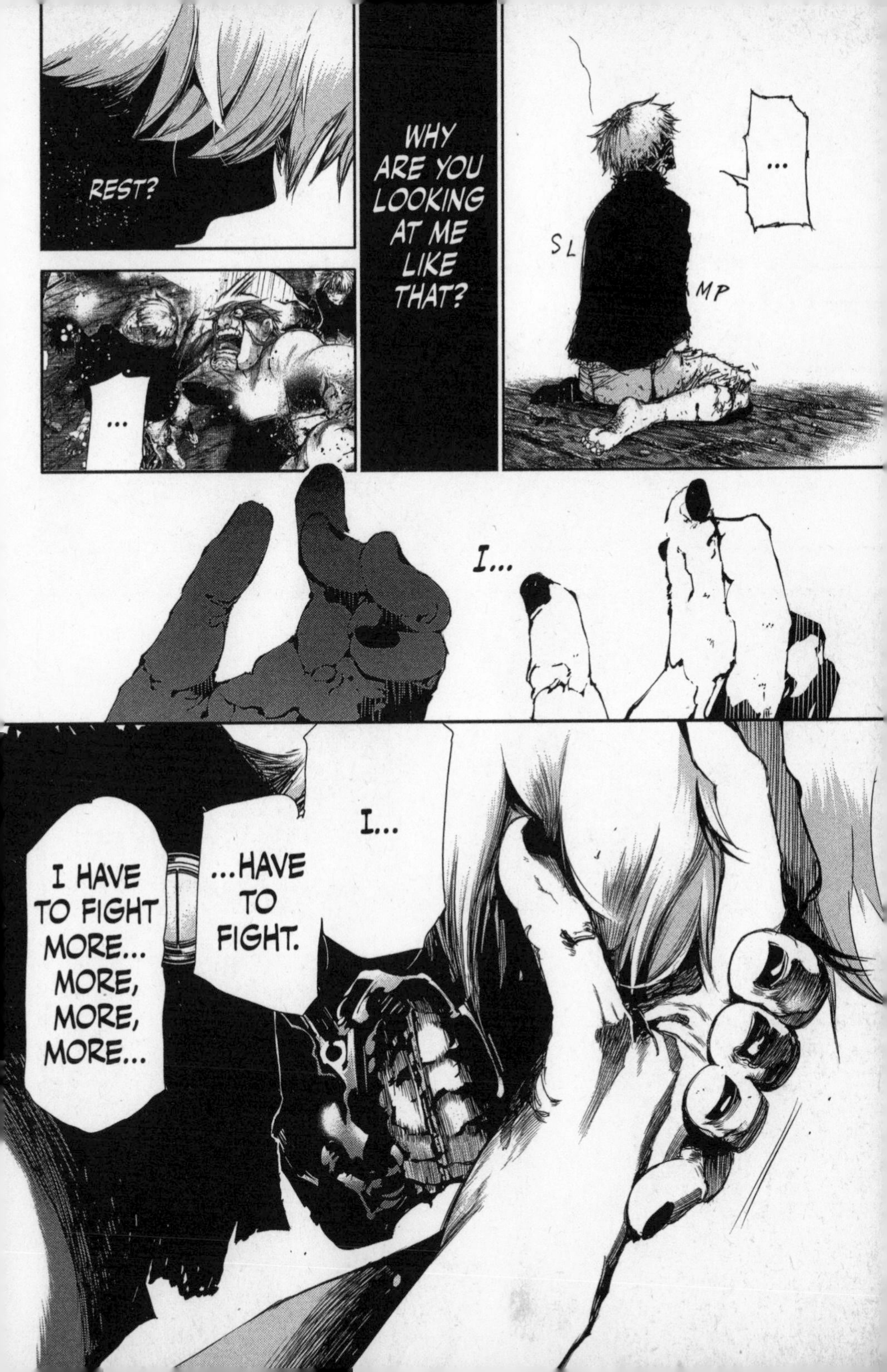
...
SL
MP
WHY ARE YOU LOOKING AT ME LIKE THAT?
REST?
...
I...
I...
...HAVE TO FIGHT.
I HAVE TO FIGHT MORE... MORE, MORE, MORE...

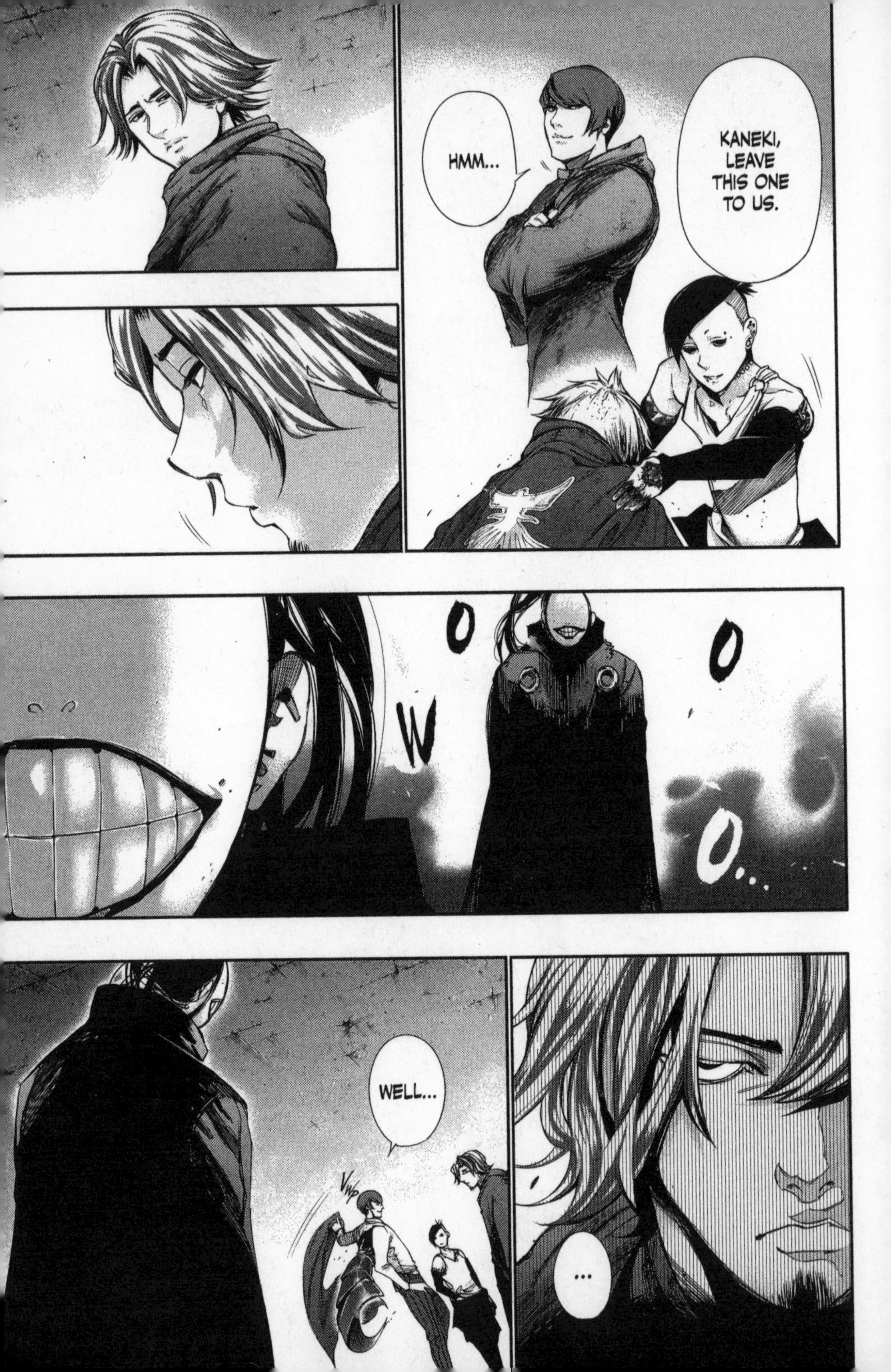
KANEKI, LEAVE THIS ONE TO US.
HMM...
WOOO...
...
WELL...
VWP

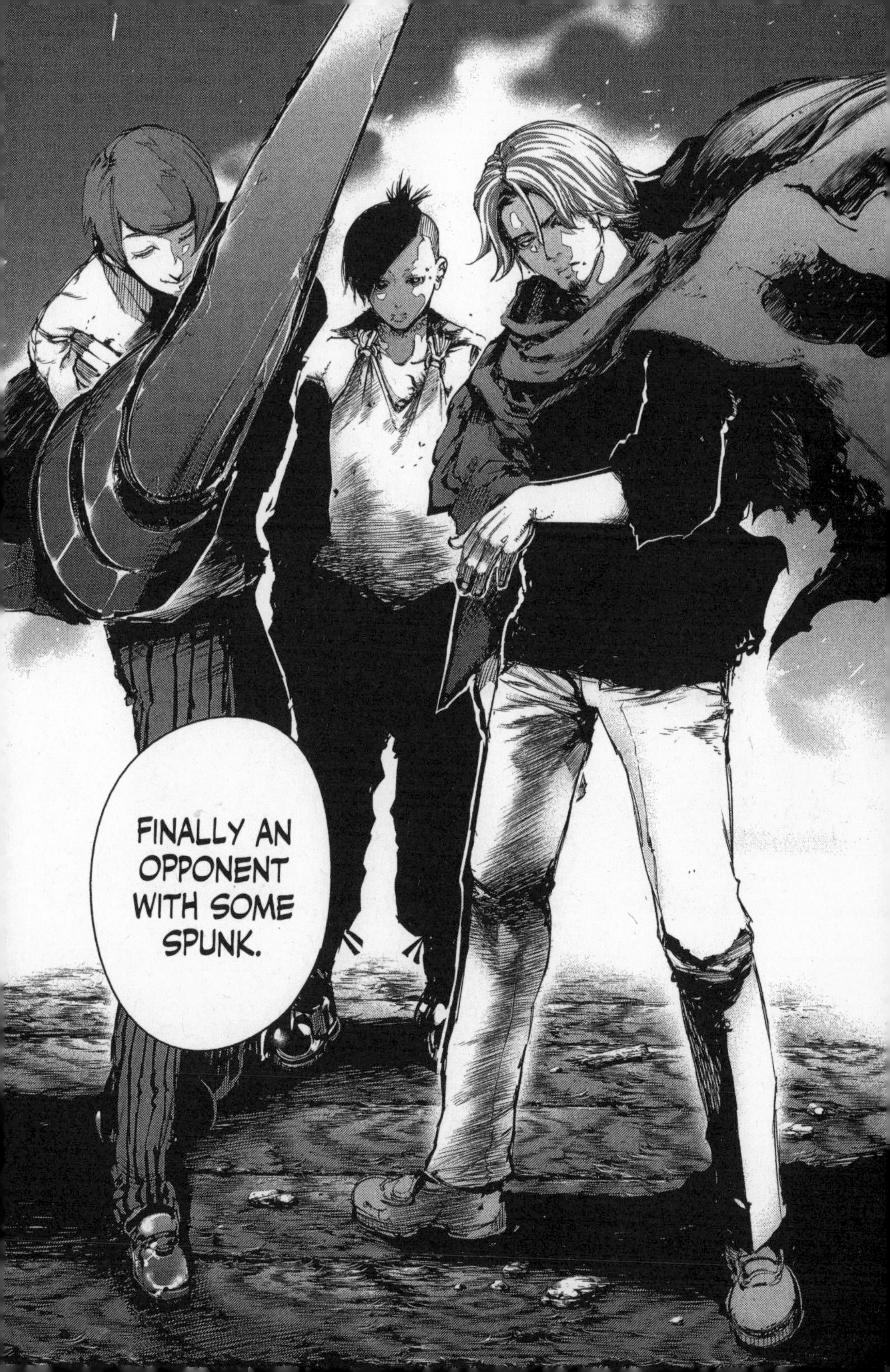
FINALLY AN OPPONENT WITH SOME SPUNK.

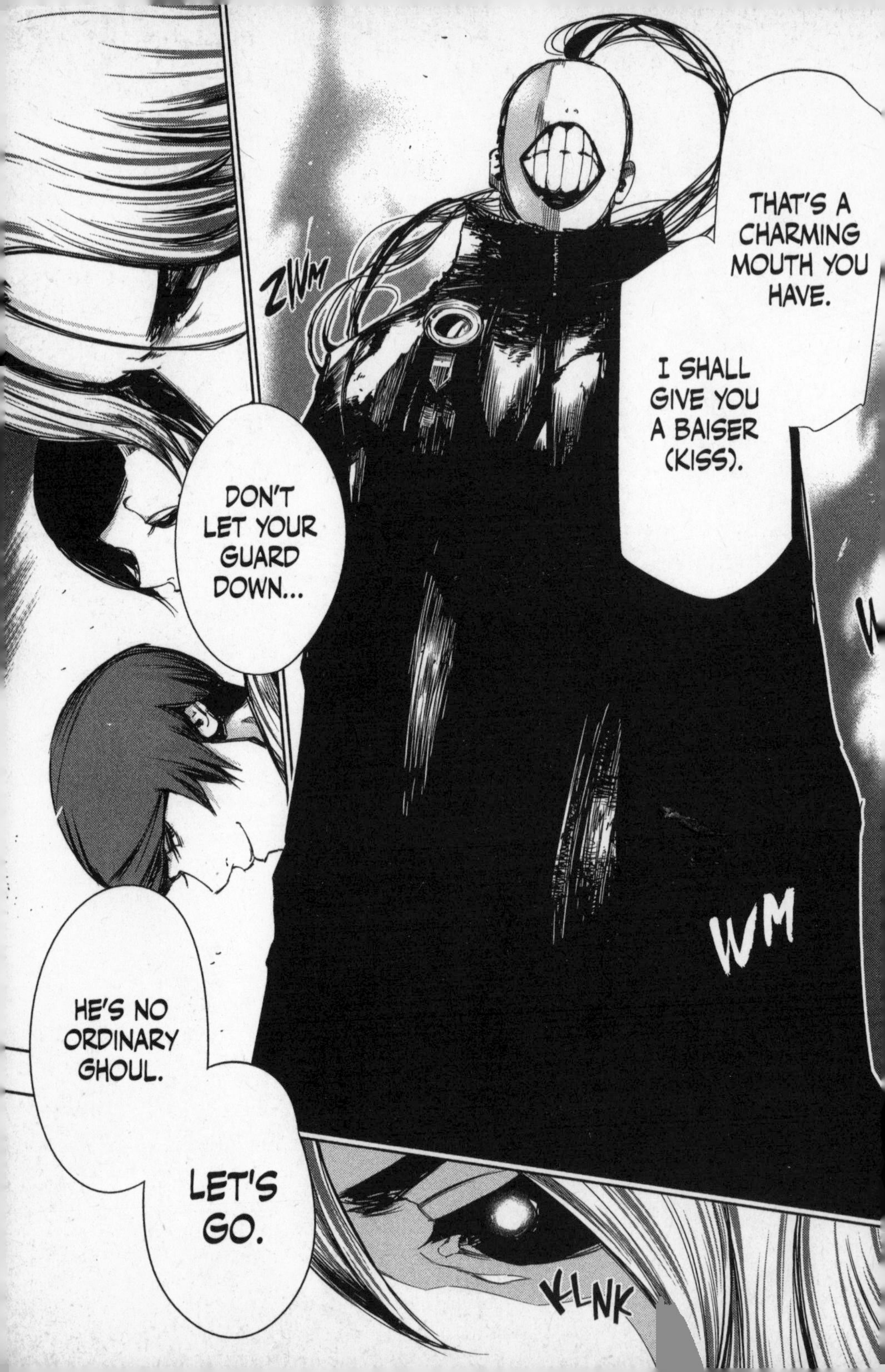
THAT'S A CHARMING MOUTH YOU HAVE.
I SHALL GIVE YOU A BAISER (KISS).
ZWM
WM
DON'T LET YOUR GUARD DOWN...
HE'S NO ORDINARY GHOUL.
LET'S GO.
KLNK

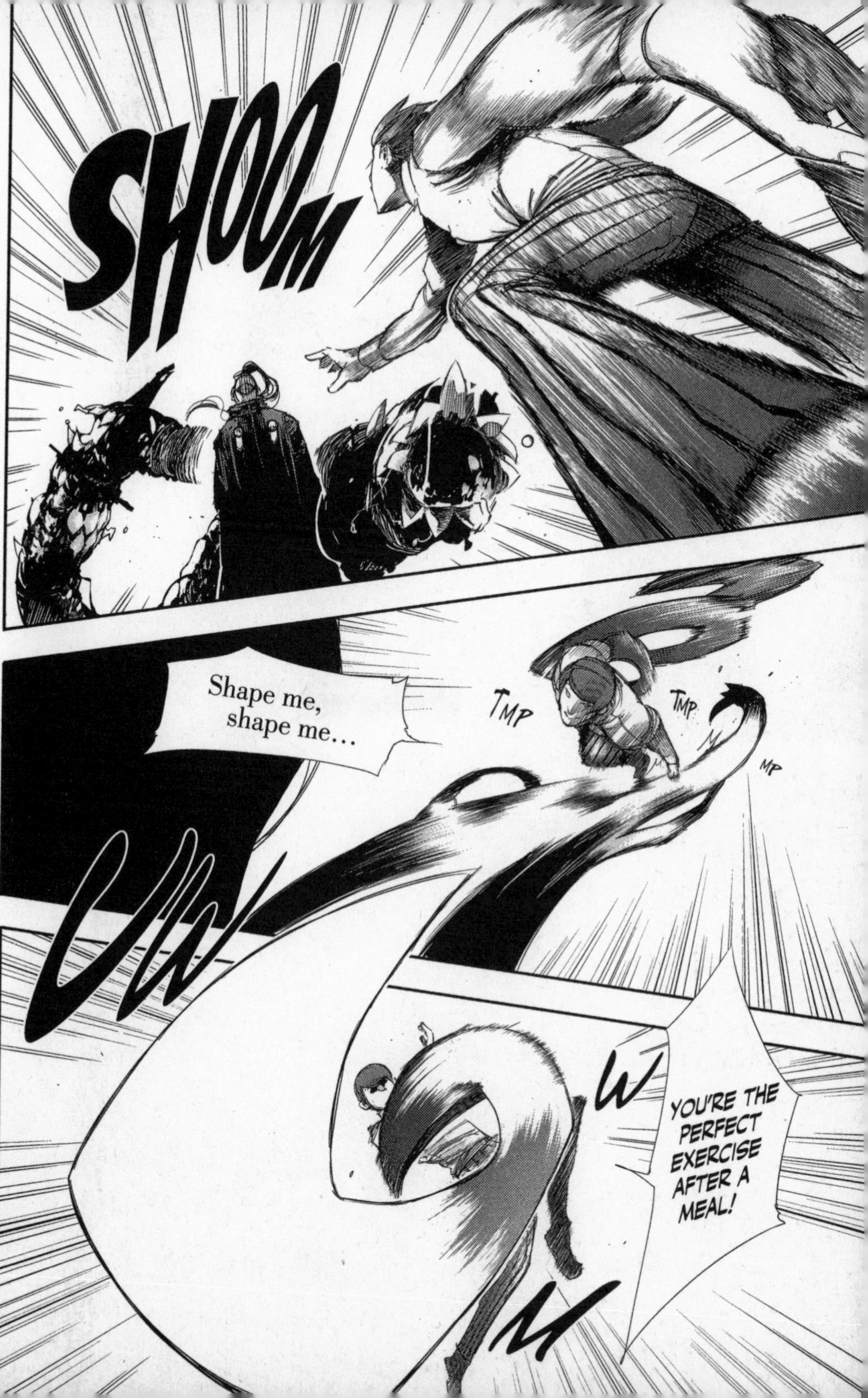
SHOOM
TMP
TMP
Shape me, shape me…
MP
YOU'RE THE PERFECT EXERCISE AFTER A MEAL!
W
M

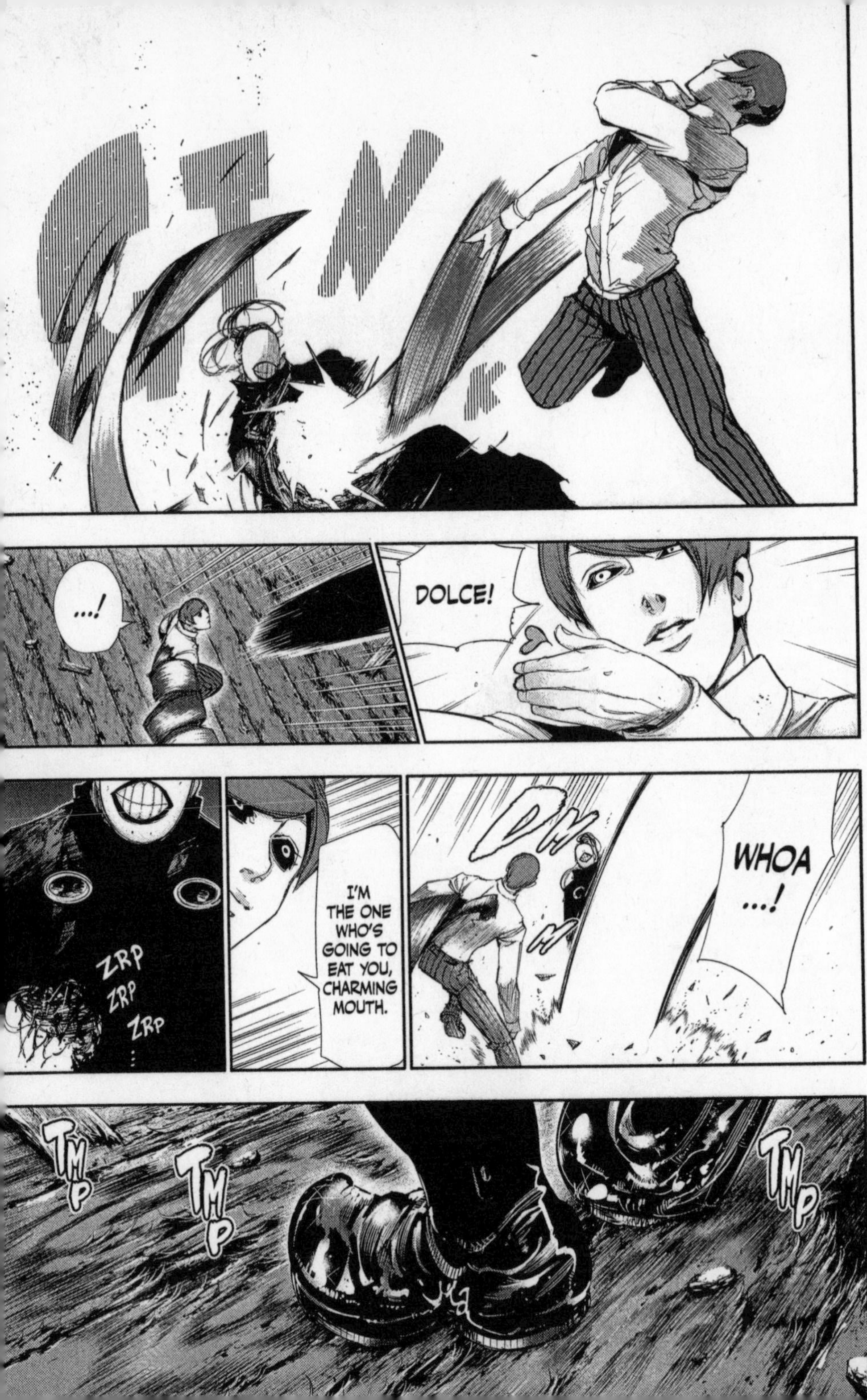
DOLCE!
...!
WHOA ...!
I'M THE ONE WHO'S GOING TO EAT YOU, CHARMING MOUTH.
ZRP ZRP ZRP ...
TMP
TMP
TMP

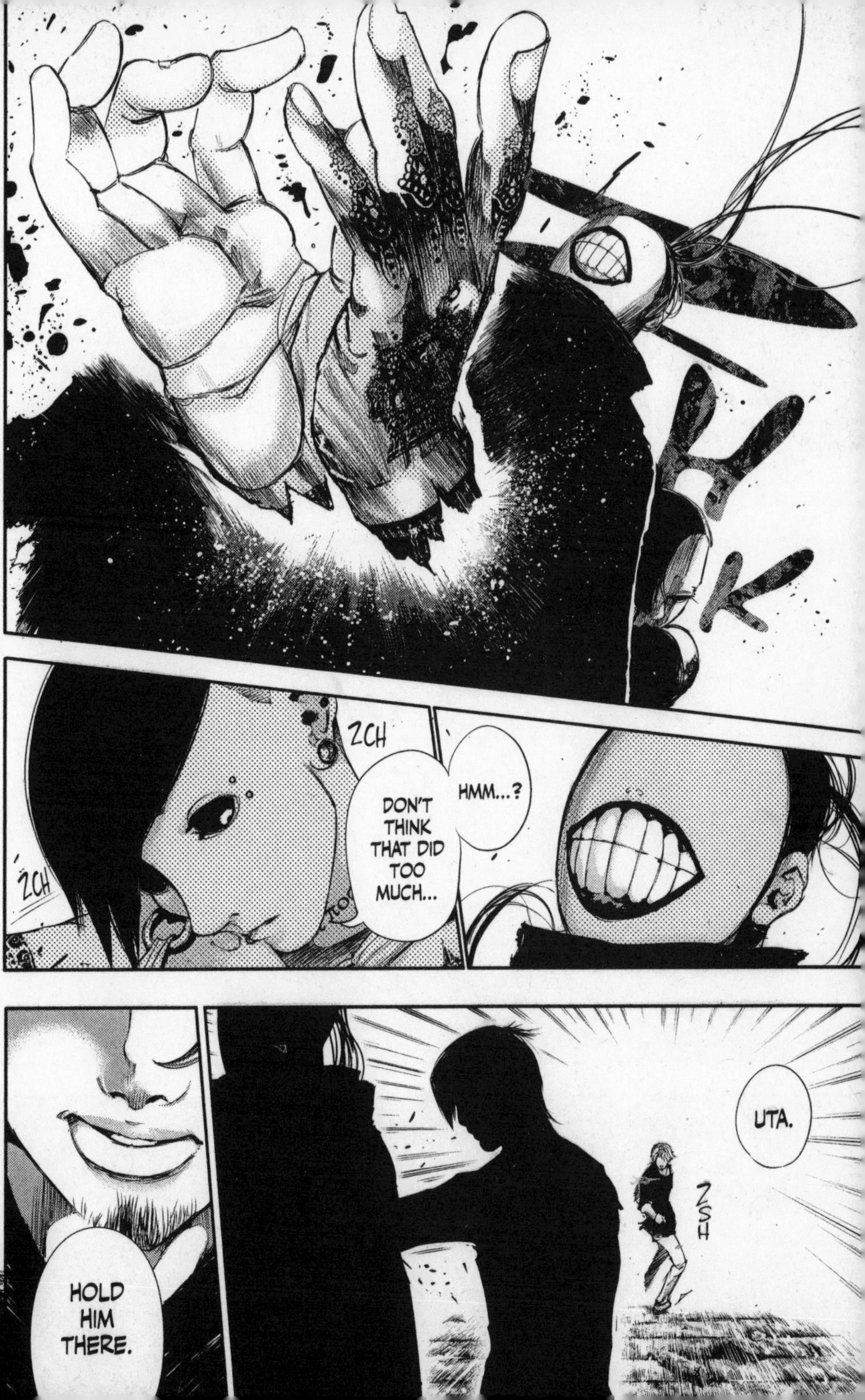
HMM...?
DON'T THINK THAT DID TOO MUCH...
ZCH
ZCH
UTA.
ZSH
HOLD HIM THERE.

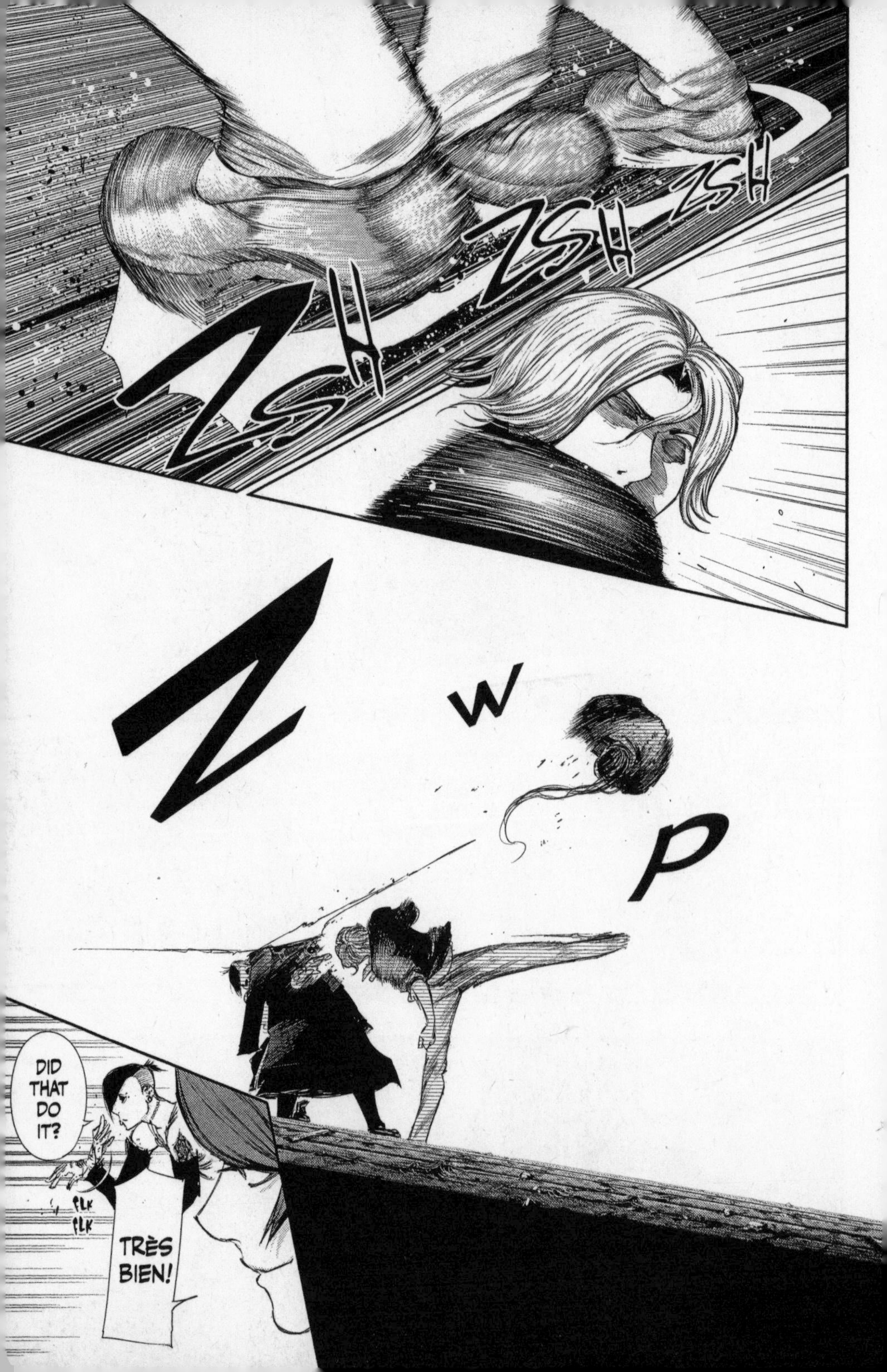
ZSH ZSH ZSH
ZWP
DID THAT DO IT?
FLK FLK
TRÈS BIEN!

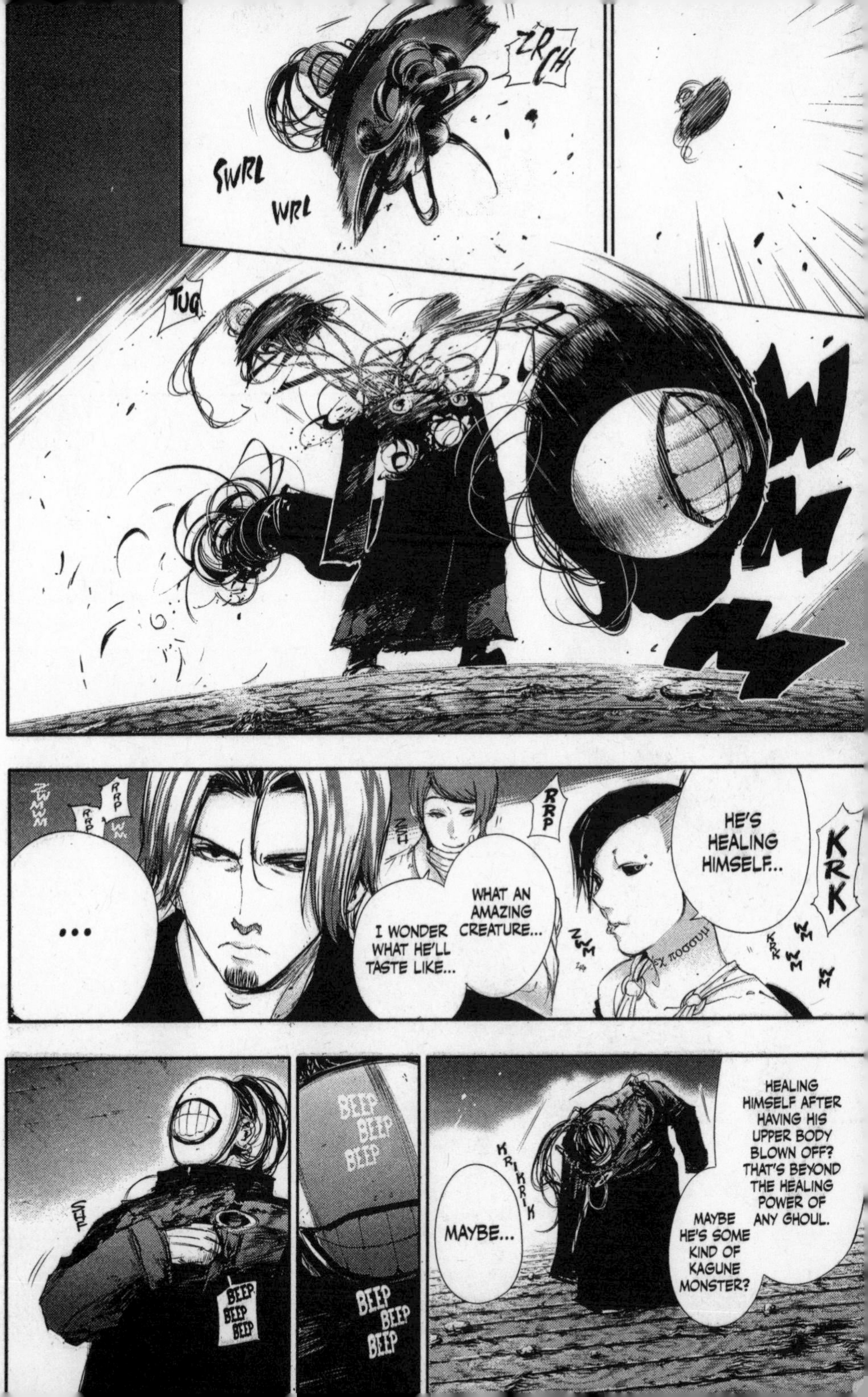
ZRCH
SWRL
WRL
TUG
WMM
KRK
HE'S HEALING HIMSELF...
KRK
WM
WM
WM
RRP
WHAT AN AMAZING CREATURE...
I WONDER WHAT HE'LL TASTE LIKE...
RRP
RRP
...
HEALING HIMSELF AFTER HAVING HIS UPPER BODY BLOWN OFF? THAT'S BEYOND THE HEALING POWER OF ANY GHOUL.
MAYBE HE'S SOME KIND OF KAGUNE MONSTER?
KRIKRIK
MAYBE...
BEEP BEEP BEEP
BEEP BEEP BEEP
BEEP BEEP BEEP

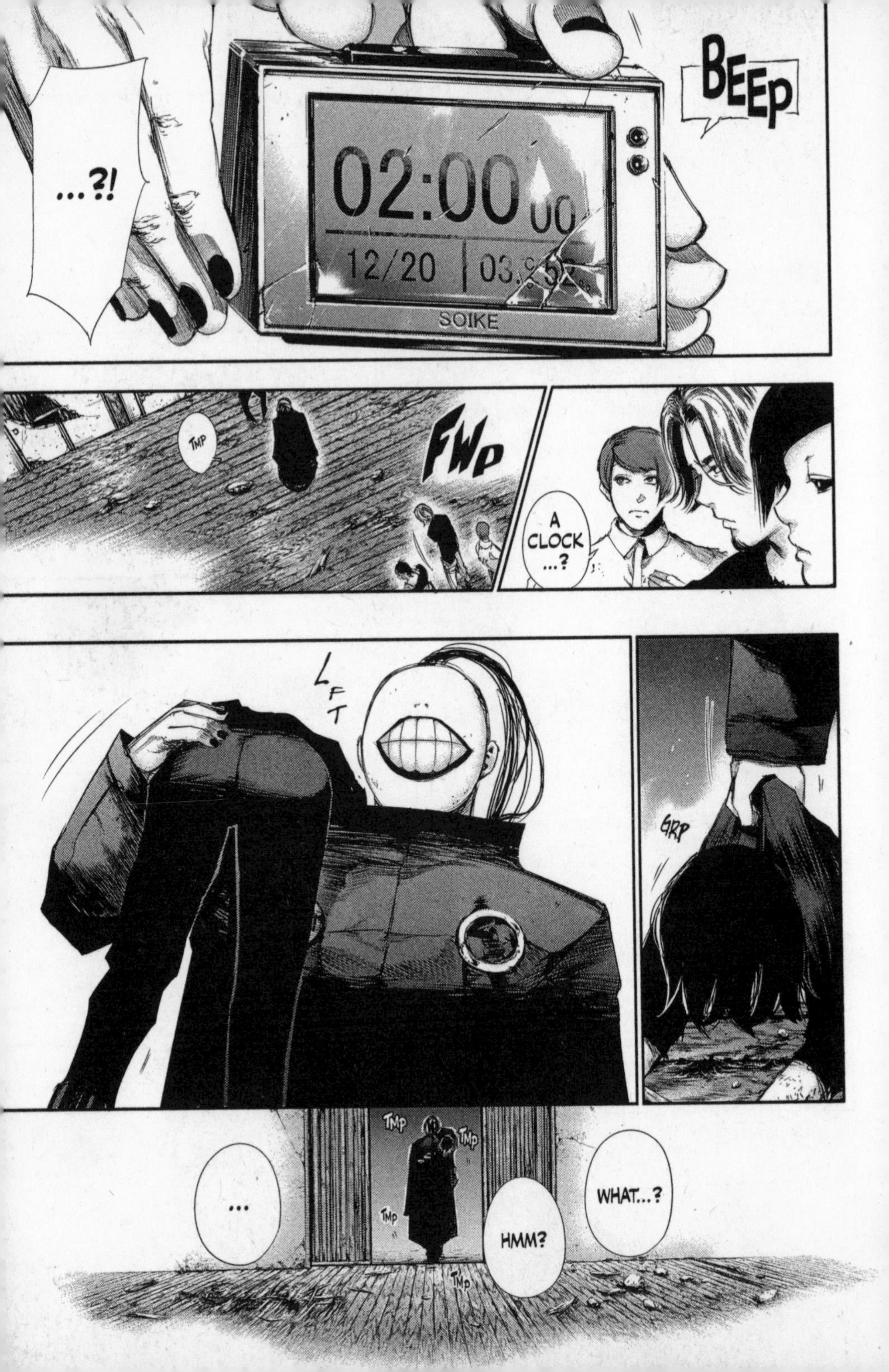
BEEP
02:00 00
12/20
SOIKE
...?!
A CLOCK ...?
FWP
TMP
GRP
LFT
WHAT...?
TMP
TMP
HMM?
TMP
TMP
...

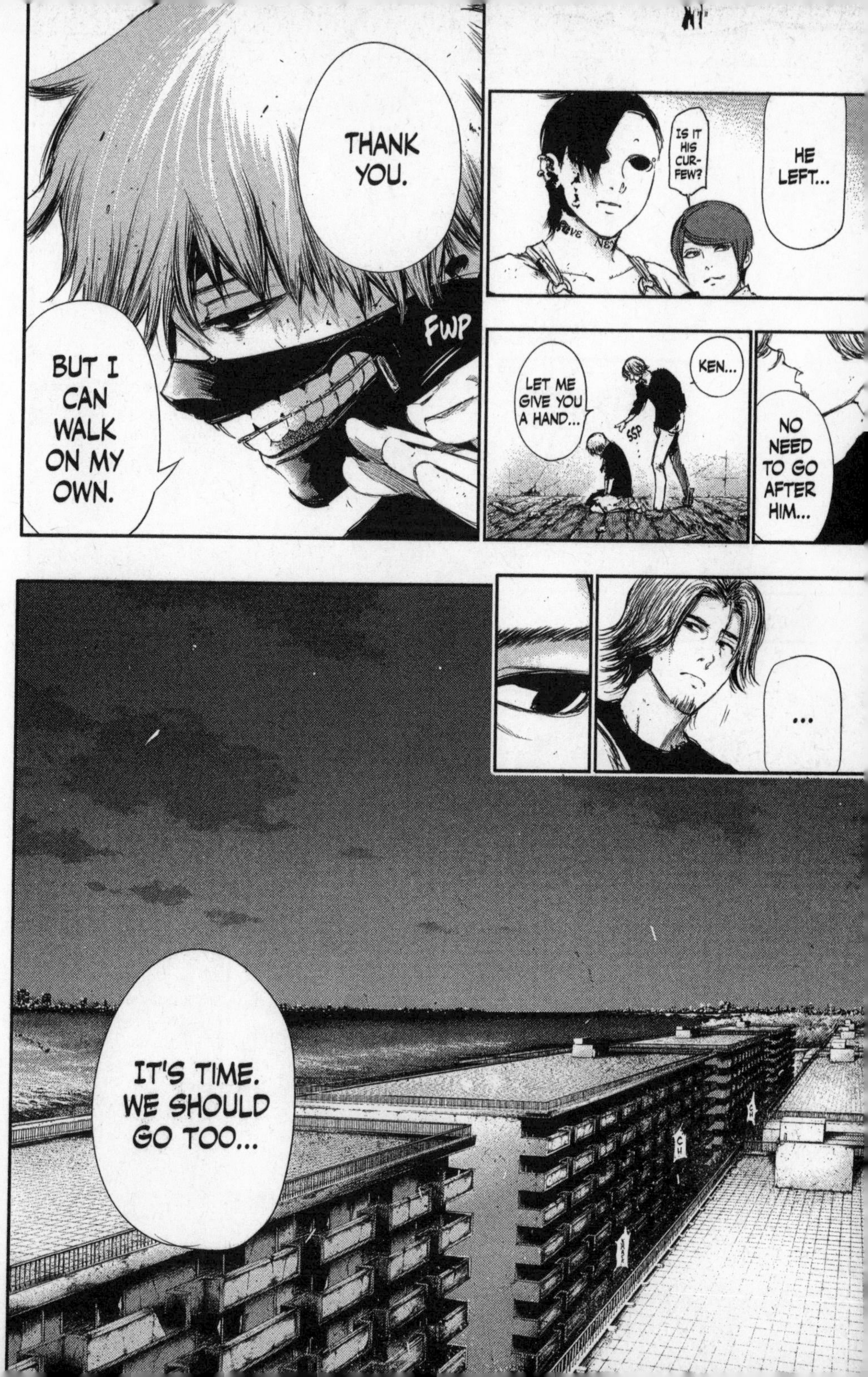
HE LEFT...
IS IT HIS CUR-FEW?
NO NEED TO GO AFTER HIM...
KEN...
LET ME GIVE YOU A HAND...
SSP
THANK YOU.
FWP
BUT I CAN WALK ON MY OWN.
...
IT'S TIME. WE SHOULD GO TOO...

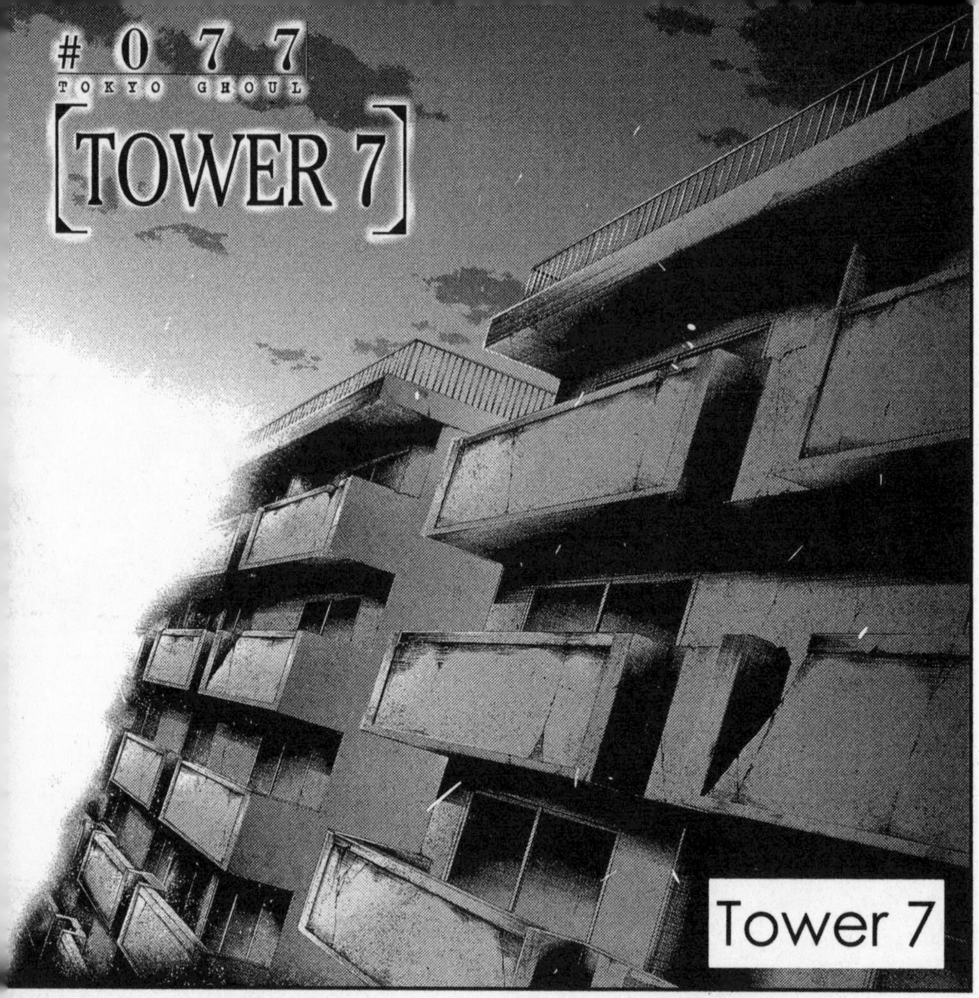
#077
TOKYO GHOUL
[TOWER 7]
Tower 7

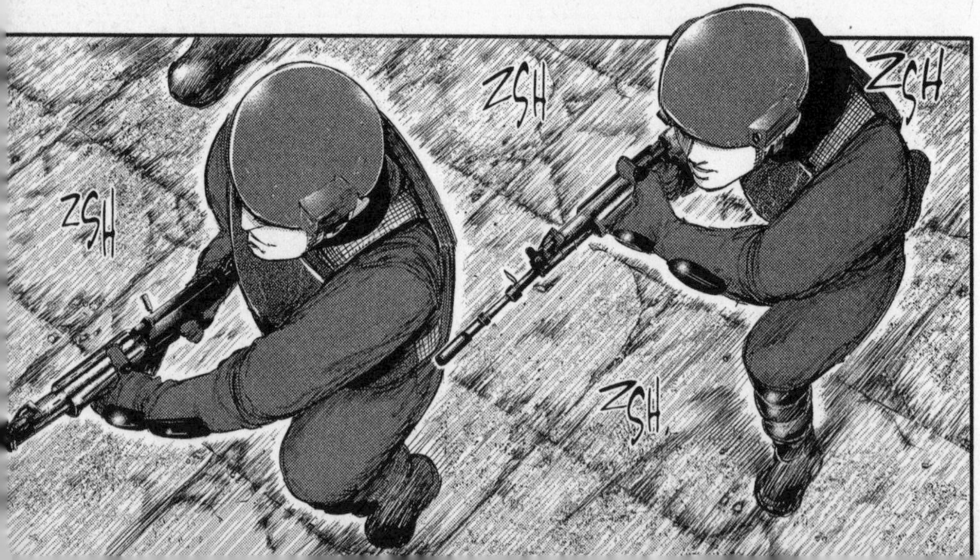
ZSH
ZSH
ZSH
ZSH

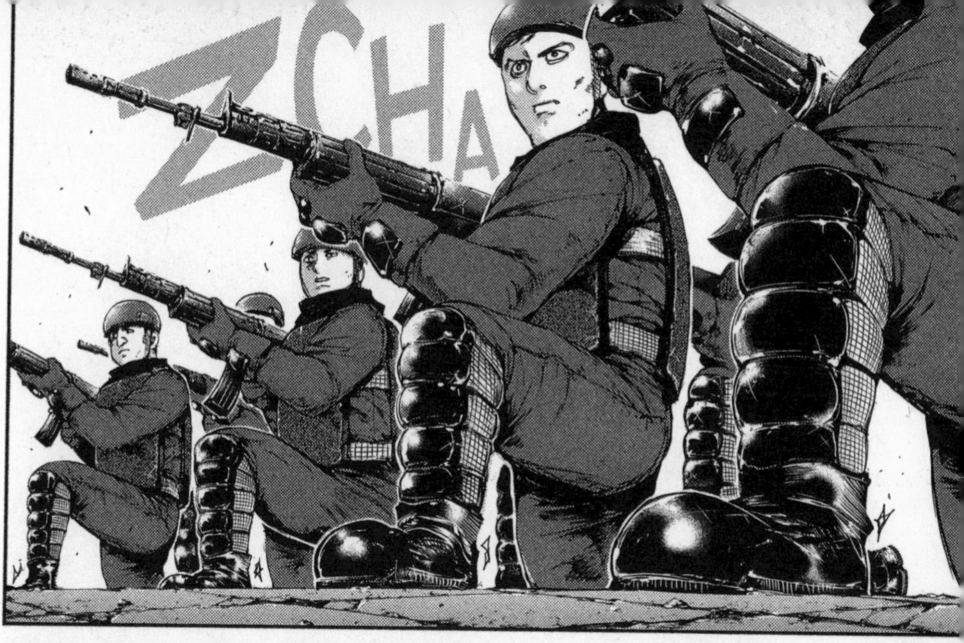
ZCHA

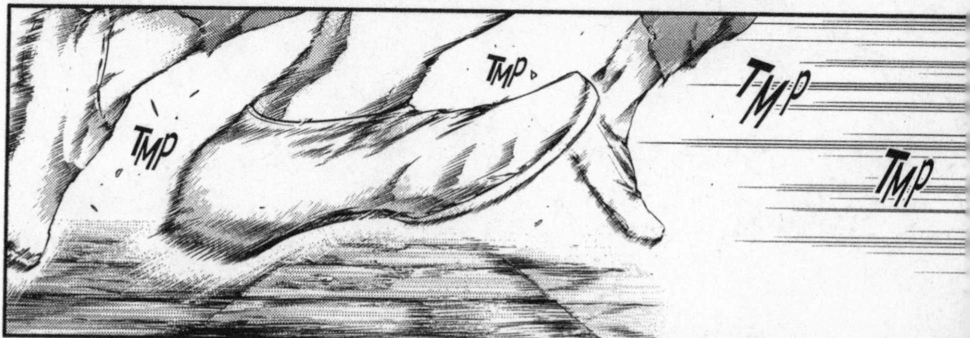
TMP
TMP
TMP
TMP

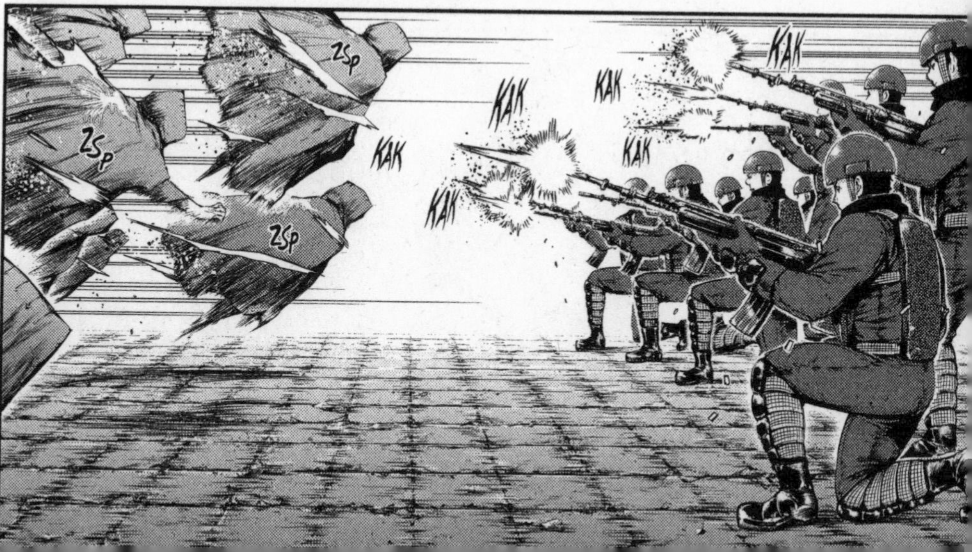
KAK
KAK
KAK
KAK
KAK
KAK
ZSp
ZSp
ZSp

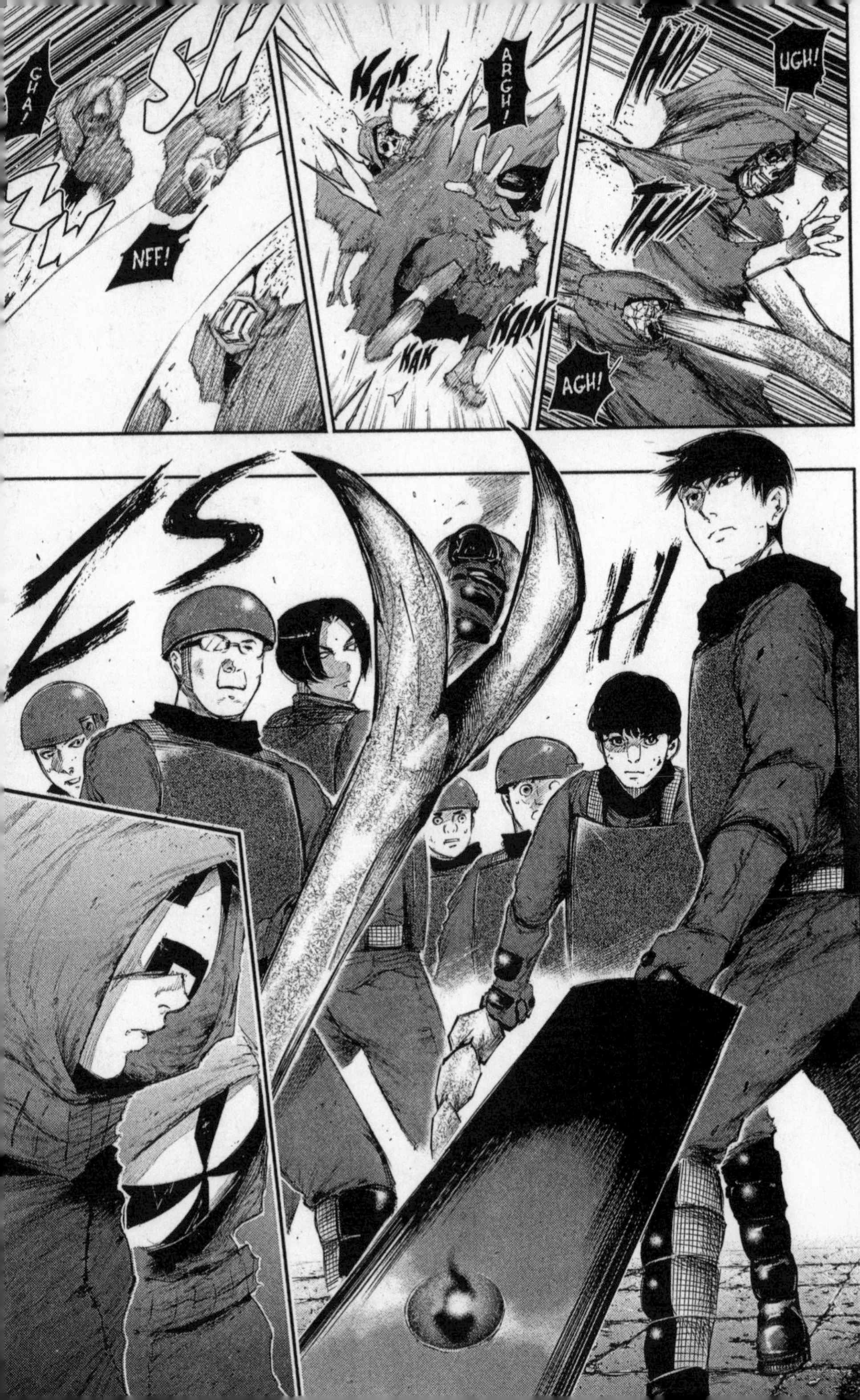
UGH!
AGH!
ARGH!
KAK
KAK
KAK
GHA!
NFF!

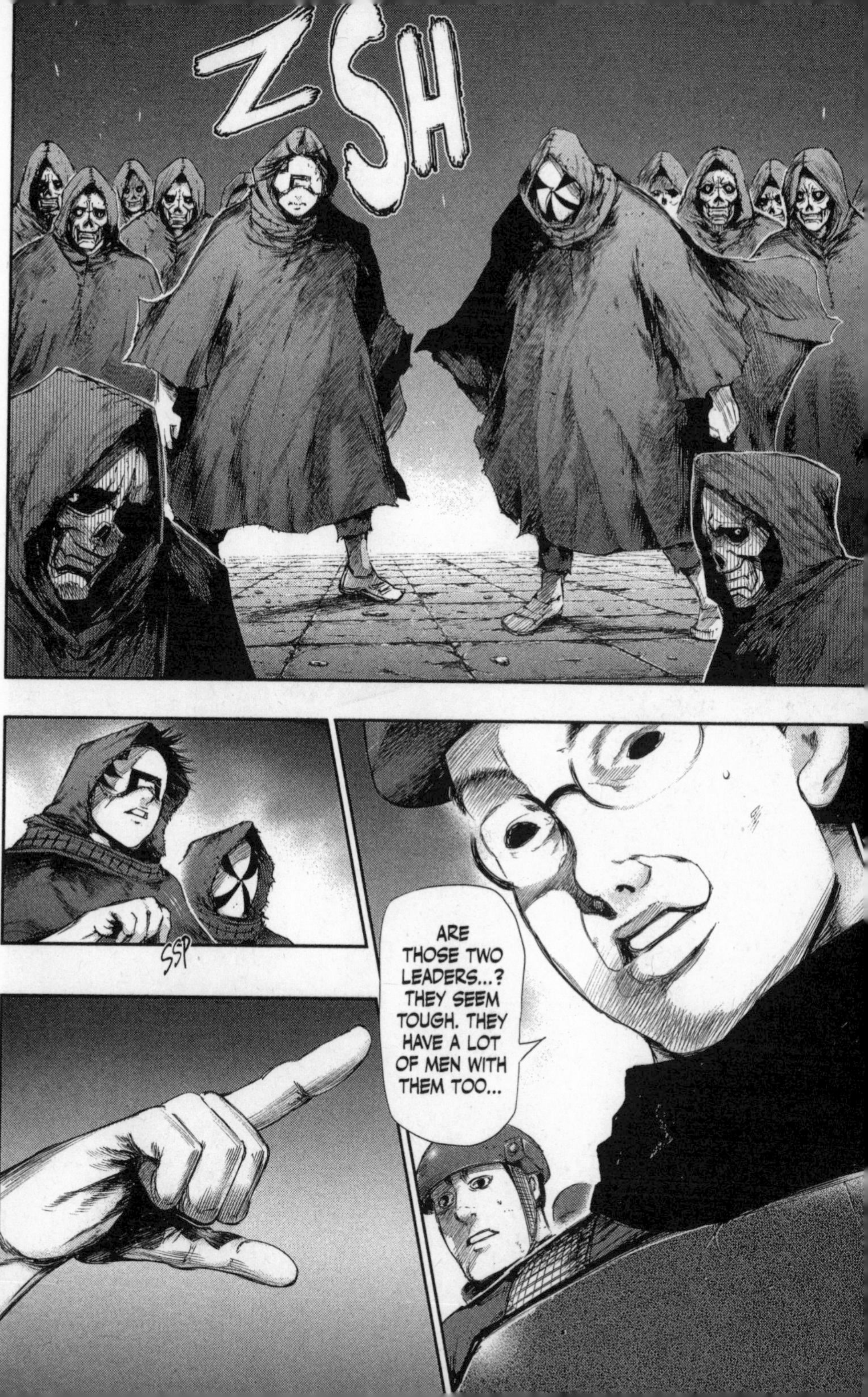
ZSH
ARE THOSE TWO LEADERS...? THEY SEEM TOUGH. THEY HAVE A LOT OF MEN WITH THEM TOO...
SSP

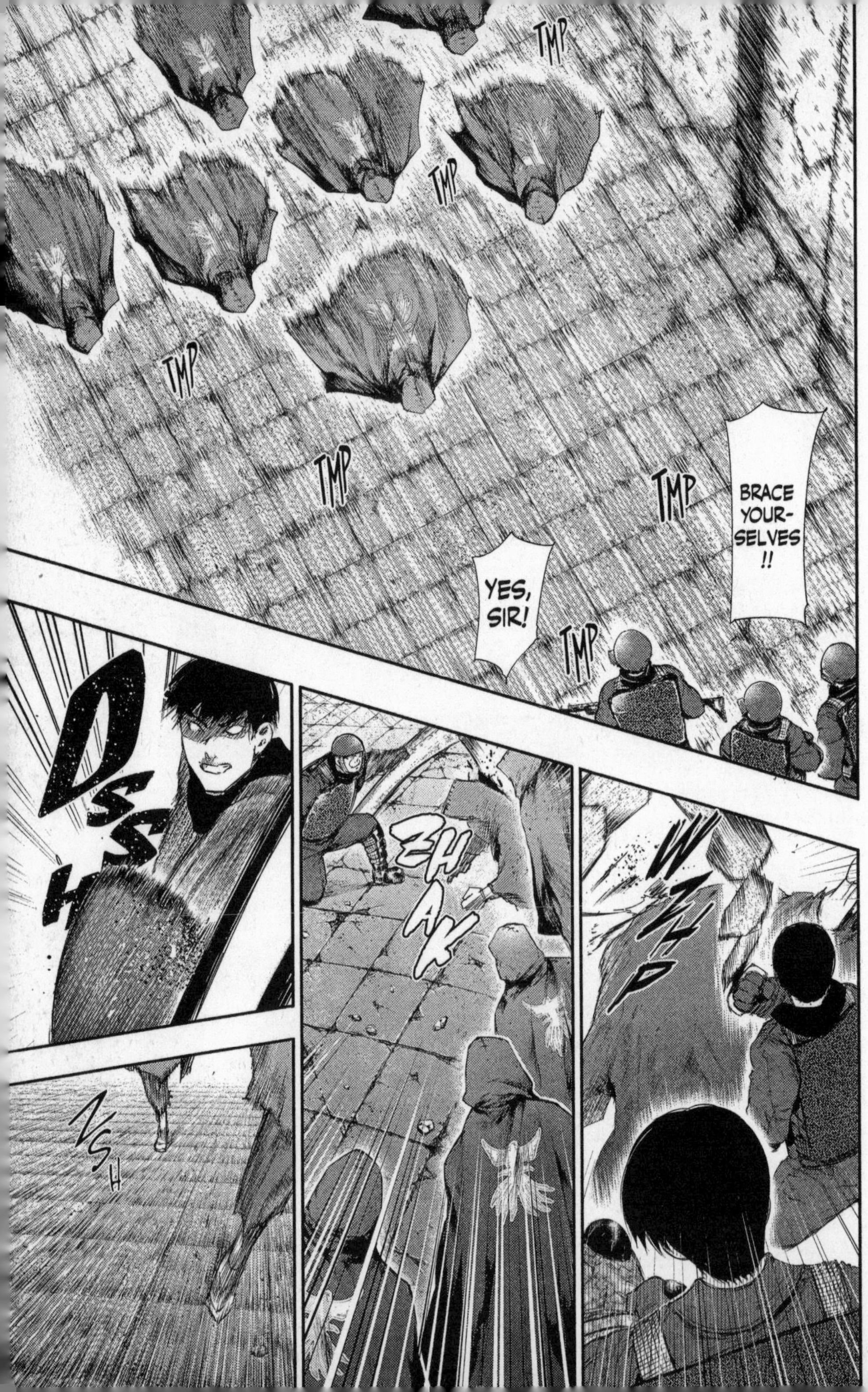
TMP
TMP
TMP
TMP
TMP
BRACE YOUR-SELVES!!
YES, SIR!
TMP
WHAP
ZHAK
DSSH
NSH

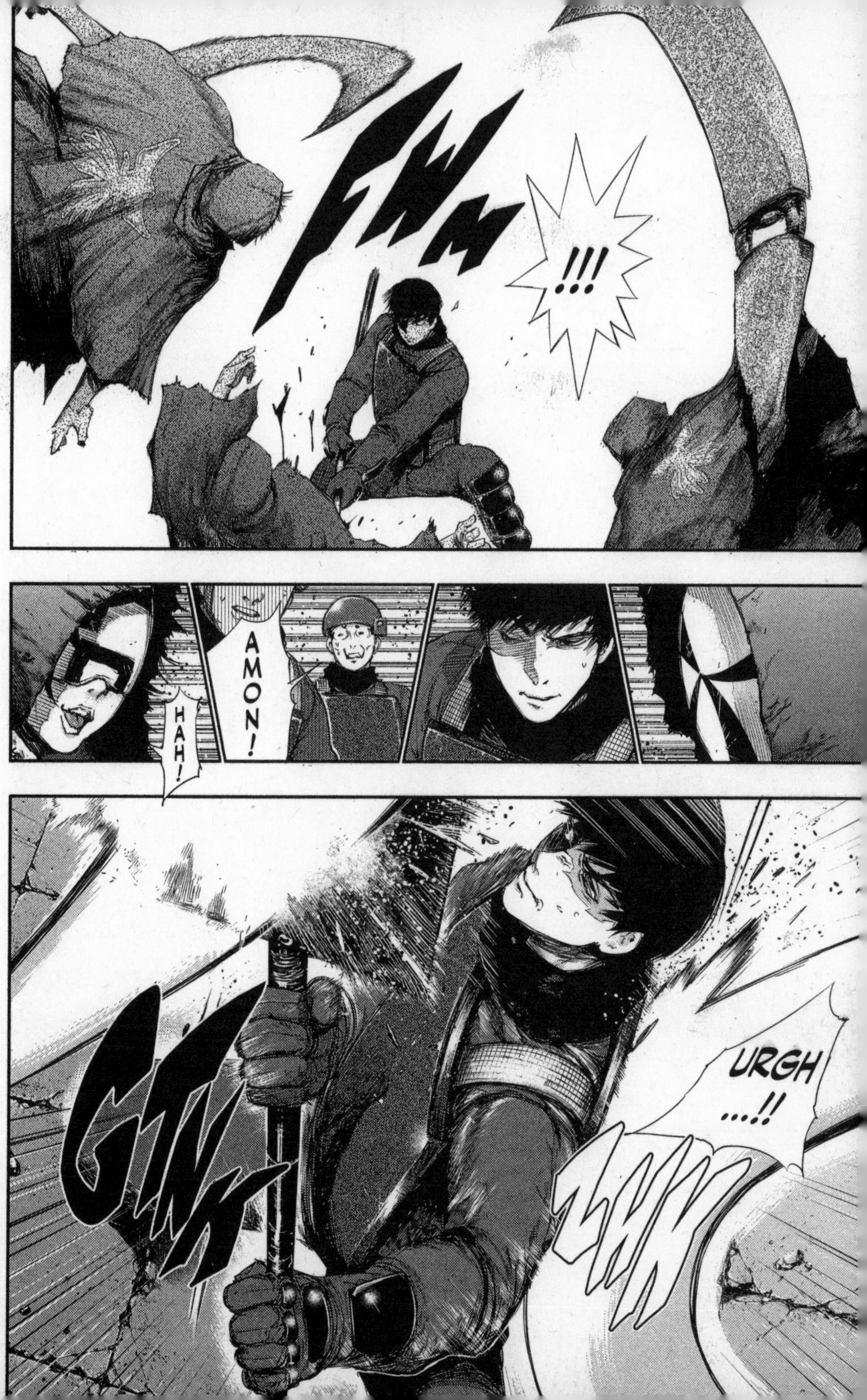
FWM
!!!
AMON!
HAH!
URGH ...!!

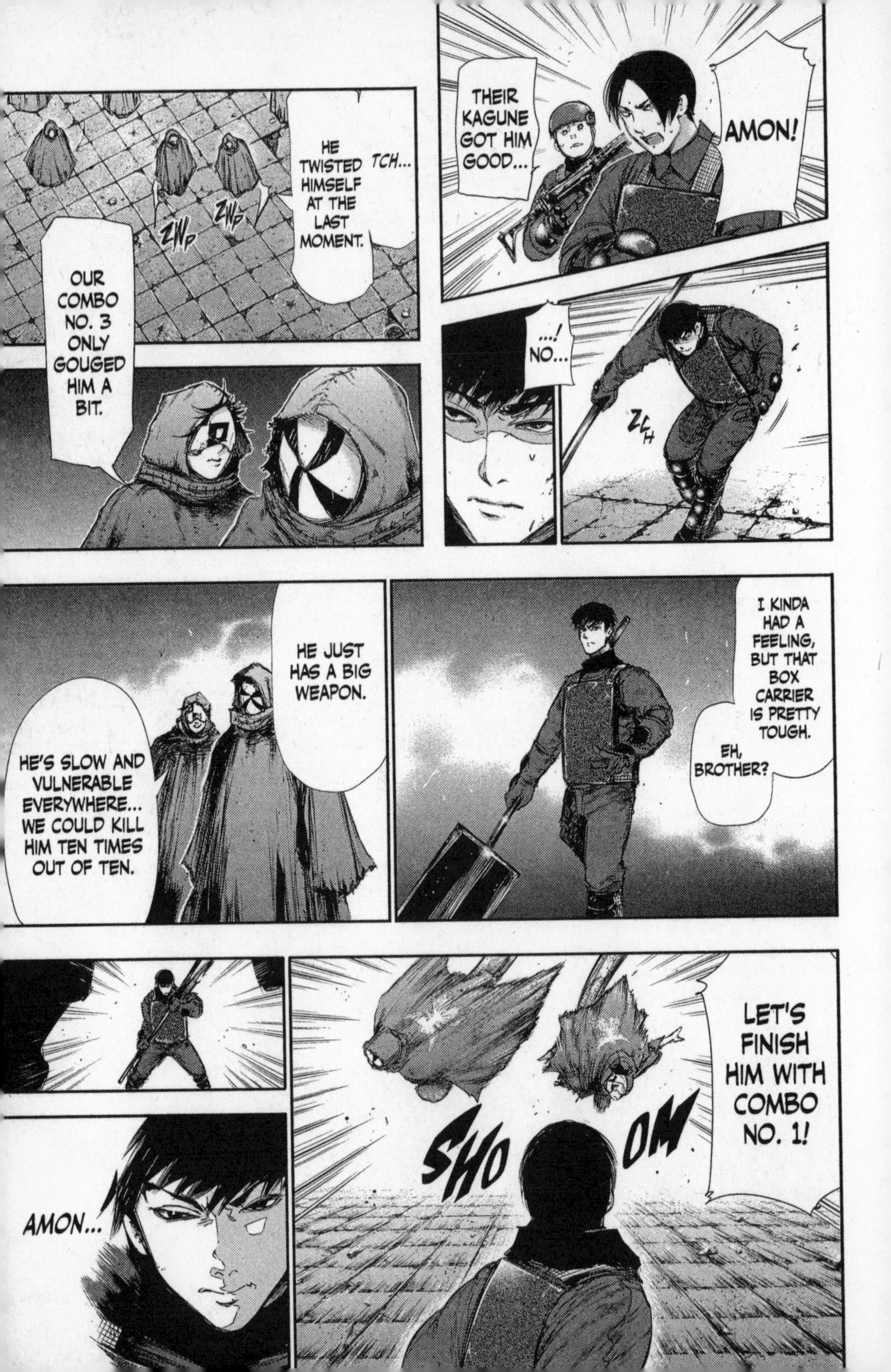
AMON!
THEIR KAGUNE GOT HIM GOOD...
TCH...
HE TWISTED HIMSELF AT THE LAST MOMENT.
ZWP
ZWP
OUR COMBO NO. 3 ONLY GOUGED HIM A BIT.
...! NO...
ZCH
I KINDA HAD A FEELING, BUT THAT BOX CARRIER IS PRETTY TOUGH.
EH, BROTHER?
HE JUST HAS A BIG WEAPON.
HE'S SLOW AND VULNERABLE EVERYWHERE... WE COULD KILL HIM TEN TIMES OUT OF TEN.
LET'S FINISH HIM WITH COMBO NO. 1!
SHOOM
AMON...

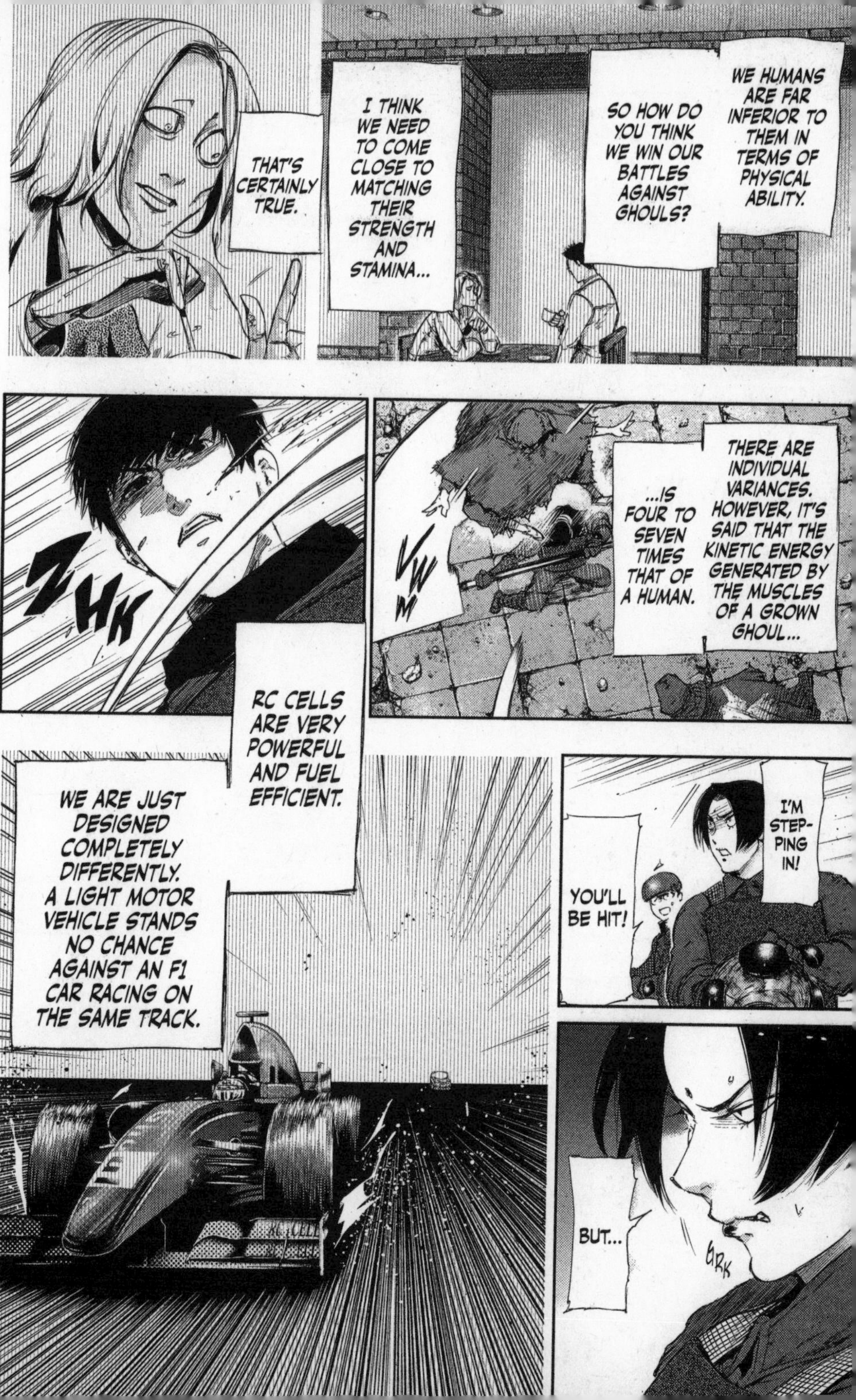
WE HUMANS ARE FAR INFERIOR TO THEM IN TERMS OF PHYSICAL ABILITY.
SO HOW DO YOU THINK WE WIN OUR BATTLES AGAINST GHOULS?
I THINK WE NEED TO COME CLOSE TO MATCHING THEIR STRENGTH AND STAMINA...
THAT'S CERTAINLY TRUE.
THERE ARE INDIVIDUAL VARIANCES. HOWEVER, IT'S SAID THAT THE KINETIC ENERGY GENERATED BY THE MUSCLES OF A GROWN GHOUL...
...IS FOUR TO SEVEN TIMES THAT OF A HUMAN.
VWWM
ZHK
RC CELLS ARE VERY POWERFUL AND FUEL EFFICIENT.
I'M STEP-PING IN!
YOU'LL BE HIT!
BUT...
GRK
WE ARE JUST DESIGNED COMPLETELY DIFFERENTLY. A LIGHT MOTOR VEHICLE STANDS NO CHANCE AGAINST AN F1 CAR RACING ON THE SAME TRACK.

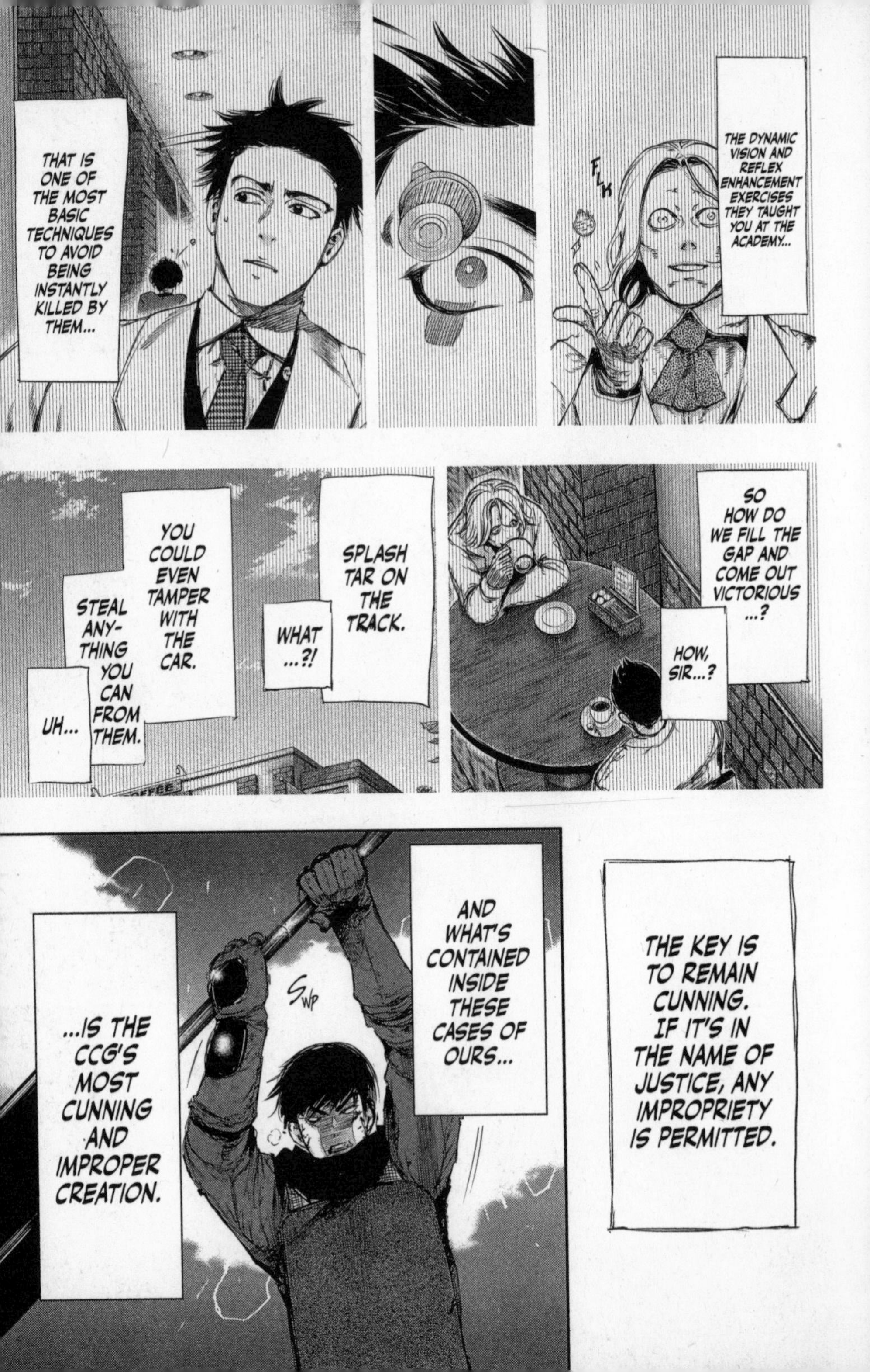
THE DYNAMIC VISION AND REFLEX ENHANCEMENT EXERCISES THEY TAUGHT YOU AT THE ACADEMY...
FLK
THAT IS ONE OF THE MOST BASIC TECHNIQUES TO AVOID BEING INSTANTLY KILLED BY THEM...
SO HOW DO WE FILL THE GAP AND COME OUT VICTORIOUS ...?
HOW, SIR...?
SPLASH TAR ON THE TRACK.
WHAT ...?!
YOU COULD EVEN TAMPER WITH THE CAR.
STEAL ANYTHING YOU CAN FROM THEM.
UH...
THE KEY IS TO REMAIN CUNNING. IF IT'S IN THE NAME OF JUSTICE, ANY IMPROPRIETY IS PERMITTED.
AND WHAT'S CONTAINED INSIDE THESE CASES OF OURS...
SWP
...IS THE CCG'S MOST CUNNING AND IMPROPER CREATION.

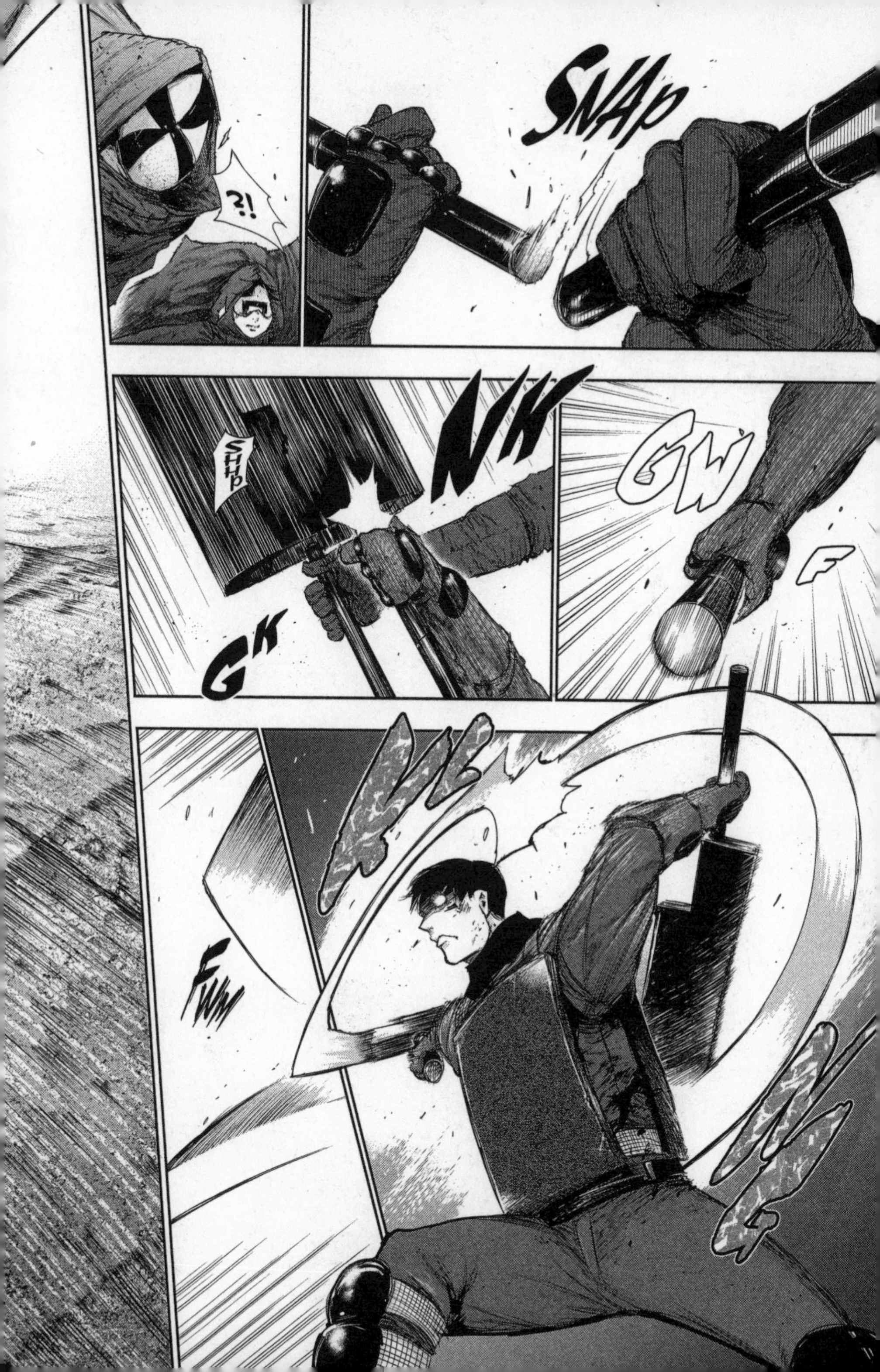
SNAp
?!
GW
F
SHHp
NK
GK
FWM

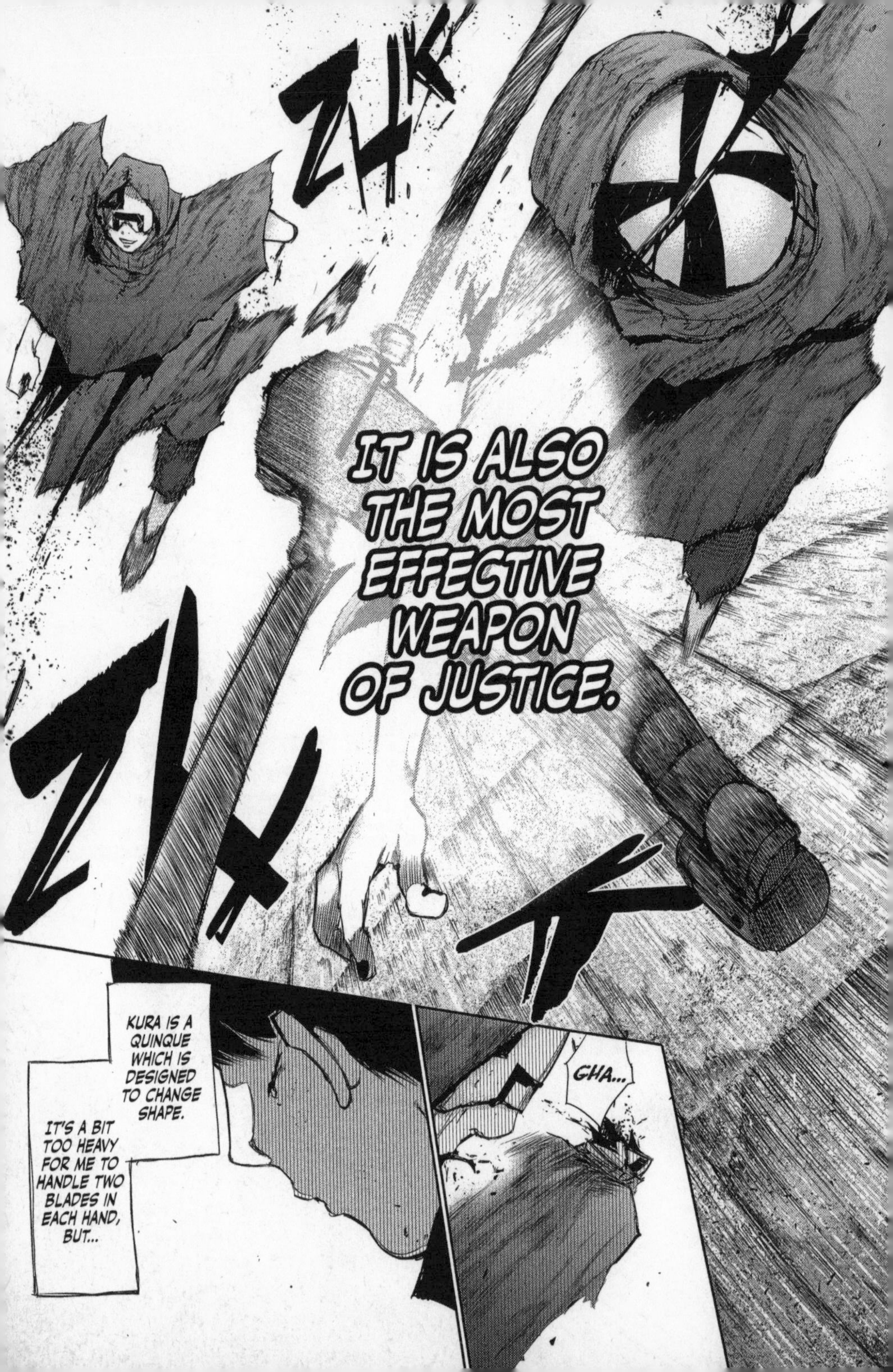
ZKK
IT IS ALSO THE MOST EFFECTIVE WEAPON OF JUSTICE.
ZKK
GHA...
KURA IS A QUINQUE WHICH IS DESIGNED TO CHANGE SHAPE.
IT'S A BIT TOO HEAVY FOR ME TO HANDLE TWO BLADES IN EACH HAND, BUT...

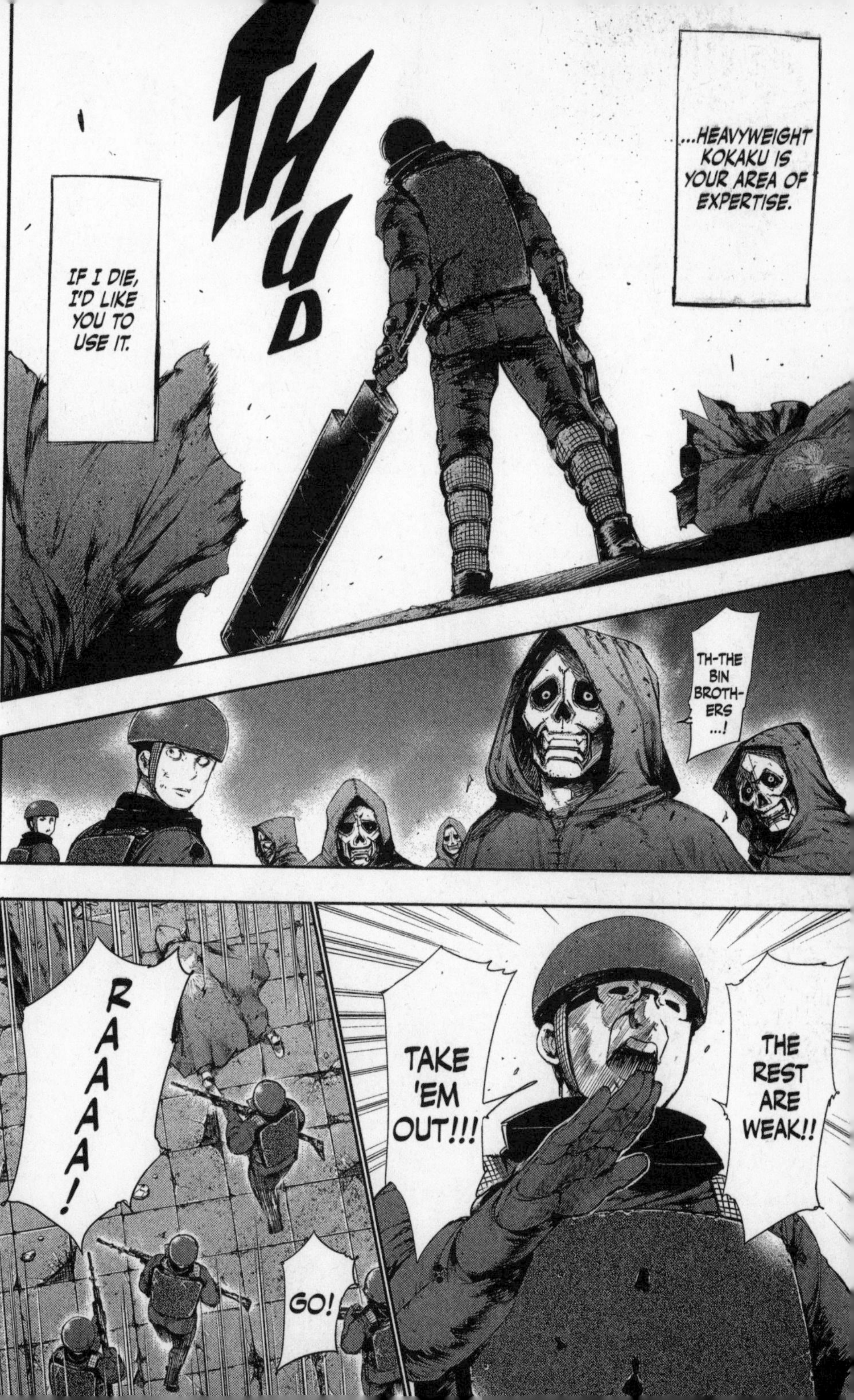
...HEAVYWEIGHT KOKAKU IS YOUR AREA OF EXPERTISE.
THUD
IF I DIE, I'D LIKE YOU TO USE IT.
TH-THE BIN BROTHERS ...!
THE REST ARE WEAK!!
TAKE 'EM OUT!!!
RAAAAA!
GO!

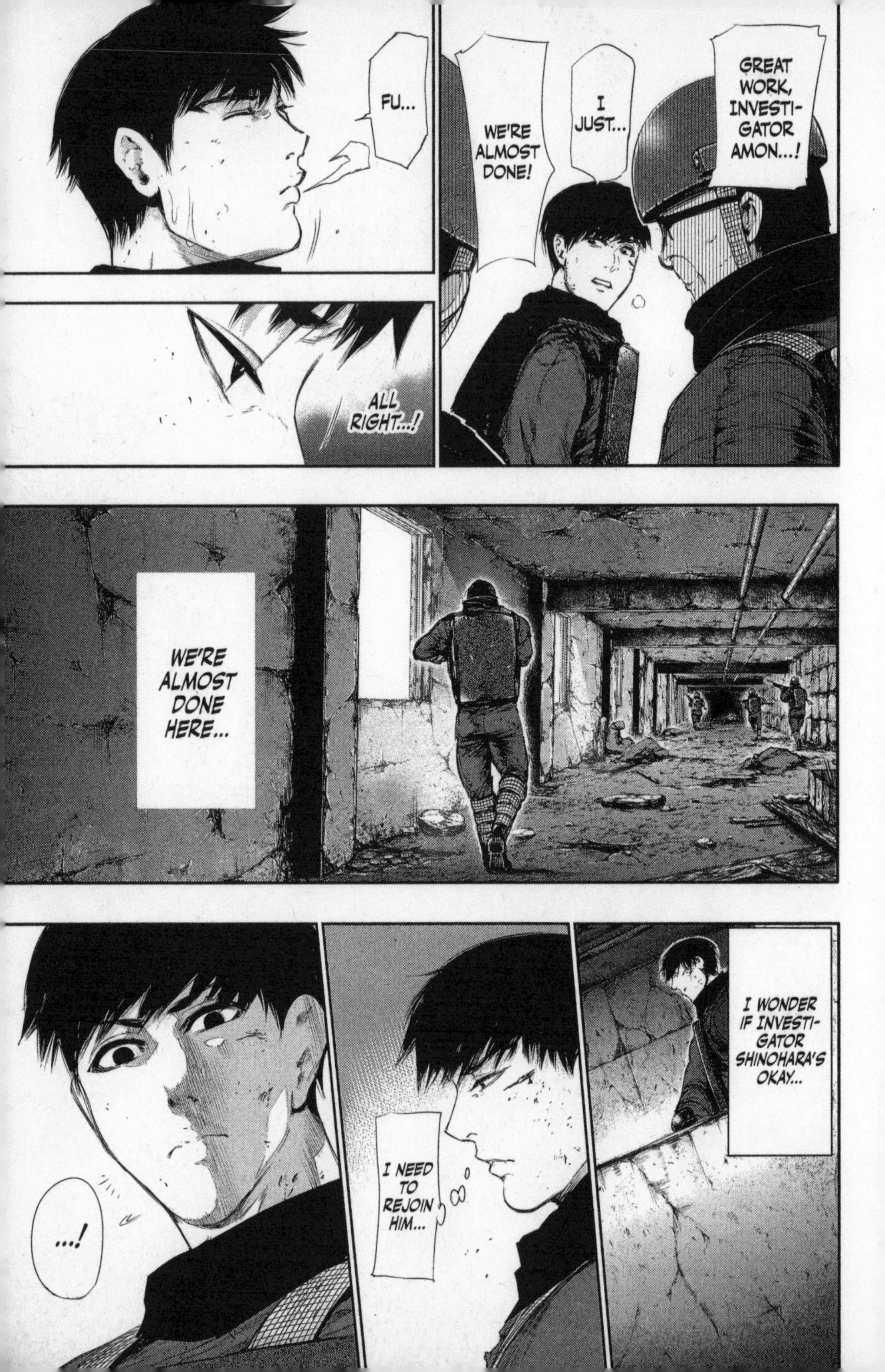

GREAT WORK, INVESTIGATOR AMON...!
I JUST...
WE'RE ALMOST DONE!
FU...
ALL RIGHT...!
WE'RE ALMOST DONE HERE...
I WONDER IF INVESTIGATOR SHINOHARA'S OKAY...
I NEED TO REJOIN HIM...
...!

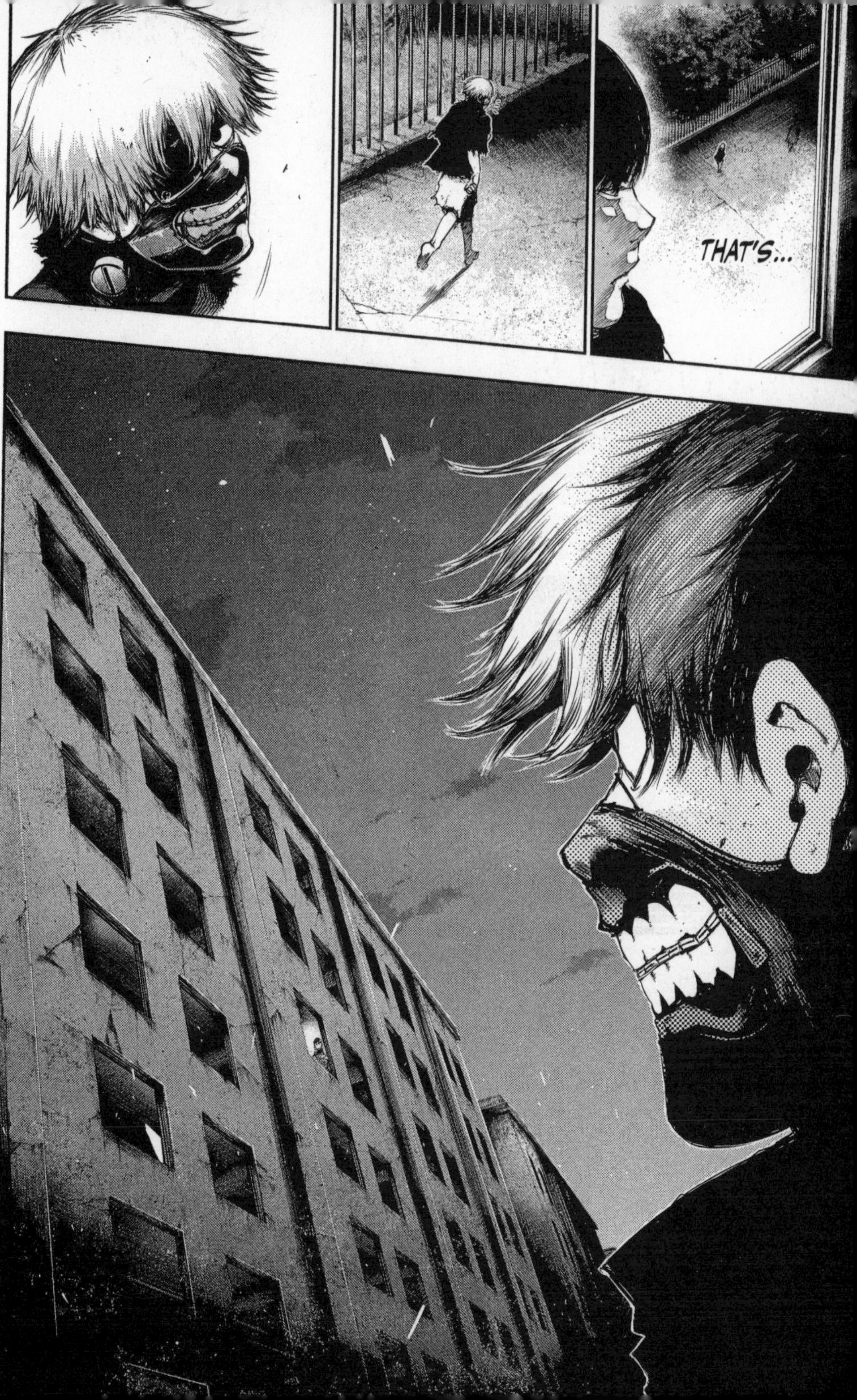
THAT'S...

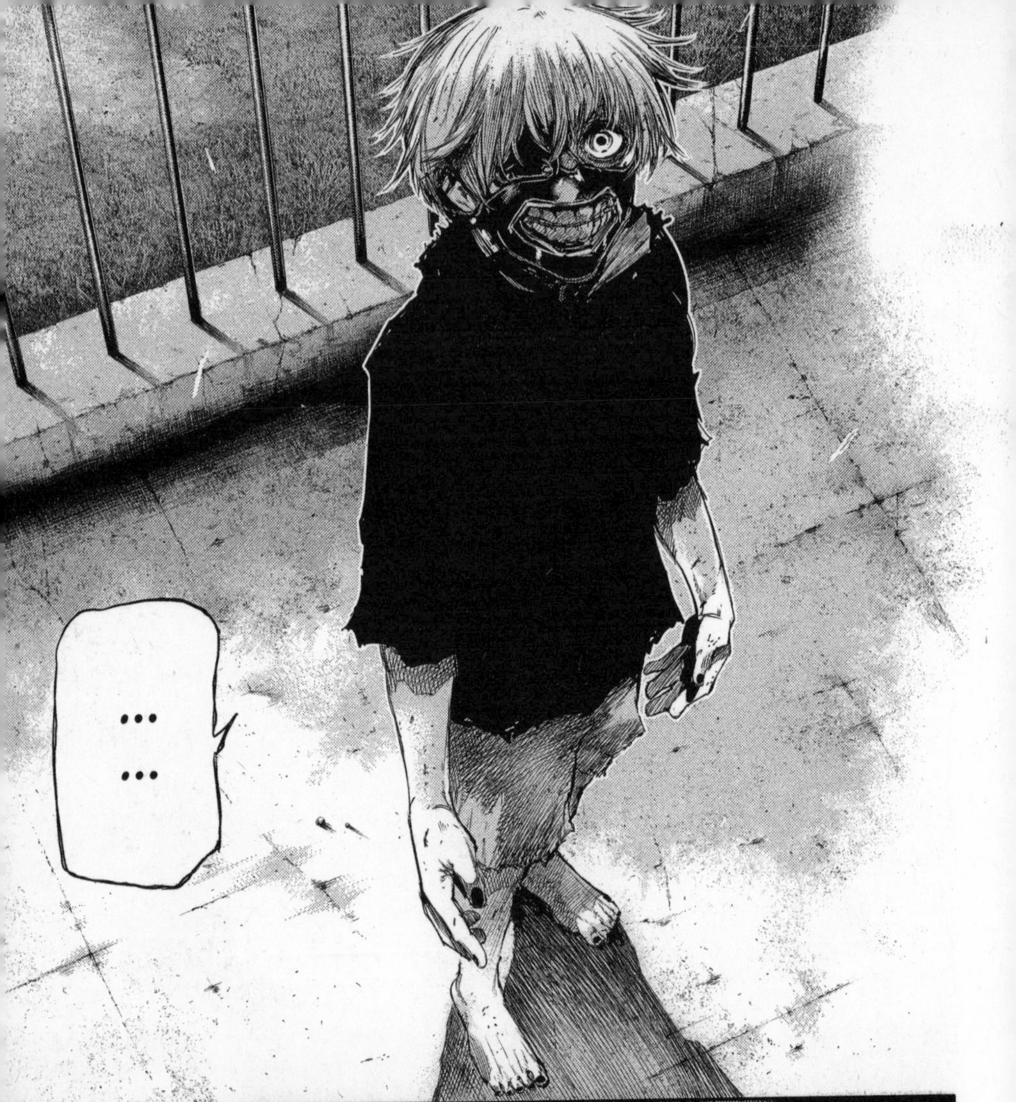
... ...

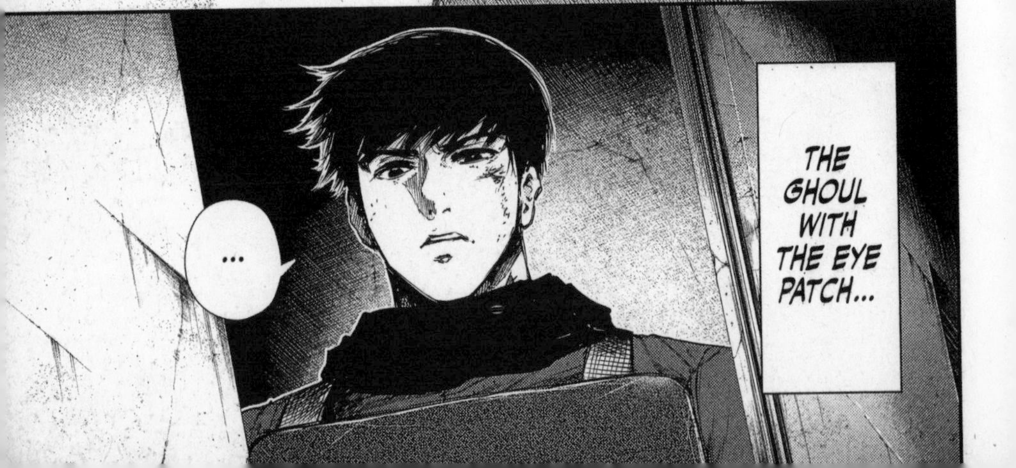
THE GHOUL WITH THE EYE PATCH...
...

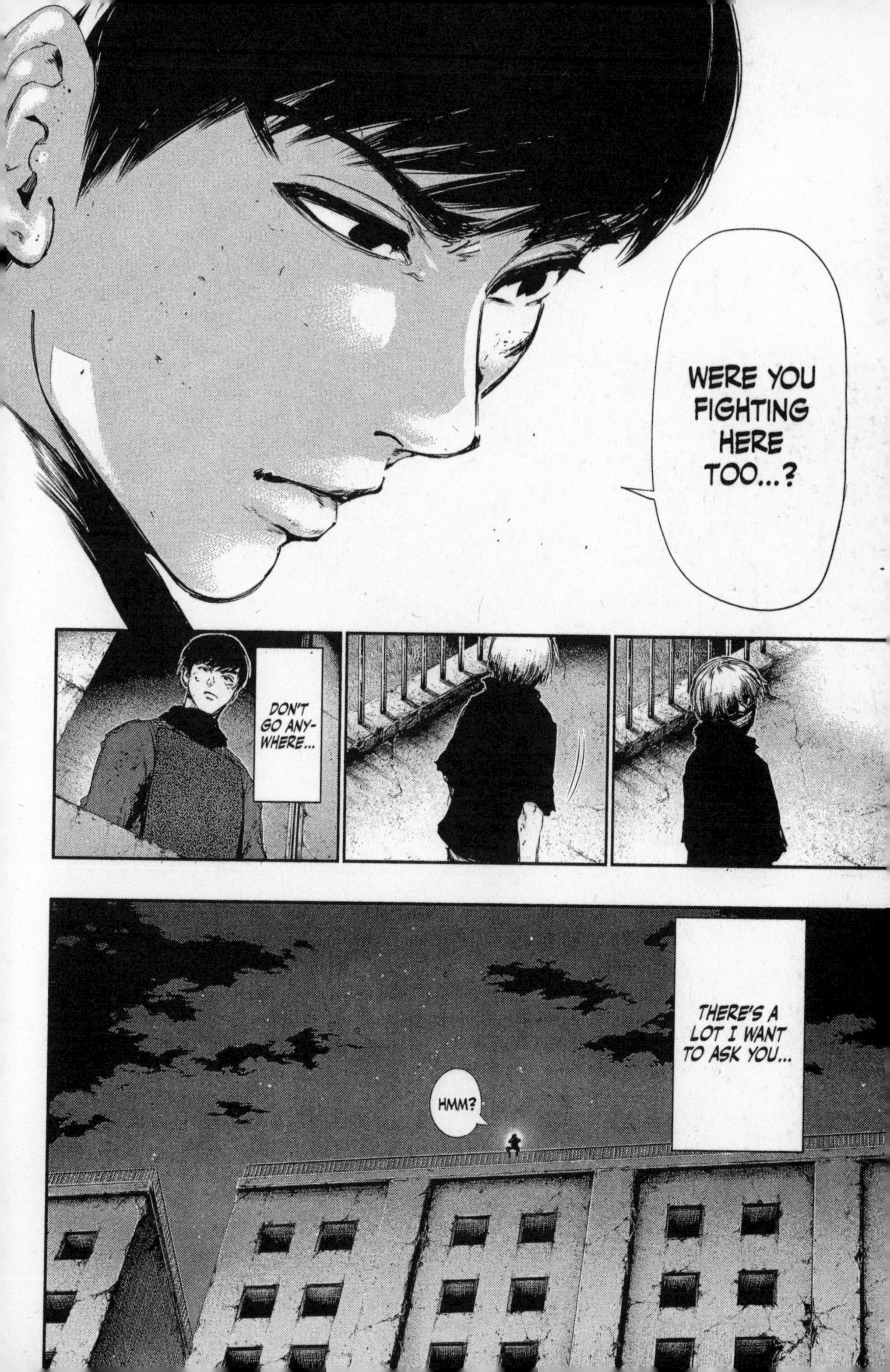
WERE YOU FIGHTING HERE TOO...?
DON'T GO ANYWHERE...
THERE'S A LOT I WANT TO ASK YOU...
HMM?

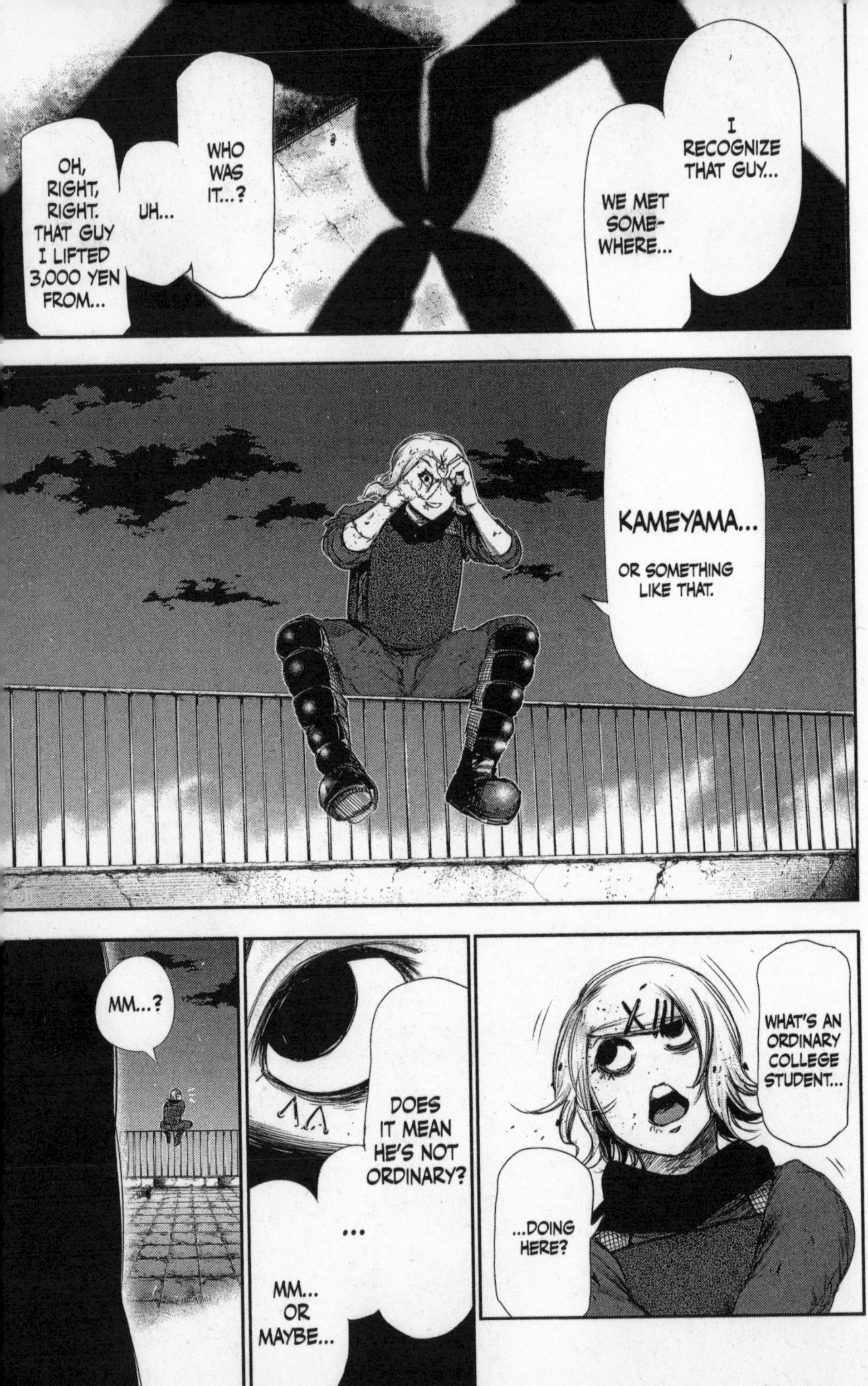
I RECOGNIZE THAT GUY...
WE MET SOME-WHERE...
WHO WAS IT...?
UH...
OH, RIGHT, RIGHT. THAT GUY I LIFTED 3,000 YEN FROM...
KAMEYAMA...
OR SOMETHING LIKE THAT.
WHAT'S AN ORDINARY COLLEGE STUDENT...
...DOING HERE?
DOES IT MEAN HE'S NOT ORDINARY?
...
MM... OR MAYBE...
MM...?

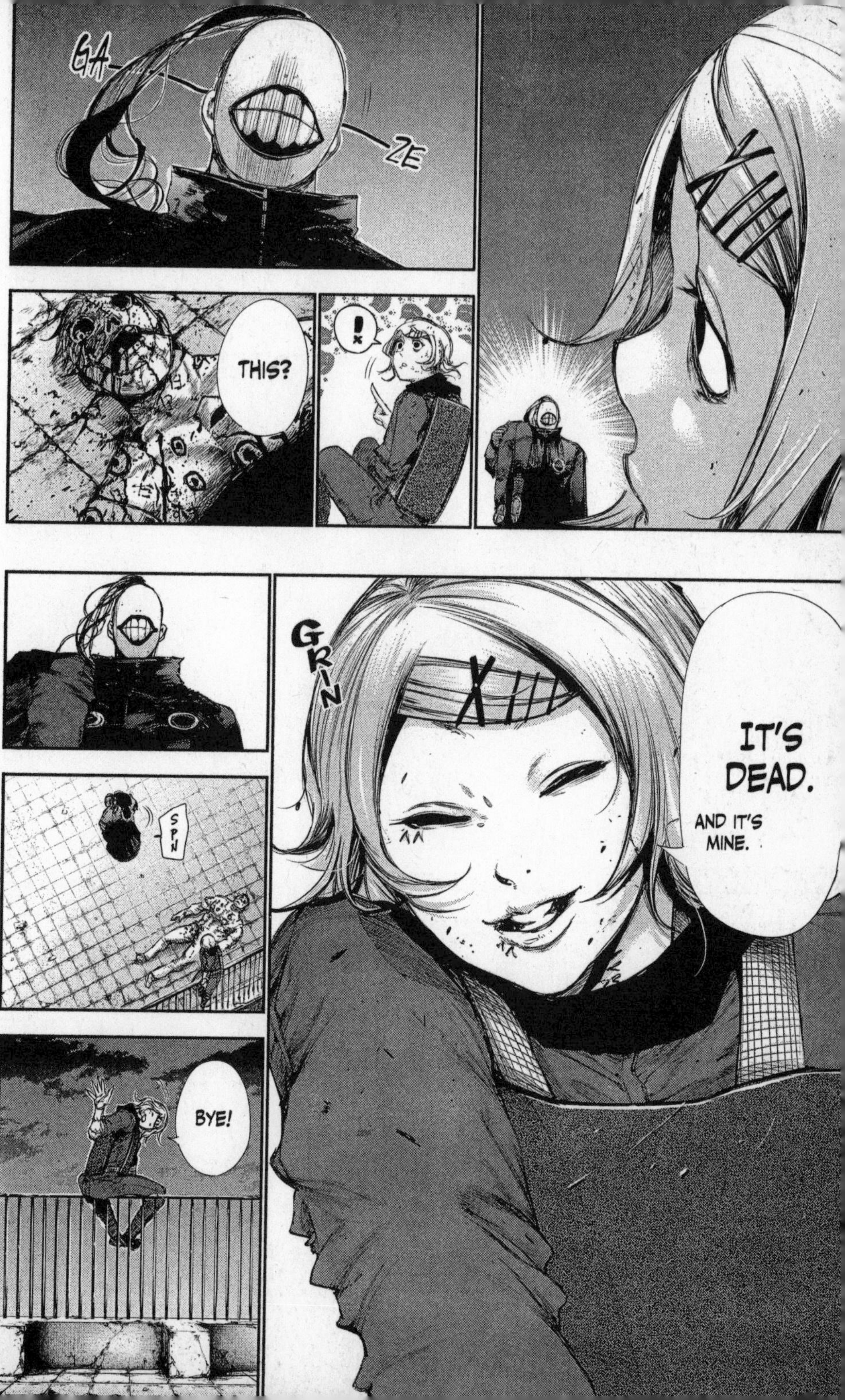
GA
ZE
!
THIS?
GRIN
IT'S DEAD.
AND IT'S MINE.
SPN
BYE!

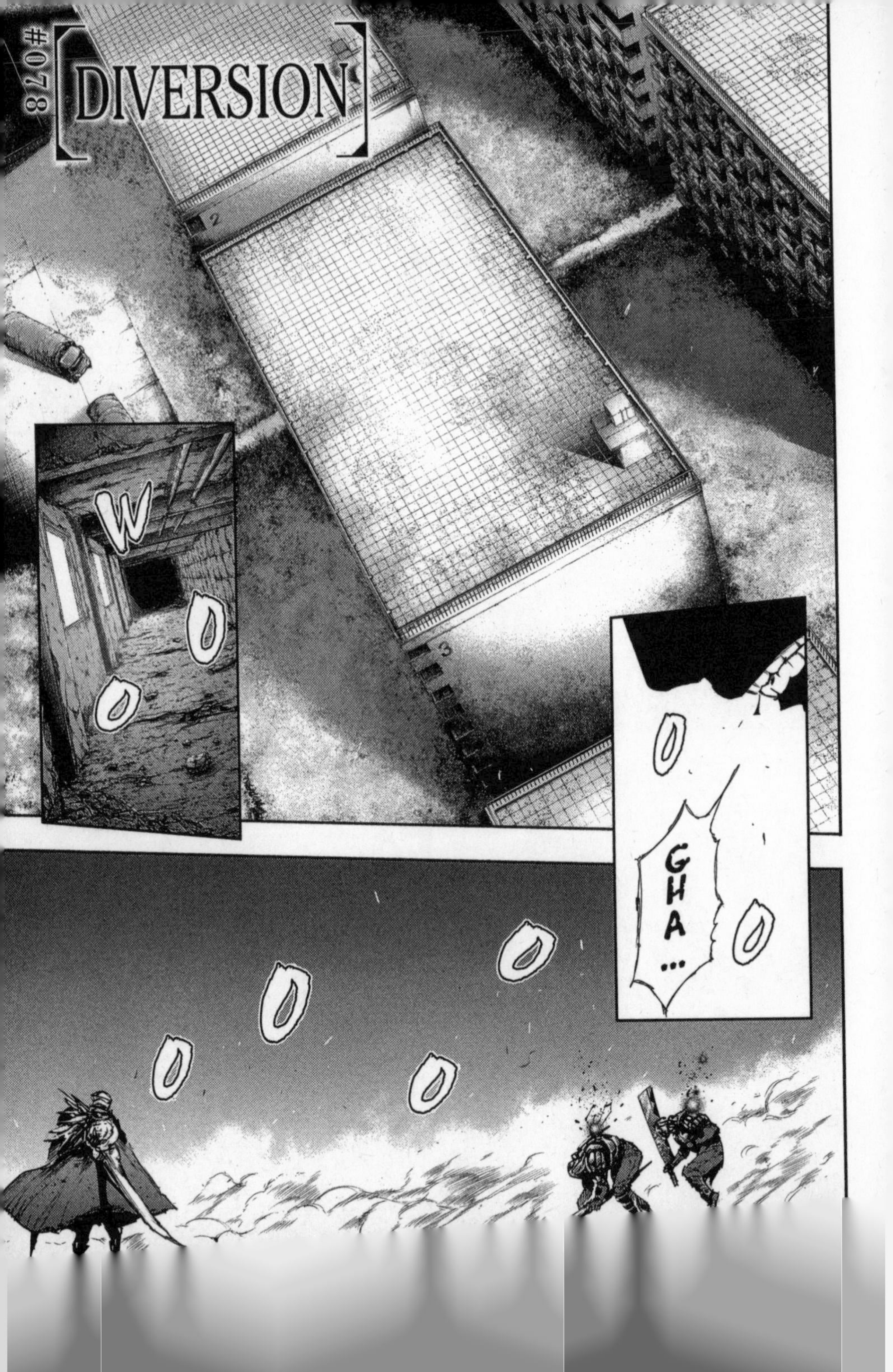
#078
DIVERSION
GHA...
WOOO
OOOOOO

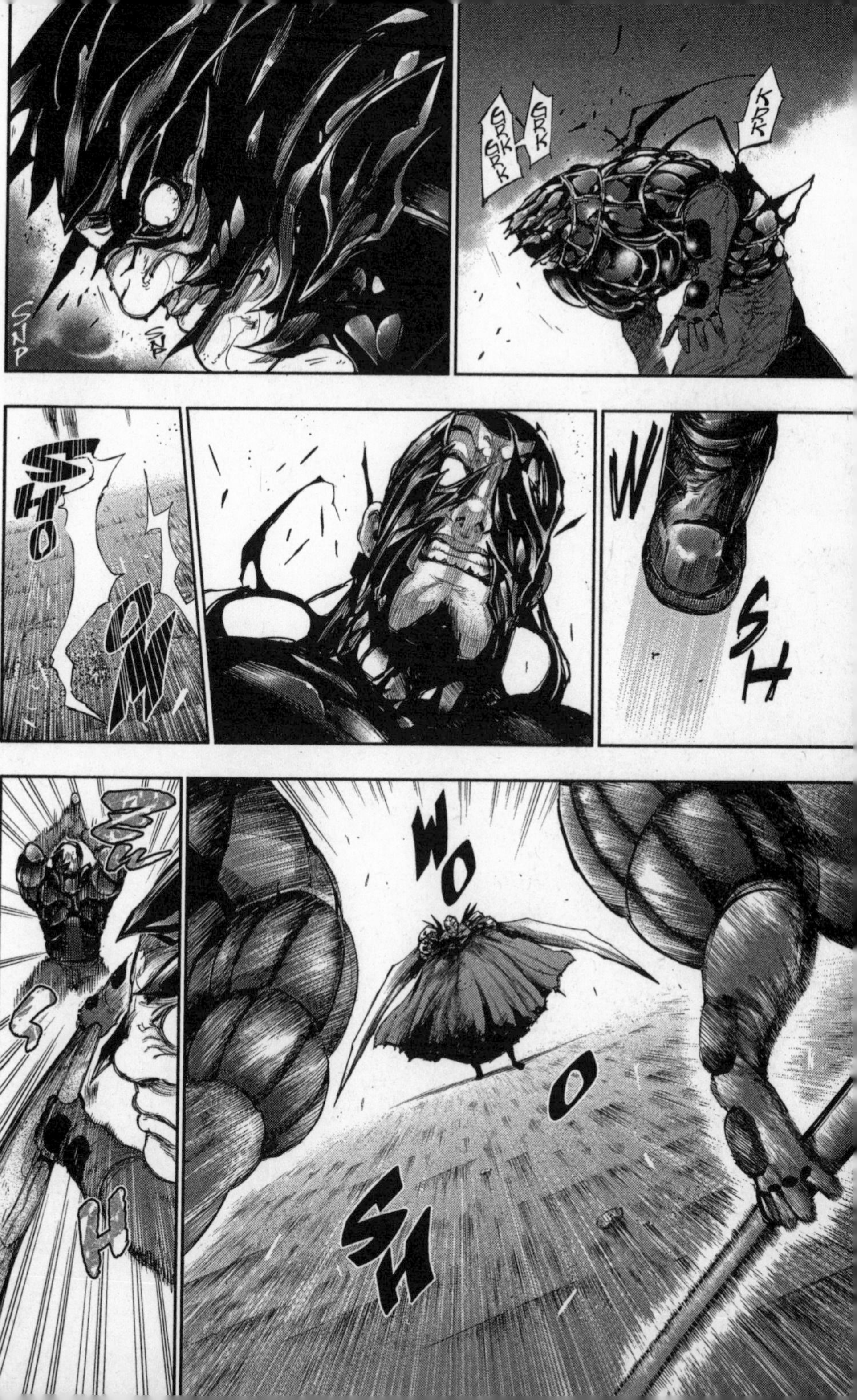
KRK
GRK
GRK
GRK
SNP
SNP
WSH
SHOOM
WOOSH

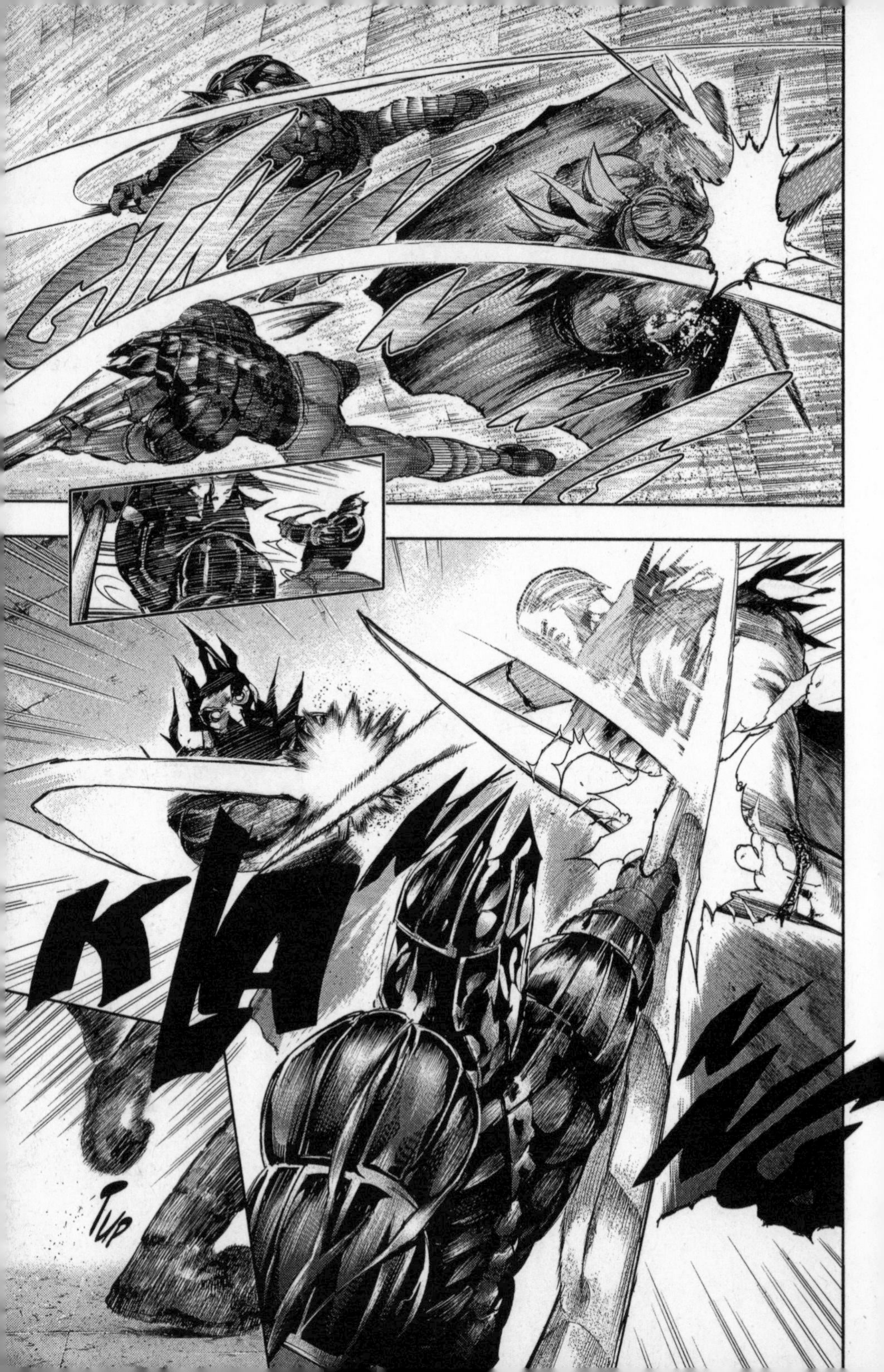
KLA
TUP

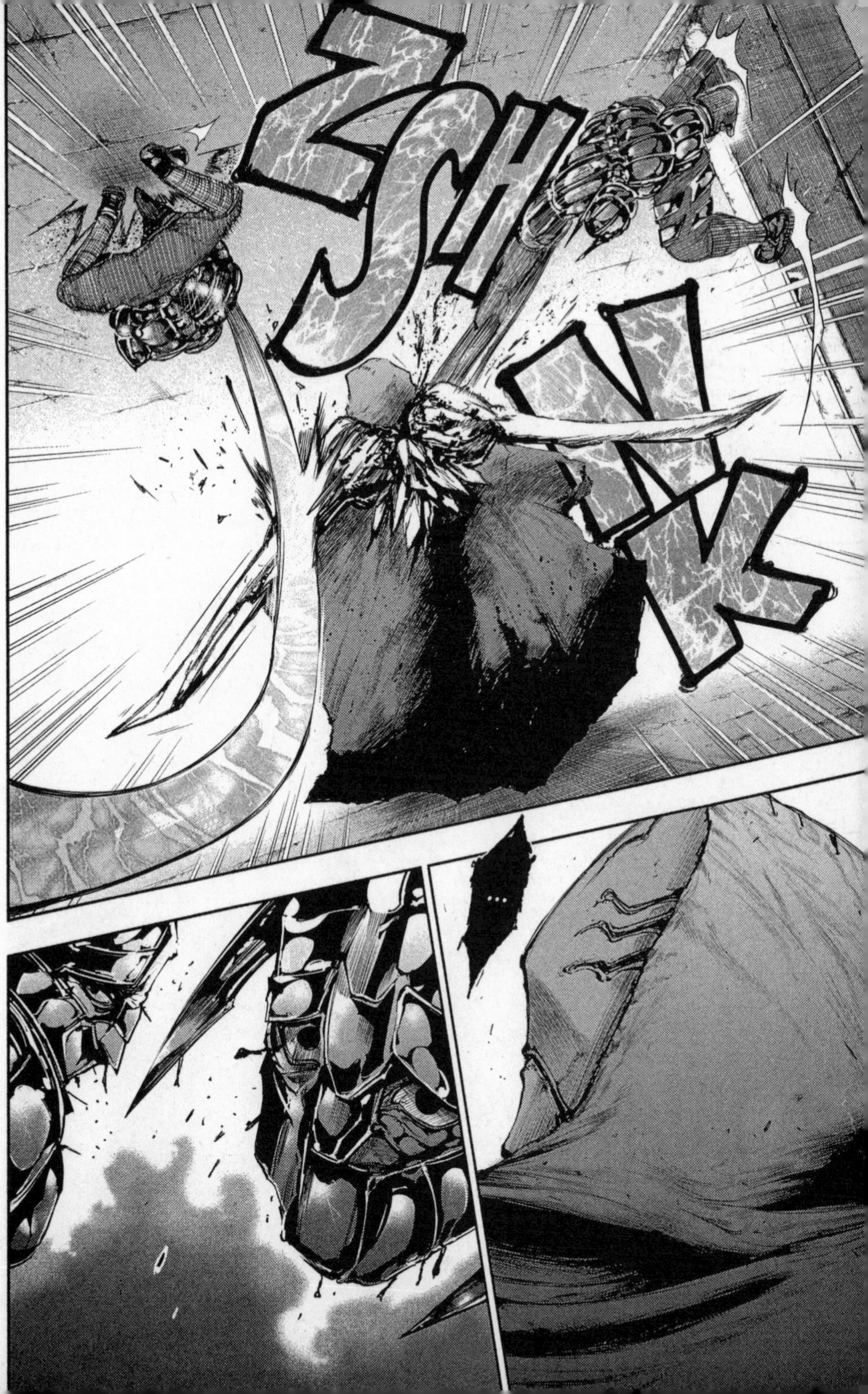
ZSHNK
...

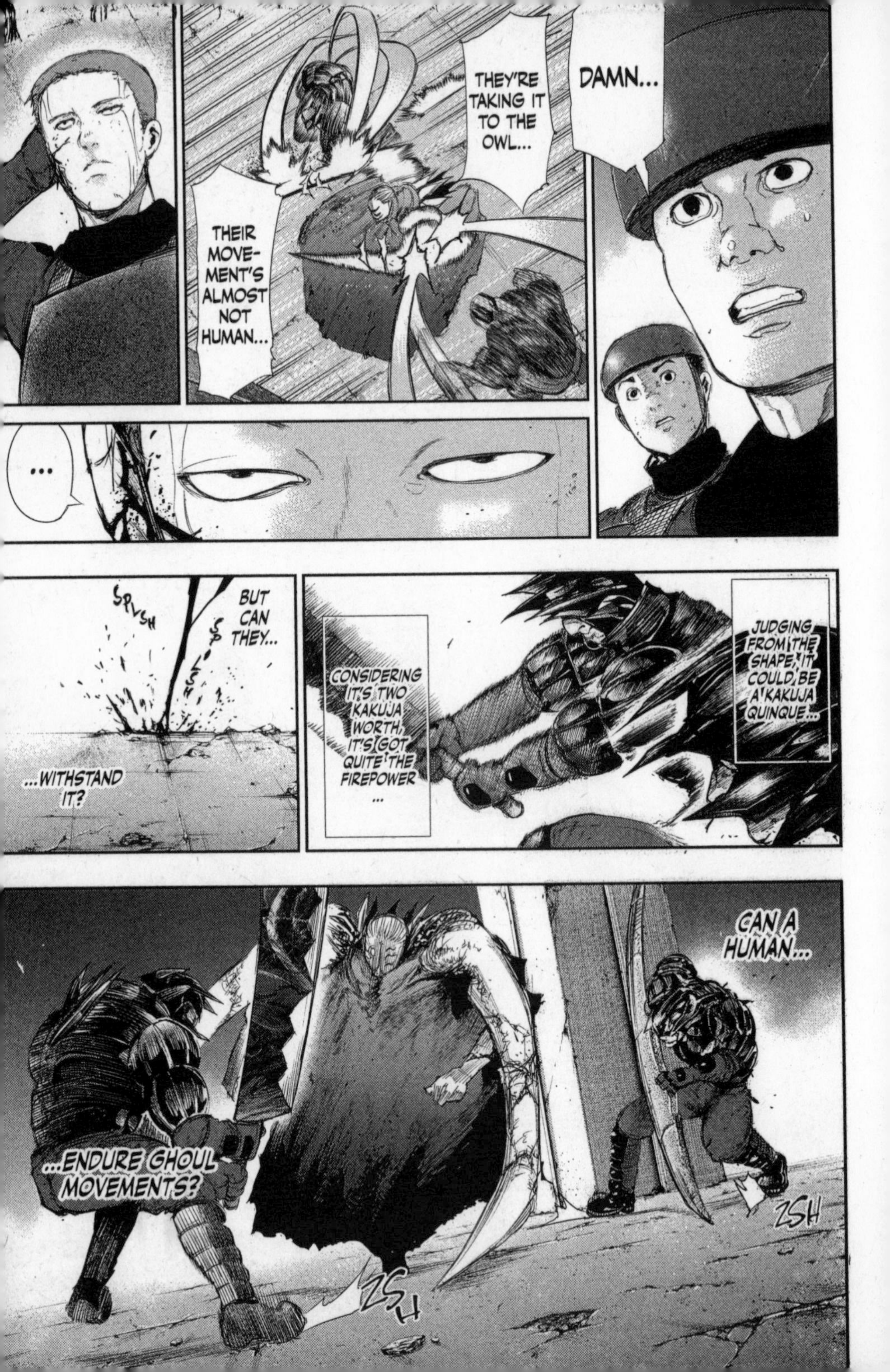
DAMN...
THEY'RE TAKING IT TO THE OWL...
THEIR MOVEMENT'S ALMOST NOT HUMAN...
...
JUDGING FROM THE SHAPE, IT COULD BE A KAKUJA QUINQUE...
CONSIDERING IT'S TWO KAKUJA WORTH, IT'S GOT QUITE THE FIREPOWER ...
SPLSH
BUT CAN THEY...
SPLSH
...WITHSTAND IT?
CAN A HUMAN...
ZSH
...ENDURE GHOUL MOVEMENTS?
ZSH

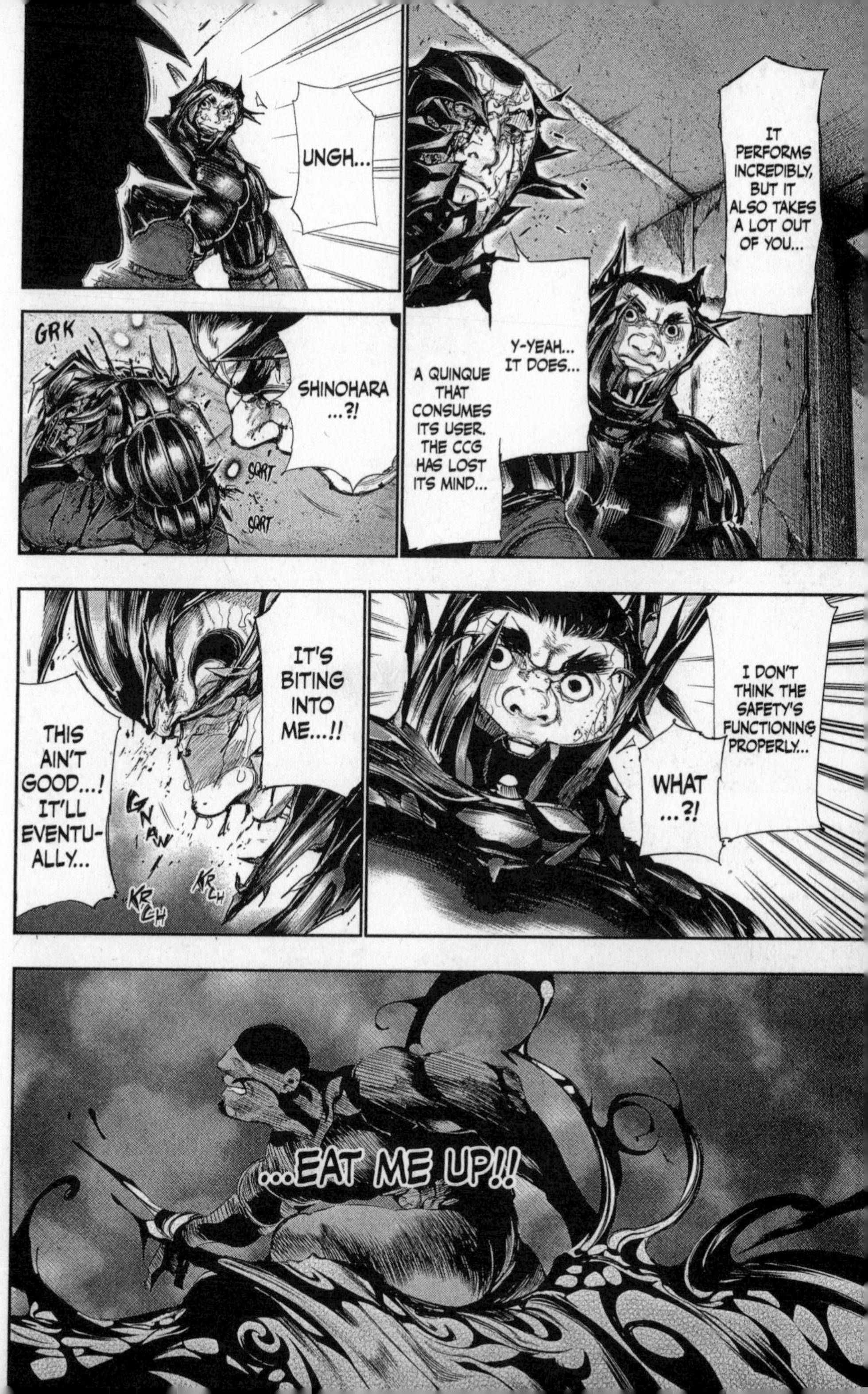
IT PERFORMS INCREDIBLY, BUT IT ALSO TAKES A LOT OUT OF YOU...
Y-YEAH... IT DOES...
A QUINQUE THAT CONSUMES ITS USER. THE CCG HAS LOST ITS MIND...
UNGH...
GRK
SHINOHARA ...?!
SQRT
SQRT
I DON'T THINK THE SAFETY'S FUNCTIONING PROPERLY...
WHAT ...?!
IT'S BITING INTO ME...!!
THIS AIN'T GOOD...! IT'LL EVENTU-ALLY...
GNAW
KRCH
KRCH
...EAT ME UP!!

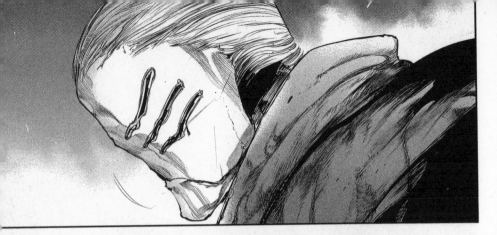

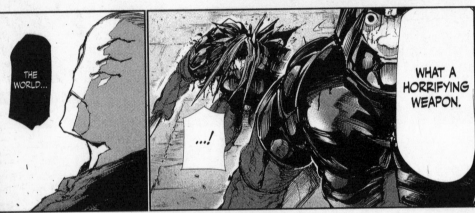

WHAT A HORRIFYING WEAPON.
...!
THE WORLD...
... CONTINUES TO BREED ANGER AND SADNESS.
PILFERING, KILLING.
WE JUSTIFY THOSE ACTS TO CONVINCE OURSELVES THAT WE ARE ONLY DOING WHAT WE ARE SUPPOSED TO.
YOUR WEAPON IS A SYMBOL OF THAT.

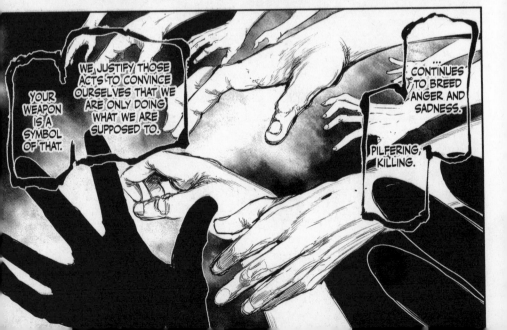

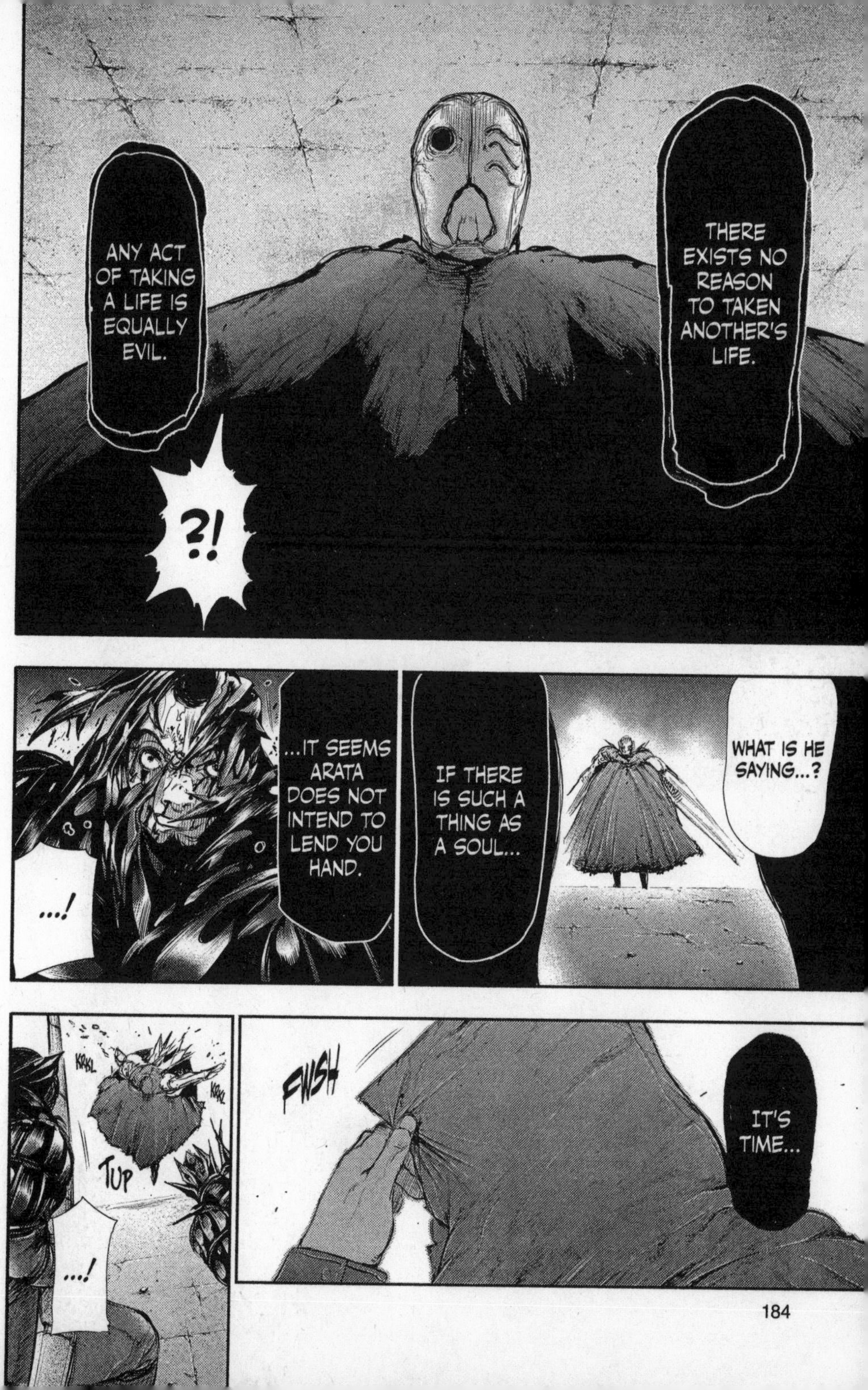
THERE EXISTS NO REASON TO TAKEN ANOTHER'S LIFE.
ANY ACT OF TAKING A LIFE IS EQUALLY EVIL.
?!
WHAT IS HE SAYING...?
IF THERE IS SUCH A THING AS A SOUL...
...IT SEEMS ARATA DOES NOT INTEND TO LEND YOU HAND.
...!
FWSH
IT'S TIME...
KRKL
KRKL
TUP
...!

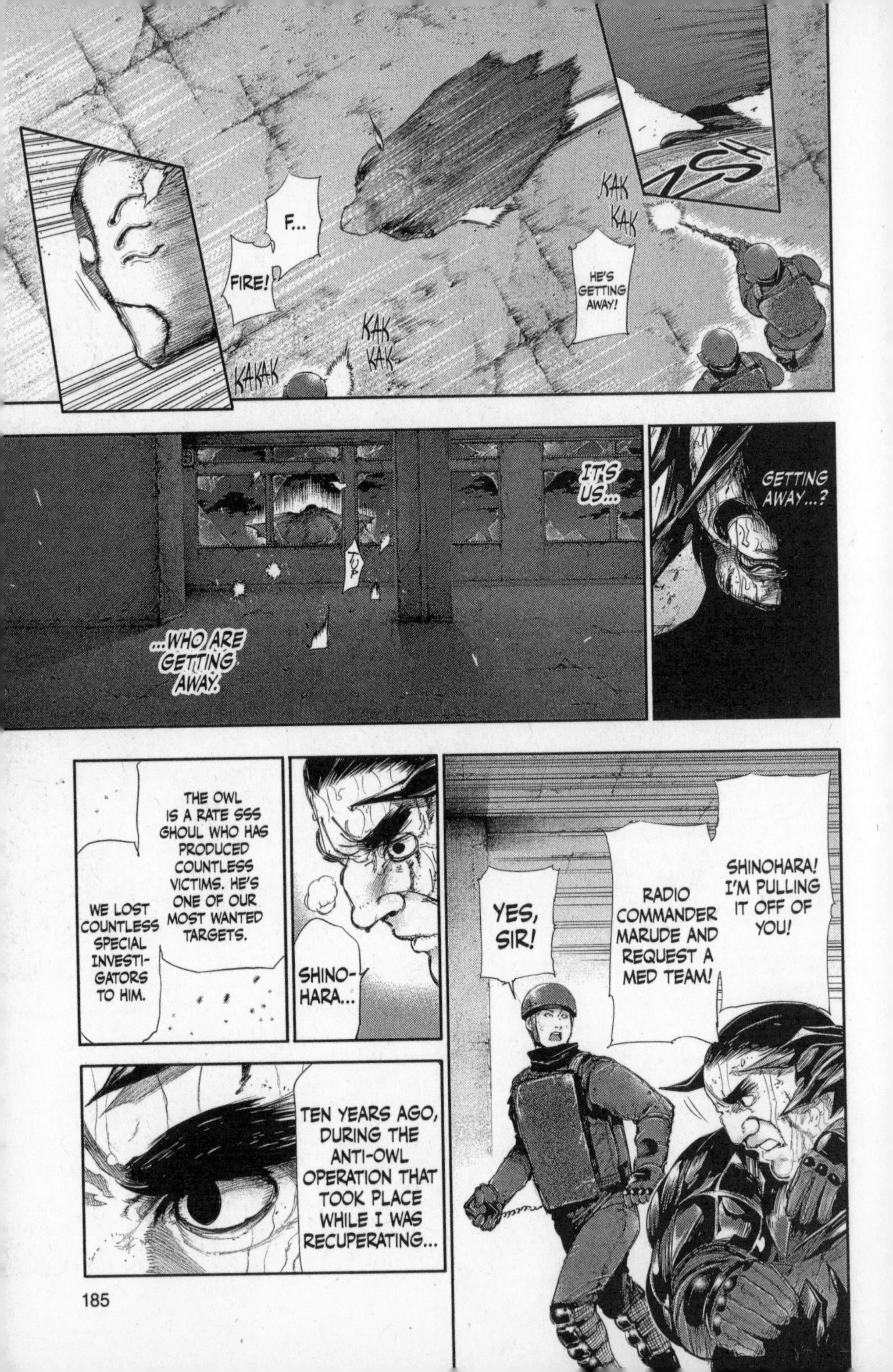
KAK
KAK
HE'S GETTING AWAY!
F...
FIRE!
KAK
KAK
KAKAK
GETTING AWAY...?
IT'S US...
TUP
...WHO ARE GETTING AWAY.
SHINOHARA! I'M PULLING IT OFF OF YOU!
RADIO COMMANDER MARUDE AND REQUEST A MED TEAM!
YES, SIR!
SHINO-HARA...
THE OWL IS A RATE SSS GHOUL WHO HAS PRODUCED COUNTLESS VICTIMS. HE'S ONE OF OUR MOST WANTED TARGETS.
WE LOST COUNTLESS SPECIAL INVESTI-GATORS TO HIM.
TEN YEARS AGO, DURING THE ANTI-OWL OPERATION THAT TOOK PLACE WHILE I WAS RECUPERATING...

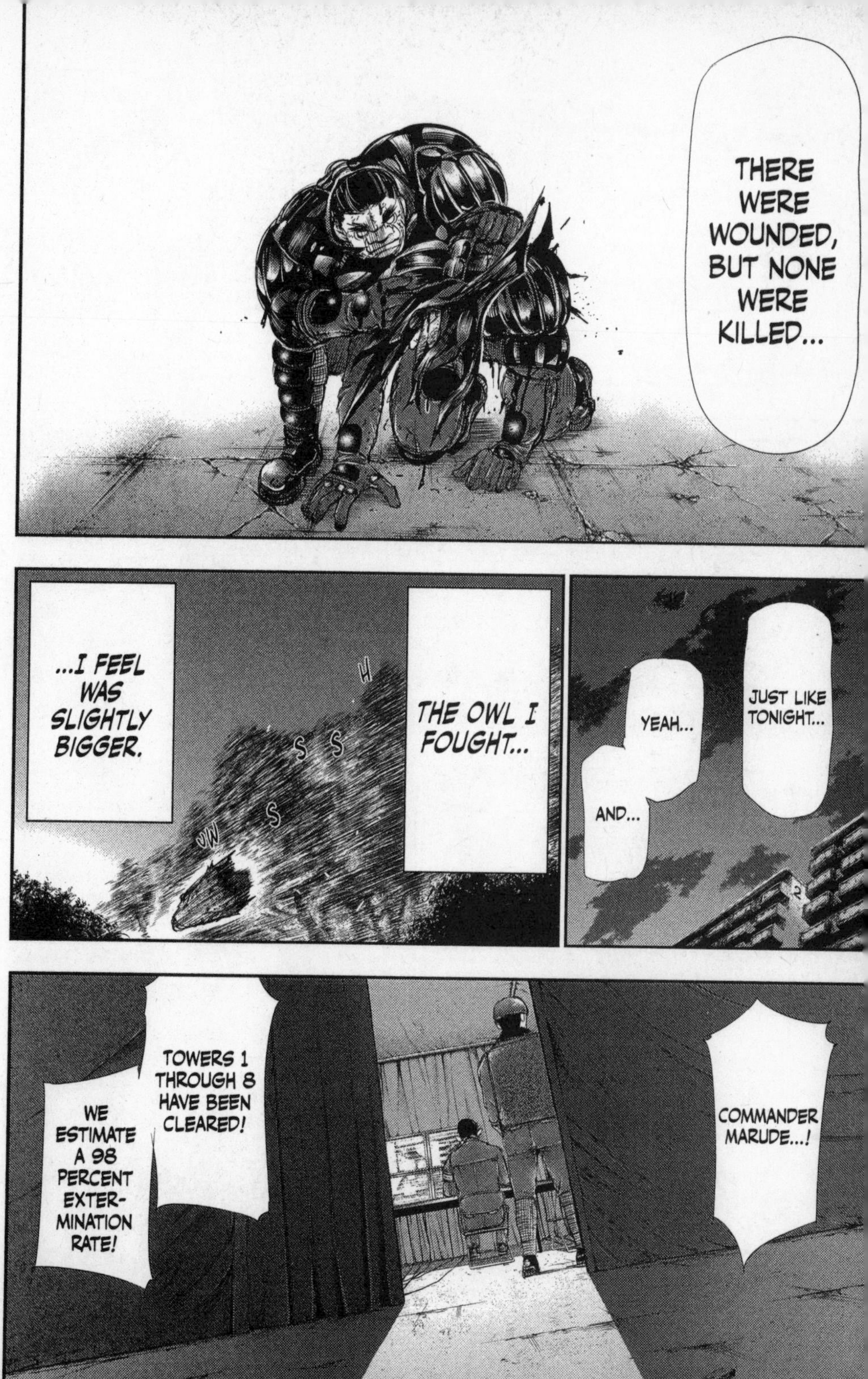
THERE WERE WOUNDED, BUT NONE WERE KILLED...
JUST LIKE TONIGHT...
YEAH...
AND...
THE OWL I FOUGHT...
...I FEEL WAS SLIGHTLY BIGGER.
COMMANDER MARUDE...!
TOWERS 1 THROUGH 8 HAVE BEEN CLEARED!
WE ESTIMATE A 98 PERCENT EXTER-MINATION RATE!

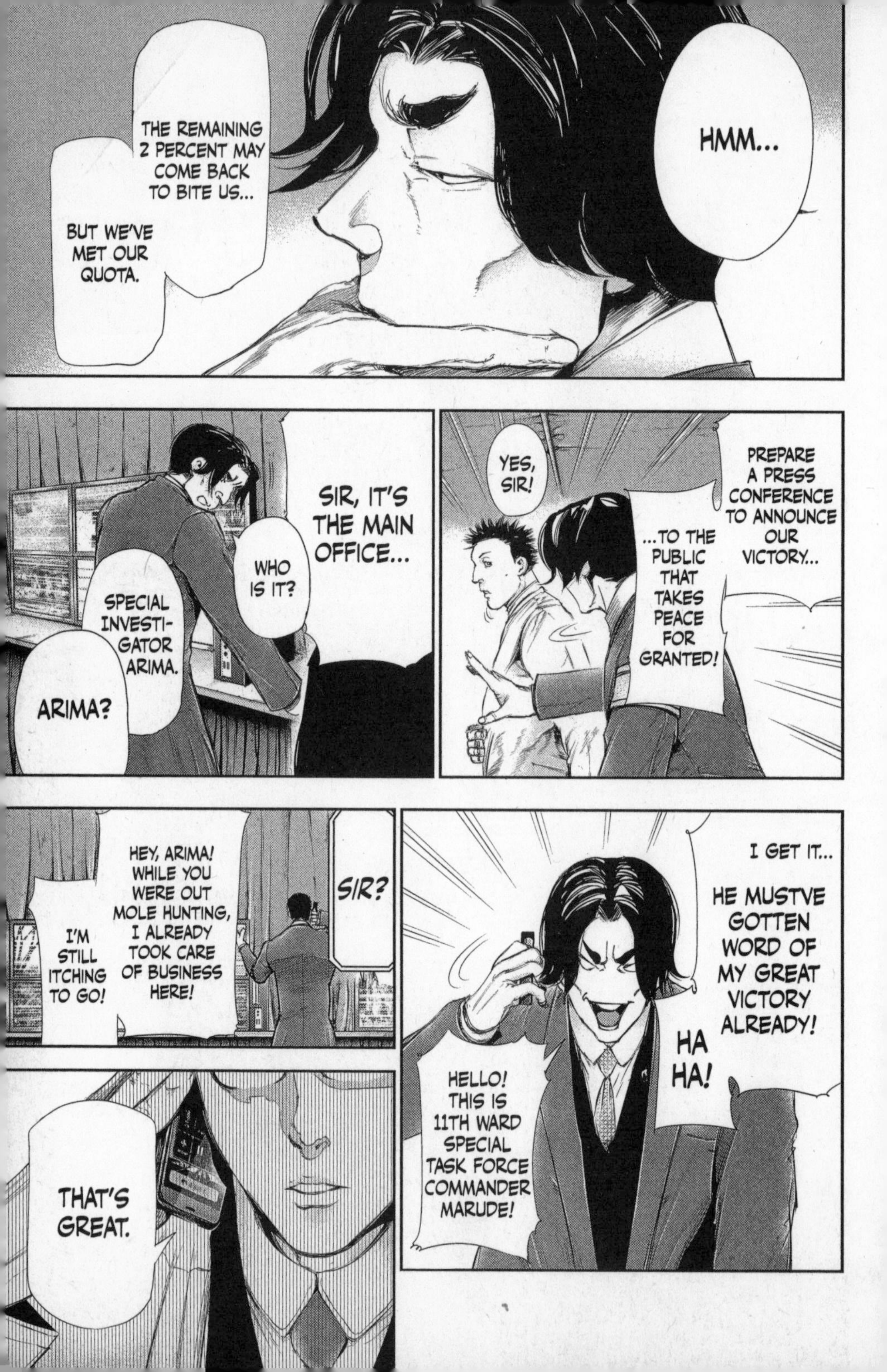
HMM...
THE REMAINING 2 PERCENT MAY COME BACK TO BITE US...
BUT WE'VE MET OUR QUOTA.
PREPARE A PRESS CONFERENCE TO ANNOUNCE OUR VICTORY...
...TO THE PUBLIC THAT TAKES PEACE FOR GRANTED!
YES, SIR!
SIR, IT'S THE MAIN OFFICE...
WHO IS IT?
SPECIAL INVESTI-GATOR ARIMA.
ARIMA?
I GET IT...
HE MUSTVE GOTTEN WORD OF MY GREAT VICTORY ALREADY!
HA HA!
HELLO! THIS IS 11TH WARD SPECIAL TASK FORCE COMMANDER MARUDE!
SIR?
HEY, ARIMA! WHILE YOU WERE OUT MOLE HUNTING, I ALREADY TOOK CARE OF BUSINESS HERE!
I'M STILL ITCHING TO GO!
THAT'S GREAT.

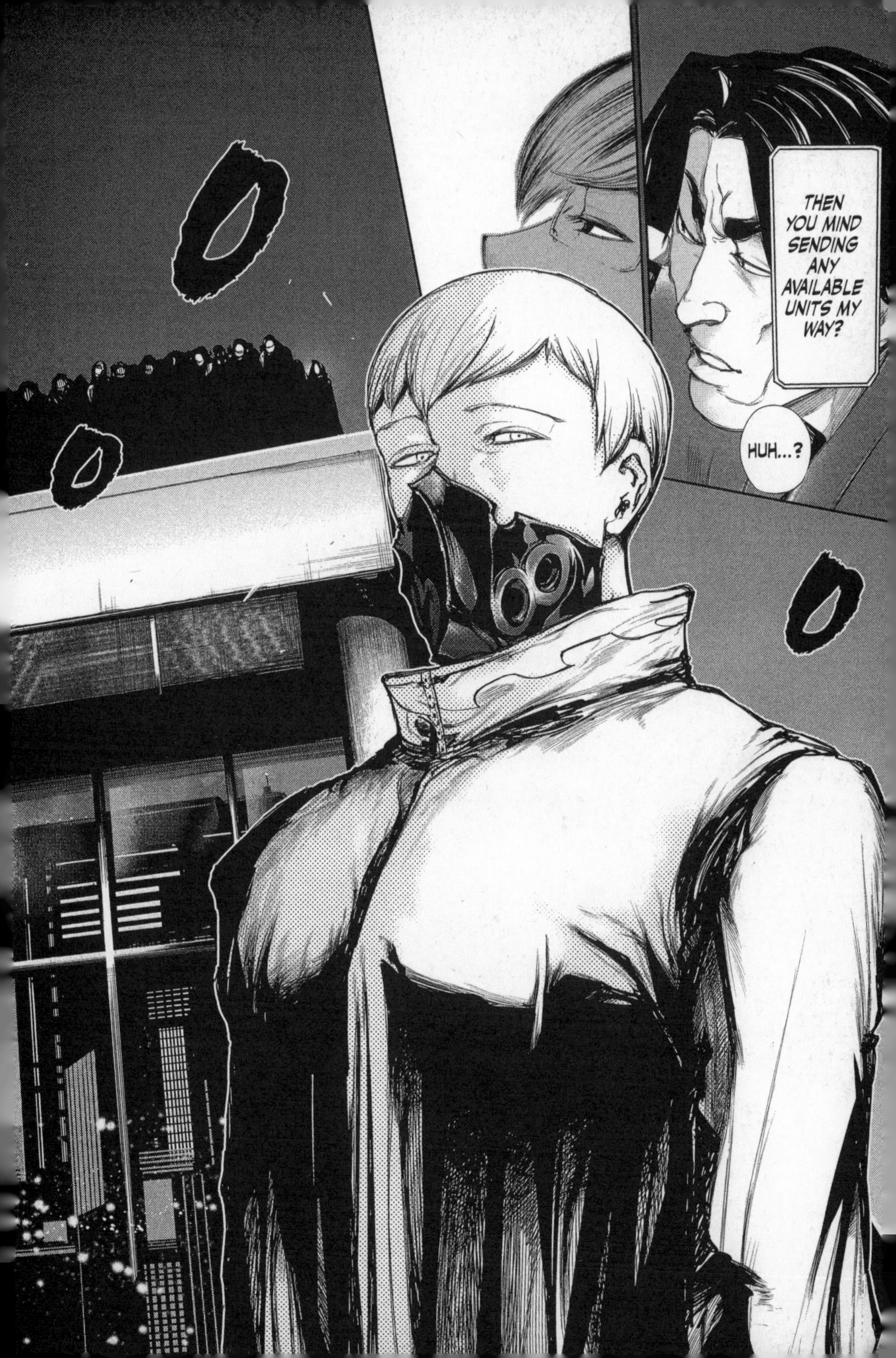
THEN YOU MIND SENDING ANY AVAILABLE UNITS MY WAY?
HUH...?

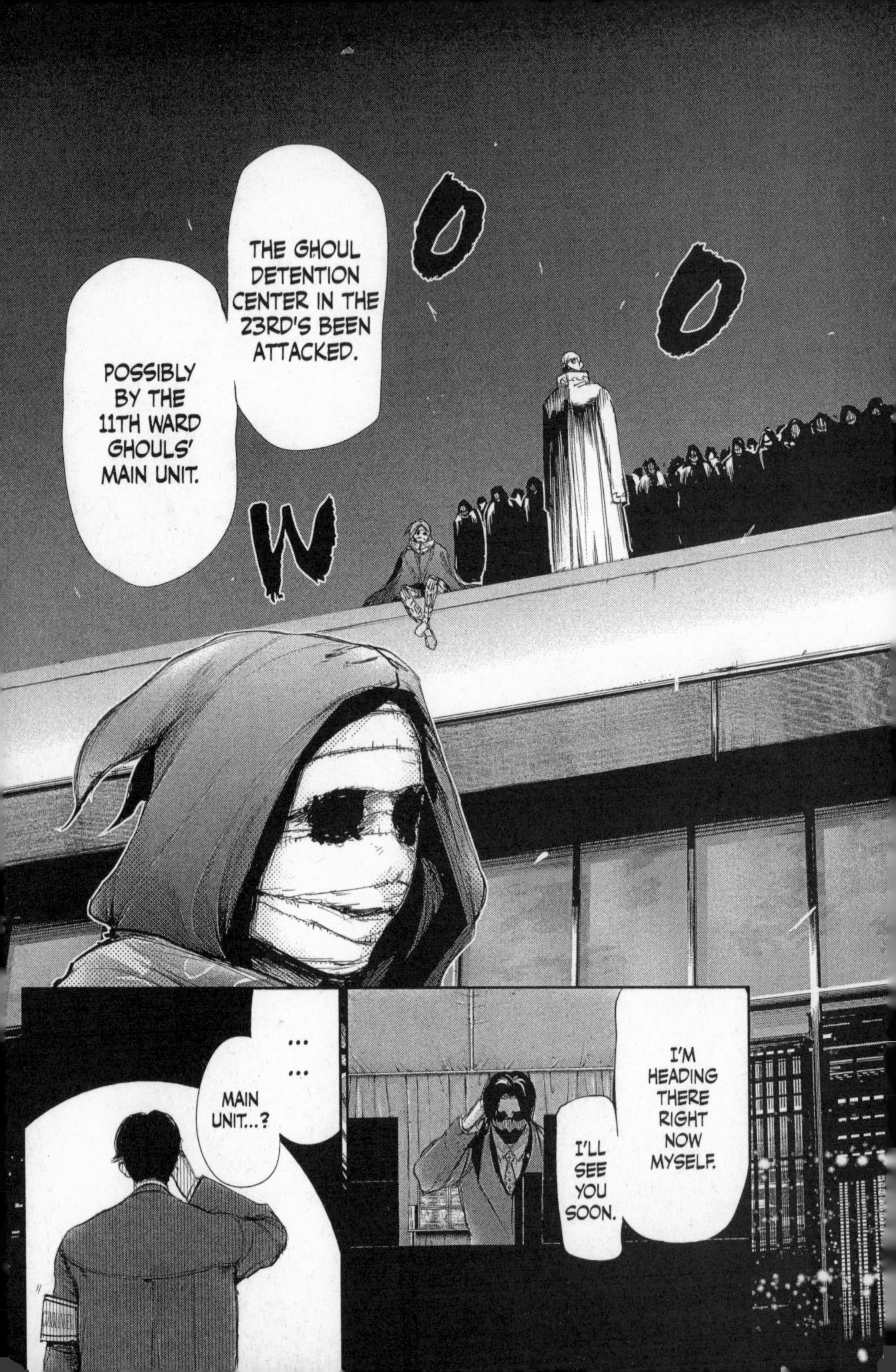
THE GHOUL DETENTION CENTER IN THE 23RD'S BEEN ATTACKED.
POSSIBLY BY THE 11TH WARD GHOULS' MAIN UNIT.
WOO
I'M HEADING THERE RIGHT NOW MYSELF.
I'LL SEE YOU SOON.
... ...
MAIN UNIT...?

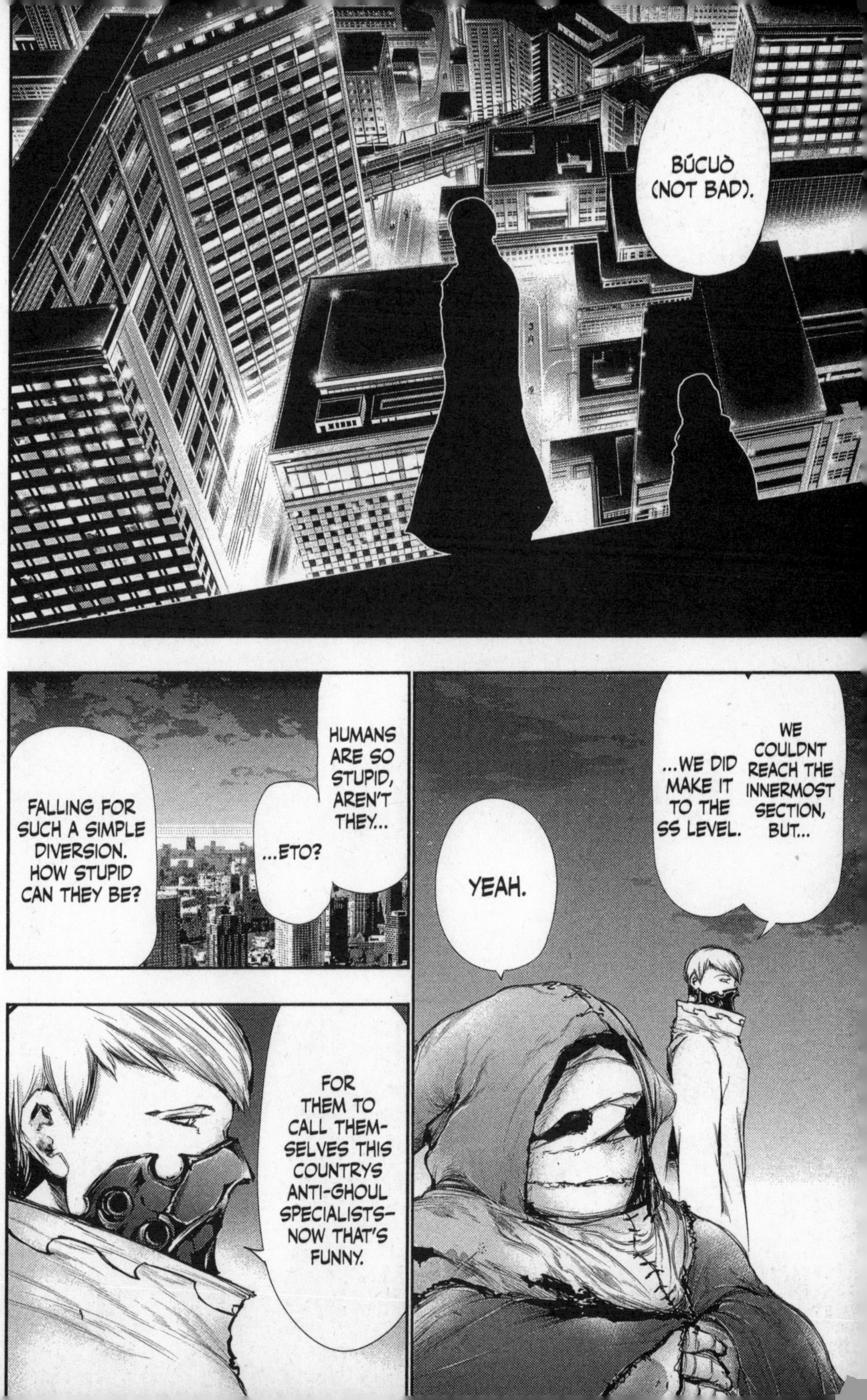
BÚCUÒ (NOT BAD).
WE COULDNT REACH THE INNERMOST SECTION, BUT...
...WE DID MAKE IT TO THE SS LEVEL.
YEAH.
HUMANS ARE SO STUPID, AREN'T THEY...
...ETO?
FALLING FOR SUCH A SIMPLE DIVERSION. HOW STUPID CAN THEY BE?
FOR THEM TO CALL THEMSELVES THIS COUNTRYS ANTI-GHOUL SPECIALISTS—NOW THAT'S FUNNY.

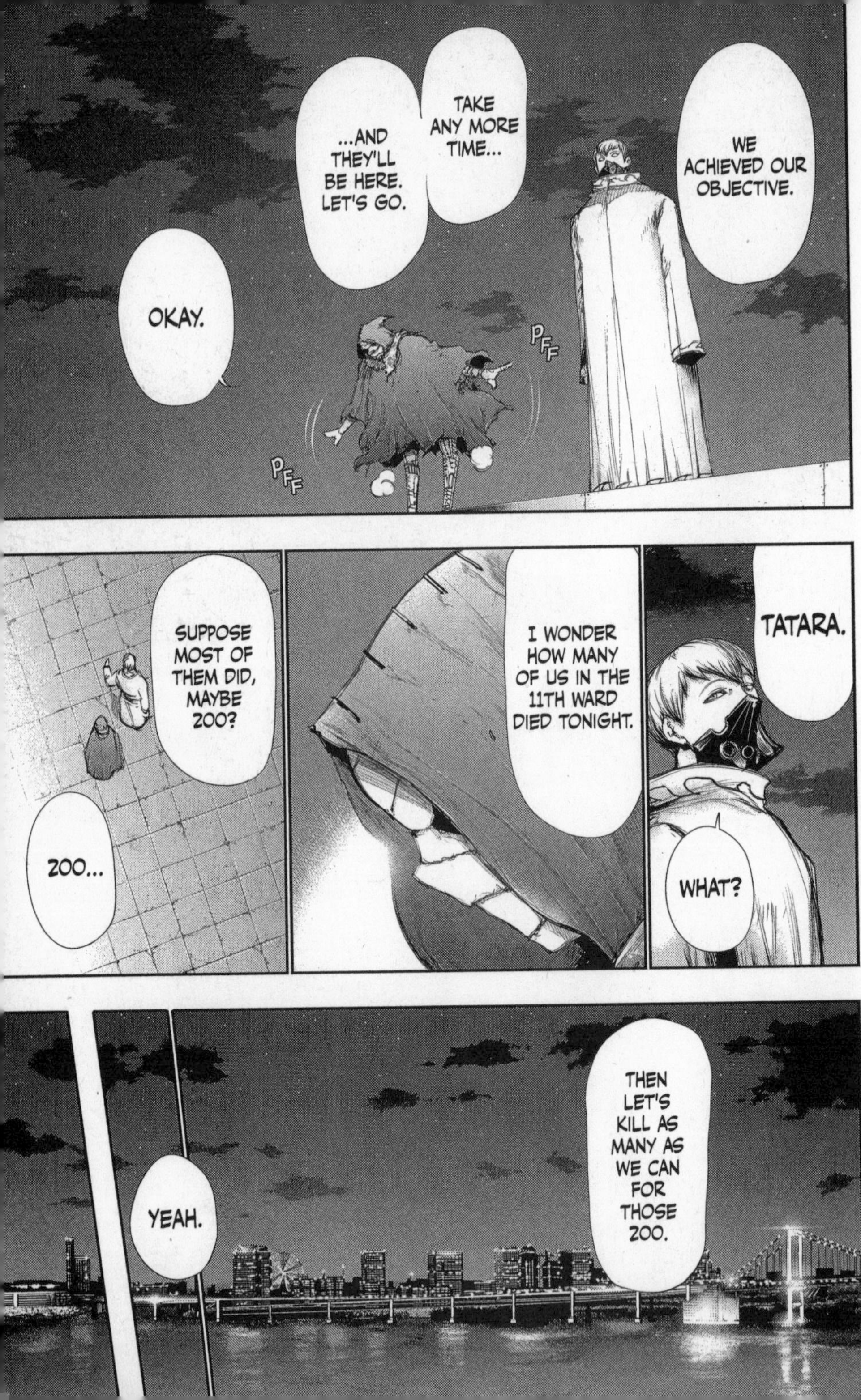
WE ACHIEVED OUR OBJECTIVE.
TAKE ANY MORE TIME...
...AND THEY'LL BE HERE. LET'S GO.
OKAY.
PFF
PFF
TATARA.
WHAT?
I WONDER HOW MANY OF US IN THE 11TH WARD DIED TONIGHT.
SUPPOSE MOST OF THEM DID, MAYBE 200?
200...
THEN LET'S KILL AS MANY AS WE CAN FOR THOSE 200.
YEAH.

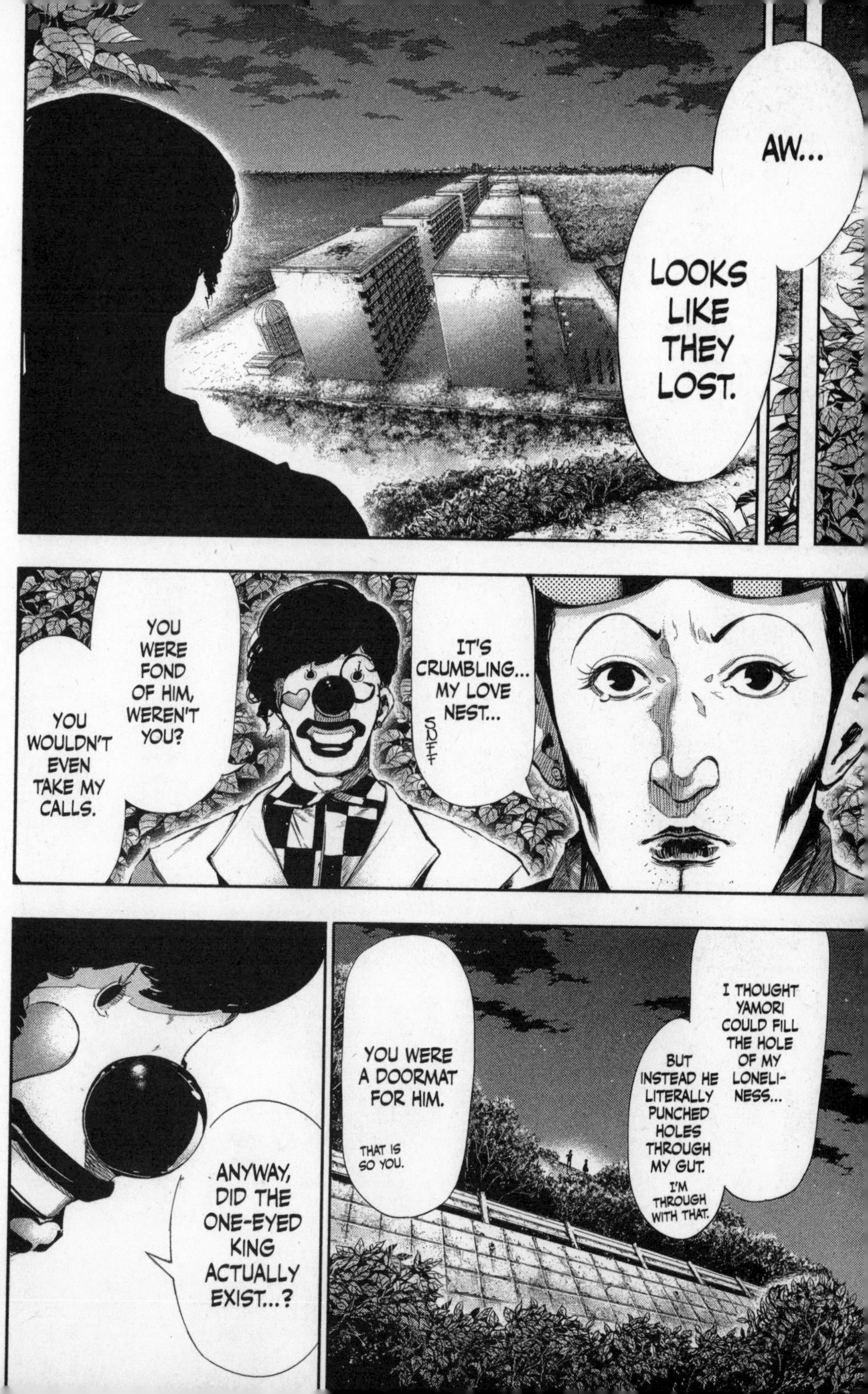
AW...
LOOKS LIKE THEY LOST.
IT'S CRUMBLING... MY LOVE NEST...
SNFF
YOU WERE FOND OF HIM, WEREN'T YOU?
YOU WOULDN'T EVEN TAKE MY CALLS.
I THOUGHT YAMORI COULD FILL THE HOLE OF MY LONELI-NESS...
BUT INSTEAD HE LITERALLY PUNCHED HOLES THROUGH MY GUT.
I'M THROUGH WITH THAT.
YOU WERE A DOORMAT FOR HIM.
THAT IS SO YOU.
ANYWAY, DID THE ONE-EYED KING ACTUALLY EXIST...?

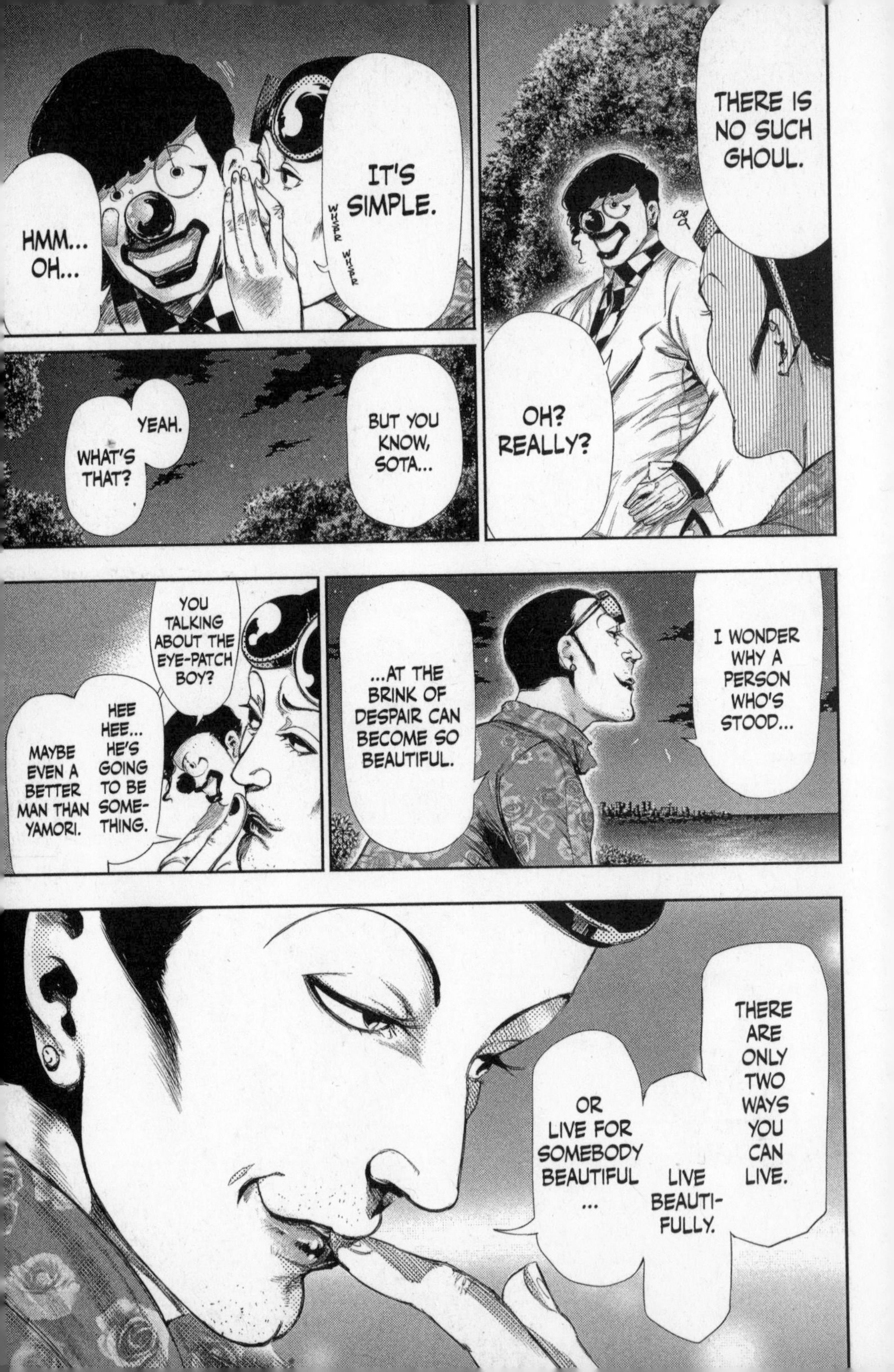
THERE IS NO SUCH GHOUL.
OH? REALLY?
IT'S SIMPLE.
WHSPR WHSPR
HMM... OH...
BUT YOU KNOW, SOTA...
YEAH. WHAT'S THAT?
I WONDER WHY A PERSON WHO'S STOOD...
...AT THE BRINK OF DESPAIR CAN BECOME SO BEAUTIFUL.
YOU TALKING ABOUT THE EYE-PATCH BOY?
HEE HEE... HE'S GOING TO BE SOME-THING.
MAYBE EVEN A BETTER MAN THAN YAMORI.
THERE ARE ONLY TWO WAYS YOU CAN LIVE.
LIVE BEAUTI-FULLY.
OR LIVE FOR SOMEBODY BEAUTIFUL ...

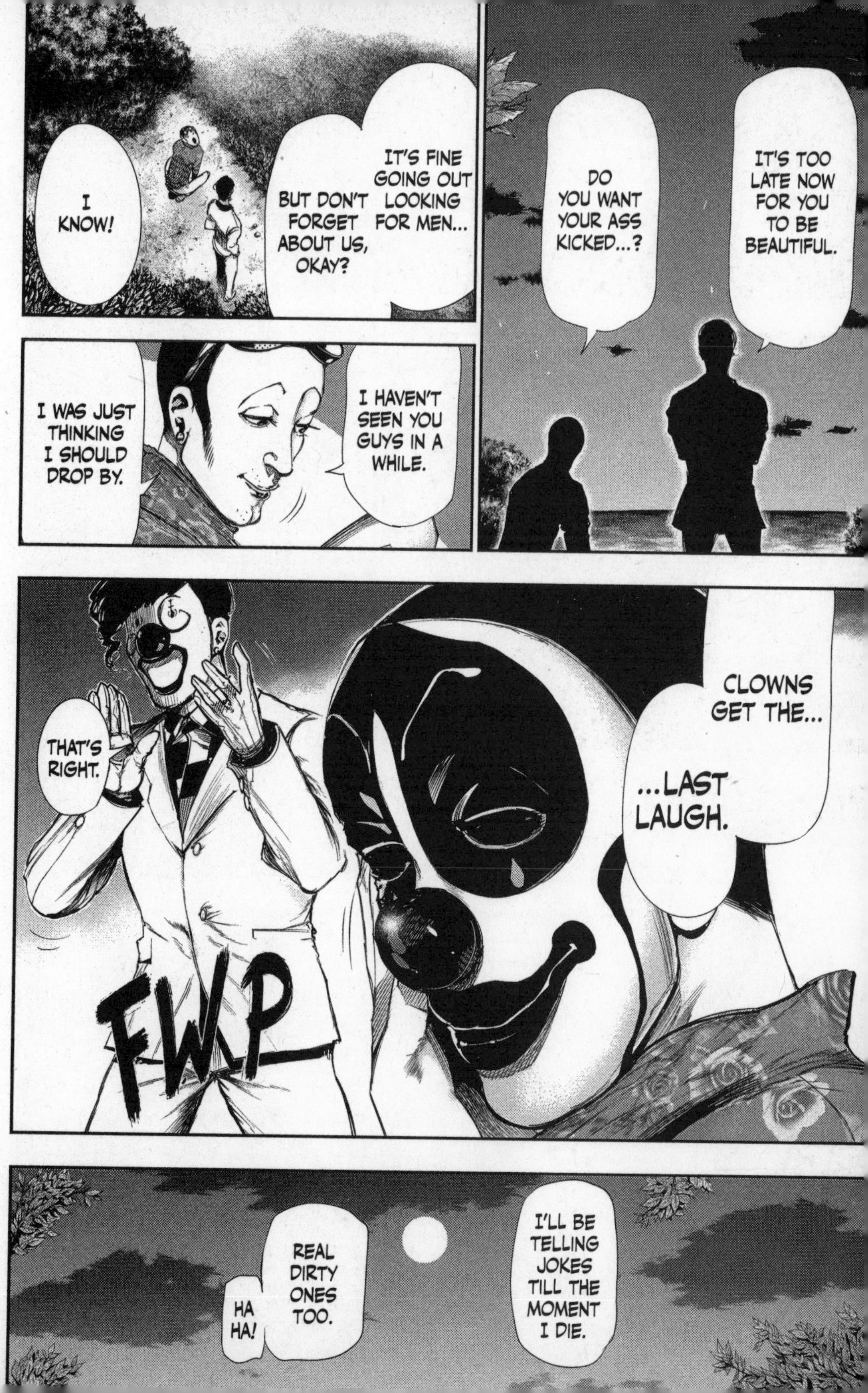
IT'S TOO LATE NOW FOR YOU TO BE BEAUTIFUL.
DO YOU WANT YOUR ASS KICKED...?
IT'S FINE GOING OUT LOOKING FOR MEN...
BUT DON'T FORGET ABOUT US, OKAY?
I KNOW!
I HAVEN'T SEEN YOU GUYS IN A WHILE.
I WAS JUST THINKING I SHOULD DROP BY.
CLOWNS GET THE...
...LAST LAUGH.
FWP
THAT'S RIGHT.
I'LL BE TELLING JOKES TILL THE MOMENT I DIE.
REAL DIRTY ONES TOO.
HA HA!

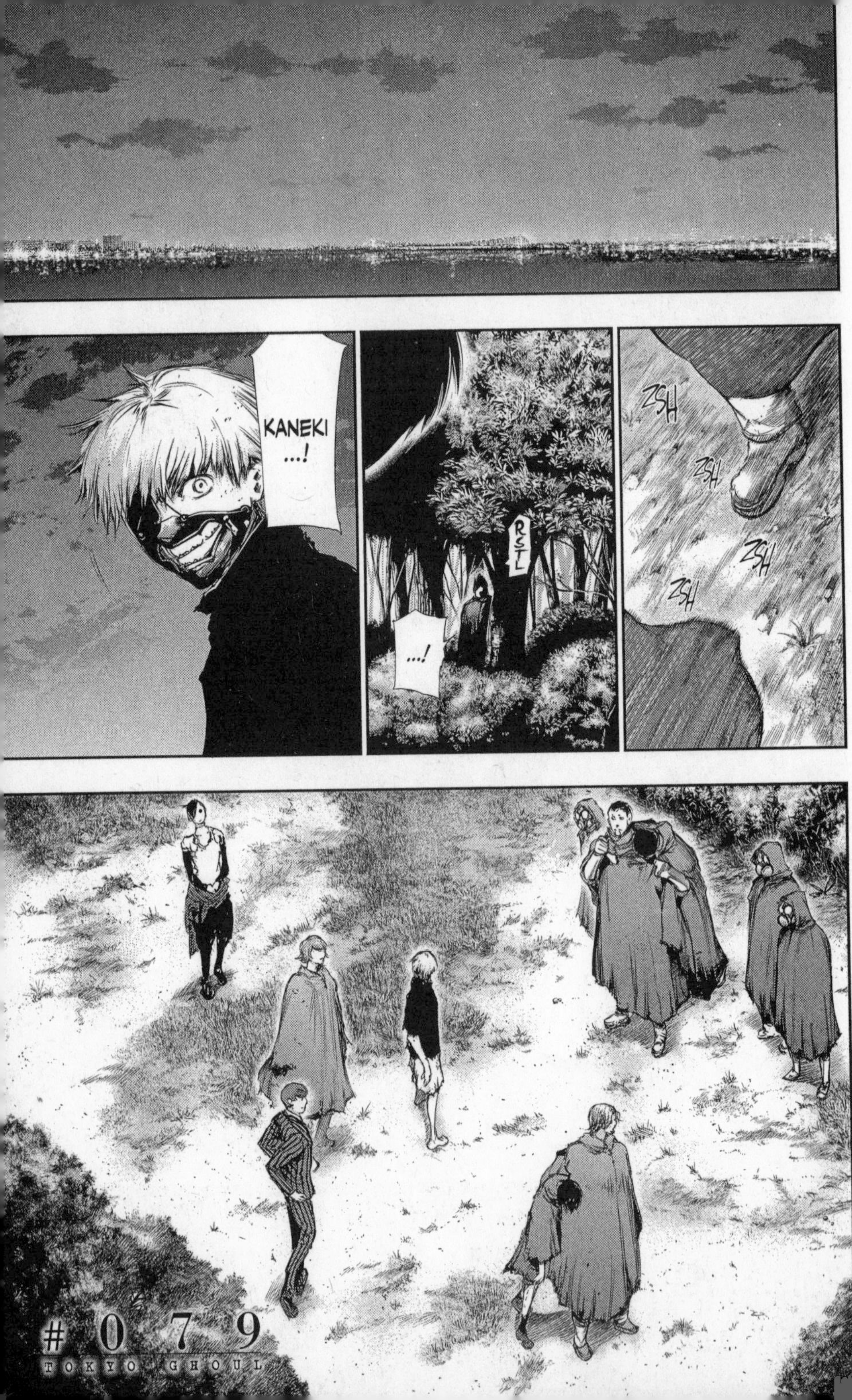
ZSH
ZSH
ZSH
ZSH
RSTL
...!
KANEKI ...!
#079
TOKYO GHOUL

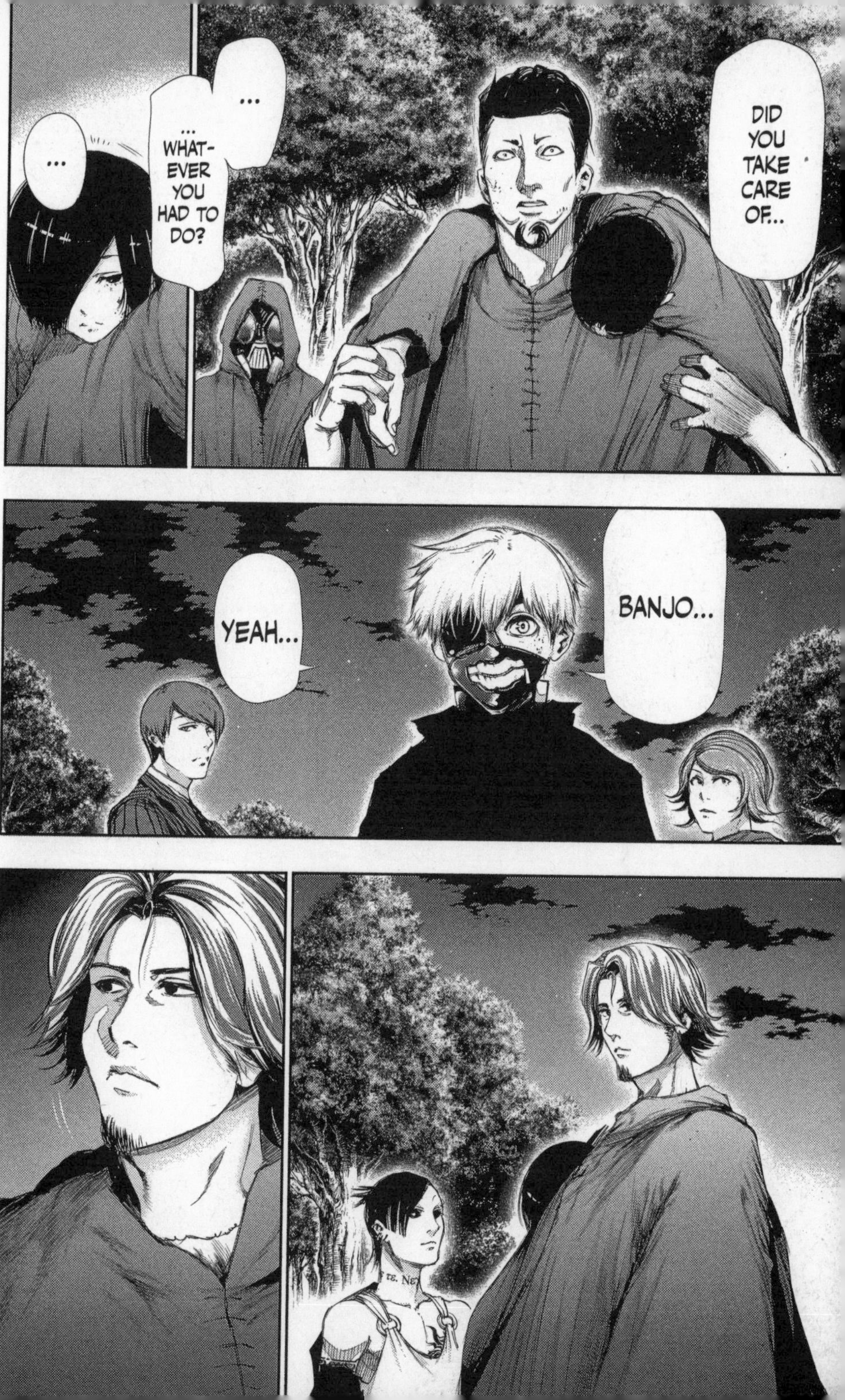
DID YOU TAKE CARE OF...
...
... WHATEVER YOU HAD TO DO?
...
BANJO...
YEAH...

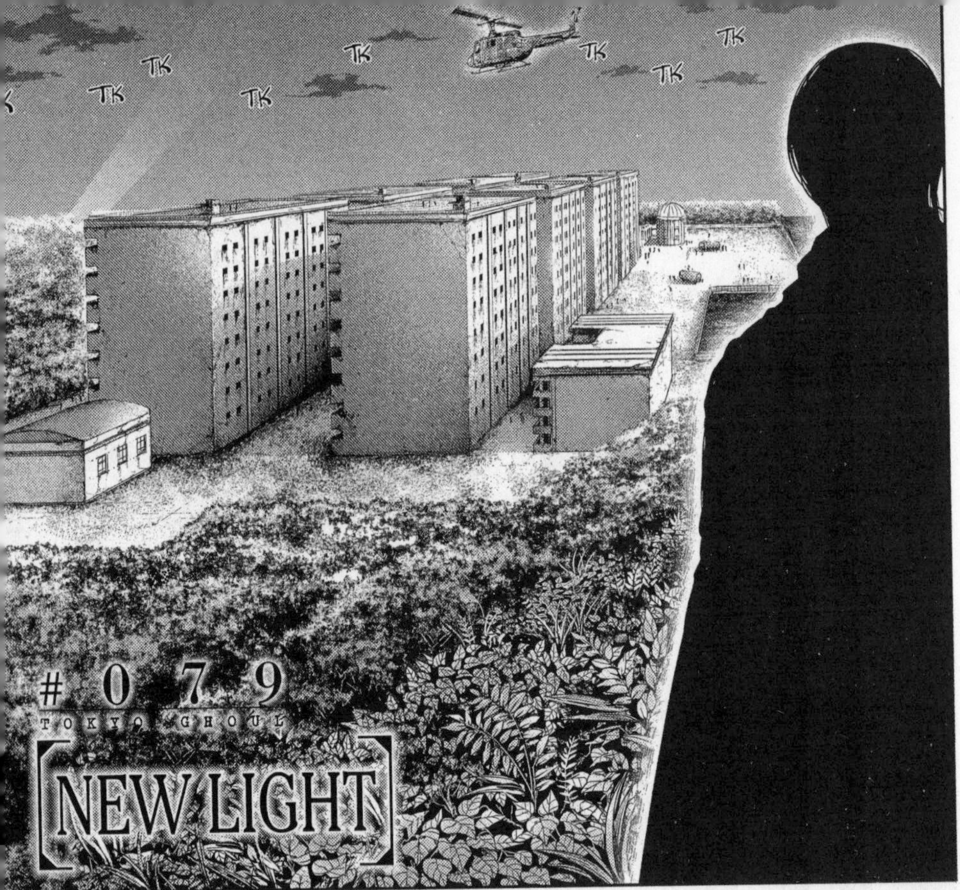
TK
TK
TK
TK
TK
TK
TK
#079
TOKYO GHOUL
NEW LIGHT

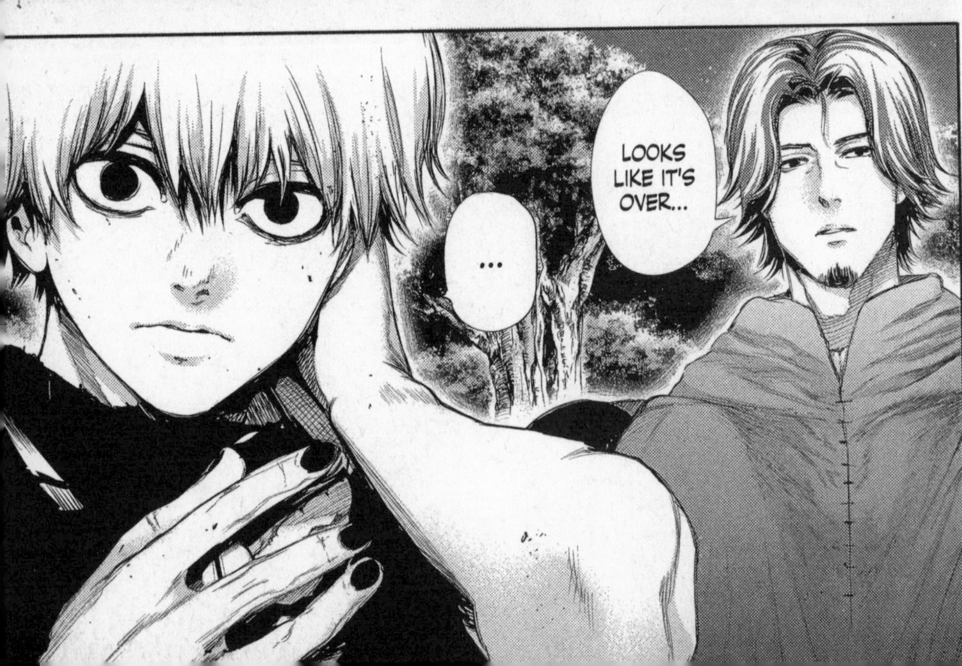
LOOKS LIKE IT'S OVER...
...

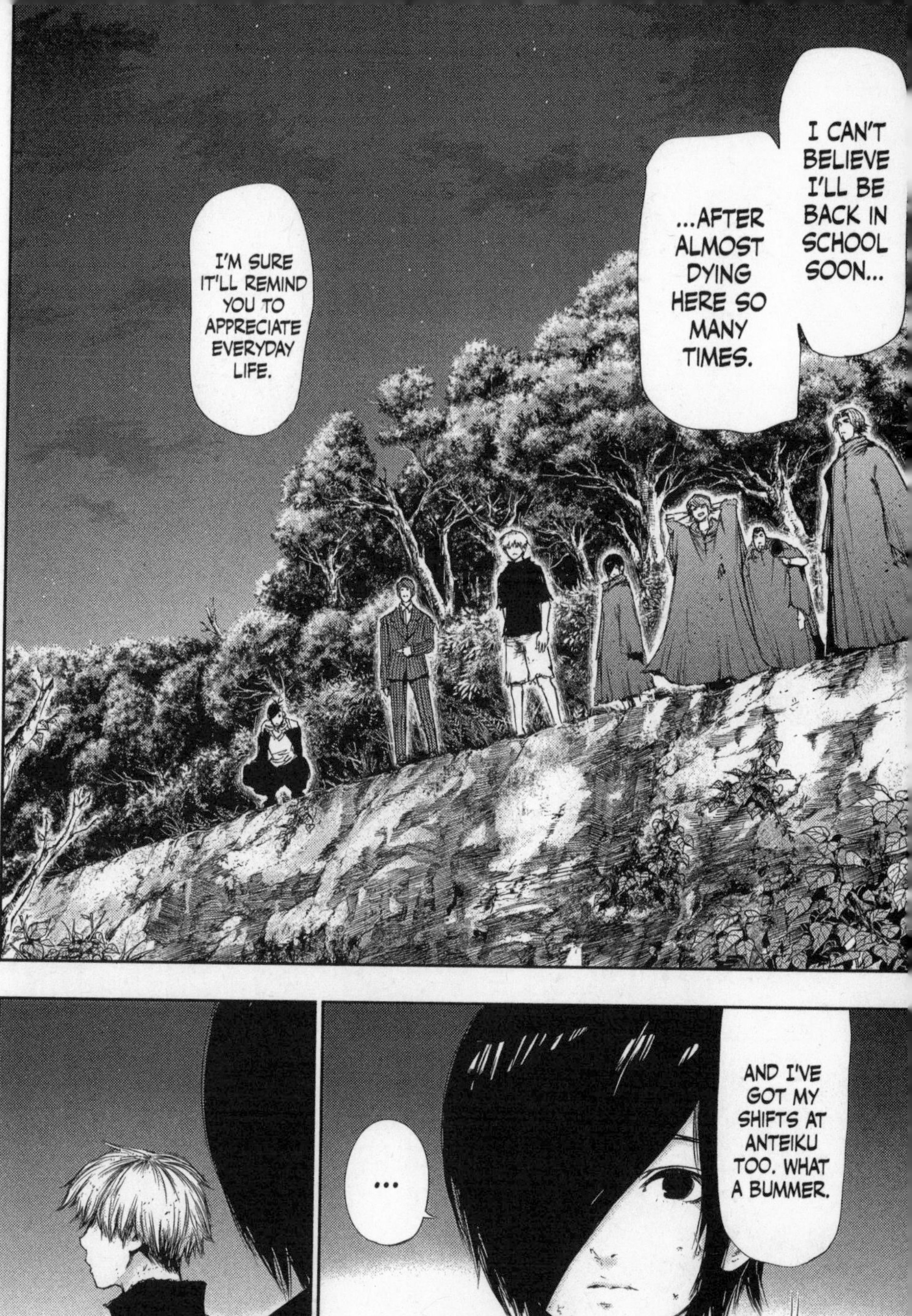
I CAN'T BELIEVE I'LL BE BACK IN SCHOOL SOON...
...AFTER ALMOST DYING HERE SO MANY TIMES.
I'M SURE IT'LL REMIND YOU TO APPRECIATE EVERYDAY LIFE.
AND I'VE GOT MY SHIFTS AT ANTEIKU TOO. WHAT A BUMMER.
...

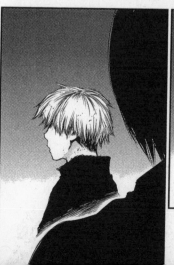

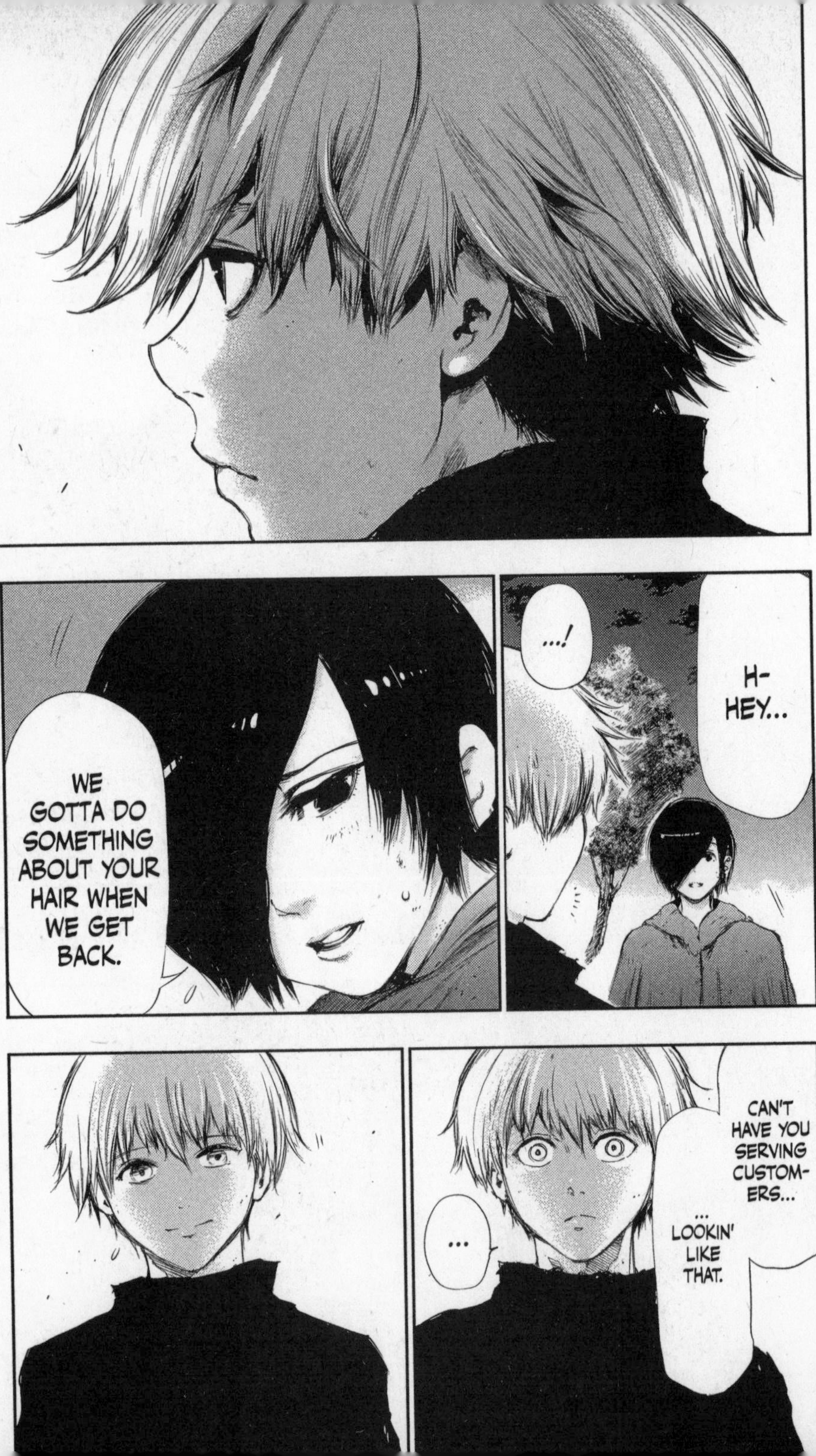
H-HEY...
...!
WE GOTTA DO SOMETHING ABOUT YOUR HAIR WHEN WE GET BACK.
CAN'T HAVE YOU SERVING CUSTOMERS...
... LOOKIN' LIKE THAT.
...

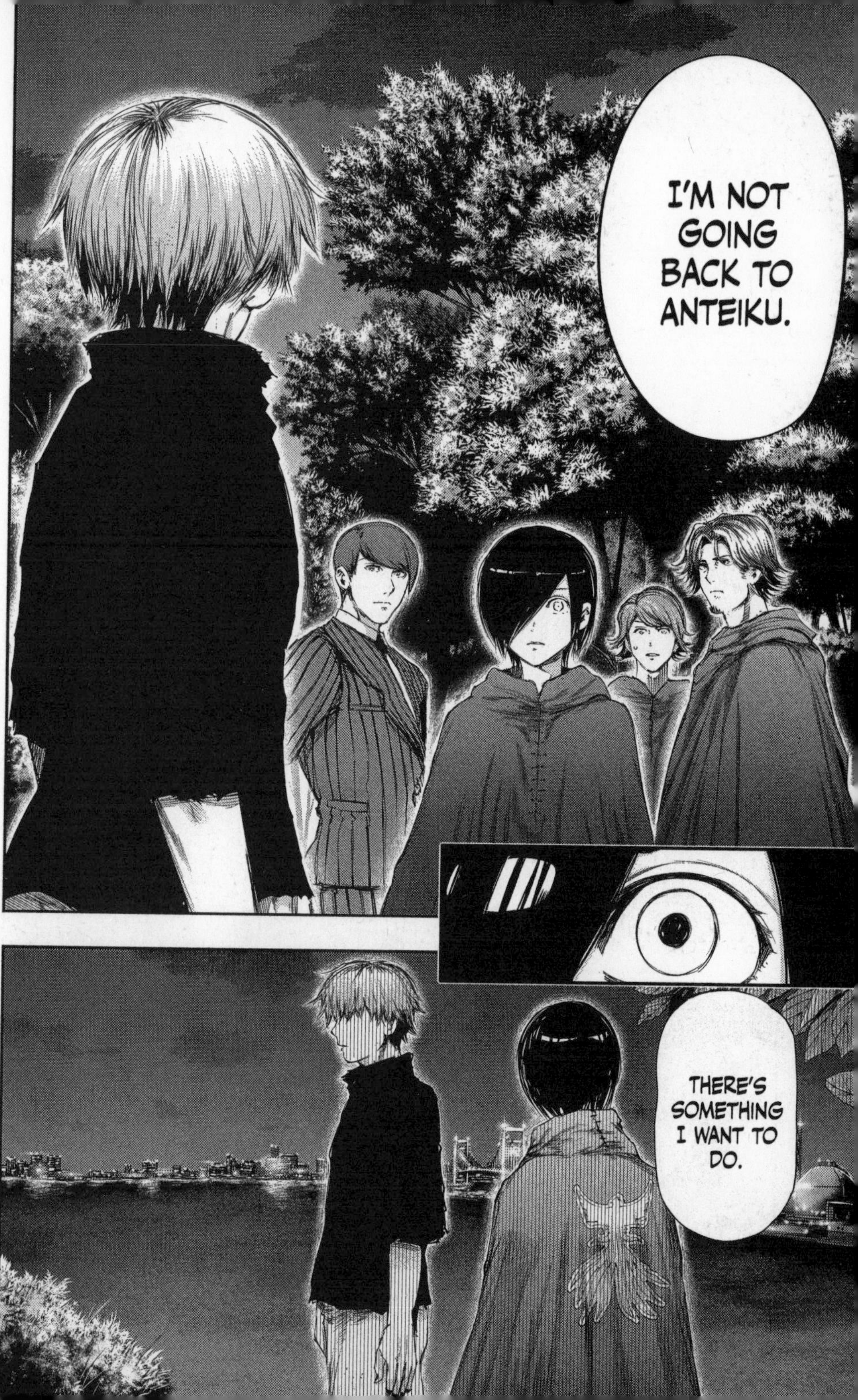
I'M NOT GOING BACK TO ANTEIKU.
THERE'S SOMETHING I WANT TO DO.

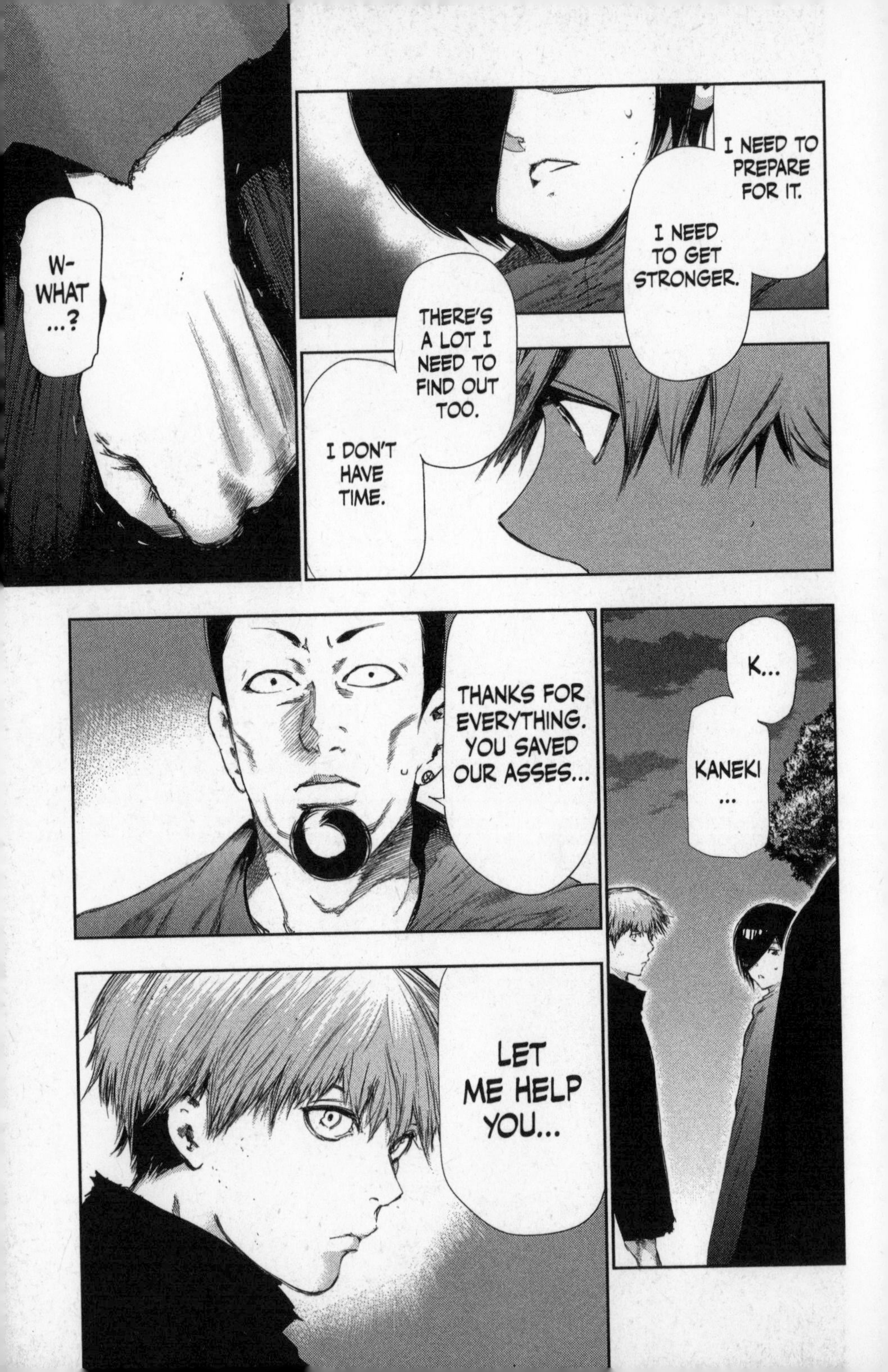
I NEED TO PREPARE FOR IT.
I NEED TO GET STRONGER.
THERE'S A LOT I NEED TO FIND OUT TOO.
I DON'T HAVE TIME.
W-WHAT ...?
K...
KANEKI ...
THANKS FOR EVERYTHING. YOU SAVED OUR ASSES...
LET ME HELP YOU...

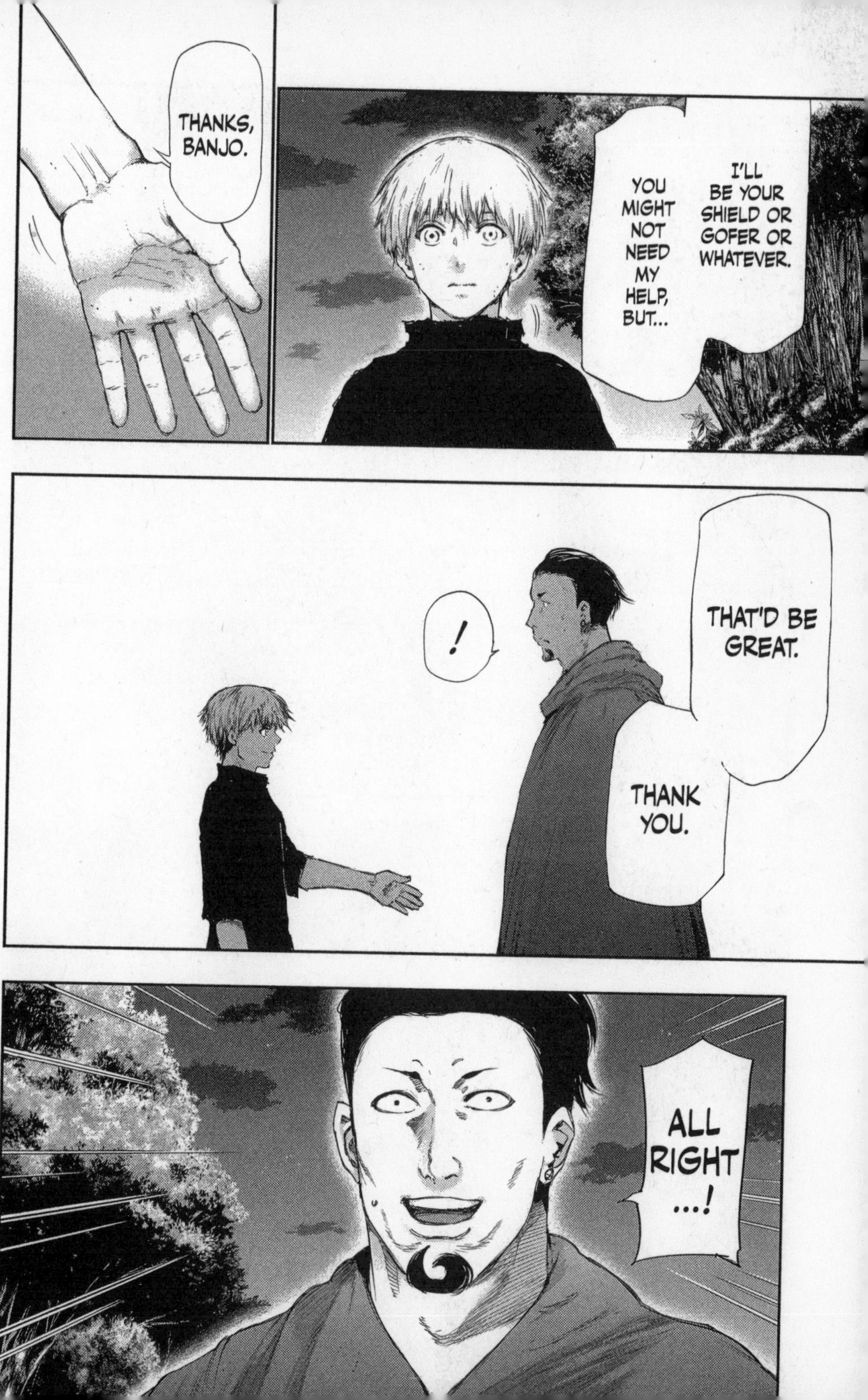
I'LL BE YOUR SHIELD OR GOFER OR WHATEVER.
YOU MIGHT NOT NEED MY HELP, BUT...
THANKS, BANJO.
THAT'D BE GREAT.
THANK YOU.
!
ALL RIGHT ...!

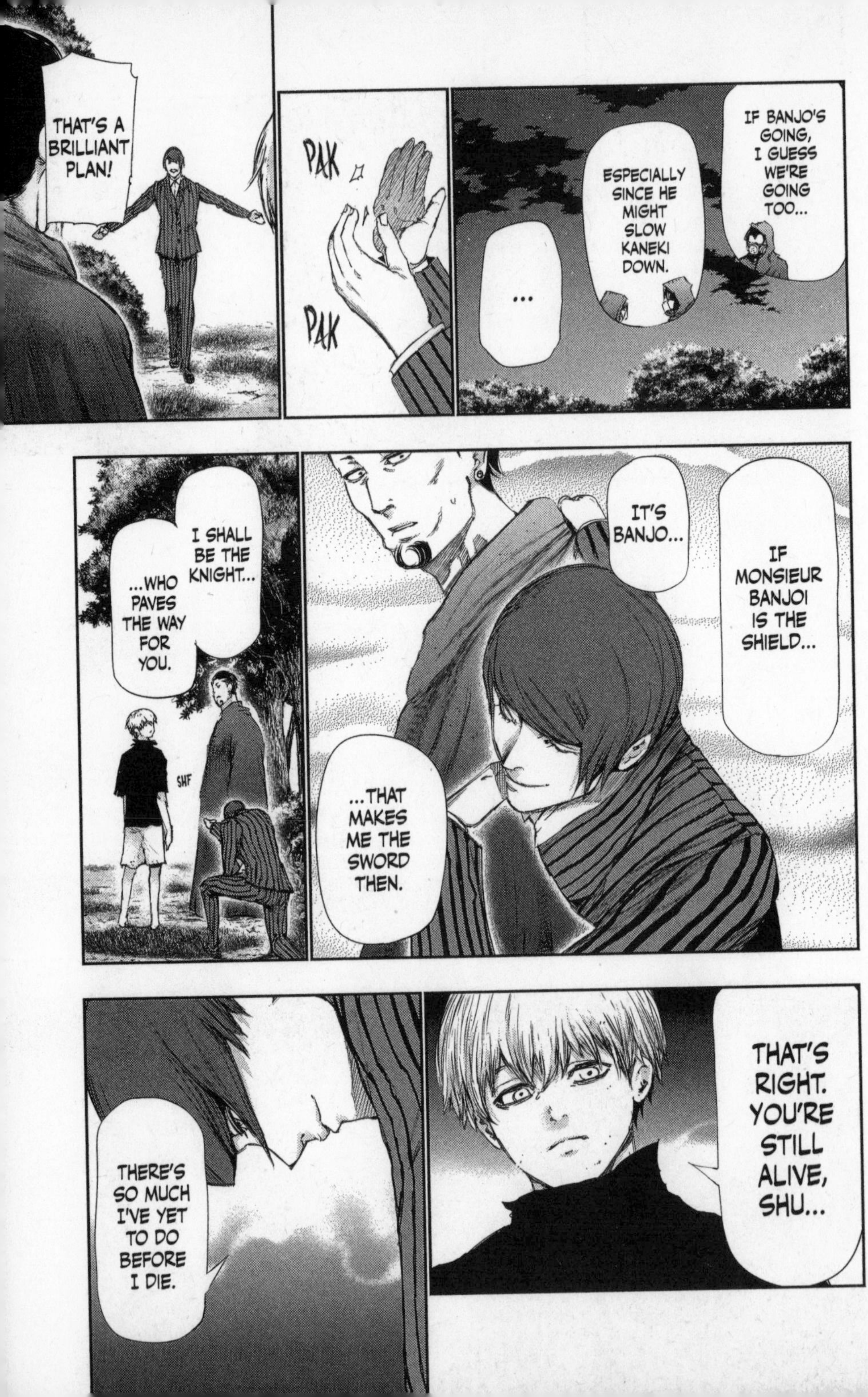
IF BANJO'S GOING, I GUESS WE'RE GOING TOO...
ESPECIALLY SINCE HE MIGHT SLOW KANEKI DOWN.
...
PAK
PAK
THAT'S A BRILLIANT PLAN!
IF MONSIEUR BANJOI IS THE SHIELD...
IT'S BANJO...
...THAT MAKES ME THE SWORD THEN.
I SHALL BE THE KNIGHT...
...WHO PAVES THE WAY FOR YOU.
SHF
THAT'S RIGHT. YOU'RE STILL ALIVE, SHU...
THERE'S SO MUCH I'VE YET TO DO BEFORE I DIE.

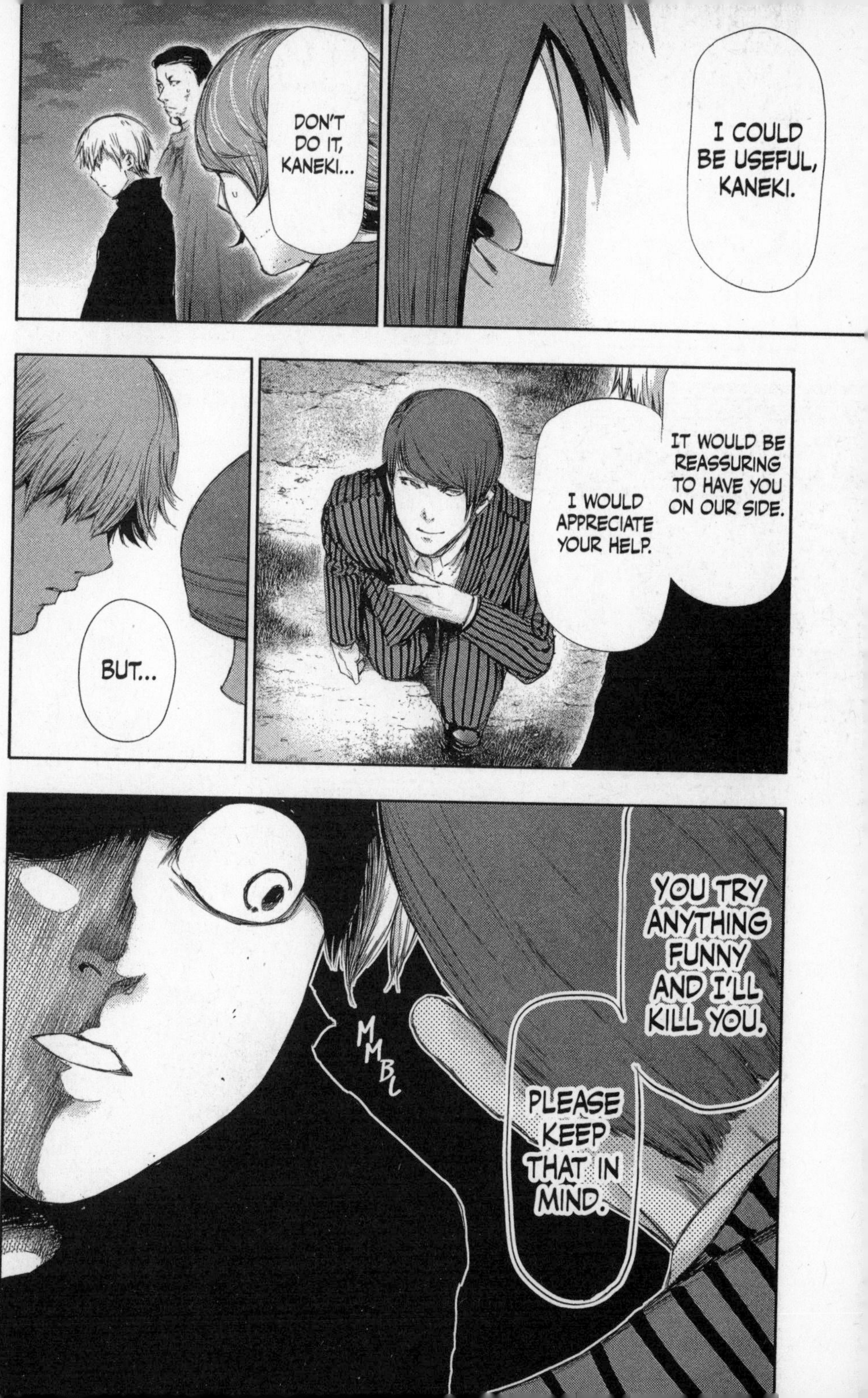
I COULD BE USEFUL, KANEKI.
DON'T DO IT, KANEKI...
IT WOULD BE REASSURING TO HAVE YOU ON OUR SIDE.
I WOULD APPRECIATE YOUR HELP.
BUT...
YOU TRY ANYTHING FUNNY AND I'LL KILL YOU.
PLEASE KEEP THAT IN MIND.
MMBL

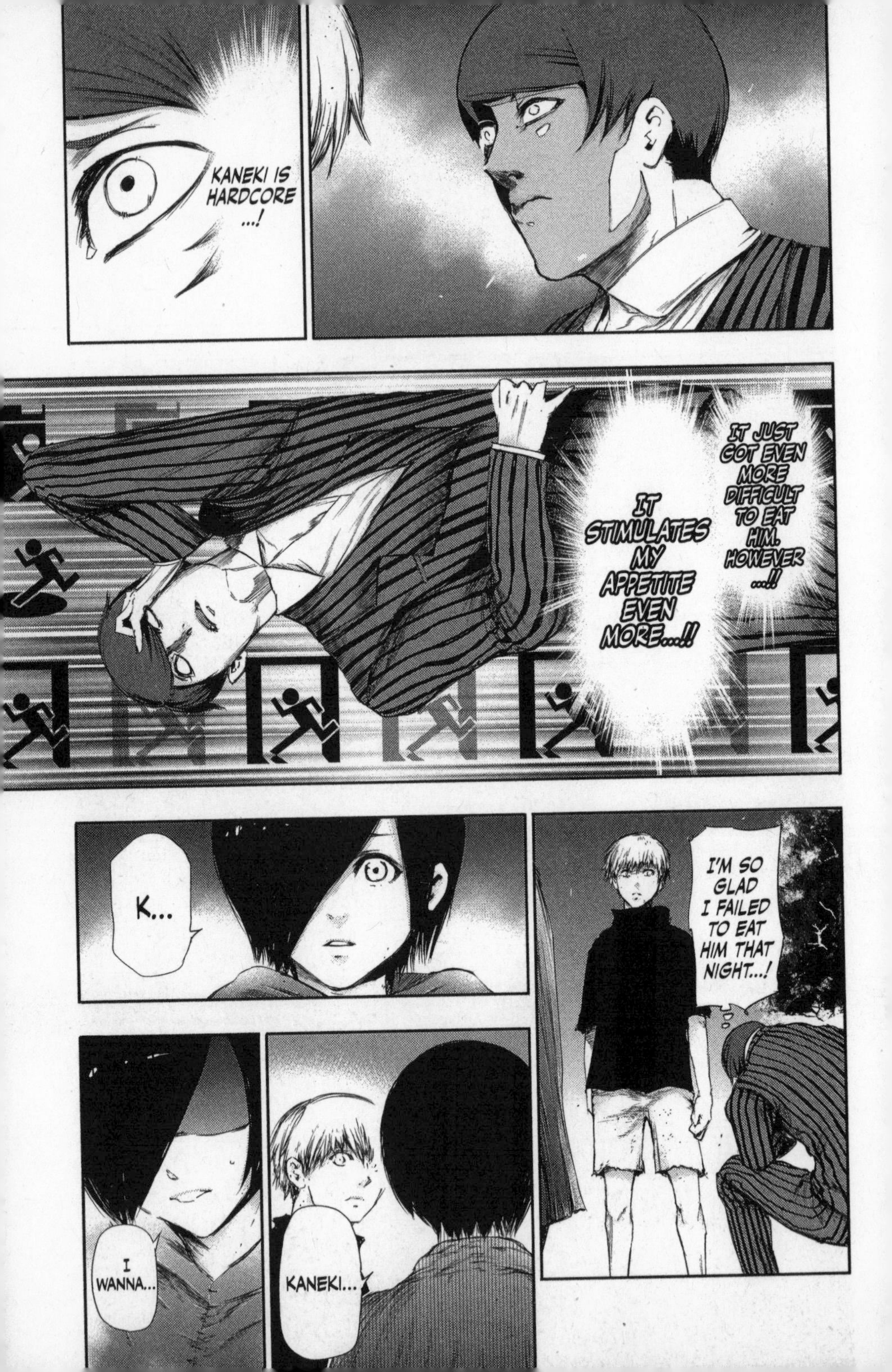
KANEKI IS HARDCORE ...!
IT JUST GOT EVEN MORE DIFFICULT TO EAT HIM. HOWEVER ...!!
IT STIMULATES MY APPETITE EVEN MORE...!!
I'M SO GLAD I FAILED TO EAT HIM THAT NIGHT...!
K...
KANEKI...
I WANNA...

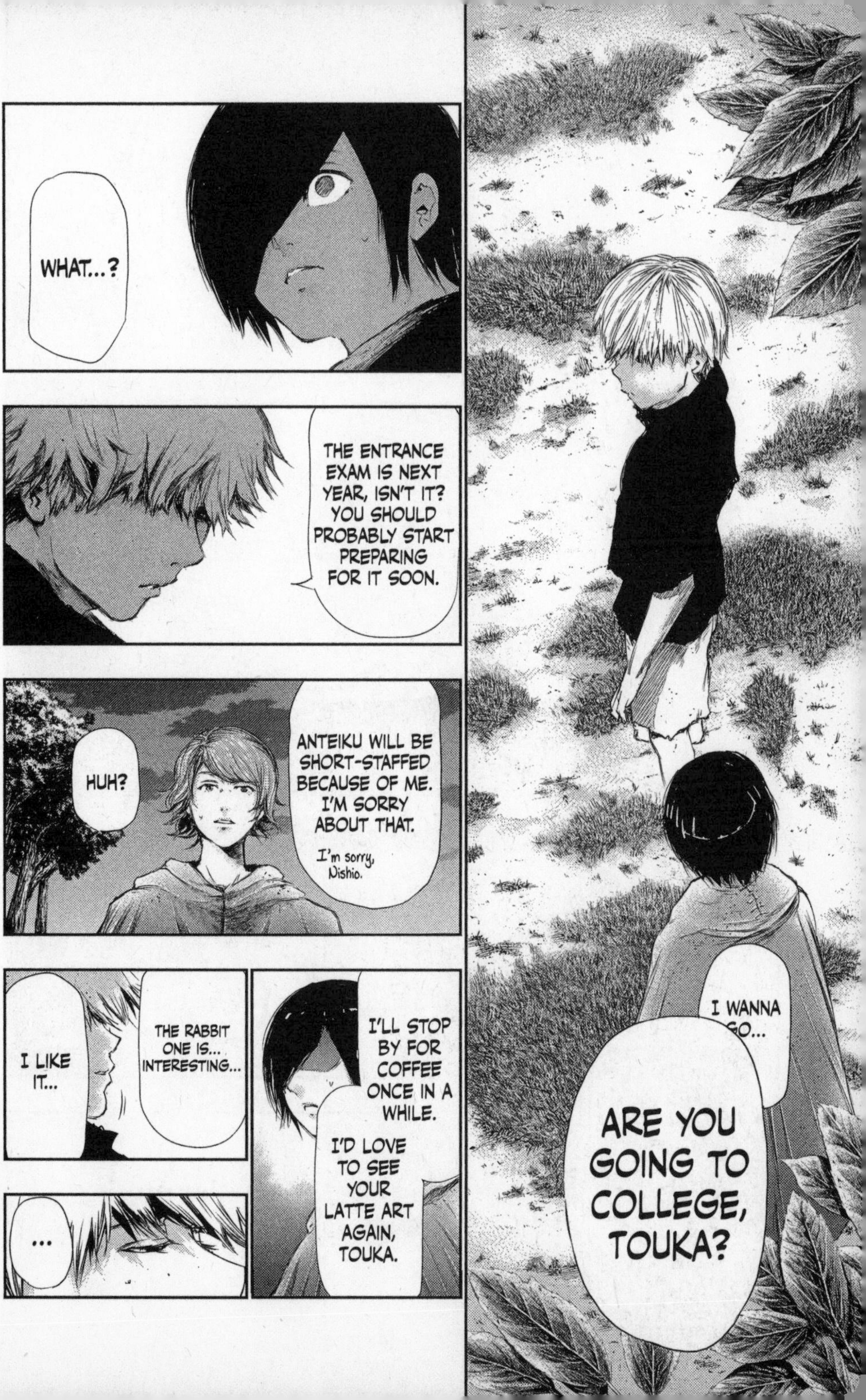
I WANNA GO...
ARE YOU GOING TO COLLEGE, TOUKA?
WHAT...?
THE ENTRANCE EXAM IS NEXT YEAR, ISN'T IT? YOU SHOULD PROBABLY START PREPARING FOR IT SOON.
ANTEIKU WILL BE SHORT-STAFFED BECAUSE OF ME. I'M SORRY ABOUT THAT.
I'm sorry, Nishio.
HUH?
I'LL STOP BY FOR COFFEE ONCE IN A WHILE.
I'D LOVE TO SEE YOUR LATTE ART AGAIN, TOUKA.
THE RABBIT ONE IS... INTERESTING...
I LIKE IT...
...

I'LL SEE
YOU...

TOUKA...

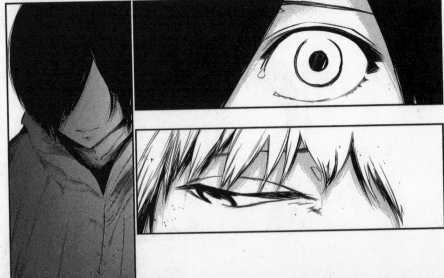

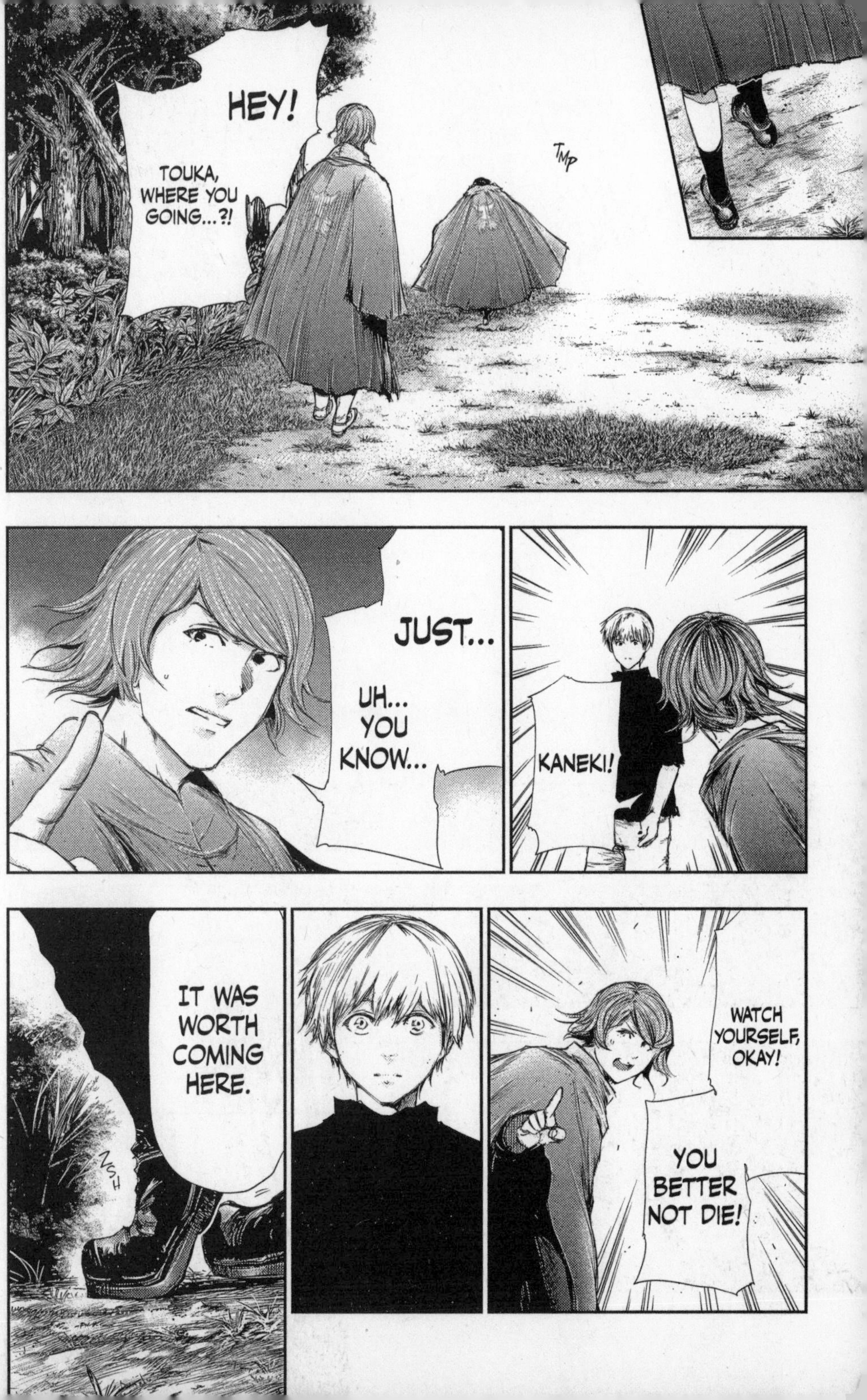
HEY!
TOUKA, WHERE YOU GOING...?!
TMP
KANEKI!
JUST...
UH... YOU KNOW...
WATCH YOURSELF, OKAY!
YOU BETTER NOT DIE!
IT WAS WORTH COMING HERE.
ZSH

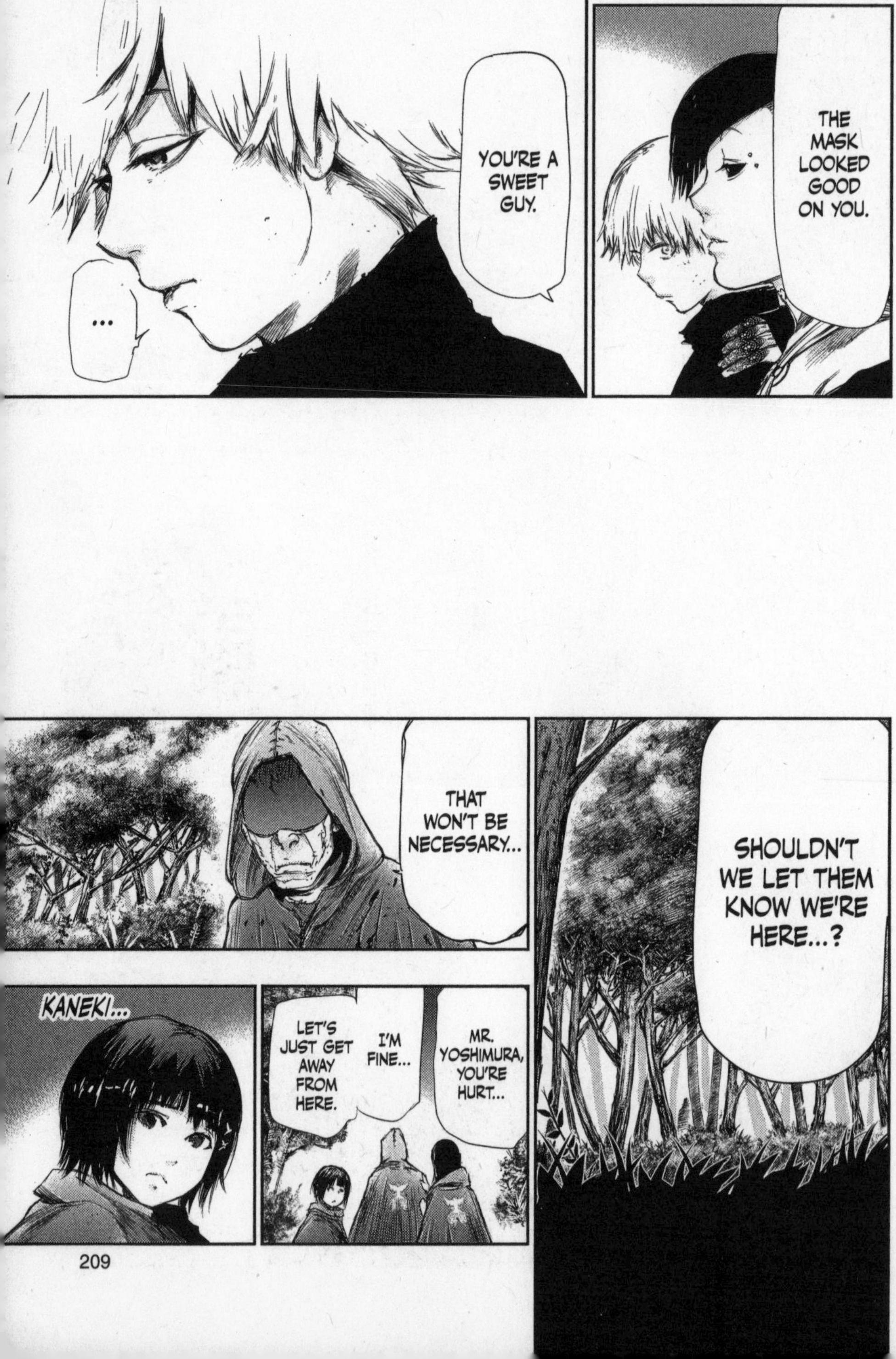
THE MASK LOOKED GOOD ON YOU.
YOU'RE A SWEET GUY.
...
SHOULDN'T WE LET THEM KNOW WE'RE HERE...?
THAT WON'T BE NECESSARY...
MR. YOSHIMURA, YOU'RE HURT...
I'M FINE...
LET'S JUST GET AWAY FROM HERE.
KANEKI...

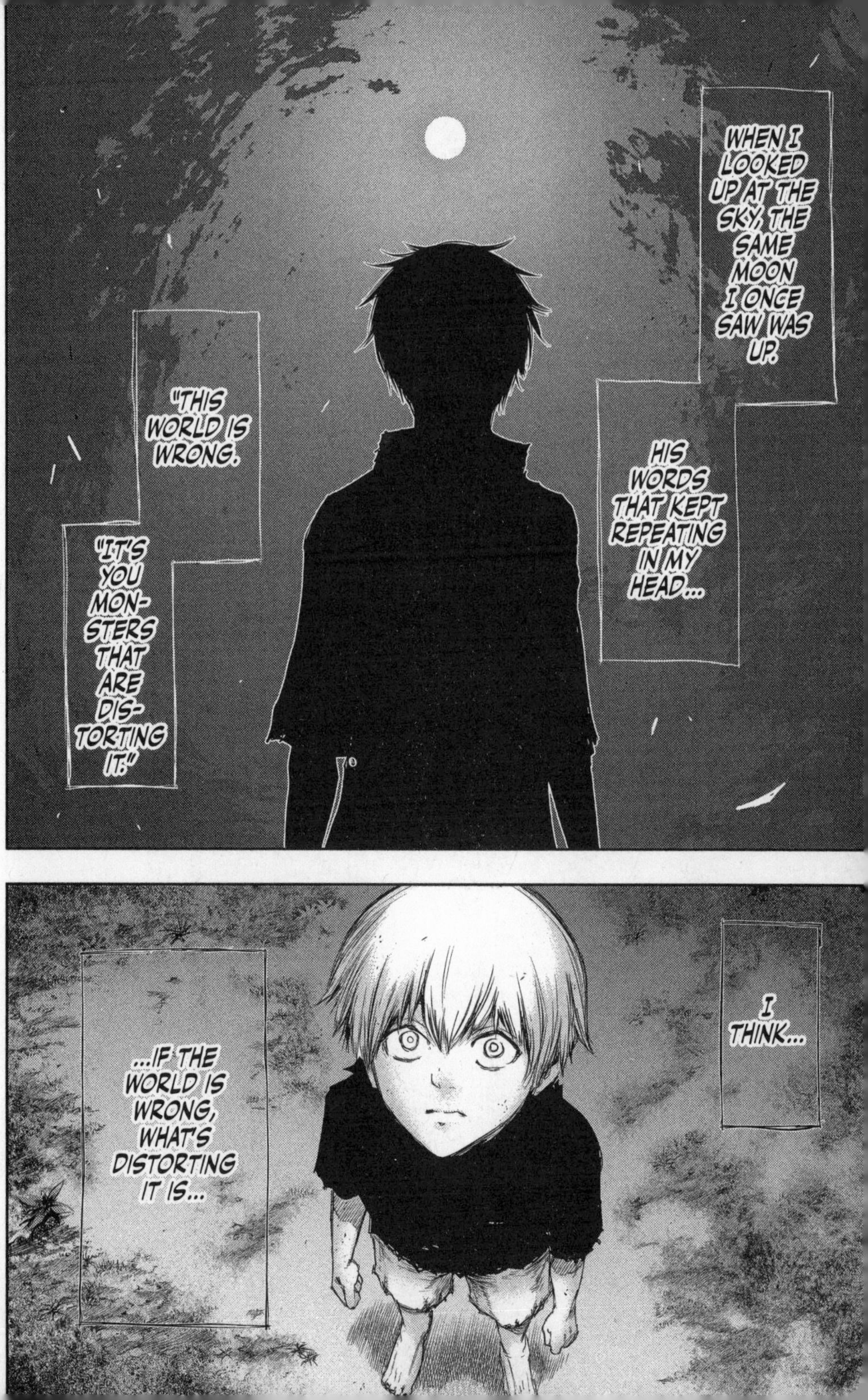
WHEN I LOOKED UP AT THE SKY, THE SAME MOON I ONCE SAW WAS UP.
HIS WORDS THAT KEPT REPEATING IN MY HEAD...
"THIS WORLD IS WRONG.
"IT'S YOU MONSTERS THAT ARE DISTORTING IT."
I THINK...
...IF THE WORLD IS WRONG, WHAT'S DISTORTING IT IS...

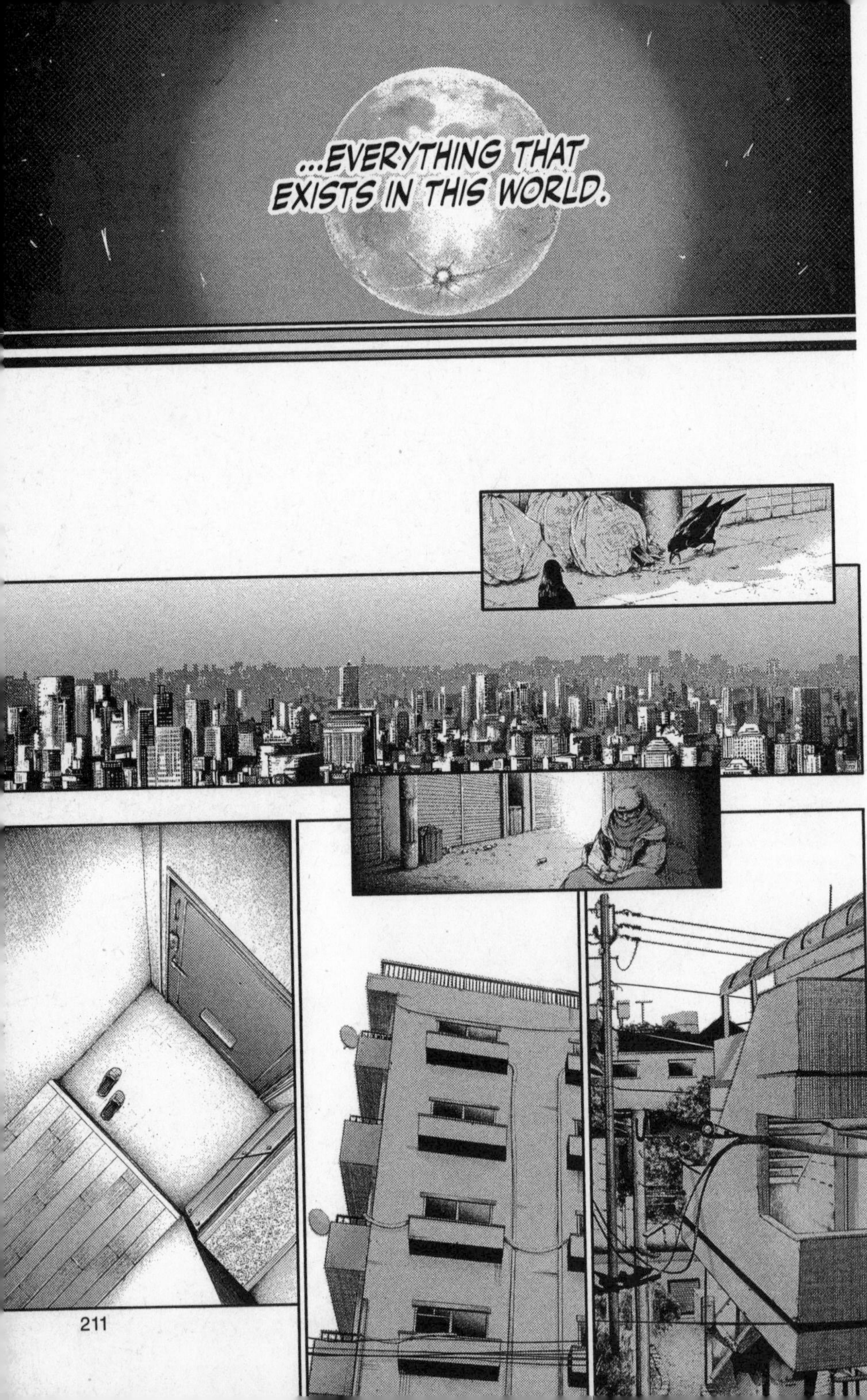
...EVERYTHING THAT EXISTS IN THIS WORLD.

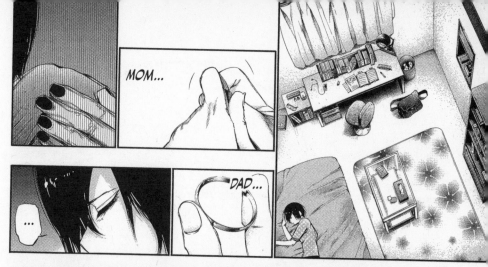

MOM...

DAD...

...

IT MADE ME...

...SO HAPPY TOO.

I WON'T BE ALONE...

WHAT DID YOU MEAN BY IT...?

HOPE YOU DIE, YOU LITTLE PUNK...

...

ARATA HIKARI

To be continued in Tokyo Ghoul Vol.9.

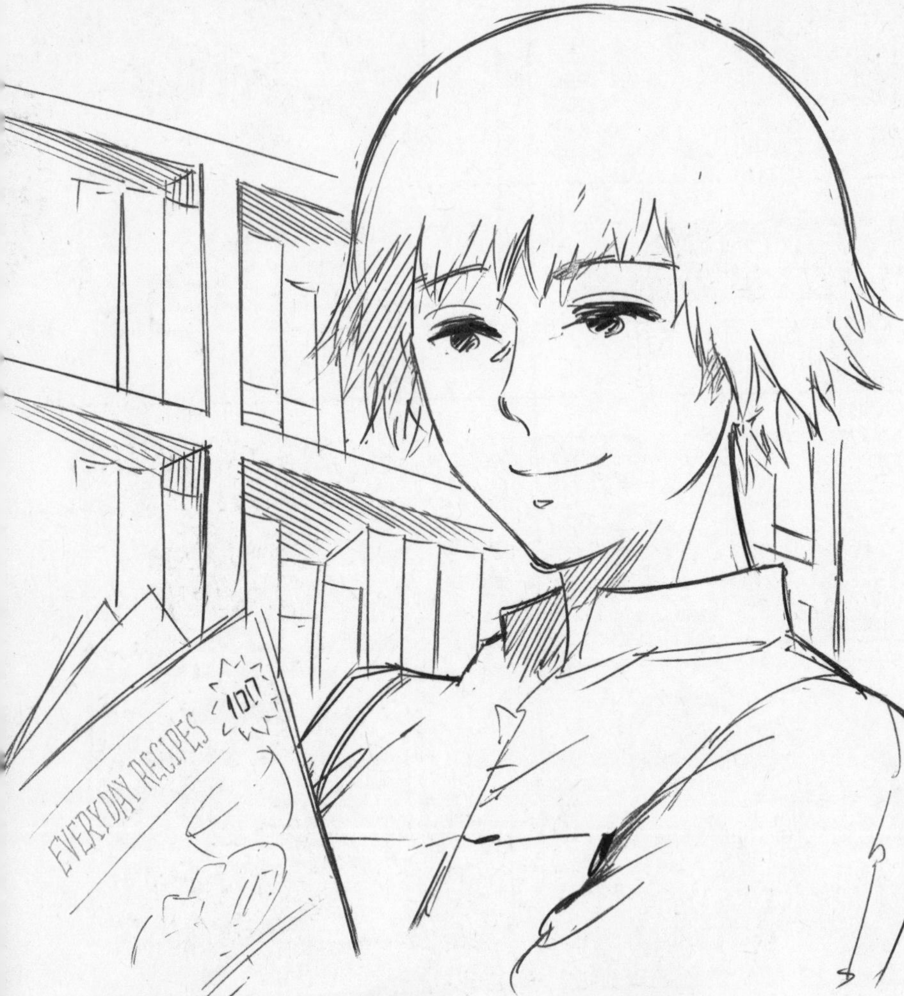
EVERYDAY RECIPES

Thanks
Eda
Ryuji Miyamoto
Mizuki Ide
Matsuzaki
Kazumi Takahsta
Nakano

Design
Hideaki Shimada (L.S.D.)

Cover
Miyuki Takaoka (POCKET)

Editor
Jumpei Matsuo

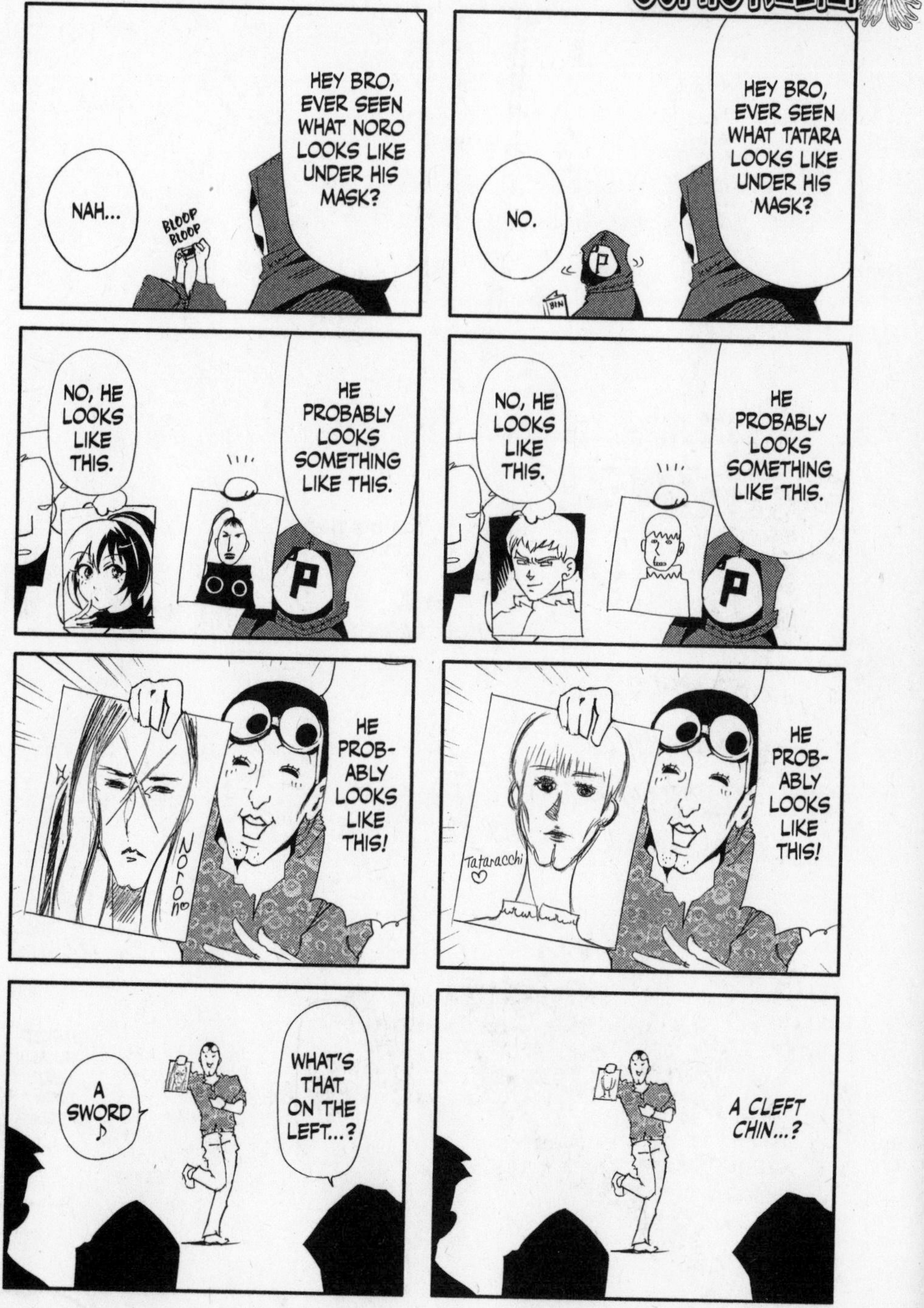
HEY BRO, EVER SEEN WHAT TATARA LOOKS LIKE UNDER HIS MASK?
NO.
BIN
HEY BRO, EVER SEEN WHAT NORO LOOKS LIKE UNDER HIS MASK?
NAH...
BLOOP BLOOP
HE PROBABLY LOOKS SOMETHING LIKE THIS.
NO, HE LOOKS LIKE THIS.
HE PROBABLY LOOKS SOMETHING LIKE THIS.
NO, HE LOOKS LIKE THIS.
HE PROB-ABLY LOOKS LIKE THIS!
Tataracchi ♡
HE PROB-ABLY LOOKS LIKE THIS!
Noron♡
A CLEFT CHIN...?
WHAT'S THAT ON THE LEFT...?
A SWORD ♪

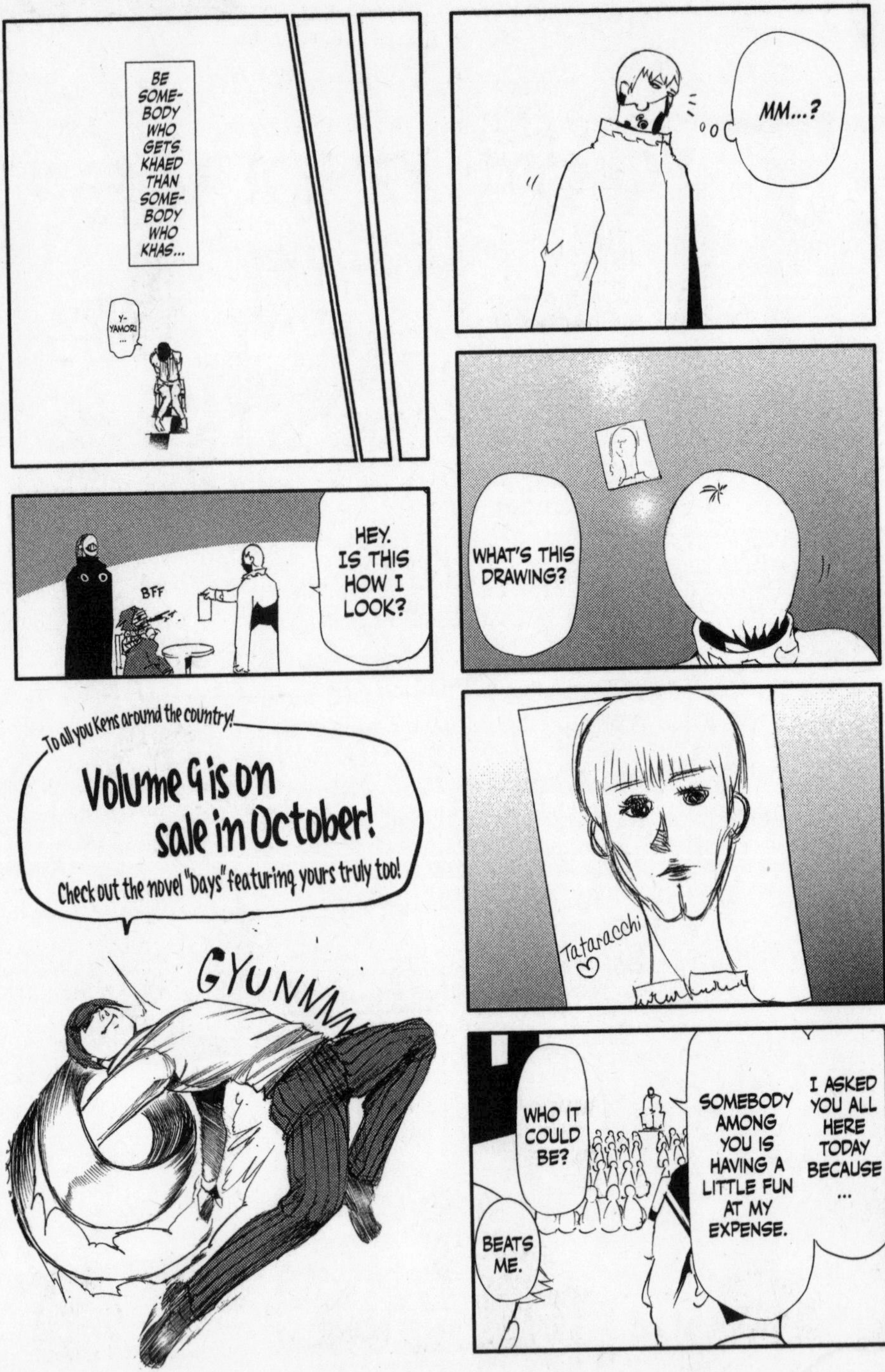
MM...?
WHAT'S THIS DRAWING?
Tataracchi
I ASKED YOU ALL HERE TODAY BECAUSE ...
SOMEBODY AMONG YOU IS HAVING A LITTLE FUN AT MY EXPENSE.
WHO IT COULD BE?
BEATS ME.
BE SOME-BODY WHO GETS KHAED THAN SOME-BODY WHO KHAS...
Y-YAMORI ...
HEY. IS THIS HOW I LOOK?
BFF
To all you Kens around the country!
Volume 9 is on sale in October!
Check out the novel "Days" featuring yours truly too!
GYUNNNN

TOKYO GHOUL

[THIS IS THE
LAST PAGE]

TOKYO GHOUL
READS
RIGHT TO LEFT

TOKYO GHOUL
東 京 喰 種

VOLUME 8
VIZ Signature Edition

Story and art by

SUI ISHIDA

TOKYO GHOUL © 2011 by Sui Ishida
All rights reserved.
First published in Japan in 2011 by
SHUEISHA Inc., Tokyo.
English translation rights arranged by
SHUEISHA Inc.

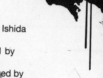

TRANSLATION. Joe Yamazaki

TOUCH-UP ART AND LETTERING. James Gaubatz

DESIGN. Fawn Lau

EDITOR. Joel Enos

Printed in the U.S.A.

Published by VIZ Media, LLC
P.O. Box 77010
San Francisco, CA 94107

10 9 8 7 6 5 4 3 2 1
First printing, August 2016

D1020385

MEDIA
www.viz.com

VIZ SIGNATURE